Dynamics of Development in Gujarat

About the Editors

Prof. Indira Hirway, is currently the Director of the Centre For Development Alternatives, Ahmedabad. Earlier she was at Mahatma Gandhi Labour Institute, Ahmedabad. She has done extensive research work in the areas of poverty and employment, labour market structures, environment and development, environment accounting, gender and development etc. She has been associated with several national and international committees and expert groups in these areas. She has a number of books and research articles published in Indian and foreign journals to her credit.

Prof. S.P. Kashyap, is currently the Director of Sardar Patel Institute of Social and Economic Research, Amedabad. During his long academic career, he has contributed extensively in the areas of agriculture and rural development, spatial and scalar dimension of industrial development in India, regional analysis and planning. He has participated in several collaborative research studies conducted by global organizations, and is a member of editorial committees of several journals and of research advisory committees of several academic bodies. He has written a number of books and published many research papers in Indian and foreign journals.

Dr. Amita Shah, an economist, has wide ranging experience of conducting research on various aspects of rural economy, such as, natural resource development with special focus on dry land agriculture and forestry, environmental impact assessment, gender and environment, agriculture-industry interface, small scale and rural industries, diffusion of technologies, and employment-livelihood issues. She has been associated with various donor agencies and has undertaken collaborative research both within and outside India. She has published about 40 research papers in professional journals and books.

DYNAMICS OF DEVELOPMENT IN GUJARAT

Edited by

INDIRA HIRWAY

Centre For Development Alternatives, Ahmedabad

S. P. KASHYAP

Sardar Patel Institute of Social and Economic Research, Ahmedabad

AMITA SHAH

Gujarat Institute of Developmnt Research, Ahmedabad

Foreword by

I. G. PATEL

Published for

CENTRE FOR DEVELOPMENT ALTERNATIVES, AHMEDABAD

by

CONCEPT PUBLISHING COMPANY, NEW DELHI-110059

ISBN 81-7022-968-5

First Published 2002

Published and Printed by
Ashok Kumar Mittal
Concept Publishing Company
A/15-16, Commercial Block, Mohan Garden
New Delhi-110059 (India)
Phones: 5351460, 5351794
Fax: 091–(11)–5357103
E-mail: publishing@conceptpub.com

Foreword

Some fifty years ago I read an article in the Diwali issue of a Gujarati publication in which the author asked the question : "What is it that constitutes the unique greatness of Gujarat?" He proceeded to answer the question thus : "Other states have other claims to greatness. Only Gujarat has produced leaders that could dream of seemingly impossible dreams, and realise them". His examples were : Dadabhoy Naoroji who first dreamt of a free India, Jamshedji Tata who first dreamt of an industrial India, Mahatma Gandhi who first dreamt of achieving freedom without violence and Mohammed Ali Jinnah who dirst dreamt of Pakistan.

There are several things about what the author said which are worth noting. His emphasis is both on vision and achievement. He is totally free from religious prejudice and can be objective even about goals or views he did not share. And he judges Gujarat and Gujaratis not by what they do for themselves but for a larger cause. Shades of Umashankar Joshi are there : "What kind of a Gujarati is he, who is only a Gujarati?"

In all these respects, things have been down the hill in Gujarat for the past several years; and in matters like religious harmony and freedom from prejudice and pre-conception, our recent behaviour is not only uncharacteristic. It is among the worst in the country.

Is there anything we can truly be proud of today? The answer that easily comes to mind is that we have achieved remarkable economic progress at least in the last ten years—so much so that we have begun to talk, of all things in this land of lions, about Gujarati tigers! Perhaps, there are rewards at least in this life for those who succeed materially. But as the following chapters on Gujarat's progress in different fields indicate even this picture is blurred. There is still poverty and much environmental degradation. Agriculture is stagnant. Our burgeoning cities and rivers are heavily polluted. In terms of social indicators such as education, nutrition, infant mortality and safe drinking water, our record is poor even by Indian standards. I read somewhere that the incidence of violence against women in India is the highest in Gujarat—by any account, it is high enough.

I have no doubt that this contrast between wealth and ill-being can be removed by appropriate policies. This book offers several pointers in that direction. While we may debate small points, there is consensus on the larger picture and what needs to be done. One ray of hope, particularly for Gujarat, is the robustness of the movement for self-helf — sometimes rather inelegantly and inappropriately referred to as non-governmental organisations. The point is not that they are not government; they need the co-operation and financial help of the government. The point is that their social workers fight against the dependency syndrome and create in ordinary men and women self-confidence as well as the desire and drive to work for their own improvement as also for the sake of their children. In the land of Gandhiji and Ravishankar Maharaj, there is still hope. What needs to be removed are the poisons spread in the minds of innocent and hard-working people by opportunistic politicians of all kinds. That is where we need not just economic reform, but social and political reform as well; not just food for the hungry, but also sustenance for the soul. Great leaders are born with the grace of God, not by the wish of men. We do not need new visions—they can sometimes be dangerous. We need to be true to the real genius of Gujarat which our author captured so well in his article some fifty years ago.

Baroda, 26th March 2001 I.G. PATEL

Contents

Introduction

Gujarat is one of the developed states in India. It ranks fourth in per capita income among the major states in the country, and with the state per capita income increasing at the highest rate in the nineties, the state is likely to progress further to the top very soon. This high growth is largely due to its fast industrial growth and the consequent growth of the tertiary sector. With relatively diversified sources of income and workforce as well as a developed capital market, the state wants to emerge as another Asian Tiger in the coming years.

It is clear that the state has taken good advantage of the new opportunities created by the new economic policies. With liberalized markets, privatization of the economy and globalization, access to economic opportunities has expanded in the state. The enterprising population of the state with its progressive leadership has accessed these new opportunities very well. The state has been at the top in the nineties in terms of attracting investments in the industrial sector, particularly in large and medium industries. According to the latest available data, the state has sanctioned more than Rs. 1,75,000 crores for industrial investments in the large and medium industries between 1991-2000 (August). The state has been almost at the top in terms of executing these projects. The state is believed to be on the path of rapid economic growth.

In spite of these achievements, however, the development in the state suffers from several weaknesses, such as almost stagnant agricultural growth, massive degradation and depletion of natural resources, heavy pollution in several industrial and urban centres, low achievements in human development, partiularly in health and education sectors and wide regional disparities. In fact, the state economy today is at the cressroads. Though the new economic policies have opened up opportunities in industries and trade for its enterprising population, the lopsided development is perhaps not sustainable. The state today has an option of either correcting the developmnt path to move towards eco-friendly and broad-based development or to eventually face disastrous consequences.

One can say that the case of Gujarat is a typical case of a developing economy struggling to grow fast to take advantages of the new global opportunities but at the cast of losing control of its environment and human development. The decade of the nineties has witnessed many such experiences in the developing world with the result that questions are being raised regarding the validity of the new LPG (liberalization, privatization and globalization) model for solving the problems of the developing world. It is important, therefore, to discuss the different dimensions of the development of Gujarat in order to understand the dynamics of its development and to infer policy interventions for a healthy and sustainable development.

Keeping this objective in mind a seminar was organised by the Centre For Development Alternatives at Ahmedabad. Selected experts were invited to write papers on the different dimensions of development of Gujarat. We are happy to present these papers in this volume.

The first three papers in the volume discuss the general pattern of economic development in Gujarat. Indira Hirway's paper, entitled "Dynamics of Development in Gujarat: Some Issues", seeks to delineate the profile of Gujarat's development with a view to understand mixed results of Gujarat's development. The paper observes that the high rate of growth of Gujarat is likely to be unsustainable, and unless the state leadership changes the course of development by making the growth broad-based and employment intensive, the state is unlikely to achieve sustainable economic growth or a significant decline in unemployment and poverty. Ravindra Dholakia's paper on "Liberalization in Gujarat" analyses the process and impact of liberalization on the state economy. He argues that the present development strategy of giving a high priority to industrialization has been their right from the inception of the state in 1960. The present success in industrialization is a result of the efforts of the past decades. The future performance of industrialization, however, depends on the commitment of the government to liberalization, improved infrastructure and a proactive bureaucracy.

Atul Sharma's paper on "Gujarat Finances: Reforms of Budgetary Management" examines the performance of Gujarat's revenue and expenditure system. It attempts to identify the basic weaknesses of the existing revenue sources and indicates a broad direction for future reforms. The major thrust of this paper, however, is on identifying the sources of inefficiencies of budgetary and expenditure policy and management, and outlining reform proposals for enhancing expenditure effectiveness. Continuing this theme Archana Dholakia's paper on "Fiscal Imbalance in

Gujarat: Non-Tax Revenue and Subsidies", argues that Gujarat needs to raise its non-tax revenue to ease its fiscal crisis. She analyses Gujarat's non-tax revenue and subsidies to find out possibilities of improvement. Contrary to the spirit of economic reforms, the state government in Gujarat is more active in the areas from which it should withdraw as shown by high economic subsidies, and it is less active in the areas where intervention is called for as shown by low social sector subsidies.

Industrialization and urbanization are two areas where Gujarat is far ahead of other states. It is one of the highly urbanized states in India with the incidence of urban poverty higher than the same of rural poverty. Amitabh Kundu, while analyzing the urbanization process in Gujarat, observes in his paper, "Globalizing Gujarat: Urbanization, Employment and Poverty", that the economic reforms are likely to give a push to the process of urbanization in the state. However, this urbanization is likely to be associated with low productive employment, poverty and a lower quality of life for the poor in cities. His analysis of the trends and patterns of urbanization in the state in the context of changing employment structures, urban governance and commercialization of basic services draws attention to the critical issues of urban growth in the state.

Dinesh Awasthi's paper on "Recent Changes in Gujarat Industry: Issues and Evidence" analyses the recent changes that have taken place in the industrial sector in Gujarat. He observes that Gujarat has responded very well to economic reforms and has experienced a rapid growth in industrial sector, particularly in large and medium size enterprises. Awasthi, however, argues that the state needs a greater emphasis on infrastructural sector for a long term industrial growth. He also observes that small-scale sector, which was lagging behind in the nineties, can be helped through the industrial cluster approach. Takashi Shinoda examines institutional changes and entrepreneurial development in the small-scale sector. The focus is primarily on the social background of small entrepreneurs whose number has grown very fast in the state. By analyzing the data on the social background of small entrepreneurs, Shinoda observes that there is a caste-based distribution of small entrepreneurs in certain industries like machinery parts, wood products, textiles, etc., which is rooted in the age old caste tradition. In contrast, relatively higher castes are more dispersed across different industries. Thus, social groups and related political aspects do play an important role in entrepreneurship development in the state.

There are three papers on agriculture and related issues. The paper on "Agriculture in Gujarat: Problems and Prospects" by Niti Mathur and S.P. Kashyap provides a statistical profile of pre and post-green revolution in agriculture. The paper analyses the changes that have taken place in the cropping pattern, land and labour productivity and input use between 1961-1993. Investment in infrastructure and strategies for sustainable resource use, according to the authors, could improve productivity in agriculture and overcome stagnancy. Parthasarathy follows up this discussion by examining participatory irrigation management in the state. The paper observes that participatory irrigation management programmes have indeed led to a better and smoother resolution of irrigation related conflicts. However, the expectation, that the programme would be cost effective, has not materialized as yet. Water Users' associations will have to be more efficient than making allocative and investment decisions to reduce the costs. A clarification of legal rights may help here. Watershed development programme is another important step for better management of natural resources in the state. Amita Shah argues that watershed development programmes have become a key strategy for sustainable economic development in large parts of Gujarat that are experiencing frequent draughts, dwindling ground water resources, increasing salinity and loss of vegetation. Amita concludes that the state has had a good beginning, but it has a long way to go to tap the full potential of the programme. These three papers taken together suggest solutions to the problem of stagnancy in agriculture exist, but efforts made so far are highly inadequate.

In spite of the rapid growth of the economy, the state suffers from employment-related problems, as pointed out by N. Lalitha and Arati Oza, in their paper entitled "Employment Trends in Manufacturing Sector of Gujarat". The authors observe that Gujarat has experienced a fairly high rate of decline in self-employment and a rapid growth in casual workers during the last decade and a half. In the post-liberalization period of rapid industrial development, particularly in large and medium enterprises, however, the state has experienced slight increase in the organized employment along with a marginal decline of employment in the unorganized sector. This is accompanied by increasing labour productivity in the organized sector and stagnant declining labour productivity in the unorganized sector. There is a need, therefore, to improve the levels of productivity in the unorganized sector as also overall employment intensity of economic growth.

Health and education are the major components of human development. Darshini Mahadevia analyses the performance of the health sector and raises the question whether "health for all" is feasible in the near future. Mahadevia argues that though there has been a significant improvemnt in the status of health in the state over the years, the health situation in the state also shows unhealthy features like better facilities for secondary and tertiary health than for primary health, deteriorating urban health facilities and emergence of occupation related diseases. The development model of Gujarat, according to Mahadevia, seems to be a major factor responsible for some of the major health problems in the state. This confirms the view expressed by Hirway that development path is mainly responsible for the relatively low level of human development, and that sector specific expenditures give only a partial solution.

The role of institutional and cultural factors in the development process in the state is examined by Vidhyut Joshi, Sudarshan Iyengar and S.S. Mehta. How much have cultural factors affected development in the state? According to Vidhyut Joshi, Gujarat is not a homogeneous society, as it is often understood. There are three subcultures each with a different ethos within the broader framework of Gujarati culture: the Mahajan culture of the central belt, the semi-feudal culture of Saurashtra and the tribal culture in the eastern belt. Each has contributed differently to the development of the state. The protestant ethic or the Mahajan culture of the central belt has facilitated growth of entrepreneurship and enterprises, Saurashtra has restricted development due to its semi-feudal culture and the tribals have remained far behind due to their inherent constraints and isolation.

Gujarat is also known for its NGO culture and its long tradition of voluntary work. Sudarshan Iyengar in his paper "Role of Non-Governmental Organizations in Development of Gujarat" observes that the Gandhian influence in social reconstruction and continuing philanthropic activity has helped to cover a large field of development. After examining the contribution of NGOs to Gujarat's development during the last 80 years or so, Iyengar observes that NGOs have to play a critical role today in the context of the new challenges.

S.S. Mehta and Pratul Ahuja discuss the Panchayati Raj in Gujarat, particularly in the new environment of the 73rd Amendment of the Constitution. Though Gujarat has a very long history of Panchayati Raj institutions, Mehta and Ahuja argue that they have a long way to go to achieve the goals of decentralized democracy. Some of the major hurdles relate to lack of the financial strength and autonomy, undue delays in extending the benefits of the 73rd Constitutional Amendment to scheduled areas and absence of control of Panchayats on their lands. The authors show that there is a glaring mismatch between the means and responsibilities of the panchayat bodies with the result that panchayat bodies, including village panchayats, are not strong enough to shoulder the responsibility of strengtnening the lowest rungs of democracy in the state.

The book gives valuable insight into the dynamics of development in Gujarat. It emerges that one of the fastest growing states in India in the post-liberalization period Gujarat is facing several challenges of varying dimensions in different directions. Economic growth brought about by liberalization may not sustain for long if it is not backed by adequate infrastructural support, administrative efficiency as well as environmental sustainability. When a large number of developing economies are moving towards unsustainable rapid economic growth, the experience of Gujarat offers quite a few lesson.

We take this opportunity to thank Oxfam (India) Trust for funding partially the seminar organized by us on Dynamics of Development in Gujarat. We also thank former Minister for Narmada and Major Irrigation, Government of Gujarat, Shri Jaynarayan Vyas for inaugurating the seminar, and Prof. Y.K. Alagh, former Minister for Planning and Programme Implementation and Science and Technology, Government of India, for delivering the valedictory address. We also extend out thanks to Dr. Krishna Raj, Editor, *Economic and Political Weekly*, for giving permission for publishing the papers in this volume. And finally, we thank all the participants in the seminar who presented/discussed the papers. We are grateful to Prof. I.G. Patel for writing foreword to this book.

December, 2000

INDIRA HIRWAY
S. P. KASHYAP
AMITA SHAH

List of Contributors

Ahuja, Pratul Research Associate, School of Planning, CEPT, Ahmedabad.

Awasthi, Dinesh N. Professor (Strategic Management and Entrepreneurship) Indian Institute of Management, Prabandh Nagar, Off Sitapur Road, Lucknow-276013

Dholakia, Archana R. Reader in Economics at Post-Graduate Department of Economics, School of Social Sciences, Gujarat University, Ahmedabad-380009

Dholakia, Ravindra H. Professor of Economics, Indian Institute of Management, Vastrapur, Ahmedabad-380015

Hirway, Indira Director and Professor of Economics, CFDA, Centre for Development Alternatives, E-71, Akash, Near Chief Justice's Bungalow, Bodakdev, Ahmedabad-380015

Iyengar, Sudarshan Professor, Gujarat Institute of Development Research, Gota, Ahmedabad-380060

Joshi, Vidyut Professor of Behavioural Science, Mahatma Gandhi Labour Institute, Drive-in Road, Memnagar, Ahmedabad-380052

Kashyap, S.P. Director, Sardar Patel Institute of Social and Economic Research, Thaltej Tekra, Ahmedabad-380052

Kundu, Amitabh Professor, Centre for Study of Regional Development, Jawaharlal Nehru University, New Delhi-110067

Lalitha, N. Associate Professor, Gujarat Institute of Development Research, Near Gota Cross Roads, Ahmedabad-380060

Mahadevia, Darshini Faculty, School of Planning, Centre for Environmental Planning and Technology, University Road, Navrangpura, Ahmedabad-380009

Mathur, Niti Deputy Director (Project), and Director, Agro-climatic Regional Planning Unit, SPIER, Thaltej Hill, Ahmedabad-380052

Mehta, S.S. Professor of Economics, School of Planning, CEPT, Ahmedabad.

Oza, Arti Data Analyst, Gujarat Institute of Development Research, Near Gota Cross Roads, Ahmedabad-380060

Parthasarathy, R. Associate Professor, Gujarat Institute of Development Research, Gota, Ahmedabad-380060

Shah, Amita Associate Professor, Gujarat Institute of Development Research, Near Gota Cross Road, Ahmedabad-380060

Sharma, Atul Director SAIL and Professor of Economics, SAIL, Indian Statistical Institute, Delhi Centre, 7, SJS Sansanwal Marg, New Delhi-110016

Shah, Niresh C. Professor of Economics, Sardar Patel Institute of Social and Economic Research, Thaltej Tekra, Ahmedabad-380052

Shinoda, Takashi Professor of Economics, Faculty, International Relation, DAITO BUNKA UNIVERSITY-560. Iwadona, Higashi-matsuyamashi, Saitama, 355 Japan

1

Dynamics of Development in Gujarat
Some Issues

INDIRA HIRWAY

Gujarat was formed in the year 1960 when the erstwhile bilingual state of Bombay was split into two separate states, namely, Gujarati speaking Gujarat State and Marathi speaking Maharashtra State. With its enterprising population and committed leadership Gujarat has done well since then in terms of overall economic growth. It has progressed to acquire the fourth rank in per capita income among the major sixteen states in India and has maintained this rank for the last two decades or so. Today it is one of the prosperous states of India with about 50 million population (2001) spread over 196000 sq. km. Though the state has less than 5 per cent of the national population, it has 6.56 per cent of the national production and about 11 per cent of the national industrial output (Government of Gujarat, 1997).

The state economy, however, is peculiar in some ways. On the one hand, it enjoys a high per capita income, 35 per cent higher than the all India average (Rs. 3,717 in 1996-97 against Rs. 2,761 in India, both at 1980-81 prices); a relatively diversified sources of income (78 per cent of the state domestic product comes from non-primary sectors against 60 per cent in India) and a diversified workforce (40.3 per cent of the workforce in the state is in the non-primary sectors as against 32.6 per cent in India) as well as stable — if not rising — employment levels and developed financial and capital markets. On the other hand, however, the state has relatively poor and unevenly distributed natural resources which have been mismanaged overtime, almost stagnant long term growth in agriculture and wide regional disparities of growth. Though the incidence of poverty in the state is much lower (23.92 per cent in 1993-94) than the same in all India (35.97 per cent in 1993-94), it is still significant, as it implies that almost every fourth person in the state is living in poverty. The state lags behind in terms of quality of employment, as also in several dimensions of human development, particularly in female literacy, enrolment and retention of children in schools, infant mortality rate, etc. It seems that the development path chosen by the state has given mixed results: It has pushed up economic growth, but has not done so well on other fronts.

This paper overviews the profile of development of Gujarat in order to understand the dynamics of development underlying the mixed results and to infer the directions of development for the future.

Growth of State Domestic Product in Major Sectors

The state economy has been growing faster than the Indian economy right from the sixties (Table 1.1). It has also shown a consistent increase in the rate of growth, from 3.32 per cent in the sixties to 4.95 per cent in the seventies and to 5.67 per cent in the eighties and nineties. The state has maintained a high rank among the major 16 states in the country in terms of the growth rates of NSDP as well as per capita NSDP. Table 1.2 which presents the data on the size and the rates of growth of NSDP and per capita NSDP in the major 16 states in India between 1981 to 1998, shows that Gujarat stands fourth in per capita income through out the period.

Table 1.1 : Sectoral Growth Rates in Gujarat (CARG)

	1960-61 to 1970-71	1970-71 to 1980-81	1980-81 to 1990-91	1990-91 to 1995-96	1980-81 to 1997-98
Primary Sector	2.91	4.15	1.24	0.18	1.42
(Agriculture)	(2.27)	(4.22)	(1.10)	(0.26)	(1.34)
Secondary Sector	3.62	5.64	7.85	9.45	8.87
(Manufacturing)	(3.04)	(5.55)	(8.73)	(11.92)	(9.19)
Tertiary Sector	3.51	5.86	6.83	10.61	7.25
Overall SDP	3.32	4.95	5.30	5.41	6.00
India GDP	3.17	3.66	5.42	5.07	5.44

Source : National Accounts Statistics of India (1950-51 to 1995-96) *EPW* Research Foundation. *Social Economic Review,* Directorate of Economics and Statistics, Gandhinagar, February 1999.

The state stands third with respect to the rate of growth in the post-economic reforms period, Maharashtra being at the top with 7.35 per cent growth rate during the period. In terms of the rate of growth of per capita NSDP, however, the state stands fourth for the period from 1980-81 to 1995-96 and is at the top for the period 1990-91 to 1997-98. Indeed, the state has shown the highest rate of growth of per capita income among the major 16 states in the post liberalization period (Tables 1.2A and 1.2B).

Table 1.2 : Compound Average Rate of Growth of Net State Domestic Product and Per Capita NSDP in the 16 Major States in India (1980-81 to 1995-96)

A. CARG of Net State Domestic Product at Factor Cost (At Constant Price 1980-81)

(In Rupees crore)

Sl. No.	State	1980-81	1990-91	1995-96	CARG 80-81 To 95-96	CARG 90-91 To 95-96
1.	Maharashtra	15163	27245	38843	6.47	7.35
2.	Uttar Pradesh	14012	22780	25112	3.96	1.96
3.	West Bengal	9594	14458	19624	4.88	6.3
4.	Tamil Nadu	7218	12411	16031	5.46	5.25
5.	Gujarat	6547	10915	14211	5.3	5.41
6.	Andhra Pradesh	7324	11723	13776	4.3	3.28
7.	Madhya Pradesh	7012	11121	12931	4.16	3.06
8.	Karnataka	5587	9112	11693	5.04	5.11
9.	Bihar	6349	10314	10965	3.7	1.23
10.	Rajasthan	4126	8473	9936	6.03	6.23
11.	Punjab	4449	7505	9235	4.98	4.23
12.	Kerala	3823	5262	7295	4.4	6.75
13.	Haryana	3032	5719	6666	5.39	3.11
14.	Orissa	3443	4345	5611	3.3	5.24
15.	Assam	2298	3426	3941	3.66	2.84
16.	Jammu & Kashmir	1050	1362	*	*	*
All India		110340	190218	243617	5.42	5.07

Source : National Accounts Statistics, 1998.

Table 1.2 : *(Contd.)*

B. CARG of Per Capita Net State Domestic Product At Factor Cost (At Constant Price 1980-81)

(In Rupees Crores)

Sl. No.	Major States	80-81	91-92	95-96	CARG 81-96	CARG 91-95
1.	Maharashtra	2435	3365	4500	4.17	2.38
2.	Punjab	2674	3825	4175	3.01	1.76
3.	Haryana	2370	3499	3670	2.95	0.95
4.	Gujarat	1940	2386	3172	3.33	5.86
5.	Tamil Nadu	1498	2268	2744	4.11	3.88
6.	West Bengal	1773	2267	2668	2.76	3.31
7.	Karnataka	1520	2262	2425	3.16	1.4
8.	Kerala	1508	1826	2353	3.01	5.2
9.	Rajasthan	1222	1761	2015	3.39	2.73
10.	Andhra Pradesh	1380	1788	1913	2.2	1.36
11.	Jammu & Kashmir	1776	1775	*	*	
12.	Madhya Pradesh	1358	1538	1784	1.83	3.01
13.	Uttar Pradesh	1278	1627	1666	1.78	0.47
14.	Orissa	1314	1530	1630	1.27	1.44
15.	Assam	1284	1575	1593	1.44	0.22
16.	Bihar	917	1119	1149	1.51	0.53
	All India	1625	2226	2648	3.3	3.53

Source: National Accounts Statistics, 1998.

Looking at the sectoral growth rates, it seems that the state economy grew in a fairly balanced fashion during the sixties and seventies (Table 1.1). The rates of the growth of the primary, secondary and tertiary sectors were between 3.0 per cent and 3.6 per cent in the sixties and between 4.15 and 5.8 in the seventies. The state NSDP grew at higher rates, 3.32 per cent and 4.95 per cent in the sixties and seventies respectively than the Indian economy, which grew at 3.17 per cent and 3.66 per cent,during the same periods. This sectoral balance in the sixties and seventies also indicates close linkages between agricultural and manufacturing sectors in the state economy.

The situation has changed since the eighties with the primary sector, particularly the agricultural sector, lagging behind in this decade. The annual growth rate in agriculture fell to 1 per cent while the secondary and tertiary sectors showed a big jump to around 7 per cent during the decade (Table 1.1). During the nineties also, the annual compound growth rate in agriculture remained at less than 1 per cent while the same in the secondary and tertiary sectors rose to 9.45 and 10.61 per cent respectively. The long-term annual compound growth rates between 1980-81 and 1997-98 in the three sectors have been 1.42, 8.87 and 7.25 per cent respectively which clearly indicates the structural distortion in the economy.

Table 1.3 presents the data on the shares of the broad industry groups in the state NSDP during the past few decades. It shows that the secondary sector experienced the highest jump in the share from about 21 per cent in 1970-71 (at 1970-71 prices) to about 40 per cent in 1995-96 (at 1980-81 prices), implying a 90 per cent increase, while the share of the tertiary sector has increased from 30 per cent to 39 per cent implying a 30 per cent increase. The share of the primary sector has fallen from 49 per cent to 21 per cent during the period. That is, the share of the non-primary sector in the state NSDP has increased by about 55 per cent during the two and a half decades. It is worth noting that unlike the Indian economy, the state economy has diversified more in the manufacturing sector than in the tertiary sector.

A striking feature of the Table 1.3 is the highly fluctuating nature of NSDP from the primary sector, and particularly from agriculture. The NSDP from this sector (at constant prices) shows high fluctuations between Rs. 2,277 crores to Rs. 3,366 crores without any strong long-term trend. The non-primary sectors, however, show a consistent increase in the value of NSDP coming from the sectors. Table 1.4, which presents per capita NSDP from the three sectors also, once again shows the similar behaviour.

To sum up, the Gujarat economy has undergone a significant structural transformation during the past few decades and experienced a high rate of growth of its NSDP. However, this cannot be considered as satisfactory because the primary sector, particularly agriculture, has lagged far behind with almost stagnant long-term growth since the eighties. Also, the agriculture in the state is highly unstable due to its wide year to year fluctuations that tend to leave the small farmers and farm labour in poverty. It is clear that this pattern of growth cannot be sustained for long as it does not allow agriculture and industry to establish strong and

Table 1.3 : Net Domestic Product by Industry Group

(Rs. in Crores)

Year	At Prices	Primary Sector	A.H. & Agriculture	Secondary Sector	Manufacturing	Tertiary etc.	Trade etc.	Services Banking Insurance	Public Admini.	Total NSDP	Per Capita NSDP (Rs.)
1970-71	1970-71	1071		456		662				2189	
		48.9		20.8		30.2				100	
1980-81	1980-81	2672	2434	1784	1354	2091	892	675	524	6547	1940
		40.8	37.2	27.2	20.7	31.9	13.6	10.3	8	100	
1985-86	1980-81	2544	2277	2721	2228	2949	1352	857	741	8214	2186
		31	27.7	33.1	27.1	35.9	16.5	10.4	9	100	
1990-91	1980-81	3026	2717	3753	3128	4094	1732	1464	899	872	2659
		27.7	24.9	34.4	28.7	37.9	15.9	13.4	8.6	100	
1991-92	1980-81	2468	2158	3308	2435	4168	1670	1553	944	9944	2381
		24.8	21.6	32.9	24	42.3	16.8	15.6	10	100	
1992-93	1980-81	3685	3366	4672	3853	4653	1909	1754	990	13011	3091
		28.3	25.9	35.9	29.6	35.8	14.7	13.5	7.6	100	
1993-94	1980-81	2739	2420	5060	4125	5011	2005	1919	1087	12801	2887
		21.4	18.9	39.5	32.2	39.1	15.7	15	8.5	100	
1994-95	1980-81	3647	3300	5429	4475	5429	2210	1992	1227	14504	3496
		25.1	22.8	37.4	30.9	37.4	15.2	13.7	8.5	100	
1995-96	1980-81	2946	2630	5729	4804	5535	2302	2066	1167	14211	3375
		20.7	18.5	40.3	33.8	38.9	16.2	14.5	8.2	100	

Source : Socio Economic Review, Directorate of Economics and Statistics, Gandhinagar.

mutually reinforcing linkages which are very essential for sustained development.

Issues in Agricultural Growth

Why is agriculture lagging behind in the state?

The performance of agriculture was good during the sixties and seventies when the compound annual growth rate in agriculture was 2.27 per cent and 4.15 per cent respectively. The growth in the sixties was largely due to the extensive cultivation and expanding irrigation facilities while the growth in the seventies was mainly due to the Green Revolution or the seed-fertilizer revolution. The negative or low growth rate of agriculture in the eighties and the nineties is largely because of the saturation of results of the earlier strategies and the lack of adoption of a new approach based on new technology (Desai and Namboodiri 1997). That is, agriculture has stagnated, if not declined, during the recent decades largely due to the lack of development of new technology that can accelerate land/labour productivity in agriculture.

Table 1.4 : Per Capita NSDP in Different Sectors, Gujarat (Rs. In 1980-81 prices)

Year	Per Capita NSDP				Per Capita GDP in India
	Primary Sector	Secondary Sector	Tertiary Sector	All Sectors	
1980-81	2672	1352	2091	1940	1625
1990-91	3006	3175	4102	2659	2267
1991-92	2104	2498	4190	2386	2226
1992-93	3352	2562	4344	3060	2298
1993-94	2411	2614	4427	2960	2391
1994-95	3347	2709	4592	3292	2518
1995-96	2641	2862	4601	3172	2648

Source : National Accounts Statistics of India, CSO, *Socio Economic Review,* Gandhinagar.

The deceleration of agricultural growth in the post-Green Revolution era, particularly in the eighties and the early nineties, is associated with several technical constraints: The available new varieties seem to have lost their genetic potential, some of the other inputs that have witnessed significant growth also therefore have lowered efficiency. This is aggravated further when the use of these new inputs is not adequately combined with the scientific knowledge of their application. Also, the share of government expenditure on agriculture, irrigation and electricity has declined, particularly since the eighties. Neglect of these expenditures implies forgoing opportunities not only to increase production and productivity, but also to stabilize weather induced fluctuations in agriculture (Desai, 1997).

Gujarat receives only one rainfall from June/July to September/ October period which varies widely from a meagre 340 mm. in west Kutch to 1800 mm. in southern hills in Dangs. The rainfall is erratic and concentrated, with the average number of rainy days varying from 20 in Kutch to 40-45 in south Gujarat. In spite of this, the south Gujarat region is endowed with some perennial rivers and the north Gujarat region has, had a good ground water potential. The exploitation of water resources in the state, however, has been far from judicious. The irrigation infrastructure as well as the subsidy pattern has not taken care of sustained use of the water resources. As a result the state is facing a serious water problem today.

The area under irrigation in the state has increased from 7 per cent in 1960-61 to 27 per cent in 1995-96. Though this comes to about 65 per cent of the total irrigation potential of the state (that leaves 35 per cent unexploited), the pattern of exploitation so far has been highly uneven and unfriendly to the ground water regimes, with the result that ground water levels have gone dangerously down in some regions due to water mining. Depletion of ground water levels have raised the cost of irrigation drastically on the one hand and affected the quality of land and water on the other hand, both affecting the productivity of land adversely.

The available unexploited potential now is largely of the surface water — from watersheds and other surface irrigation systems which somehow has not been used well. Developing this irrigation and using the available water systems judiciously are critical needs of today. Equally important would be conjunctive use of water in existing command areas of irrigation projects and better utilization of available water from these projects. This will not only raise the productivity in agriculture, but it will also provide the much-needed stabilization to the sector by reducing year to year fluctuations in its production.

There is, therefore, a need to think about and devise a new strategy for agriculture from henceforth. Of the three options for agricultural growth, namely, extensive farming, intensive agriculture and technological change, the last seems to be more relevant to Gujarat today. Since extensive farming has a limited scope now and since intensive agriculture is agro-economically unsustainable (due to its diminishing rate of returns that also creates pressure on natural resources), agricultural growth in Gujarat will have to come from technological change, viz. scientific knowledge based farming (Desai, 1997). Some of the challenges in this context are integration of seed-centred new technology with resource-centred new technology, which calls for systemized efforts. The technological inputs which should play a very critical role in the agricultural growth in the coming years, are promotion of watershed planning for moisture conservation, better use of the present irrigation systems, growing drought resistant varieties on a large scale and general promotion of dry farming technology. These technical changes along with institutional and infrastructure support in the field of credit, marketing, etc. will contribute substantially to a sustainable agricultural growth in the state. This new strategy will make agriculture broad-based — it will spread agriculture to rain-fed, semi-arid and arid regions, it will stabilize agriculture by reducing year to year fluctuations and it will make agricultural growth employment intensive and broad-based. Decentralization, debureaucratisation and better synergy in government expenditure should accompany these. This task is tough but not beyond the capabilities of the state (Hirway, 1997).

Issues in Industrial Development

Gujarat is among the most industrialised states in India. The industrial sector has performed consistently well with the growth rate of the manufacturing sector continuously increasing from 3.04 per cent in the sixties, to 5.55 per cent in the seventies, 8.73 per cent in the eighties and 11.92 per cent in the nineties.

Though Ahmedabad had developed as a major centre of the textile industry at the time of the independence, Gujarat ranked eighth in industrial development in 1960. The favourable policies of the state government as well as the enterprising population of the state, however, pushed the sector up over the years with the result that the state is at the forefront of industrial development today. The factors that led to this achievement are establishment of industrial estates with all the required infrastructural facilities in several parts of the state by the GIDC (Gujarat Industrial Development Corporation), continuous availability of power to the industry, availability of water (from the major rivers) to the industry, availability of railway links with major industrial and trading centres, particularly in south Gujarat where the industries are concentrated, setting up of four important corporations, namely, GIIC (Gujarat Industrial Investment Corporation), GIDC, GSFC (Gujarat State Finance Corporation) and Indextb (Industrial Extension Bureau) to provide finance, power facilities and all other required support to industries, and generally highly positive and supportive attitude of the government to the new industries. The industrial base of Gujarat got increasingly diversified gradually with petrochemicals and fertilisers, pharmaceuticals and drugs, dyestuff as well as engineering and electronics industries developing in the state.

The process of industrialisation in Gujarat has taken a new turn since the introduction of the economic reforms in 1991. After the Government of India announced the NIP (New Industrial Policy) in 1991 with the objective of implementing the economic reforms in the industrial sector, government of Gujarat has also responded favourably and announced its own industrial policies. The State Industrial Policy 1990-95 was already in operation when the New Industrial Policy (NIP), 1991 was declared by the Central Government. The Gujarat government declared the New Industrial and Incentive Policy 1995-2000 thereafter and Gujarat 2000 AD and Beyond in 1994 for accelerated industrial development of the state. Though the policy declarations by the government of Gujarat are essentially based on the general framework of the NIP, 1991, these are more aggressive in terms of promoting and facilitating new industrial investments. According to the government of Gujarat, the new climate of economic liberalisation and globalisation has opened new opportunities to the states in India to attract industrial investments from India and abroad. The state's approach is "to compete not only with other Indian states, but also with the newly emerging high growth regions of Southeast and East Asian countries" in the industrial sector (Indextb, 1996).

As in the case of the Central Government, the main policy instruments of the state government are deregulation and liberalisation of the different markets, incentives and concessions to potential industrialists from India and abroad, and promotional and developmental work. The focus of the policy, however, has been relatively more on incentives and concessions, and on promotional and developmental works. There is also a clear emphasis on promoting larger units which are described as "Premier" (units with investment between Rs. 100 crores to Rs. 500 crores) and "Prestigious units" (Units with investment of more than Rs. 500 crores) in the policy statements.

The government has devised a generous package of concessions and incentives in turn over sales tax on a whole range of goods such as, raw materials, intermediate goods, packing materials, processing materials, consumable goods, by products, scrap and waste materials, etc. In addition, there is transport subsidy and capital investment subsidy on a large number of products. These incentives are given at the taluka level to 128 talukas and 8 regions of the total 184 talukas of the state, covering about 78 per cent area of the state. Secondly, certain industries such as electronics industry as well as the Thrust Industries, Premier Units and Prestigious Units are eligible for the special incentives throughout the state except four banned areas. Tiny units set up and managed by the persons belonging to SC/ST/OBC castes or by women are eligible for the incentives through out the state and the existing units undertaking expansion or diversification also are eligible for the special incentives as per the rules. In addition, special incentive are provided to exporting units including the EOUs, employment oriented small-scale units, units constructing project related infrastructure, units investing in social infrastructure construction and common as well as public purpose infrastructure. Special incentives are being given to NRIs that range from cash subsidies, tax concessions, out of turn allocation of sheds, power and other infrastructural facilities to various types of escort services like providing facilities to their families and children. Government of Gujarat has set up Single Point Contact, the NRI Cell in the Indextb to assist NRIs right from the stage of concept to the stage of commissioning of industrial units.

Realising that subsidies and concessions are not adequate to attract industries in the state if the required infrastructure is not available, government of Gujarat has given a high priority to the promotion of infrastructure in the state. The government has set up Gujarat Infrastructure Development Board (GIDB) in 1995 with the objectives of attracting private sector investment in infrastructure, such as roads, power plants, ports, jetties, etc., setting up guidelines for the involvement of the private sector, the banks and the financial institutions including the global financial institutions in funding infrastructural facilities in Gujarat and formulation as well as implementation of a long term infrastructure policy in Gujarat. In addition, the state government has also provided concessions to new industries in the acquisition of power, land, water and other infrastructure support, and assured these supplies within a limited time. The state government has also made special efforts to provide all required information to prospective industrialists and has used the media extensively for the purpose. In short, the state government has been aggressive and determined to attract maximum industrial investments to the state.

This approach has given rich dividends in terms of attracting industrial investments to the state, particularly in the large and medium industries. In fact, Gujarat has attracted the highest industrial investment in the large and medium sectors, more than Rs. 1,70,000 crores during 1991-1997 among all the states in India. This quantum jump implies more than 10 times increase in the industrial investment per year, five and a half time increase in the number of projects per year, and more than 60 per cent increase in the average investment per unit, from Rs. 24 crores to Rs. 40 crores (Hirway and Shah 1998) (Tables 1.5 and 1.6).

Table 1.5 : Industrial Investments: Sanctioned Projects in Large and Medium Industries in Gujarat (1983-1990 and 1991-1996)

	During 1983–1990	During 1991–1996
Projects Sanctioned		
Total Number	886	4423
No. per year	110.75	649.25
Investments (Rs. m)		
Total	213,860	1,701,169
Investment per year	26,722	319,266
Employment		
Total	141637	843673
Per year	17,704	158,287

Source: Indext (b), Government of Gujarat, Ahmedabad.

The new industrial investments are gradually introducing a set of new characteristics in the industrial scene in Gujarat: (a) there is a clear increase in the investments in large and medium industries in the state with the SSI sector lagging far behind in the post-1991 period, (b) the location pattern of industries has shifted to coastal Saurashtra with 21 per cent (instead of 2 per cent before 1991) of the new investments located in the region (Table 7), (c) though the basic pattern of industrial dispersion has not changed as the industrially rich regions have attracted larger industrial investments, several small industrial centres have developed/

strengthened in the post reform period, (d) the new investments are much more capital intensive than before, particularly in the Saurashtra and Kutch regions (Table 1.7), (e) the share of mineral-based industries is very large (9 per cent), (f) there is an export orientation in the new investments, and (g) the share of industries using non-renewable resources and pollution prone industries has remained high (Hirway and Shah 1998).

Table 1.6 : Location of the Sanctioned Industrial Investments in Large and Medium Industries 1983-1990 and 1991-1996 (% to the total)

Region	1983-1990	1991-1996
Central and South Region		
Projects	70.31	76.08
Investment	92.61	69.41
Employment	69.87	69.41
North Gujarat		
Projects	13.31	13.17
Investments	4.13	4.62
Employment	15.31	13.01
Saurashtra		
Projects	6.99	9.66
Investments	2.15	21.20
Employment	7.94	15.84
Kutch		
Projects	6.98	1.04
Investments	0.48	4.65
Employment	4.47	1.75

Source: Indext(b), Government of Gujarat, Ahmedabad.

What kind of impact will this new pattern of industrialisation have on the state economy? Several concerns have been raised regarding the impact of the new industrial investments on the state economy. Using the studies on the subject, we would like to discuss the major issues.

1. The first issue is regarding the validity of the policy of promoting or rather pushing modern industries in backward regions without

attacking the roots of backwardness in the regions. The question is not of selecting one against the other, but it is of sequencing them for the healthy development of backward regions. Backward regions are frequently suffering from severe environmental degradation and/or are poor in infrastructure. It is important therefore that the environment is protected before it is too late and agriculture is stabilised in the process. The 'agriculture first' strategy will ensure a sustained development in the region, which will help in establishing strong industry-agriculture linkages in the region. It must be reiterated that industrial development is a must for economic diversification and for economic growth. But to impose modern capital intensive industries on the fragile ecology of backward regions will not be sustainable. In short, the issue is about the development strategy of backward regions.

Table 1.7 : Investment and Employment Per Project 1983-90 and 1991-96

Region	1983-1990	1991-1996
Central and South Region		
Investment per project (Rs. m)	31.79	36.28
Employment per project	158.86	165.29
Investment per employment (Rs. m)	00.200	00.219
North Gujarat		
Investment per project (Rs. m)	7.48	13.95
Employment per project	183.80	178.94
Investment per employment (Rs. m)	00.041	00.077
Saurashtra		
Investment per project (Rs. m)	7.44	87.25
Employment per project	181.61	296.58
Investment per employment (Rs. m)	00.041	00.294
Kutch		
Investment per project (Rs. m)	1.69	177.02
Employment per project	103.98	303.52
Investment per employment (Rs. m)	00.016	00.583

Source: INDEX (b), Government of Gujarat, Ahmedabad.

2. The second issue is whether these industries enrich the region through

the functioning of factor markets and if not, what kinds of interventions are needed. Studies have shown that large industrial units in backward areas tend to exploit the region through distorted land markets that include the Land Acquisition Act (which enables industrialists to acquire cheap land from farmers, panchayats and government) and segmented labour markets (that allows the industrialists to use local cheap labour without giving them any social protection). In addition, the industries are allowed to use natural resources including non-renewables like minerals at a cheap rate. They are not even forced to pay for the pollution that they create in the region. In other words, these modern and highly capital intensive industries exploit the region without benefiting much the local people and the local economy.

In order to improve the functioning of the land market, it is important to examine carefully the validity of the Land Acquisition Act for industries. Efforts should also be made to develop the land market through promoting transparency in the market and through enforcing the laws regarding the sale of common land and forest land. In the case of the labour market it is important to keep systematic records of workers and provide them with adequate wages and a package of minimum health as well as social protection on the one hand and to provide skill training to local youths to integrate them in the new industries on the other hand.

3. The third issue is regarding the model of industrial development for the state. It is clear that the state government has initiated a new model since the inception of the reforms. The question is whether it is sustainable and whether it can generate enough employment opportunities in the economy. Theoretically, there are two approaches to industrialisation, namely, the 'textile first' approach and the 'machinery first' approach. While the former approach advocates highest priority to industries that produce non-durable consumer goods like textiles, sugar, tea, edible oil, light engineering goods, intermediate goods, and simple equipments and machines; the latter advocates heavy capital goods, basic inputs, etc. The first strategy tends to strengthen the industry-agriculture linkages, generates large-scale employment as well as higher growth rates in the short-run. The question is whether there is a need to push the second strategy through heavy incentives and concessions and promote industries that use non- renewable natural resources, frequently for exports and generate pollution that is difficult to control.

4. The next issue is pertaining to large-scale incentives given to industries in the state. There is a race going on among some major states in the country in providing incentives to attract industrial investments to their respective states. This race has created several problems. Firstly, it is not market friendly but it is anti-market in character, and therefore is likely to give wrong signals if not managed carefully. Secondly, it reduces the revenue of the state drastically, which tends to put restrictions on the allocations to the social sectors. And thirdly, such incentive to new units is unfair to the already existing units. Though it is true that the issue is not under the control of the state government, it can take stronger initiative at the national level.
5. And lastly, the issue is also of the need for expanding non-polluting industries in the state, particularly the new generating knowledge-based industries. The predominance of polluting industries in the industrial structure of the state economy is largely due to some historical facts. There is, however, a need to go into non-polluting knowledge-based industries which somehow do not seem to be attracted to the state. Though the state government has initiated some efforts in this area, there is a long way to go to be in the forefront of science and technology in the country.

Employment and Labour Market

Generation of remunerative employment is an important condition for reducing un/underemployment and poverty in an economy. In this context it will be useful to see how the development has treated the employment scene in the state.

In the year 1991, there were about 16.6 million workers in the state (the workforce participation rate was about 40 per cent), of whom 14.1 million (85 per cent) were main workers and 2.5 million (15 per cent) were marginal workers. Most of the male workers (about 99 per cent) worked as main workers while only 53 per cent of women workers worked as main workers. That is, about 47 per cent of women workers in the state worked for less than six months in the year. The incidence of chronic unemployment (i.e. unemployment measured in terms of the usual status of the population) was fairly low, 0.62 per cent and 0.30 per cent for men and women respectively in rural Gujarat and 4.7 per cent and 0.50 per cent for men and women respectively in urban Gujarat (Table 1.9). The current unemployment rates based on the daily status of the population in the state, however, were higher, 6.00 and 4.70 for men and women in rural Gujarat, and 5.70 and 7.8 for men and women in urban Gujarat during 1993-94 (Table 1.9).

The overall employment scene in Gujarat is better than the same in India in some ways. Firstly, Gujarat has not experienced any decline in the level of employment in the recent decades. In fact, the WFPR in Gujarat has shown a marginal increase between 1981 1991 while the same in India declined. And secondly, the rates, of unemployment, including the daily status unemployment rates in Gujarat are much lower for males and females both in rural and urban areas than the same in India.

The dimensions of unemployment in the state, however, are far from insignificant. It has been estimated that the backlog of unemployment in the labour force will increase and reach 1.9 million to 2.2 million in 2001. The major task therefore is to generate new employment of this size to ensure work to all in the labour force (Table 1.10). This dimension of the task identified needs to be desegregated to understand the complexities of the un/underemployment problem. Some of the major issues, still unresolved, in this context are discussed below:

Table 1.8 : Workforce Participation Rates in India and Gujarat, 1981-1991.

		Gujarat		India	
		Rural	Urban	Rural	Urban
1981	Males	54.2	50.2	53.8	49.1
	Females	26.9	6.5	23.2	8.33
1991	Males	54.91	51.08	52.4	48.94
	Females	35.60	7.21	26.7	9.2

Source: Census of Population 1981-1991.

Un/underemployment of the rural poor

The first major issue is pertaining to the un/underemployment of the rural poor, especially those living in backward regions. It has been observed that the rural poor in Gujarat are primarily concentrated in the regions that are environmentally degraded and/or are infrastructurally backward. As we shall see later, the incidence of poverty is highest in these regions, that is, in the northern dry region and the eastern tribal region. The poor from these regions migrate long distances in search of work at the cost of their health, education and welfare after the short agricultural season is over. Generation of massive employment opportunities in these regions therefore has to be the first task of any employment strategy in the state. The two activities, which can provide massive employment to the poor here, are environmental regeneration and ecological restoration of the region and creation of social and physical infrastructure. Employment in these activities will generate employment for the un/underemployed on the one hand and promote and stabilise the agriculture on the other hand, resulting in a broad-based development of the region. It will also create socio-economic infrastructure, which will provide a sound foundation for long-term development.

Table 1.9 : Unemployment rates, Gujarat and India

	Rural				Urban			
	Gujarat		India		Gujarat		India	
	Male	Female	Male	Female	Male	Female	Male	Female
Chronic unemployment rates by usual status								
1972-73	0.74	0.11	1.16	0.48	2.85	0.86	4.8	6
1977-78	0.63	0.81	1.27	2.01	2.38	0.58	5.4	12.4
1983	0.84	0.46	1.51	0.82	4.16	0.43	5.1	4.9
1987-88	0.62	0.3	1.8	2.41	4.7	0.5	5.2	6.2
By current daily status								
1972-79	5.45	6.6	7.15	11.37	5.78	1.37	8	13.7
1977-78	6.34	5.69	7.56	9.5	3.49	0.82	9.4	14.5
1983	5.15	5.15	7.95	10.38	5.5	0.67	9.2	11
1987-88	6.24	5.34	6.51	8.24	4.75	1.26	8.8	12
1993-94	6.00	4.70	5.60	5.60	5.70	7.8	6.70	10.5

Source: NSS Rounds.

Though wage employment programmes such as Employment Assurance Scheme (EAS), Jawahar Rojgar Yojana (JRY) and the large-scale scarcity works are expected to perform these tasks and integrate the poor in the development process of these regions, somehow this has not happened. It is important therefore that the government pools the funds of these wage employment programmes and uses it in a systematic way so as to generate short term as well as long term sustainable employment for the poor on the one hand and to promote development of the backward regions on the other.

Table 1.10 : Population, workforce, labourforce and unemployment projections (millions)

Year	Population		Workforce		Labourforce		Unemployment	
	P1	P2	P1	P2	P1	P2	P1	P2
1991	41.0	42.0	15.3	15.3	15.7	15.9	0.4	0.6
1992	43.3	45.6	16.5	16.5	17.7	18.3	1.2	1.8
1996	43.8	46.1	16.8	16.9	18.1	18.8	1.3	1.9
1997	44.4	47.1	17.1	17.4	18.6	19.3	1.5	1.9
1998	44.9	47.9	17.4	17.8	19	19.9	1.6	2.1
1999	45.4	48.8	17.7	18.4	19.5	20.5	1.8	2.1
2000	46.0	49.1	0	0	0	0	0	0
2001	46.5	49.7	18.0	18.8	19.9	21.0	1.9	2.2

Notes :

- P1, W1, L1 and U1 are based on the population projections by the Expert Committee that used 1981 data.
- P2, W2, L2 and U2 are based on the revised population projections.
- The difference between the labourforce and the workforce indicate the extent of employment.

Improving quality of existing employment

Poor are too poor to remain idle, and most of them take up whatever work is available even at a very low skill/productivity level or at a very low wage rate. Many of the non-poor workers belonging to the unorganised sector also are deprived of fair wages and even a minimum level of social protection. About 41 per cent of men workers and more than 55 per cent of women workers in rural areas are engaged in such activities, which need to be upgraded. In the case of urban areas, many of the 17 per cent of men workers and 28 per cent of women workers who are engaged in casual employment may need upgraded employment. These workers are almost totally unprotected and need a minimum social protection. Also, 40 per cent of male workers and 40 per cent of the female workers in rural areas, and 38 per cent of male workers and 35 per cent of female workers in urban areas are self-employed, again mostly in petty activities and need upgradation of employment as well as social protection. Informalisation of the labour market over time, particularly of the urban economy in the recent years, has occurred much faster in Gujarat than in India. The higher incidence of poverty in urban Gujarat is a result of this process.

The high incidence of self-employment also implies the need for strengthening the self-employed by improving their access to better skill training, credit and other infrastructure facilities on the one hand and providing social protection on the other hand. The ongoing policies and programmes in this field need to be strengthened qualitatively as well as quantitatively. It is also important that (a) the government pays more attention to the enforcement of minimum wages, (b) provides old age pension/provident fund, (c) covers workers under some minimum health insurance and (d) ensures maternity benefits to women workers.

National Renewal Fund and frictional unemployment

Workers in Gujarat have suffered a lot in the past decades due to the closure of a large number of textile mills in the state (Patel, 1996). Since the phenomenon of industrial sickness and industrial mortality is likely to increase further in the post-reforms phase resulting in several incidents of frictional unemployment, it is important that proper policies and programmes are formulated for the workers who are affected by unemployment originating from industrial sickness and mortality

The National Renewal Fund (NRF), which has been designed for the purpose, needs to be strengthened qualitatively and quantitatively. So far the NRF has (a) focused mainly on public sector textile units (by giving the workers VRS benefits) and neglected thousands of workers who lost their jobs without receiving their legal dues, (b) done very little in the field of training/retraining quantitatively and qualitatively, (c) has not introduced any unemployment insurance, (d) rehabilitated only a very small number of workers and (e) neglected the area regeneration part of the NRF almost totally. Consequently, the NRF has not yet developed into a programme that provides a significant relief to the workers of closed textile mills (Hirway, 1996). Setting up of a State Renewal Fund, implementation of area regeneration schemes that aim at using the land and machinery of the closed mills to revitalise the urban economy of Gujarat, expanding and improving training/retraining machinery, etc. can help considerably in the coming years.

Linking of education and employment

Gujarat is one of the most industrialised states in India and the pace of industrialisation in the coming years is likely to be faster than before. This huge investment will need a variety of labour trained in different skills and professions. It is important, therefore, that the state government reorients its education and training policy to meet the variety of demands generated for the skills and professions in the state.

The present situation, however, is of a mismatch of the demand and supply of educated labourpower in the state. On the one hand, the army of educated unemployed people is increasing continuously, while on the other hand, there is, and there will be, a serious shortage of technical labour. Over time, from 1980 to 1995, the strength of the educated unemployed has increased from 2.70 lakhs to 6.82 lakhs, that is more than two and half times increase. The share of the educated unemployed in the total unemployed has increased from 57 per cent in 1980 to 75 per cent in 1994, which is indicative of the low and declining employability of the educated labourpower in the state. It is interesting to note that the unemployment of technically qualified persons, including engineering degree holders, has increased over the last decade and a half. (Table 11)

As against this, the rapid industrialisation of the state is likely to generate demand for a variety of technical skills, not all of, which are available in the state. It has been estimated that the percentage share of technically qualified labourpower in the total main workers in Gujarat was less than one in 1981 while the percentage of educated labourpower above matriculation was 15 in the same year (Census of India, General Economic Tables 1981, Gujarat). The percentage has increased to 9 today. However, there is an urgent need to plan for the required technical labourpower carefully and systematically. There is an urgent need (a) to improve the employability of the already educated persons by undertaking skill training programmes and (b) to reorient the education system to meet the future demand for labour in the state. Though the committed industrial investments in the state may not be able to ensure full employment, it can

Table 1.11 : Number of Job Seekers by Level of Education

Sr. No.	Level of Education	As on 31st December						
		1980	1985	1990	1994	1995	1996	1997
1	2	3	4	5	6	7	8	9
1	S.S.C.	199588	337826	435429	441546	439642	463715	458316
2	Inter	23906	55404	81724	111191	127454	126545	119540
3	Diploma	3720	5000	8766	10750	10787	10992	11599
4	Graduates	39489	45986	55007	66368	76483	84523	94656
	(a) Arts	14891	15721	16443	24133	29366	33878	39031
	(b) Science	4520	5332	8479	9406	10974	11839	13524
	(c) Commerce	13239	17695	20584	20069	22603	23594	25131
	(d) Others	6839	7238	9501	12760	13540	14812	16970
5	Engineering Graduates	694	1042	4085	4298	3725	3681	3742
	(a) Civil	216	410	2368	1952	1431	1428	1327
	(b) Mechanical	232	290	681	731	630	638	754
	(c) Electrical	118	177	370	574	619	624	681
	(d) Others	128	165	666	1041	1045	993	980

(Contd.)

Table 1.11 *(Contd.)*

Sr. No.	Level of Education	As on 31st December						
		1980	1985	1990	1994	1995	1996	1997
1	2	3	4	5	6	7	8	9
6	Post Graduates	2855	4027	8129	11194	12184	12928	14296
	(a) Arts	1229	1538	2355	4401	5452	5914	6851
	(b) Science	686	1117	2050	2548	2369	2433	2733
	(c) Commerce	553	781	1891	2363	2475	2485	2630
	(d) Others	387	591	1833	1882	1888	1996	2082
7	Engineering Post Graduates	1	3	15	25	6	2	2
	(1) Total Educated Unemployed	270253	449288	563155	645352	670281	702386	702151
	(2) Total Uneducated Unemployed	200635	284550	363826	260975	241901	229896	240444
	Grand Total (1+2)	470888	733838	926381	906327	912182	932282	942595

Source: Directorate of Employment and Training, Gujarat State, Gandhinagar.

definitely reduce the extent of the unemployment, of the educated people if the required efforts are made.

Environment and Ecology

Gujarat has lost heavily on its environment and ecology during the process of economic growth. It shows wide diversity of physiography, climate and hydrology. It can be described as arid, semi-arid and to an extent sub-humid in character. The state has been divided into seven agroclimatic zones: In the south there are Southern Hills which is part of Saputara range (Dangs and Valsad districts) which receives more than 1800 mm. of average annual rainfall; the rest of south Gujarat (Bharuch and Surat districts) that receives about 970 mm. of average annual rainfall; middle Gujarat (Kheda and Vadodara) with more than 900 mm. of average annual rainfall; north Gujarat that is arid and semi-arid in character with an annual rainfall of 735 mm., (covering five districts, namely, Ahmedabad, Gandhinagar, Mehsana, Sabarkantha and Banaskantha), North-west arid zone (Kutch district), that receives extremely low rainfall of about 340 mm.; north Saurashtra, close to Kachchh which is arid and semi-arid in character with 530 mm. of annual rainfall (covering northern parts of Amreli, Bhavnagar, Rajkot, Jamnagar and Surendranagar districts) and south Saurashtra or coastal Saurashtra which is dry and sub-humid in character.

The diversity has resulted in uneven distribution of land, water and vegetation in the state. Unfortunately, the state has mismanaged these resources.

Water Resources in the State

There is a general belief that in any arid and semi-arid region, water shortage is a gift of nature. This argument is frequently put forth to explain the water shortage of Gujarat. However, this is quite far from the truth. The combination of climate, physiography and geology in different regions of the state did provide naturally favourable conditions for water resources in most regions of the state about three decades ago (Hirway and Patel, 1994). For example, the north Gujarat alluvial area has low rainfall, but has good topographic conditions of recharge and ideal conditions of aquifers, which has rendered the region with rich ground water reservoir. In fact, this storage has supported thousands of tube-wells for more than

35 years in this region. In the same way, the hilly areas of the east have adverse physiographic and geological conditions inhibiting large ground water storages, but these areas have been provided with ideal sites for creating surface storage dam reservoirs. The arid areas of Kutch have favourable geological formations, which have provided confined aquifers in consolidated formations of sweet water up to 200 m. depth. Finally, the coastal areas of Saurashtra are capable of storing the rainfall run-off from the upland rocky terrain thereby naturally conserving the precipitation of the region.

The shortage of water felt by the state is to a great extent man-made, originated in overdrafting of ground water without any adequate recharge systems. The coastal Saurashtra enjoyed sweet (ground) water regime, but the overdrafting of ground water from coastal Saurashtra has pushed in saline water resulting in salinity ingress in the region on the one hand and deterioration in the quality of water supply on the other hand. The indiscriminate withdrawal of ground water in north Gujarat, Kutch and northern Saurashtra has depleted its water resources badly leading to water mining on a large scale. Even in the south, where the rainfall is high, the canal irrigation and the consequent overuse of water has pushed up water logging and salinity in this region. In short, the total mismanagement of the water resources, basically arising from the pricing and subsidy policy of irrigation, has brought the state to a level where water has become one of the most scarce items in the state.

The rapid loss of ground water resources in the state can be seen from the Table 1.12 which shows that while in 1984 about 164 talukas (88 per cent) were "white", i.e. "safe" in terms of ground water position, today the number has dwindled to 95 (about 51 per cent). About 31 talukas are overexploited and 64 are dangerous in terms of ground water withdrawal.

Overdrafting of ground water leading to water mining and salinity ingress has resulted in the deterioration of the quality of water available in the different regions of the state. The most important quality problems are pertaining to excessive salinity and excessive fluoride in water. About 14 per cent villages in the state have ground water with excessive fluoride. Mehsana has the highest proportion of such villages (28.78 per cent) followed by Banaskantha (24.8 per cent), Ahmedabad (22.01 per cent) and Jamnagar (20.41 per cent). About 6 per cent villages have excess salinity in the ground water. Kheda is at the top in salinity followed by Ahmedabad and Mehsana. The excess salinity in the ground water in

Table 1.12 : Talukawise Level of Ground Water Development

Sr. No	District	*Number of Talukas in each category*														
		1984					1991					1997				
		W	G	D	OE	S	W	G	D	OE	S	W	G	D	OE	S
1	Ahmedabad	6	0	0	0	0	2	0	0	4	0	2	0	2	3	0
2	Amreli	7	2	1	0	0	9	0	0	1	0	9	0	0	1	0
3	Banaskantha	11	0	0	0	0	5	2	1	3	0	1	1	2	4	3
4	Baroda	12	0	0	0	0	11	0	1	0	0	10	1	0	1	0
5	Bhavnagar	12	0	0	0	0	12	0	0	0	0	10	2	0	0	0
6	Bharuch	11	0	0	0	0	9	0	1	1	0	6	2	0	3	0
7	Valsad	8	0	0	0	0	8	0	0	0	0	7	1	0	0	0
8	Dangs	1	0	0	0	0	1	0	0	0	0	1	0	0	0	0
9	Gandhinagar	1	0	0	0	0	0	1	0	0	0	0	0	0	1	0
10	Jamnagar	9	1	0	0	0	8	2	0	0	0	7	3	0	0	0
11	Junagadh	9	4	2	0	0	8	4	2	1	0	3	8	2	2	0
12	Kheda	10	0	0	0	0	6	1	2	1	0	4	4	0	2	0
13	Kutch	9	0	0	0	0	2	4	1	2	0	2	3	0	4	0
14	Panchmahals	11	0	0	0	0	8	3	0	0	0	10	1	0	0	0

(Contd.)

Table 1.12 *(Contd.)*

Sr. No	District	1984					1991					1997				
		Number of Talukas in each category														
		W	**G**	**D**	**OE**	**S**	**W**	**G**	**D**	**OE**	**S**	**W**	**G**	**D**	**OE**	**S**
15	Rajkot	8	4	0	1	0	10	2	0	0	1	5	7	0	0	1
16	Sabarkantha	10	0	0	0	0	5	3	1	1	0	1	6	2	1	0
17	Surat	13	0	0	0	0	13	0	0	0	0	13	0	0	0	0
18	Surendranagar	8	0	0	0	1	4	4	0	0	1	4	4	0	0	1
19	Mehsana	6	2	3	0	0	0	0	1	10	0	0	0	0	9	2
	Gujarat	**162**	**13**	**6**	**1**	**1**	**121**	**26**	**10**	**24**	**2**	**95**	**43**	**8**	**31**	**7**

W – White; G – Grey; D – Dark; OE – Overexploited; S – Saline.

Source: Narmada and Water Resources Department, GOG 1986, 1992 & 1998.

Table 1.13 : Forest Cover in Gujarat (by main types of crown density and mangroves)

(In million hectares)

A. De sc.	1972-75	1983-85	1985-87	1987-89	1989-91	1991-93	1993 95	1972-75 to 1983-85	1983-85 to 1985-87	1985-87 to 1987-89	1987-89 to 1989-91	1989-91 to 1991-93	1991-93 to 1993-95	1972-75 to 1993-95
Dense forest	0.70	0.69	0.54	0.62	0.63	0.63	0.63	-1.43	-21.74	14.81	1.61	0.00	0.00	-10
% share to total forst	73.68	57.85	45.06	52.27	52.32	51.70	50.38							
Open forest	0.20	0.46	0.61	0.53	0.53	0.53	0.52	130.00	32.61	-13.11	0.00	0.00	-1.89	160.00
% share to total forest	21.05	39.00	51.41	44.39	44.20	42.71	41.74							
Mangroves	0.05	0.04	0.04	0.04	0.04	0.07	0.09	-20.00	0.00	0.00	0.00	75.00	28.57	80.00
% share to total forest	5.27	3.14	3.53	3.33	3.48	5.59	7.88							
Total Forest	0.95	1.19	1.19	1.19	1.20	1.23	1.25	25.26	0.00	0.00	0.84	2.50	1.63	31.58

Source : State of Forest Reports, 1987, 1989, 1991, 1993, 1995 & 1997, FSI, Dehradun, The Citizen's Fifth Report, State of India's Environment, CSE, 1997.

Kheda is because of the overuse of canal water and the consequent waterlifting while the excess salinity of Mehsana is due to the overdrafting of ground water. Excessive nitrate in ground water is observed only in about 3 per cent of villages in the state, Bhavnagar and Amreli topping the list followed by Kheda. In short, the excessive levels of nitrites, salinity and fluoride are observed in almost all the districts of the state.

Shortage of potable drinking water is one of the serious problems that the state is facing today. It has been estimated that about half the villages in the state face serious shortage of potable drinking water in the summer. The GWSSB (Gujarat Water Supply and Sewerage Board) has declared more than 75 per cent villages in the state as 'No Source Villages' implying villages with no dependable or sustainable source of water. The state government has adopted a policy of installing regional water pipelines to carry water to distant villages, located 100 km to 200 km or even 300 km. away. It has been observed, however, that such schemes are environmentally non-sustainable (since they use ground water which is continuously sinking), economically expensive, administratively non-feasible and technologically non-manageable at the village level (Hirway and Patel, 1994). The quality of water supplied through such schemes is also under question as often the source tapped has high salinity or fluoride content or in the course of transport of the water, it gets contaminated.

The best solution to the problem is to encourage local traditional (modified as per the new technology) systems of rainwater collection for the purpose of ensuring water supply to the village. Several NGOs have developed successful models in this field. Recently, the GWSSB also has shown interest in supporting such activities if undertaken by NGOs and community organisations. These efforts need to be strengthened.

The main sources of urban water supply in the state today are ground water, which is drafted by builders and developers indiscriminately, and surface water, which is acquired through nearby irrigation dams. With the increasing demand for water, the urban authorities go deeper in water excavation or go farther in accessing water from distant irrigation dams. Though considerable water supply can be conserved by controlling leakages of water taps (about 30 per cent); standardising fixtures such as toilet, flush, water pipes, water taps, corks in water tanks, etc. (by upto 50 per cent), recycling of used water and ground water recharging; the efforts are generally focused on acquiring ground water from still deeper acquifers and irrigation dams located farther away. It is clear that these solutions will never solve the problem of urban water supply unless supplemented by the measures of water conservation.

Forest Cover

As compared to the norm of about 30 per cent forest cover for Gujarat (the norm depends on the topography and physiography of the region), the forest area in the state cover about 10 per cent of its area. The actual forests, however, cover only 6 per cent of the area (Forest Survey of India, 1997). This is clearly a gross shortage from the environmental point of view. Another indicator of the adequacy of forest cover is per capita forest cover, which is 0.47 ha. for "every individual to meet his basic needs" (Forest Survey of India, 1997). Gujarat has the per capita cover of 0.042 ha. which is less than 10 per cent of the norm.

Though Gujarat experienced a loss of forest cover till about seventies, the decline has been arrested to an extent in the sense that the actual forest cover is stabilised around 63 m. ha. In terms of quality of forest, however, the state shows a declining trend as the percentage of dense forests has consistently declined, from 73.68 in total forest in 1972-75 to 50.4 in 1993-94 (Table 1.13). There is some improvement in mangroves, after a consistent loss for decades, in the recent years. This gain, however, is limited only to a few regions, around the gulf of Kutch (Forest Survey of India, 1997).

In short, Gujarat has experienced an overall declining trends in forests, which are supposed to play a critical role in protecting and stabilising its environment and ecology.

Salinity ingress is another serious environmental problem of the state. It has affected adversely the quality of water supply on the one hand, and agricultural productivity of land on the other. Government of Gujarat conducted the first survey on salinity in 1960, the year when the state was formed. According to this survey, the salinity was observed mainly in some coastal villages located right on the sea coast covering about 1,232 sq. km. area in the six districts of Saurashtra. The pace of salinisation accelerated between 1960-1975 and particularly between 1975-1993. The saline area in the state increased more than 8 times during this period. This was primarily because of (a) the destruction of mangroves on the sea coast, (b) overdrafting of (sweet) ground water in the coastal regions and (c) overdrafting of ground water in other regions. The extent of salinity has increased also in canal irrigated area due to the overuse of (cheap) canal water resulting in water logging in these regions. It has been estimated by the Gujarat Ecology Commission (GEC) that about 30 per cent area of the state will be affected by excess salinity by 2001 AD if radical actions are not taken to control its ingress. The most damaged area will be the region around the Gulf of Khambhat and the coastal Saurashtra (GEC 1997).

Government of Gujarat has set up several committees and task forces on salinity since 1970 when the first committee was set up for salinity ingress in Saurashtra and Kutch. This was followed by Kapoor Committee (1974), the Shivraj Committee (1978), the Dutch Mission in early nineties, and the recent Coastal Zone Management Plan (CZMP) (1996).

Somehow, the recommendations of these committees and task forces have not been implemented seriously, as a result increasing salinity of land and water is a major environmental problem of agricultural growth of the state threatening the sustainability of agricultural growth on the one hand and worsening the problem of drinking water on the other.

Waste Lands and Coverage of DPAP/DDP Programmes

According to the recent environmental statistics, published by the CSO, more than 40 per cent area in the state is wasteland (CSO, 1997). This is slightly higher than the all India average of 38-39 per cent. The high percentage of the wasteland in the state is a consequence of the long history of environmental degradation in the state. Deforestation and degradation of forests, salinity ingress and desertification are some of the major factors responsible for this. A recent study of the GEC on the process of desertification in Kutch and Banaskantha districts between 1961 and 1991 shows that the desertification in the region has occurred primarily because of the overexploitation of the natural resources in the region through overcultivation, overgrazing, overirrigation practices, deforestation and poor natural resource management. In short, the desert has advanced considerably during the past few decades. This is reflected in the large coverage of the DPAP (Drought Prone Area Programme) and DDP (Desert Development Programme) in the state. Of the total 184 blocks (talukas) of the state 99 blocks (54 per cent) are either under DPAP or under DDP. Except for the three districts, namely, Kheda, Surat and Gandhinagar, all the districts have some coverage under one of these programmes. Even the districts of the South Gujarat such as Dangs and Valsad have some areas under DPAP in spite of the more than 1800mm annual rainfall. The coverage of these programmes was much less in mid-seventies when the programmes covered about 27.7 per cent of the area of the state. The increased coverage is a clear indication of the severe environmental degradation that the state has experienced in the recent decades.

Pollution of Natural Resources

The economic growth process in the state has also increased pollution of air, water and land in the state. About 60 per cent of the factories in the state generate pollution which, unfortunately, is not controlled adequately. According to the official data, some of the major industrial centres in the "golden corridor", such as Ahmedabad, Vadodara, Ankleshwar, Vapi and Surat have much higher proportion of sulphur dioxide, nitrogen dioxide and SPM than the standard norms (CSO, 1997). These are known to be some of the major pollution centres in the country. Several micro and regional studies, PILs and movements/actions of NGOs show that the state does not have the required ability to control the polluting industries in the state.

Pandya's studies of Vapi, Ankleshwar, Panoli and surrounding areas, for example, throw useful light on the dangers of industrial pollution that the state is facing (Pandya 1988, 1992). His studies point out that (a) about 3 per cent to 4 per cent chemicals produced in Ankleshwar and surrounding areas are banned in the industrialised countries on the ground that they are too hazardous, (b) plant designs of the units, particularly of small units, are frequently undertaken by non-qualified persons, as a result they do not have the equipment and appliances for ensuring safety and security of workers, for measuring the technical specifications including hazards and risks, for monitoring the environment and for taking actions in emergency, (c) the technical personnel is far from adequate in small factories since there is a shortage of such persons, consequently unqualified or half qualified staff manage production and supervision without even realizing the dangers involved and (d) there is no scientific and systematic monitoring of potential hazards and pollution in all the areas and the pollutory effects of the production processes and waste disposal systems have increased the pollution of air, water and land in the region; rivers are polluted, underground water is polluted, and the air has higher proportion of harmful gases.

Another regional study of mineral-based industries conducted in coastal Saurashtra also warns against rapid industrialization at the cost of environmental health (Hirway and Shah, 1997). The study shows that the rapid growth of mineral-based industries in general and the cement industry in particular has not paid adequate attention to environmental aspects: (a) Units of this industry are located in one of the greenest regions, Nagher, in Saurashtra, (b) The industry does not seem to be following the rules and regulations of the process of quarrying as well as of the regeneration of quarries, with the result that the quarrying results directly into degeneration of the ecology in the region, (c) The industry also frequently does not observe the norms of safety and pollution during the production process.

It is important to note that the Government of Gujarat has set up two important organisations in this field, namely, Gujarat Ecology Commission (GEC) and Gujarat Pollution Control Board (GPCB). The GEC was set up in 1992 with the main objective of integrating environmental and developmental concerns to facilitate fulfilment of basic needs, improving living standards and a better prosperous future for the state by working as a state level nodal agency for (a) ecological restoration, (b) organising people's action to prevent ecological degradation, (c) planning for sustainable development and (d) establishing appropriate institutions. GEC strives to develop a holistic overview of the region, replacing the traditional sectoral approach through a comprehensive, multidisciplinary data base compiled from various sources. Within a short span of its inception the GEC has done good work in the areas of research and studies, data bank, networking of NGOs conservation and biodiversity; and undertaken a few pilot interventions. GEC is now involved with preparing an Environment Action Plan for the state.

The GPCB was constituted in 1974 to control pollution in the state. Recently, the GPCB has taken several initiatives in controlling industrial pollution in the state: identification of severe pollution problems and regions, identification and development of sites for disposing hazardous wastages, evolving better strategies for pollution control, proper selection of sites for new industries, etc. The judiciary of the state and the centre also forced the Board to change to an extent. However, as far as the control over pollution is concerned, the state has a long way to go.

To sum up, the process of economic growth has encroached upon the environmental health of the state very badly. Though actions have been designed for correction, these are not yet adequate in terms of content and coverage. A lot is still to be done.

Income Poverty and Human Poverty in Gujarat

As far as income poverty is concerned, Gujarat is not in a very bad position. The incidence of poverty in Gujarat was 23.92 in 1993-94 and the state ranked third inverse ranking among the major states in India. As the adjoining table shows Gujarat has improved its rank from 6 in 1977-78 to 5 in 1983 to 3 in 1993-94, implying a relatively better performance of poverty reduction in the state (Table 1.14).

Table 1.14 : Poverty in Gujarat

	Number in Lakhs			Number in Lakhs		
Year	Rural	Urban	Total	Rural	Urban	Total
1972-73	94.61	41.09	135.7	46.35 (5)	49.31 (7)	47.21 (5)
1977-78	92.53	41.33	133.86	41.76 (5)	43.13 (6)	42.17 (6)
1983	73.49	47.26	120.75	29.8 (5)	40.63 (9)	33.27 (5)
1987-88	75.95	52.63	128.58	28.67 (5)	39.63 (8)	32.33 (6)
1993-94	62.16	41.77	103.93	22.18 (3)	27.07 (6)	23.92 (3)

Note : Figures in the brackets indicate the rank of the state economy among the major 16 states in India.

Source : Planning Commission, New Delhi.

Gujarat has experienced considerable reduction in the incidence of poverty, from 46.35 per cent in 1972-73 to 22.18 per cent in 1993-94, about by 53 per cent in rural areas and from 47.21 per cent in 1972-73 to 27.07 per cent in 1993-94, by 45 per cent in urban areas. This is much more than the averages decline at the all India level. In fact, the state stands fourth in terms of the rate of decline in poverty. In terms of absolute numbers, however, the decline in poverty is a mere 23 per cent in the last two decades (1973-74 to 1993-94), from 135 lakhs to 103 lakhs, and the number of urban poor has actually increased.

Urban poverty is emerging as a relatively serious problem in the state. Gujarat has always had a very high incidence of urban poverty, the

State's rank being 8 or 9 in the eighties. The incidence of urban poverty declined only marginally during the eighties with the absolute number of the urban poor increasing from 41.33 lakhs in 1977-78 to 47.26 lakhs in 1983 and to 52.63 lakhs in 1987-88. The likely reasons for this are (a) decline in the organised textile industry (economy of some small towns was centred around a composite textile mill or two) leading to direct and indirect unemployment, (b) declining quality of employment arising from informalisation of the labour market and (c) urbanisation originating from migration from rural areas. The incidence of urban poverty, however, has declined very sharply between 1987-88 and 1993-94, by 32 per cent during this period, as against the 23 per cent decline in the incidence of rural poverty during the same period. This primarily seems to indicate resilience of the urban economy due to a high growth of investment and employment opportunities in the secondary and tertiary sectors.

Table 1.15 throws useful light on the intrastate variations in the incidence of poverty in the state across the NSS regions. The table shows that there are wide variations in the incidence of poverty across the five regions in Gujarat. The incidence varies from 18.8 per cent in Saurashtra to 25.06 per cent in the eastern tribal region. The variations are much larger in rural areas as compared to urban areas. The table also shows that though the Gujarat Dry Region was the poorest region in 1987-88, the Eastern Tribal Belt is the poorest region today. The Eastern Belt is the poorest in rural, urban as well as in the total poverty. It seems that tribals have emerged as the poorest group in the state.

One observes a decline in poverty in all the regions, the decline varying widely from 12.29 per cent in the northern plains to 42 per cent in the dry region. The Saurashtra is the least poor region in the state as far as the total poverty and rural poverty are concerned. However, as far as urban poverty is concerned, the Southern Plains — "the golden corridor" of industries — is the least poor region. It is important to note, however, that the rural areas of this golden corridor are very poor ranking second from the bottom. In fact, this is the only region where the incidence of poverty has increased between 1987-88 and 1993-97. In other words, industrial development has helped the urban population, but not so much the rural population of this region. Lastly, the inter NSS region differences in the incidence of poverty have declined only marginally during 1987-88 and 1993-94. The coefficient of variation has declined in rural, urban as well as total area between these two years, but only marginally.

Table 1.16 : Literacy in Major Indian States

States	1991			2001			Difference		
	Male	Female	Total	Male	Female	Total	Male	Female	Total
A.P.	55.13	32.72	44.09	70.85	51.17	61.11	15.72	18.45	17.02
Assam	61.87	43.03	52.89	71.93	56.03	64.28	10.06	13	11.39
Bihar	52.49	22.89	38.48	60.32	33.57	47.53	7.83	10.68	9.05
Gujarat	73.13	48.64	61.29	80.5	58.6	69.97	7.37	9.96	8.68
Haryana	69.1	40.47	55.85	79.25	56.31	68.59	10.15	15.84	12.74
J & K				65.75	41.82	54.46	65.75	41.82	54.46
Karnataka	67.26	44.34	56.04	79.29	57.45	67.04	12.03	13.11	11
Kerala	93.62.	86.17	89.81	94.2	87.86	90.92	0.58	1.69	1.11
M.P.	58.42	28.85	44.2	76.8	50.28	64.11	18.38	21.43	19.91
Maharashtra	76.56	52.32	64.87	86.27	67.51	77.27	9.71	15.19	12.4
Orissa	69.09	34.68	49.09	75.95	50.97	63.61	6.86	16.29	14.52
Punjab	65.66	50.41	58.51	75.63	63.55	69.95	9.97	13.14	11.44
Rajasthan	54.99	20.44	38.55	76.46	44.34	61.03	21.47	23.9	22.48
T.N.	73.45	51.33	61.66	82.33	64.55	73.47	8.58	13.22	10.81
U.P.	55.73	25.31	41.6	70.23	42.98	57.36	14.5	17.67	15.76
W. Bengal	67.81	46.56	57.7	77.58	60.22	69.22	9.77	13.66	11.52
India	64.13	39.29	52.21	76.46	54.37	65.50	12.33	15.08	13.29

Source : Census of Population, 1991 and 2001.

Table 1.15 : Incidence of Poverty According to NSS Reporting

		Max – Min x 100 Max + Min EOPL (Total)	
		1987-88	1993-94
1	Gujarat Eastern	34.49	25.06
2	Northern Plains	29.03	24.58
3	Southern Plains	25.85	22.45
4	Gujarat Dry Regions	40.2	23.3
5	Saurashtra	28.18	18.8
	RURAL		
1	Gujarat Eastern	34.19	24.12
2	Northern Plains	25.87	20.52
3	Southern Plains	22.85	23.51
4	Gujarat Dry Regions	46.95	22.52
5	Saurashtra	18.95	10.03
	URBAN		
1	Gujarat Eastern	39.32	34.33
2	Northern Plains	34.23	30.05
3	Southern Plains	30.89	20.89
4	Gujarat Dry Regions	53.88	27.03
5	Saurashtra	53.77	34.04

Note : EOPL = Estimates based on the Expert Group Official Proverty Line.

It seems that the poverty in the degraded regions is a major issue. Works of environmental protection through well designed wage employment programmes are likely to help in reducing poverty in the short run as well as in the long run as these works can promote sustainable employment intensive activities.

Human Development

It is now well established that economic growth does not automatically get translated into human development. Human development is primarily achieved through rapid economic growth of the type that is favourable and conducive to human development as well as through direct and well-planned state interventions.

Has Gujarat been able to translate its economic growth into a higher level of human development?

Though Human Development Index (HDI), as proposed by the UNDP, is not a fully satisfactory index for measuring human development (Hirway and Mahadevia, 1996), the index does provide a broad measure of human development. The HDI of Gujarat, computed for the Indian states, shows that Gujarat has a fairly low HDI. The HDI of Gujarat, as computed by JBG Tilak (Socio Economic Review, Gujarat State 1996-97), was 0.566, which was way behind Kerala (0.775), Punjab (0.744), Maharashtra (0.655) and Haryana (0.624). Since education and health are the two important components of human development, we shall examine the performance of Gujarat in these two sectors.

Education and Literacy : Table 1.16 presents data on the literacy rates (2001) in the major states in India. The table shows that though Gujarat ranks fourth in the literacy rate, the rate (69.9) is much lower than the same in Kerala (90.2). The rate indicates that 3 persons in every 10 in the state are illiterates. The table also shows that the state has a much lower literacy of females (58.6), particularly in rural areas with the state ranking 7th among the major fifteen states.

The state's performance in terms of improvement in literacy has been less than satisfactory. The percentage increase in the Gujarat was 17.4 between 1961-1971, 22.1 between 1971-1981 and 43.3 between 1961-1981 against 22.9, 22.7 and 50 at the all India level respectively. As a result the rank of the state has decelerated over the decade. The performance for females has been much worse with the state experiencing 69 per cent increase against 92 per cent at the all India level. In short, there is a deceleration in the field of literacy improvement in the state in relative sense.

The enrolment and retention data presented in Table 1.19 of school children upto standard V confirms this phenomenon. As shown in Table 24, about 95.97 per cent from the age group 6-14 enrol in schools in the state. Of these only 53.75 per cent children complete standard V. This implies that just about half of the children in the age group 6-14 in the state complete their education up to the fifth standard. The table shows that though Gujarat stands 4th among the major states in enrolment of children to primary school, it stands 12th in their retention up to standard V and therefore 9th in terms of the percentage of children completing the education up to standard V.

Table 1.17 : Enrolment and Retention of Children (6-14) up to Standard V in the Major States in India

State	Enrolment(6-14)	Retention (up to Std. V)	Per cent Completing V Standard
Andhra Pradesh	86.38	57.82	49.94
Assam	88.50	60.95	53.94
Bihar	75.04	36.64	27.49
Gujarat	95.97(4)	53.75(12)	51.58(9)
Haryana	98.58	96.07	95.08
Karnataka	84.38	59.22	49.96
Kerala	100.00	104.23	100.00
Madhya Pradesh	74.97	71.64	53.70
Maharashtra	94.48	72.38	68.38
Orissa	83.29	47.46	39.52
Punjab	96.17	78.26	75.26
Rajasthan	74.35	51.07	38.48
Tamil Nadu	95.53	82.7	79.00
Uttar Pradesh	74.70	80.06	60.28
West Bengal	76.46	59.57	45.54
India	86.79	67.45	58.54

Note : *Figures in the bracket indicate the rank of Gujarat.
Source: Directorate of Economics and Statistics, and Department of Primary Education, Gandhinagar).

The dropout rate increases as one moves from primary education to secondary and higher education, the dropout rates being 59.57 upto standard 8 and 67.57 upto standard 10. When one looks at these data in the background of the huge industrial investments in modern industries coming to the state, one can realise the inadequacy of the local manpower to take advantage of the new opportunities.

Studies have shown that the causes for this are related not only to the supply side factors, such as educational infrastructure, quality of education, etc., but also to the demand side factors which include poverty, social norms, perception towards education, etc. It has been observed that environmental degradation tends to affect the enrolment and retention rates of children in schools adversely in the state (Hirway and Mahadevia, 1998). People living in environmentally degraded areas tend to occupy children in the collection of fuel, fodder and water leading to their low level of attending the school. Also, degradation-induced migration tends to increase dropout rates from schools. In short, the level of literacy in the state is not only affected by micro level factors such as infrastructure, quality of education, etc., but it is also affected by macro level factors such as environmental degradation, poverty and the related factors like the poor quality of employment of adults.

Table 1.18 : Percentage Change in Literacy Rates in India 1961-81

(Percentage Change)

Rank	States	1961 Both*	1971 Both	1981 Both	1961-1971	1971-1981	1961-1981
1.	J&K	11	18.6	26.7	69.1	43.5	142.7
2.	Haryana	19.9	26.9	36.1	35.2	34.2	81.4
3.	Madhya Pradesh	17.1	22.1	27.9	29.2	26.2	63.2
4.	Rajsthan	15.2	19	24.4	25.0	28.4	60.5
5.	Maharashtra	29.8	39.2	47.2	31.5	20.4	58.4
6.	Orissa	21.7	26.2	34.2	20.7	30.5	57.6
7.	U.P.	17.7	21.7	27.2	22.6	25.3	53.7
8.	Punjab	26.7	33.7	40.9	26.2	21.4	53.2
9.	Karnataka	25.4	31.5	38.5	24.0	22.2	51.6
10.	Kerala	46.9	60.4	70.4	28.8	16.6	50.1
11.	Tamil Nadu	31.4	39.5	46.8	25.8	18.5	49.0
12.	Gujarat	30.5	35.8	43.7	17.4	22.1	43.3
13.	Bihar	18.4	19.9	26.2	8.2	31.7	42.4
14.	Andhra Pradesh	21.2	24.6	29.9	16.0	21.5	41.0
15.	West Bengal	29.3	33.2	40.9	13.3	23.2	39.6
	All India	24	29.5	36.2	22.9	22.7	50.8

*Ranking is based on percentage change in literacy rate from 1961 to 1981.
Source: As used by Malini Karkal in her article " Progress in Literacy in India - A Statistical Analysis.

Life Expectancy at Birth (LEB) and Infant Mortality Rate (IMR)

Life expectancy at birth and IMR are known to be two robust indicators of health of a population. Gujarat ranks low in both these indicators. In the case of LEB, the rank of the state is 9th (1991) while in the case of IMR the rank is 6th.

The LEB in Gujarat is 62.9 as against an all India average of 62.7. The highest value of LEB is in Kerala (71.3), followed by Punjab (68),

Maharashtra (66.5), Haryana (66.2), Tamil Nadu (64.4) and others. In the case of male LEB, the state ranks at the 8th position (61.7), while in the case of female LEB the state stands at the 9th position (64.3). LEB in rural areas is much lower (62.1) than the same in urban area (64.6), which implies that as in the case of literacy, rural areas are worse off.

It is important to note, however, that the rank of the state in LEB was 13th in 1971 with the value of LEB at 53.4 which was lower than the all India value (54). The state has recorded 17.8 per cent increase during 1971-1991 and improved its position to the 9th rank. In terms of improvement, Gujarat stands in the fourth place, much above the all India increase of 16 per cent. The highest improvement has been achieved by U.P. (21.2 per cent), followed by Rajasthan (20.79 per cent) and Maharashtra (18.54 per cent). The rate of increase in LEB, however, has declined between 1981 and 1991 in Gujarat (as well as in the other states). In fact, Gujarat experienced only a small increase of 5.36 per cent during the decade which is much less than the all India increase of 6.45 per cent. The rank of the state in terms of increase in LEB fell to 9 in this decade. Females achieved a much smaller increase of 3.21 per cent than the males who achieved 4.22 per cent increase.

In the case of the IMR, Gujarat ranks seventh (with inverse ranking) among the major fifteen states in India. The IMR in the state is 63 (1994-96) as against 73 in India. Kerala has the lowest IMR, 15, followed by Maharashtra (53) and Punjab (53), Tamil Nadu (55), West Bengal (58) and Karnataka (61). The IMR in rural Gujarat (69) is more than 40 per cent higher than the same in urban Gujarat (48). Gujarat ranks 10th in rural IMR and 8th in urban IMR among the major states. This once again reflects the lower health status in rural areas.

In the case of IMR also the state has performed relatively better during 1971-1996 by reducing the IMR by 56.05 per cent in rural areas and 54.72 per cent in urban areas. The state stands second in the rate of decline, the first position being occupied by Kerala by reducing the IMR by 75 per cent during this period. It is to be noted that the IMR in Kerala is one-fifth of the same in Gujarat, which implies that Gujarat has a long way to go to improve the health status of its population.

The rate of decline in IMR appears to have declined during the nineties, particularly in late nineties. The rate has come down to 42 per cent during 1981-83 and 1994-96. If one goes by the annual SRS data, one observes an increase in the rural IMR in the state between 1995 and 1997 from 68 to 69. In the case of urban areas, the rate has remained stagnant at 46. Though similar trends have been noted in other states, the case of Gujarat is important as Gujarat had experienced a fairly high rate of decline in the past.

Table 1.19 : Life Expectancy at Birth in Major States in India (1971–1991)

Rank	Major States	1971	1981	1991	% Change 1971-81	% Change 1981-91	% Change 1971-91
1.	U.P.	48.9	53.5	59.3	9.41	10.84	21.27
2.	Rajasthan	50.5	54.6	61	8.12	11.72	20.79
3.	Maharashtra	56.1	65.3	66.5	16.40	1.84	18.54
4.	Gujarat	53.4	59.7	62.9	11.80	5.36	17.79
5.	Tamil Nadu	54.8	60.2	64.4	9.85	6.98	17.52
6.	Karnataka	56.3	66.7	66	18.47	-1.05	17.23
	INDIA	54	58.9	62.7	9.07	6.45	16.11
7.	Orissa	52.6	57.7	60.7	9.70	5.20	15.40
8.	Assam	51.3	55.5	58.5	8.19	5.41	14.04
9.	Kerala	62.8	74	71.3	17.83	-3.65	13.54
10.	Andhra Pradesh	56.6	61.6	63.9	8.83	3.73	12.90
11.	Haryana	60.6	61.9	66.2	2.15	6.95	9.24
12.	M.P.	55.9	51.1	59.5	-8.59	16.44	6.44
13.	Punjab	64.3	67.6	68	5.13	0.59	5.75
14.	Bihar	—	55.5	59.7	—	7.57	—
15.	J & K	61.8	66.4	—	7.44	—	—
16.	West Bengal	—	60.5	64.6	—	6.78	—

Note : Ranking is based on percentage change in LEB (1971-91).

In short, there is a deceleration in the performance of the two health indicators in the recent past. Though no firm reasons have been presented by scholars about these developments, it is observed that the fault does not necessarily lie only with the direct efforts at the state level. The health status of a society depends on two sets of factors, namely, health and medical services of different kinds and general nutrition level of the population. The latter is influenced by poverty and unemployment levels, environment and pollution status, women's position in the family, etc. which are macro variables influenced by the development path of the economy. For example, a decline in IMR takes place due to (a) improved neo-natal facilities, better immunisation, extension of healthcare system to take care of complications of deliveries, etc., and (b) improved health status of mothers through better nutrition of girls, higher age of marriage, higher age at the time of first child birth, spacing of children and the general improvement in the status of women, including their improved literacy. A state achieves the initial gains through the first set of factors, but it has to depend on the second set of factors to experience consistent gains.

Table 1.20 : Infant Mortality Rate in the Major Indian States (1994-96)

State	Infant Mortality Rate		
	Rural	Urban	Combined
Kerala	15	13	15
Jammu & Kashmir	—	—	—
Haryana	70	64	69
Karnataka	69	38	61
Maharashtra	64	34	53
Andhra Pradesh	72	45	66
Punjab	57	38	53
Tamil Nadu	62	42	55
Rajasthan	89	61	85
Orissa	104	65	100
Assam	78	56	76
Gujarat	69	48	63
Madhya Pradesh	104	60	98
Uttar Pradesh	90	66	86
West Bengal	61	47	58
Bihar	72	57	71
India	79	49	73

Source: Vital Rates of India, 1971 to 1996, Based on SRS, Registrar General, New Delhi.

Since the second set of variables depends on the development process, direct interventions can go only up to a limit. This implies that in the case of Gujarat the factors like environmental degradation, low quality of employment and poverty are once again relevant.

Population and Demography

The status of health in the state is reflected in the demographic behaviour of the population. Gujarat had 41.3 million population in 1991. The Expert Committee on Population, set up by the Government of Gujarat, has projected 46.5 million (49 million by the revised estimates) population for 2001 AD.

Table 1.21 : Percentage Change in Infant Mortality Rate by Residence in India (Three years moving average, 1971-1973 to 1994-1996)

Rank	Major States	1971-73 Total	81-83 Total	94-96 Total	% Change 71-73 to 81-83	% Change 81-83 to 94-96	% Change 71-73 to 93-96
1.	Kerala	60	34	15	-43.33	-55.88	-75.00
2.	Gujarat	144	111	63	-22.92	-43.24	-56.25
3.	U.P.	182	151	86	-17.03	-43.05	-52.75
4.	Punjab	112	79	53	-29.46	-32.91	-52.68
5.	Tamil Nadu	114	87	55	-23.68	-36.78	-51.75
6.	Maharashtra	107	76	53	-28.97	-30.26	-50.47
	INDIA^	134	107	73	-20.15	-31.78	-45.52
7.	Assam	137	100	76	-27.01	-24.00	-44.53
8.	A.P.	109	81	66	-25.69	-18.52	-39.45
9.	Rajasthan	131	105	85	-19.85	-19.05	-35.11
10.	Karnataka	93	68	61	-26.88	-10.29	-34.41
11.	M.P.	145	134	98	-7.59	-26.87	-32.41
12.	Orissa	134	131	100	-2.24	-23.66	-25.37
13.	Haryana	90	95	69	5.56	-27.37	-23.33
14.	Bihar	—	110	71	—	-35.45	—
15.	J & K	71	70*	—	-1.41	—	—
16.	West Bengal	—	87	58	—	-33.33	—

*Excludes J&K due to non-receipt of return for the year 1996.

Source: Vital Rates of India 1971 to 1996 based on the Sample Registration System (SRS), Registrar General, India, New Delhi 1998.

The population in the state has grown from 9.1 million in 1901 to 41.3 million in 1991, almost 4.5 times increase in the space of 90 years. The inter-census annual growth rates show that the fastest increase was between 1951 and 1981, primarily due to the rapid decline in the mortality rate from 23.5 in 1951 to 16.8 in 1971 and to about 12 in 1981. The rate of population growth has constantly fallen after 1971 from 2.6 per cent between 1961-1971 to 2.4 per cent between 1971-1981 and to 1.9 per cent between 1981-1991. The growth rate was expected to fall below 1.5 per cent by the end of the century. The results of the Census of Population

2001 has shown that the population of Gujarat is now 50.6 m/t and the annual compound rate of growth between 1991-2001 has been 2.03 as against 1.93 of all India.

Table 1.22 : Trends in Population and its Characteristics

Census Year	Population (Millions)		Sex Ratio (Females/ 1000 Males)		Annual Inter-censal Growth Rate (%)		Density of Population per (Sq.Km.)		Per cent of Urban Population	
	Gujarat	India	Gujarat	India	Gujarat	India	Gujarat	India	Gujarat	India
1901	9.1	238.3	954	972	—	—	46	77	22.3	10.8
1911	10.0	252.0	946	964	0.8	0.6	50	82	19.2	10.3
1921	10.2	251.2	944	955	0.4	0.03	52	81	20.2	11.2
1931	11.5	278.9	945	950	1.2	1.1	59	90	20.5	12.0
1941	14.5	318.5	941	945	1.8	1.3	70	103	23.8	13.9
1951	16.3	361.0	952	946	1.7	1.3	83	117	27.2	17.3
1961	21.0	439.1	940	941	2.4	2.0	105	142	25.8	18.0
1971	27.0	548.2	934	930	2.6	2.2	136	178	28.1	19.9
1981	34.1	683.3	942	933	2.4	2.2	174	221	31.2	23.3
1991	41.3	846.3	934	927	1.9	2.1	211	273	34.5	26.1
2001	50.6	1027.1	921	933	2.03	1.93	258	324	—	—

Note : Growth rate for 1961-71 and 1971-81 was calculated taking into the fact that the reference date of 1971 Census was April 1,whereas 1961 and 1981 Censuses had the usual reference date *i.e.* March 1.

Sources : 1. Census of India, 1961, Vol. 1, India, Part II-A (i), General Population Tables, 1975, and II-C(ii) Social and Cultural tables, 1977.

2. Census of India, 1971, Series 1, India, Part II-A(i), General Population Tables, 1957, and II-C(ii) Social and Cultural Tables, 1977.
3. Census of India, 1981, Series 1, India, Paper 1 of 1982, Final Population Tabies; Part II, Special report and tables, based on 5 per cent sample date, 1984, Part II-B(i), Primary Census Abstract; General Population 1983.
4. Census of India, 1991, Series 1, Paper 2 of 1992, Final Population Tables: Brief Analysis of Primary Census Abstract.

The main reason for the decline in the population growth rate after 1971 was the fall in the birth rate, from 41.6 during 1961-1971 to 34.8 during 1980-82 and to 26.7 in 1995. The average pattern of population growth indicates that the state is now passing through the third stage of demographic transition with the falling death rate and the rapidly falling birth rate. This is definitely a positive development. However, the results of the Census of Population, 2001 indicate that the demographic transition is now delayed.

Concluding Observations

The enterprising population of Gujarat, supported by its progressive leadership, has brought the state in the forefront of development in the country. The state has not only acquired and maintained its fourth rank in per capita NSDP, but it has also taken quantum jump in the post-liberation period by attracting the highest industrial investment, particularly in large and medium industry, and experienced the highest growth in per capita NSDP during this period. In the process the economy of Gujarat achieved a highly diversified economic structure.

The process of this economic diversification, however, does not seem to be sustainable as the primary sector, particularly agriculture, has lagged far behind distorting the agriculture-industry linkages. Along with agricultural near stagnation, environment has also experienced severe degradation, both of which have created constraints to the sustainability of economic growth in the state. The limited achievements of the state in the fields of employment and poverty, as well as in human development are closely related to the macro development path. That is, these developments are not independent on each other, but are the consequences of the dynamics of development of the state.

The corrective interventions on a programme basis have therefore a limited role to play. Since the decline in the rate of decline in poverty, the backlog of unemployment, the poor quality of employment, the fast degrading environment as well as the deceleration in the rate of progress in human development are all related to the path of the development selected by the state, the corrections are needed in the path of the development. Though direct interventions are necessary and there is a good scope for their improvement in the state, these are not sufficient for achieving the goals of development. In the final analysis therefore the solution lies in correcting the path of development of the state.

There are possibilities in Gujarat for broadening the base of development through employment intensive and environment friendly development path. Such a path is conducive to rapid poverty reduction as well as to rapid human development. It is important that the state shifts towards this path. It is high time that the political leadership in the state should realise that attracting industrial investments to the state at any cost will not serve the long-term interests of the state. It will neither lead to sustainable development nor to a rapid reduction of income and human poverty in the state.

REFERENCES

Chadha, G.K. (1995), "Employment, Earnings and Poverty", Sage Publication, New Delhi.

Desai, Bhupat (1997), *Colloquium on Development of Agriculture and Allied Sectors in Gujarat : A Strategic Perspective for the Ninth Plan.*

Desai, Bhupat, Shah, Anil C. and Singi, Prakash (1999), "Raising Agricultural Productivity in Gujarat", *EPW,* February 1999.

DES (1995,98), *Govt. of Gujarat Socio-Economic Reviews.*

EPW Research Bureau (1998), National Income Statistics, Mumbai.

Gujarat Ecology Commission (1997), "Ecological Degradation Around Gulf of Khambat, Gujarat: A Status Report", GEC and Baroda.

Indext-B (1998), Industrial Policy Statements of Govt. of Gujarat.

Industries Commisssionerate *(1997),* Investment in Large Projects in Gujarat, Government of Gujarat, Gandhinagar.

Industries Commisssionerate (1997), Industries in Gujarat, Government of Gujarat, Gandhinagar.

Hirway, Indira and Shah, Amita (1998), *Liberalization, Globalization and Industrialization: Conflict and Resolution in a Regional Context.*

Hirway, Indira and Mahadevia, Darshini (1999), Human Development Report, Gujarat.

Hirway, Indira (1995), "Selected Development and Widening Disparities in Gujarat", *Economic and Political Weekly.*

Hirway, Indira (1997), "Issues in Special Employment and Agricultural Development: Perspective" in Bhupat Desai's *Agricultural Development Paradigm for the Ninth Plan Under New Economic Environment.*

Oza, A.N. (1997), "Role of Agriculture in Industrialization", in Desai B.M.(Ed.) *Agricultural Development Perspective for the Ninth Plan,* Oxford and IBH Co. Ltd., New Delhi.

Kashyap, S.P. (1995), "Industrial Scene in Gujarat: A Contrast of Two Patterns", *Anveshak,* Vol. 25, No.1.

Singh, Gurdev (1997), "Employment Potential of Wastelands Development in India", in Desai B.M. (Ed.) *Agricultural Development Perspective for the Ninth Plan,* Oxfor and IBH Co. Ltd., New Delhi.

Lakdawala, D.T. (1972), "Growth of Saurashtra Economy", *SPIESR,* Ahmedabad.

Hirway, Indira (1995), "Safety Net of the National Renewal Fund: Some Basic Issues", *The Indian Journal of Labour Economics,* Vol.38, No.2, 1995.

Hirway, Indira and Patel, P.P. (1993), *Dynamics of Drinking Water in Rural Gujarat,* Utthan, Ahmedabad.

Forest Survey of India (1986, 1991, 1997), "State of Forest in India", *FSI,* Dehradoon.

2

Liberalization in Gujarat

Review of Recent Experience

RAVINDRA H. DHOLAKIA

Introduction

With democratic federal structure, it is possible to find different Indian states having distinct economic objectives and goals. It is also shown that they were actually following their own development strategies within the overall broad national plan strategy even during the period when the country seriously followed the development strategy based on central planning to a large extent (Dholakia, 1994). During the process of economic policy reforms and liberalization, the constraints and regulation of economic activities by the Centre in different segments of the economy got relaxed. The states found more freedom and flexibility to pursue their own socio-economic agenda. It is not surprising that different states took advantage of this increased flexibility according to their physical capabilities, economic environment and ability to evaluate opportunities and risks involved. States may be required to reconsider their development strategies, alter necessary policy decisions and change institutional structure to attract more economic activities in their economies. Liberalization in Gujarat during the nineties has to be seen in this context.

Development strategy in Gujarat has been very clear and unambiguous ever since its inception in 1960 in according a high priority to industrialization as can be seen from various state plans documents and the socio-economic reviews carried out annually. The state had made a clear choice of encouraging the secondary sector activities over the primary and tertiary sectors' activities (Dholakia, 1994). It is a well-known fact that Gujarat lags behind several states in the country in terms of human capital and related indices. Between the human capital and physical capital related government expenditures also, the Gujarat government had consistently accorded higher priority to the latter (Archana Dholakia, 1990). Thus, the development strategy of Gujarat for industrialization has been unbalanced growth with emphasis on Directly Productive Activity (DPA) rather than on creating Social Overhead Capital (SOC). The impact of liberalization on the state economy should, therefore, be examined in terms of the performance of industrialization in the state. The next section is devoted to this examination. In the third section, recent measures of liberalization and deregulation taken by the Gujarat government are described after discussing the concept of liberalization at the state level. The fourth section is then devoted to the initiatives and policy changes effected by the Gujarat government in the Small-Scale Industry (SSI) sector during the nineties.

Impact of Liberalization on the State Economy

Gujarat is above the national average in terms of its per capita income and as a result, it can be considered relatively better off. But in terms of the growth, its performance is not very impressive. Table 2.1 provides the comparison of the indices of net State Domestic Product (SDP) and Net National Product (NNP) at constant (1980-81) prices from 1980-81 to 1997-98. During the 18 year period, there are as many as seven years when the total real income (SDP) in Gujarat declined as compared to the previous year. As against this, the national real income (NNP) marginally dropped only once during the 18 years. The economic growth in Gujarat is more volatile and lacks stability. It is clearly brought out that it is the primary sector and more particularly agriculture which has been the principal cause of this instability (Dholakia, 1983; Iyengar, 1996). Agriculture and related activities is a declining sector in Gujarat. Its share in SDP was about 41 per cent in 1980-81 which sharply declined to around 19 per cent in 1997-98. This is indicative of significant structural changes in Gujarat's economy over the short period of 18 years.

Table 2.1 : Index Number of Net State Domestic Product of Gujarat and Net National Product at Constant (1980-81) Prices

Sr. No.	Year	Index of SDP in Primary Sector (Gujarat)	Index of Net State Domestic Product (Gujarat)	Index of Net National Product at Factor Cost
1.	1980-81	100.0	100.0	100.0
2.	1981-82	117.5	109.9	105.8
3.	1982-83	100.6	108.3	108.1
4.	1983-84	122.5	129.1	116.9
5.	1984-85	124.1	129.0	120.9
6.	1985-86	95.2	125.5	125.6
7.	1986-87	94.9	133.2	130.3
8.	1987-88	51.5	118.4	135.3
9.	1988-89	134.0	166.1	149.7
10.	1989-90	118.9	163.1	160.2
11.	1990-91	112.0	165.6	168.4
12.	1991-92	92.4	151.9	168.2
13.	1992-93	137.9	200.8	176.7
14.	1993-94	104.7	194.6	187.3
15.	1994-95	147.8	237.5	200.0
16.	1995-96	114.2	240.7	216.8
17.	1996-97	132.9	264.5	233.5
18.	1997-98	134.0	281.5	244.6

Sources : 1. Directorate of Economics and Statistics, Gujarat.
2. Central Statistical Organisation, New Delhi.

After 1990-91, the economic policy reforms and the speeded up liberalization at the national level had considerable impact on the Gujarat economy. It can be seen from Table 2.1 that the growth of real income in Gujarat during the eighties marginally lagged behind the national average. But during the nineties, it is considerably higher than the national average. Moreover, the experience of the year 1995-96 reveals that the state has also developed capabilities to absorb the relatively large adverse shock on its primary sector not allowing its aggregate real income to fall. Thus, national liberalization process seems to have stabilizing and growth accelerating impact on the Gujarat economy.

The impact of liberalization is not expected to be uniform across different sectors. In order to identify the impact-sectors in the Gujarat state economy, the following spline trend function or a piece-wise trend is fitted to the income originating in different sectors at constant 1980-81 prices in Gujarat over the period 1980-81 to 1997-98 (see, Gujarati, 1995):

$$\ln Y = a + bt + c\,(t - t^*)\,D + U$$

Where the year 1990-91 is taken as t^* which represents the break point; U is the random error term; ln Y is the natural logarithm of the real income originating in the given sector; a is the intercept parameter; b is the basic trend-rate; and c is the parameter showing acceleration or deceleration in the basic trend-rate during the nineties. The results are presented in Table 2.2.

Table 2.2 : Trend Rate of Growth, 1980-81 to 1997-98

Sr. No.	Sectors	Basic Trend Rate		Acceleration/ Deceleration		R^2
		Co-efficient	Standard errors	Co-efficient	Standard errors	
1.	Primary Sector	-0.0037	(0.01942)	0.0475	(0.04352)	0.1668
1.1	Agri. & Animal Husbandry	-0.0076	(0.02166)	0.0556	(0.04856)	0.1484
2.	Secondary Sector	0.0695*	(0.00673)	0.0412*	(0.01509)	0.9737
2.1	Manufacturing	0.0716*	(0.00947)	0.0435*	(0.02122)	0.9525
2.2	Reg. Manufacturing	0.0722*	(0.01082)	0.0539*	(0.02424	0.9446
2.3	Unreg. Manufacturing	0.0709*	(0.00874)	0.0043	(0.01959)	0.9403
3.	Trade, Transport etc.	0.0616*	(0.00626)	0.0034	(0.01403)	0.9585
4.	Banking etc.	0.08317*	(0.00439)	0.0177	(0.00984)	0.9897
5.	Public administration & other services	0.0552*	(0.00304)	-0.0060	(0.00682)	0.9858
6.	Tertiary sector	0.0673*	(0.00282)	0.0072	(0.00633)	0.9929
7.	Total NSDP	0.0440*	(0.00663)	0.0381*	(0.01486)	0.9478

* Significant at 5 per cent level of significance.

Note: The year of break in the trend is taken to be 1990-91.

It can be seen from the results that the primary sector in general and agriculture, including animal husbandry, in particular do not show any systematic time trend over the 18 year period in Gujarat. Similarly, the liberalization of the nineties has hardly any significant perceptible steady impact on the growth performance of these sectors in the state. On the contrary, the secondary and tertiary sectors in Gujarat not only have well-behaved positive basic time-trend but also show statistically significant high rates of growth over the period. Thus, the economic growth of the state is sustained by its secondary and tertiary sectors, which is quite consistent with the development strategy followed by the state. The results reported in Table 2.2 also clearly reveal that it is only the secondary sector in Gujarat, which shows positive and significant growth acceleration during the nineties. The manufacturing sector in Gujarat has shown the real impact of liberalization in the nineties. The trend rate of growth in the real income in the sector is about 11.5 per cent during the nineties. Within the manufacturing sector, however, it is the registered manufacturing, which shows significantly high growth acceleration with liberalization. The unregistered manufacturing sector, which includes the cottage and tiny sector units along with several small-scale units, does show high and statistically significant growth acceleration. Thus, liberalization and economic policy reforms have impacted the production and income of mostly the large-scale manufacturing in the state. It seems that the state has not contradicted the centre's initiatives in liberalization and economic policy reforms but has facilitated through its own action the large-scale manufacturing activities in Gujarat. In the democratic federal structure of India, the major role of the state governments is to control and regulate the activities of the small-scale, cottage and tiny sector units. The state level initiatives in liberalization should have their impact on the performance of such units in the state. In the next section, we turn to a brief review of the liberalization measures taken by the Gujarat government during the nineties.

Liberalization in Gujarat

Liberalization, as discussed above, is a process of relaxing or reducing the direct restrictions, regulations and controls on the economic activities by the government. These direct interventions are conceptually similar to the quantitative restrictions. As against this, the government can also control and regulate the economic activities indirectly by imposing tariffs, charging fees, levying taxes, etc., which are conceptually similar to the price-based interventions. Economic policy reforms include changes in the government policies of both these types. Liberalization, however, covers only a part of the economic policy reforms inasmuch as it pertains to the relaxation of the measures of quantitative nature. At the central government level, the policy of economic liberalization was seriously followed and speeded up since 1991. The state governments were expected to cooperate by following consistent policies and further facilitate liberalization by taking measures within their control.

In the context of influencing industrial activities at the state level, the states have been using three distinct instruments, viz. (a) providing tax and cost related incentives; (b) provision of infrastructure and input supplies; and (c) granting approvals and clearances to the units (Sengupta, 1996). The tax and cost related incentives are essentially the price-based interventions. The other two are quantity-based interventions where the progress of liberalization at the state level can be examined.

In the second half of the nineties, there have been major liberalization initiatives in Gujarat in terms of providing infrastructural support and input supplies to the productive units in the state. Following certain recommendations from the report of the Gujarat State Finance Commission (1994), major reforms in the power sector were initiated around 1995-96 with continuous improvements taking place in the policy up to now. The power sector is opened up to the private sector. There have been now clear statements on the Captive Power Policy (CPP) for the own use and Independent Power Policy (IPP) for the suppliers to the grid. These policies still leave some scope for modifications and improvements, but the basic statements are made and implemented. As a result, within a period of only three years 2,300 MW additional power generation capacity was installed in the state out of the target of 5,000 MW in ten years. Gujarat has, therefore, not experienced any major power-cut in the last 3 years. As a result of this significant liberalization initiative, the state, which faced severe shortage of electric power in the past, experienced marginal oversupply of electric power recently. The state government, therefore, introduced the Tatkal Yojana with high registration fees for new agricultural connections.

Similarly, in the other infrastructural sectors like ports and roads the private participation is now encouraged. Build-Operate-Transfer (BOT) policy on the lines of the Philippine's and Chilean experiences is being adopted. Concepts of private ports or the private companies owning their jetties are being implemented. Liberalization to allow private participation in the matter of storage of specialized cargo is under consideration. The road network to link the port and construction of underground pipes to transport commodities to and fro ports are important infrastructural development where clearer policy initiatives are expected (See, Gujarat Chamber of Commerce and Industries, 1998).

Gujarat Industrial Development Corporation (GIDC) has been providing comprehensive infrastructural facilities to the industrial units through their estates and sheds in selected locations in the state. It has now started handing over the management of these estates to the users. Generally, the association of the shed-holders in the particular location is given the responsibility. Thus, GIDC has started transferring the operation and management of the estates to the private sector after building the same. Similarly, since 1998-99, there has been a systematic effort to involve representatives of the private sector from the Gujarat Chamber of Commerce and Industries on the Boards of the state government entities playing vital role in the infrastructure and related matters of importance to the industry and trade in the state, e.g. Gujarat Electricity Board, Gujarat Infrastructure Development Board, Gujarat Pollution Control Board, Gujarat Environment Management Institute, etc.

Another major liberalization initiative is the abolition of the urban land ceiling in the state from April 1999. This measure is expected to restore the legitimacy of the transactions in the land market in the urban areas. Now, the land can be freely transacted. It is hoped that the excess land locked up with several industrial units in the state can now be released for sale and development purposes. The effective land prices in the urban areas may, therefore, fall in the short run and housing and construction activities in the urban areas are likely to boom. Moreover, the sale of excess land with industries in deep trouble can provide very vital doze of fresh resources for their rehabilitation. However, recently the government has introduced the Town Planning Act, which requires the buyer to surrender 50 per cent of the land for various purposes including infrastructure development. Previously the proportion was 33 per cent. There is already some protests and controversies regarding this Act. It is too early for quantitative assessment of the impact of all these measures on the urban economy of Gujarat.

In the matter relating to making the land available to industries, the unique measure taken by the Gujarat government in 1997 is to grant permission to convert agricultural land to non-agricultural (NA) uses upto the limit of 10 hectares almost automatically. This cuts down the elaborate process and delays in obtaining the NA permission for land and encourages rapid industrialization. Considering low agricultural productivity and high density of industries with necessary infrastructural support in the state, this measure may be justified.

The state government has also abolished the turnover tax in 1997. If octroi is abolished from the state, it would be considered a major initiative towards increasing the efficiency of movements of goods within the state by the trade and industry. However, the abolition of octroi has become a highly controversial issue since the local bodies and the bureaucrats have not been able to find a satisfactory solution in terms of reliable and implementable alternative to octroi in the state. But the state government has at least stopped granting new monopoly contracts to private parties (*Thekas*) to collect octroi in the state since 1st April 1999. This measure in itself has given some relief to the trade and industry in Gujarat.

Liberalization in the SSI Sector

As seen in Section II Gujarat has continued to achieve high growth in the registered and unregistered manufacturing sectors during the nineties. 14,063 SSI units were registered during 1996-97 and 14,631 SSI units were registered during 1997-98 in the state. The cumulative SSI registration in Gujarat as on 30th November 1998 stands at 2.21 lakh units. The regional spread of the new SSI units registered in the state during 1997-98 shows that hardly 5.5 per cent of the units are located in the metropolitan areas. About 57.3 per cent of the new units are located in the urban areas excluding the metropolitan areas. Thus, only 37.2 per cent of the new units are located in the rural areas (Government of Gujarat, 1999). The emerging urban centres and smaller towns are largely attracting the new SSI units in the state. The district and nagar panchayats are, therefore, likely to play important role in attracting the industry and trade. The state industrial policy upto 2000 A.D. accords priority to promote identified thrust industries including electronics, engineering, ancillaries, garments, gems and jewellery, food and agro-processing industries, leather goods, other labour intensive industries and 100 per cent export oriented units (EOU). A separate incentive scheme including speedy approval has been introduced for promotion of such thrust industries in the state.

At the district level, it is the District Industries Centre (DIC) which plays a pivotal role for promotion of industries. The principal objective of establishing the DIC is to provide all assistance under one roof to the entrepreneurs engaged in different types of industries and to those proposing to establish small and cottage industries in the district (Government of Gujarat, 1999). The state government has made the DICs more effective and operational by delegating the powers concerning registration for several developmental and subsidy purposes. Thus, registration for cash subsidy, SSI registration certificate for sales tax exemption, recommendation of loans and loans under artisan scheme, etc. have been delegated to the DICs. This not only simplifies procedures but also effectively decentralizes the developmental decisions providing further incentives to the administration to become people oriented. As a result, District Industrial Executive Committee under the chairmanship of either the Member of Parliament from the district or the Collector meets periodically to discuss and resolve problems of industrialists to the extent possible with the help of the DIC. Similarly, to ensure better co-ordination among various agencies working in the district, a Single Window Industries Follow-up Team (SWIFT) is constituted in 1996-97 in each district under the chairmanship of the district Collector. Moreover, at the state level a monitoring cell is established in the office of the Industries Commissioner to monitor the working of the DICs on monthly basis.

The DICs provide registration for both the tiny and the small-scale sectors. The validity for registration under tiny sector is for 5 years. Thereafter, the unit has to either renew the registration or get conversion to the SSI registration. Since January 1999, there has been a major simplification introduced to expedite the registration of small and tiny sector units. Units with investment up to Rs. 40 lakhs in plants and machinery can now be registered without inspection. Officials at DICs feel that more than 90 to 95 per cent of the small and tiny sector units would be covered here. This would cover not only the new units but also the hitherto unregistered existing units. There is a drive to register small entrepreneurs, rural artisans, cottage industries, etc. so as to enable them to get incentives available for such activities and also to strengthen the database in the sector.

For the registration under SSI sector, the procedures are also fairly simplified with only the following papers required to be submitted in general:

(a) application form in duplicate
(b) notorised declaration on Rs. 20 stamp paper
(c) rent receipt copy and copy of municipal tax bill in urban area
(d) copy of the partnership deed or memorandum of articles
(e) copy of the licence under Shop and Establishment Act

(f) power NOC or copy of the power bill
(g) sales tax number
(h) affidavit of machinery ownership or the list of machinery
(i) copy of the first sales bill

Moreover, the SSI registration is now available almost on the same day of application.

However, if the unit is in the following specified sectors, the necessary approval/permission is additionally required from the respective authority:

	Sectors	*Authority granting Approval*
(i)	Pharmaceutical	Food and Drug Control Administration
(ii)	Chemical	Pollution Control Board
(iii)	Explosives	Department of Explosives, Faridabad
(iv)	Pesticides/Insecticides	Central Insecticide Board

For larger units, environmental clearance is also required and for 100 per cent Export Oriented Units, a letter of permission is needed from the Secretariat of Industrial Approval (SIA) in the Ministry of Industry, Government of India to claim any benefits.

A major step is taken in Gujarat in 1999 to prepare and publish citizen's charter for all DICs. In this charter, not only all procedural requirements are enlisted but also even the time limits are prescribed for various clearances and approvals needed, when all necessary documents and evidences are provided by the applicants. Moreover, this is also monitored strictly by the Industry Commissioner's office almost every week since all this is computerised. Thus, unnecessary delays and harassment in undertaking productive activity in the state are likely to reduce and quick disposal of applications and cases can be expected.

The trade and industry often bitterly refer to the inspection visits by different government officials to the units during the year. Confederation of Indian Industries (CII), Gujarat chapter, has estimated that on an average about 46 visits of the government officials take place during a year to a registered manufacturing unit for "inspection" purposes. Out of these, about two-third visits are from the central government offices and the remaining one-third visits are from the state government offices. For an unregistered manufacturing unit the number of visits is estimated to be about 28. This excessive number of visits point to the continuation of the "inspector raj" and high degree of regulation and control leading to often unproductive and otherwise avoidable "transaction costs". Although the state government recognises the point made by the trade and industry, the government bureaucracy has not made any significant effort to reduce these visits by the inspectors. This is also the area where the central government has not made any progress for addressing the problem. This is a complicated issue because the inspections are necessary for (a) enforcement of certain standards and laws, and (b) development and entitlement for incentives based on assets, production, etc. Those units, where incentives are either claimed or sought, most of the approvals and several of the inspections become necessary. Otherwise, several of the approvals/permissions and inspections are not necessary. The government officials at the state and the district levels in Gujarat, however, are not very clear about the proportion of the inspection visits between enforcement and development.

Currently, the following Acts and Ordinances need inspection for their satisfactory enforcement in a production unit: PF Act, Boiler Act, ESI Act, Factory Act, Labour Act, IDR Act, Pollution Control Act, Food and Drugs Control Act, ISO/ISI Act, Aggmark/FPO Act, Essential Commodity Act, Lubricating Oil and Greeze Control Order, Molasses Control Order, Explosive Act, etc. Similarly for development and incentives, the inspection visits are required from banks, financial institutions, sales tax department, excise department, etc. Although it is generally agreed that duplication in inspection visits should be avoided, everybody feels that the inspection visits by the government officials cannot be reduced to zero. Even the concept of a Single Inspection Unit is not generally considered feasible under the prevailing conditions. Deregulation and liberalization in this regard will require to be innovative and bold because the objective of inspection for enforcement is the welfare and safety of population and workers, and for developmental incentives is the reduction of costs to the entrepreneurs.

Concluding Remarks

Gujarat's secondary sector has certainly gained from the national policy of liberalization, particularly after 1990-91. The state has also followed consistent policies and taken further measures to liberalize the state economy and simplify certain procedures to promote industrial activities in the state. However, most of these initiatives have been taken very recently — after 1996. It is, therefore, too early to examine their impact on the state economy quantitatively. Centre's efforts at liberalizing the industrial economy to a large extent are confined to the early nineties. Gujarat, as we have discussed above, has started its major efforts at the state level liberalization only after the mid-nineties. It is perhaps because of this reason that the impetus to accelerated growth in the industrial sector in Gujarat continued significantly throughout the nineties. It is to be seen whether the trend of liberalizing the state economy continues at the same rate or accelerates in future. The state government's commitment to liberalize and provide greater transparency in administration, control and regulation will be the deciding factor, besides the attitude and co-operation of the state bureaucracy.

Acknowledgement

[Grateful thanks are due to various officials from Gujarat Chamber of Commerce and Industries, CII Gujarat Chapter, Industrial Extension Bureau, District Industries Centre, Ahmedabad and Bureau of Economics and Statistics, Gandhinagar for useful discussions and valuable material.]

REFERENCES

Dholakia, Ravindra H. (1994), *Spatial Dimension of the Acceleration of Economic Growth in India, EPW*, Vol. 29, No. 35, August 27, pp. 2303-9.

Dholakia, Archana R. (1990), *Benefits from Government Expenditure in India - A Welfare Indicator Approach*, Bombay, Himalaya Publishing House.

Dholakia, Ravindra H. (1983), *Economic Growth and Fluctuations in Gujarat*, in D.T. Lakdawala (ed.): *Development of Gujarat - Problems and Prospects*, SPIESR, Ahmedabad Monograph Series 10.

District Industries Centre, Ahmedabad. (1999), *Nagarik Adhikar Patra* (Citizen's Charter), Office of Industries Commissioner, Government of Gujarat, February.

Government of Gujarat (1999), *Gujarat State: Socio-Economic Review, 1998-99*, Budget Publication No. 30.

Government of Gujarat (1994), *Report of The Gujarat State Finance Commission*, April.

Gujarat Chamber of Commerce and Industry (1998), *Proposal for Discussion in Sectoral Meetings*, Gujarat Trade and Industry Conference 1998 held in Ahmedabad on 28th March.

Gujarati, Damodar (1995), *Basic Econometrics*, 3rd Edition, McGraw-Hill International Edition.

Iyengar, Sudarshan (1996), *Level and Pattern of Economic Growth in Gujarat, 1980-94*, Gujarat Institute of Development Research, Working Paper No. 72, March.

Sengupta, D.N. (1996), *Deregulation at the State Level*, IIMA Working Paper No. 1327, August.

3

Gujarat Finances Reform of Budgetary Management*

ATUL SHARMA

This paper examines the performance of Gujarat's revenue and expenditure systems. It attempts to identify the basic weaknesses of the existing revenue sources and indicates the broad direction of future reforms that is desirable. Its major thrust, however, is on identifying the sources of inefficiencies of budgetary and expenditure policy and management, and preparing reform proposals for enhancing expenditure effectiveness.

Budgetary Policy Making in Federal Background

The budgetary policy of Gujarat like any other states', that has culminated in its revenue and expenditure systems, evolved in the planning process in the mixed economy framework. Being a part of the federal system, central government policies, particularly in regard to fiscal transfers, pricing of goods produced by its enterprises and interest rates have also influenced, to an extent, Gujarat's revenue and expenditure systems. In the reform period, beginning from the mid-1991, the central government's several reforms measures have adversely impacted state's budgets. For example, in its efforts to curb fiscal deficits, the central government reduced fiscal transfers to states in some years. Its tax reforms, liberalization of interest rates and prices of goods such as coal and petroleum products produced by its public sector undertakings also induced direct or indirect impact on

---

* This paper, based on the ADB project on Gujarat's Reform of Public Finances, was presented at the Seminar on Dynamics in Gujarat held at the Centre for Development Alternatives, Ahmedabad during April 23 and 24, 1999.

Gujarat's budgets. Recent pay revision of the state government employees along the central pay revision of its employees is another example of how some of the central government policy decisions impact the state's transactions. The actual impact of some such policy decisions on Gujarat's budget will find a mention in appropriate places. The short point is that some of the sources of strain on Gujarat's finances fall outside its realm of decision making.

Worsening Fiscal Balances

Almost all states in India have witnessed a secular deterioration in their fiscal balances. As the Tenth Finance Commission has noted, states have passed through three phases of deterioration in the revenue account balance. In the first phase until 1986-87, the non-plan account surplus was larger than the plan deficit, and to that extent, contributed to an overall revenue surplus. Between 1986-87 and 1991-92, the plan deficit rose sharply and far exceeded the shrinking non-plan surplus. The third phase from 1991-92 marked the beginning of growing deficit on non-plan revenue account.[1]

Gujarat does not exactly follow the pattern. The plan revenue account yielded deficit beginning from 1985-86. There existed, however, surplus on non-plan account except for 1990-91. Yet the fact remains that the revenue expenditure outstripped revenue receipts almost continuously from 1985-86 barring three years (1996-1997) in the reform period (Table 3.1 and Appendix).

The gap between revenue receipts and current expenditure came to account for 2.90 per cent of NSDP in 1990-91. Though declined in subsequent years, it still stood at 1.01 per cent of NSDP in 1997-98. But it is the growing interest liability, which has essentially driven the wedge between revenue receipts and current expenditure. This means that the state's revenue was adequate to meet its non-interest current expenditure.

But interest liability alone cannot explain the growing fiscal deficit of Gujarat, as the trend of primary deficits, particularly since 1993-94, suggests.

With growing revenue deficit, the fiscal deficit widened. The fiscal deficit which stood at 7.37 per cent of NSDP in 1990-91 came down to 1.34 per cent NSDP in 1993-94 but started claiming once again to reach the level of 4.15 per cent in 1996-97 and further to 4.44 per cent in 1997-98 (R.E.) (Table 2-A). This means that the state government has trailed far behind the target of 3.5 per cent of NSDP set for 1997-98. The fiscal deficit came down during 1993-94 and the following year essentially as a result of capital expenditure continued while the fiscal deficit kept moving up. In fact, the revenue deficit on the average contributed 11.3 per cent of gross fiscal deficit during 1990-95 (Table 3A).

Table 3.1 : Major Deficit Indicators as per cent of NSDP

Sl. No.	Itmes	Years 1980-81	1985-86	1990-91	1996-97	1997-98
1.	Balance on Revenue A/c	0.06	0.02	(-)Neg	(+)Neg	N.A
2.	Budget Deficit	-0.62	0.16	0.56	-0.01	0.32
3.	Fiscal Deficit	3.77	4.23	7.37	4.15	4.44
4.	Fiscal Deficit	4.34	4.61	7.91	2.41	4.61
5.	Primary Deficit	2.72	2.68	5.19	1.32	1.45
6.	Revenue Deficit	-1.86	0.58	2.90	-1.04	1.01
7.	Interest Adjusted Revenue	0.81	-2.13	-5.07	-1.79	-4.00
8.	NSDP Estimates	65.47	121.47	242.69	568.64	632.90

Note : [(-) Sign Indicated Surplus]: NSDP for 1997-98 assumed GDP growth rate in that year.

Sources : (1) GoG, DOES, Budget in Brief, Various Issues.
(2) R.B.I. Bulletin, Various Issues.

This suggests that revenue expenditure continued to grow far in excess of revenue receipts. Gujarat's aggregate revenue receipts, as per cent of NSDP was higher than aggregate revenue expenditure as per cent of state income till 1984-85. This trend reversed since then except for 1993-94 and 1994-95. During these two years, revenue-income ratio was a little higher than expenditure-income ratio (Table 4A).

Rising Unit Cost of Public Service

The important implication of growing revenue deficit is that the unit cost of public services rises to the extent the interest liability increases due to financing revenue expenditure with borrowed fund. This method of financing revenue expenditure further fuels the growth of already bulging public debt which, in turn, adds to the fast growing interest and thus to revenue expenditure growth.

Releasing Budget Constraint

In the Indian federal system, a state functions under a hard budget constraint. A state cannot borrow on its own as long as it is indebted to the central government. Nor can it resort to deficit financing. Even so, all states in India have rising fiscal deficit. This is financed by central loans, market loans and other loans as well as using the surplus on Public Accounts. It is the latter source, which has given the states some leeway in their fiscal adjustment because other sources are determined exogenously. Frequent use of surplus on Public Account, though has relaxed budget constraint, to an extent, has important consequences on state's allocative efficiency.

Understanding the Weaknesses of the Revenue System

Gujarat's aggregate revenue receipts rose to 17.26 per cent of its NSDP in 1997-98 from 15.66 per cent in 1980-81—just one and a half percentage points over more than one and a half decades. The state's own tax revenue increase alone has contributed this growth. The other two broad components, viz. non-tax revenue and central transfers in terms of tax shares and grants as percentage of NSDP declined during the same period. The former dipped from 2.83 per cent in 1980-81 to 2.66 per cent in 1997-98 and the latter from 4.71 per cent to 3.85 per cent over the same period. Their contributions to aggregate revenue also slashed overtime.[2]

Table 3.2 : Composition of Gujarat's Aggregate Revenue

Components	1980-81		1990-91		1997-98 (RE)	
	As % of aggregate revenue	As % of NSDP	As % of aggregate revenue	As % of NSDP	As % of aggregate revenue	As % of NSDP
Revenue transfer from the Centre	30.09	4.71	17.05	2.37	22.30	3.85
State's own tax revenue	51.81	8.11	71.02	9.89	62.31	10.75
State's non-tax revenue	18.10	2.83	11.94	1.66	15.40	2.66
Aggregate revenue receipt	100.00	15.66	100.00	13.92	100.00	17.26

Source: GoG, DOES, Budget in Brief.

Gujarat's tax performance as measured by tax-income ratio is higher than three states (Haryana, Punjab and Maharashtra) which are above it in income scale. Some other studies have also made similar observation on Gujarat's relative tax performance even in earlier years [3]. But relatively less developed states like Kerala, Karnataka and Tamil Nadu have realized much higher tax-income ratio. Gujarat, however, lags far behind Haryana and Punjab but not Maharashtra in tapping non-tax sources (Table 3.3).

Table 3.3 : Comparison of States' Own Tax and Non-Tax Revenue

Sr. No.	States	1984-85		1995-96		1995-96	
		States' Own Tax Revenue As % of its Own Total Revenue	States' Non-Tax Revenue As % of its Own Total Revenue	States' Own Tax Revenue As % of its Own Total Revenue	States' Non-Tax Revenue As % of its Own Total Revenue	States' Own Tax Revenue As % of its NSDP	States' Non-Tax Revenue As % of its NSDP
1.	Andhra Pradesh	51.16	48.84	72.00	28.00	6.64	2.59
2.	Assam	27.08	72.92	67.70	32.30	4.59	2.19
3.	Bihar	25.87	74.13	67.70	32.30	5.05	2.41
4.	Gujarat	55.39	44.61	76.90	23.10	10.76	3.24
5.	Haryana	51.29	48.71	49.80	50.20	8.67	8.74
6.	Karnataka	52.27	47.73	81.00	19.00	12.24	2.87
7.	Kerala	55.26	44.74	86.30	13.70	13.63	2.16
8.	Madhya Pradesh	39.34	60.66	66.40	33.60	7.36	3.72
9.	Maharashtra	53.61	46.39	79.80	20.20	8.31	2.11
10.	Orissa	27.64	72.36	64.20	35.80	5.39	3.00
11.	Punjab	60.79	39.21	59.90	40.10	7.73	5.18
12.	Rajasthan	39.71	60.29	54.80	45.20	6.92	5.72
13.	Tamil Nadu	58.25	41.75	89.30	10.70	10.81	1.30
14.	Uttar Pradesh	36.25	63.75	69.50	30.50	6.06	2.66
15.	West Bengal	52.68	47.32	92.70	7.30	7.16	0.57

Note : Non-tax revenue here includes central transfers and thus not comparable with that in Table 3.2.

Source: *RBI Bulletin*, Various Issues.

Growth

Aggregate revenue of the state grew almost at the same rate (14.47 per cent per annum) both in pre-reform period of about twenty years (1978-91) and the past seven years in the reform period. However, the state's own tax revenue growth slumped from 15.66 per cent per annum in the preceding period to 13.44 per cent per annum in the latter period. Non-tax revenue growth declined to a much lower rate of 8.55 per cent in the reform period as compared to its growth of 15.69 per cent per annum in the pre-reform period (Table 3.4).

Table 3.4 : Growth and Buoyancy of Broad Revenue Sources

Sr. No.	Items	Growth Rates		Buoyancy	
		1978-91	1991-98	1978-91	1991-98
1.	Aggregate Revenue Receipts	14.47	14.47	1.09	0.98
2.	State's Own Tax Revenue	15.66	13.44	1.19	0.95
3.	State's Own Non-Tax Revenue	15.69	8.55	1.19	0.63
4.	Receipts from Shared Taxes	8.58	18.99	0.63	1.38
5.	Grants from the Centre	13.07	13.07	0.96	0.86

Source: Estimated.

Buoyancy coefficients clearly suggest that different revenue components' growth has not kept pace with the state income growth in the reform period. For example, the aggregate revenue of the state rose only by 0.98 per cent in response to one per cent increase in state income in the 1991-98 period as compared to 1.09 per cent in the preceding period. More important, State's own tax revenue response is still weaker at 0.95 per cent in the reform period in comparison with 1.19 per cent in the 1978-91 period. It implies that the design of the state's tax system is not wide enough to mop up a part of the incremental income. This is the most serious weakness of the state's tax system.

Decomposing State's Own Tax Revenue : Single Tax Dominance

Gujarat has levied nine major taxes: three direct taxes — profession tax, land revenue and stamp duty and registration and six indirect taxes —

sales tax, state excise, motor vehicles tax, goods and passenger tax, electricity duty and entertainment tax. There are still a few minor taxes such as luxury tax and mineral rights tax. Among these, sales tax alone contributes around two-thirds of the state's own tax revenue (Table 5A). The only other tax, which contributes one-tenth or more of the state's own tax revenue is electricity duty. Stamp duty and registration as well as motor vehicles tax add more than 5 per cent each but less than 10 per cent to Gujarat's own tax revenue. The other taxes provide no more than 2 per cent of state's own revenue receipts.

The most dominant tax, which is sales tax, has become sluggish in the reform period. The revenue growth dipped from 16 per cent in 1978-91 to 13 per cent per annum during 1991-98. Its response to state income also declined in the later period. The growth of revenue from electricity duty, the tax next in importance, however, improved its growth performance from 18 per cent per annum during 1978-91 to 2 per cent in the reform period. So did its buoyancy from 1.37 to 1.52 per cent in the corresponding periods. Among the remaining taxes, motor vehicle tax, and stamp duty and registration improved both growth and buoyancy while the rest slumped or remained stagnant (Table 3.5).

Table 3.5 : Growth and Buoyancy of State Taxes

Sr. No.	Items	Growth Rates		Buoyancy	
		1978-91	1991-98	1978-91	1991-98
1.	Sales Tax	16.00	13.00	1.24	0.96
2.	Electricity Duty	18.00	21.00	1.37	1.52
3.	Motor Vehicle Tax	15.00	20.00	1.10	1.38
4.	Stamp and Registration Duties	15.00	19.00	1.10	1.32
5.	Goods and Passenger	11.00	-3.00	0.87	-0.17
6.	Land Revenue	12.00	12.00	0.91	0.91
7.	Tax on Entertainment	7.00	10.00	0.52	0.67
8.	State Excise	13.00	12.00	0.97	0.84

State excise deserves a special mention in the context of Gujarat. The state has never considered state excise as a source of revenue and remains the lone state in the country to continue to enforce prohibition ever since 1931.

The Gujarat government has initiated certain tax reform measures. These are in right direction but yet to go to the root of poor tax elasticity. As a result, these have not contributed much to improving tax buoyancy as the above analysis shows.

Box 1
Tax Reforms Since 1992-93

Sales Tax Reforms

- The process of the reforms was initiated in 1992.

(i) Additional tax was abolished from 1-4-1992.

(ii) New Schedules in the Act were prepared.

(iii) Barring a few commodities, the levy of tax was brought to the first stage and single point.

- From 1-4-1996, the number of tax rates was reduced from 23 to 17.
- From 1-4-1997.

(i) Turn over tax was abolished.

(ii) Number of rates of tax was consolidated to six.

(iii) From 1-4-1997, the number of items in the list of prohibited goods was reduced to 33 from 63.

(iv) Rate of input tax was brought down from 2.4 per cent to 2 per cent.

- Budget 1998-99 has introduced a number of tax reform measures which are dealt with in the Volume two.

Profession Tax

The rate structure was made progressive from 1-4-1997.

Stamp Duty

From 1-4-1997 rates of stamp duty on certain commercial transactions was reduced.

Ready reckoners updated implemented from August 1998.

Budget 1998-99 proposed immediate implementation of updated ready reckoners for valuation of immovable properties. Other reform and rationalization measures are discussed in the chapter on stamp duty.

Transport Taxes and Goods Taxes

From 1-4-1993, composite tax based on number of seats in private buses was introduced in place of additional tax, which was leviable on the basis permits and numbers of passengers. The elements of motor vehicles and additional tax were merged. This has resulted in the elimination of corruption and permits system, less administrative work, transparent tax system and more revenue.

From 1-4-1997, goods tax and motor vehicle tax were merged in respect of

(Contd.)

goods vehicles.

Budget 1998-99 has replaced weight based rate structure by ad valorem rate: 4 per cent on the ex-factory price of motor cars and jeeps, though proposed no change in tax structure for two wheelers.

Luxury Tax

Budget 1998-99 has raised the exemption limit and introduced some minor adjustment in tax rates to encourage tourism.

Creation of Directorate of Taxation

GoG has created a nodal organisation called Directorate of Taxation to accelerate the process of tax reforms.

The tax analysis clearly drives home four important points :

(i) The state operates in a multiple tax regime.

(ii) The state overwhelmingly depends on one single tax, viz. sales tax, for its resource mobilization.

(iii) Gujarat's tax performance is essentially based on tax deepening rather than on base widening. Gujarat State Finance Commission (GFC) has also made a similar observation.

(iv) The existing tax design does not provide an adequate tax base that yields revenue in response to income growth.

To sum up, it is not that Gujarat has not used the tax instruments to mobilize resources. It has done, and done even better in comparison to some of the more advanced states. But the tax designs as they exist at present are seriously faulty. These have led to the over dependence on one single source, viz. sales tax. Even this is not buoyant. An in-depth study of the working of the present sales tax system has identified the major reasons for its being so.[4] These are: narrow tax-base, excessive dependence on input taxation, cumbersome administrative procedures and outlandish administration, provision of a long list of tax-free goods and numerous industrial incentives and exemptions. The examination of the other state taxes has also highlighted similar drawbacks. As a consequence, the entire tax revenue has failed to grow with the state's income growth. This clearly suggests the direction of future tax reforms: simplify and rationalize tax system and thus widen tax-base. Modernize tax administration and facilitate compliance. The thrust of tax reforms in the state has to be on widening tax base while keeping the tax design simple and transparent that facilitates better tax administration and compliance.

Shrinking Non-Tax Receipts

Receipts from state-owned enterprises (SOEs) and departmentally run schemes, user charges inclusive of receipts from irrigation, royalty on mines and minerals, revenues from forest and interest recovery are the broad sources of non-tax revenue. With considerably low forest coverage, there is hardly any scope for enlarging much receipt from forest in Gujarat. The state is endowed with a wide range of mines and minerals, but the union government determines the royalty on major minerals. The royalty on minor minerals, which are fixed by the state government, is passed on to the Panchayats. Receipts from the other non-tax sources fall within the realm of state decision making.

Non-tax revenue contributes in normal years less than one-fifth of Gujarat's total revenue. Royalty on crude oil alone accounted for more than one-fifth of the state's non-tax revenues in 1996-97. This indicated still lesser state efforts to mobilize resources from its other sources. Non-tax share even inclusive of oil royalty from the centre has slumped gradually to only 15.40 per cent in 1997-98 (RE). As noted earlier, its growth dropped to 8.55 per cent per annum in the 1991-98 period. Neglect of these sources for resource mobilization is common to almost all states in the country[5] (Table 3.3). The basic reason lies in state's reluctance to take hard decisions that affect some deeply entrenched interest groups. Low water charges and power tariff, low cost recovery of non-merit public services and poor interest are largely due to this constraint.

The Vaidyanathan Committee made several realistic recommendations for water rate fixation. The GFC has considered and endorsed these recommendations for implementation. The Gujarat government is, however, yet to implement them.

State-Owned Enterprises

Gujarat has 40 government companies inclusive of 7 subsidiaries, 6 deemed companies and five statutory corporations. Five statutory corporations, which employed capital of Rs. 66.16 billion as on March 31, 1995, earned a total return of Rs. 5.43 billion or 8.19 per cent rate of return during 1994-95. This rate of return includes the subsidy of Rs. 6.562

billion provided to Gujarat Electricity Board (GEB). Without this subsidy, GEB's return on capital employed worked out at (-) Rs.1929.2 million. In any case, two of the five corporations, viz. Gujarat Road Transport Corporation and Gujarat State Warehousing Corporation earned negative return of Rs. 431.6 million and Rs.3 million respectively in 1994-95. Again, 40 government companies earned Rs. 392.4 million or 2.4 per cent rate of return during 1994-95 on the capital of Rs. 16.39 billion employed on these companies.[6] All the SOEs (54) reported losses of about Rs. 1.33 billion in 1994-95. The poor performance of SOEs has caused heavy drain in the form of capital contributions, loans and subsidy on the state's exchequer year after year (Table 3.6).

Table 3.6 : Budgetary Outgo for SOEs (Rs. Million)

Types of Outgo	1993-94		1995-96	
	Govt. Cos.	Statutory Corpn.	Govt. Cos.	Statutory Corpn.
1. Equity/capital contributions	2436.2	111.0	767.2	
2. Loans from budget	296.0	2572.1	4310.1	1884.8
3. Subsidy	716.6	8781.2	813.4	7350.0
4. Total	3448.8	11464.3	12740.7	9234.8

Source: Report of the Comptroller and Auditor General of India for the year ended 31 March 1996, No. 2 (Commercial).

The GFC examined closely the working of SOEs and made important specific recommendations for restructuring/privatization/merger/divestment. The Government of Gujarat (GoG) is seized of the problem of restructuring and privatization of SOEs and has taken several initiatives under Public Sector Restructuring Programme (PSRP). It constituted a Standing Committee under the Chairmanship of Chief Secretary to operationalize the recommendations of GFC on SOEs. Subsequently, it set up an independent Technical Secretariat to advise the Finance Department and other line ministries and SOEs in developing restructuring/divestment proposals for the SOEs selected under PSRP.

The GoG has constituted a High Powered Cabinet Sub-Committee with Chief Minister as Chairman for the purpose of smooth, transparent and timely implementation of SOE reforms. This committee is vested with decision-making powers for restructuring SOEs. The Technical Secretariat, as mentioned above, provides support to the Committee.

The state government has identified under the PSRP 28 SOEs for the purpose of their restructuring, closure, merger, privatization and divestment (Table 7A). Subsequently, as part of Asian Development Bank (ADB) technical assistance, the Price Waterhouse studied 10 SOEs and submitted restructuring programmes for them.

The GoG has also created a State Renewal Fund to provide a social safety net mechanism for restructuring of SOEs. These initiatives are in right direction, and their successful completion would have favourable impact on Gujarat's Finances.

Interest Receipts

In the current regime, the government has to borrow at the market determined interest rate. As a result, the cost of borrowing has gone up. Even so, government lending is at a highly subsidized rate. For example, the loan and advances given by the Gujarat government stood at Rs. 42.65 billion as on March 31, 1995. The total interest realized on this huge sum during 1995-96 was only Rs. 71.3 million and the average interest worked out was only 0.17 per cent. This realized interest rate is abysmally lower than even the modest rate of 4 per cent recommended by the Tenth Finance Commission on the loans outstanding to third-parties as on March 31, 1995.[7] The implementation of various types of restructuring in SOEs, which are under consideration of the Gujarat government, is likely to have favourable impact on further accretion of loans and advances at subsidized interest rate for certain purposes such as vehicle purchase or house building advance to government employees in the new economic environment.

Cost Recovery

The GFC has made a very detailed examination of the issue of subsidies. It has estimated the recovery rate of different types of public services and shown that the average cost recovery rate of total social services was no more than 5.08 per cent in 1980-81. What is worse, it further declined to 2.23 per cent a decade later (1990-91)[8]. The Report of National Development Council on Austerity put the ratio of cost recovery to the cost of public services for Gujarat at 14.26 per cent as against 26.35 per cent for Maharashtra in 1987-88[9]. All this clearly calls for a strategy to improve cost recovery of public services.

.This brief discussion brings out the following important points. First, the non-tax sources have not received desired attention of GoG as a source of revenue. Second, there is a considerable scope for resource mobilization from some of these sources and expenditure reduction in respect of some others. For example, successful implementation of restructuring and privatization of SOEs, as is being attempted by GoG, will have the latter effect in terms of reduced subsidies and budgetary support. Third, there exists long prevailing practice of providing public services at a low or no price. This leads to a resistance to any price hike. Therefore, the success of resource mobilization from some of these sources will call for imaginative schemes combining proper pricing and improved delivery system as well as effective public information programmes. Fourth, some of the existing schemes, loans and advances for certain purposes, as indicated earlier, have lost their relevance in the new economic context.

Focusing on the Expenditure Effectiveness

Growing at the rate of 16.53 per cent per annum for more than a decade (1978-91), the revenue expenditure growth slowed down to 13.31 per cent per annum in the reform period (1991-98). Even so, the level of revenue expenditure continued to surpass revenue receipts in the reform period. Capital expenditure which expanded at a much lower rate of 10.70 per cent per annum further slowed down (9.66 per cent per annum) in the reform period (Table 3.7). As a result, capital expenditure as percentage of NSDP dripped to 3.55 in 1997-98 from 5.01 in 1990-91, while the corresponding ratio for revenue expenditure shot up to 18.26 from 16.82 with some year to year fluctuations in between. This indicates that the reduction in fiscal deficit was achieved largely by compressing capital expenditure.

When total (revenue and capital outlay and lending) expenditure is decomposed into development and non-development, similar disturbing behaviour is observable: development expenditure as percentage of state's NSDP tended to decline while the ratio relating to non-development expenditure clearly rose [10] (Table 3.8). More importantly, non-development has recorded a rapid growth of 15.77 per cent per annum during 1991-98 as compared to 11.24 per cent during the same period (Table 3.7). However, unlike most states, Gujarat allocated larger proportion—more than two-third of its revenue expenditure for development activities although non-development activities claimed increasingly rising share overtime (Table 3.9). In fact, Gujarat along with Maharashtra apportioned highest proportion of their respective revenue expenditure for development activities during 1990-98 in comparison to the other major states. This holds even when the relative share is examined combining both revenue and capital expenditure.

Table 3.7 : Growth of Different Fiscal Aggregates

Sr. No.	Item	Growth Rates 1978-91	1991-98
A	Total Revenue Expenditure	16.41(15.01)	13.31(12.72)
1	Development Expenditure	17.85(14.83)	12.36(11.24)
(a)	Social Services	15.21(14.84)	11.66(11.43)
(b)	Economic Services	16.42(14.83)	12.00(11.13)
2	Non-Developmental Expenditure	16.54(15.77)	16.67(15.77)
(a)	Interest	22.15	16.85
(b)	Establishment	13.32	15.43
B	Total Capital Outlay	10.70	9.66
1	Developmental Expenditure	10.91	7.72
(a)	Social Services	10.32	7.87
(b)	Economic Services	10.79	8.03
2	Non-Developmental Expenditure	10.09	19.37

Note : Figures in brackets indicate the growth rate of revenue and capital expenditure combined.

Source: Computed.

Table 3.8 : Broad Expenditure Categories as per cent of NSDP and Total Expenditure*

Sr. No.	Categories	1980-81 As % of	As % of	1990-91 As % of	As % of	1997-98 (R.E.) As % of	As % of
A.	Total Expenditure	20.00	-	21.83	-	21.82	-
(a)	Revenue Expenditure	13.80	(68.99)	16.82	(77.04)	18.26	(83.72)
(1)	Development	15.35	(76.76)	16.25	(74.45)	15.38	(70.48)
(i)	Eco. Services	9.27	(46.34)	9:31	(42.64)	8.39	(38.46)
(ii)	Social Services	6.08	(30.42)	6.95	(31.82)	6.99	(32.02)
(2)	Non-Development	4.56	(22.80)	5.50	(25.19)	6.35	(29.13)
(i)	Interest	1.05	((5.24)	2.18	(9.98)	2.99	(13.70)
(ii)	Establishment	2.59	(12.95)	2.70	(12.35)	2.67	(12.23)
(b)	Capital Expenditure	6.20	(31.01)	5.01	(22.96)	3.55	(16.28)

* Total expenditure comprises revenue expenditure, capital outlay and govt. lending. Figures in brackets indicate total expenditure inclusive of repayment as % of NSDP.

Source : Computed.

Within development expenditure, economic services have an edge over social services in revenue expenditure allocation. As for capital expenditure, social services received not only lesser share but that was also shrinking overtime. Even economic services' share in capital expenditure was almost continually falling with the latter's shrinking share in Gujarat's aggregate public expenditure. This should be a matter of great concern for the state. For, as a leading industrialized state in the country, Gujarat has to improve not only provision but also the quality of the goods and services as well as skill that allow the markets to flourish. But the weighted index of "Relative Development of Infrastructure"[11] of Gujarat plunged to 124 in 1990-95 from 132 in 1966-68 and Gujarat's relative position among the states is fifth which is lower than its fourth position in per capita income scale. It is conceivable that physical and social infrastructure constraints would hinder sustaining Gujarat's growth at higher trajectory.

Among the economic services, irrigation together with flood control and energy have received higher priority in non-interest expenditure allocations. Transport and communication is losing its share overtime (Table 3.10). So has done the allocation for industries. This should not be a source of worry if the government has performed its role as a facilitator of private sector investment.

Of social services, education has claimed the highest share in non-interest expenditure but its share has tended to decline overtime. On the other hand, a wide variety of welfare programmes have received an increasingly larger share in the nineties (Table 3.10). In fact, the expenditure under various welfare programmes is far more than that for agriculture, rural development, transport and communication and industry. In an unequal society like Gujarat's as much as India's welfare schemes do receive policy makers' attention. But the fact is that these are loosely targeted and implemented. Consequently, these fail to achieve the desired objectives. Smaller number but well targeted and easy to administer programmes will be cost effective as well as more beneficial.

Gujarat has trailed behind other comparable states in regard to the performance of some of the health and education indicators. Their improvement will be supportive of rapid industrial growth.

Of non development expenditure comprising more than one-quarter of Gujarat's revenue expenditure, interest liability and establishment are the two major components. Interest as percentage of NSDP moved up to 2.99 in 1997-98 (RE) from only 1.05 in 1980-81. The corresponding proportion for establishment remained more or less steady below 3 in the entire period (Table 3.8).

Table 3.9 : Broad Composition of States' Expenditure – 1990-98

Sr. No.	States	As % of Total Revenue Expenditure				Developmental		Developmental
		Develp. Exp.	Social Services	Economic Services	Non-Devlp. Exp.	Interest Payment	Capital Outlay As % of Total Capital Outlay	Expenditure As % of Total Expenditure
1.	Andhra Pradesh	67	39	28	32	14	99	70
2.	Assam	66	41	24	34	14	97	68
3.	Bihar	61	37	24	39	19	99	63
4.	Gujarat	69	35	34	31	15	98	72
5.	Haryana	48	23	25	50	11	97	51
6.	Karnataka	67	38	29	31	13	90	70
7.	Kerala	61	41	20	.38	15	96	64
8.	Madhya Pradesh	67	37	30	30	12	99	70
9.	Maharashtra	69	35	28	34	15	98	72
10.	Orissa	64	39	25	36	20	98	69
11.	Punjab	53	27	26	46	21	95	57
12.	Rajasthan	64	39	24	36	16	98	69
13.	Tamil Nadu	68	39	29	29	11	95	70
14.	Uttar Pradesh	41	32	23	43	20	93	44
15.	West Bengal	62	41	21	36	18	96	64

Source: Reserve Bank of India Bulletin, Various Issues, "Finances of State Governments".

Table 3.10 : Composition on Non-Interest Expenditure (Total)

Categories	Year		
	1990-91	1996-97	1997-98(R.E)
1. Development Expenditure	82.70	79.00	81.66
2. Economic Services	47.36	45.27	44.56
(i) Agriculture	6.56	5.15	5.37
(ii) Irrigation and Flood Control	11.82	18.60	15.80
(iii) Rural Development	5.95	3.72	4.47
(iv) Energy	11.20	9.38	11.68
(v) Industries	4.07	3.31	2.89
(vi) Transport and Communication	7.76	5.11	4.35
3. Social Services	35.35	33.73	37.11
(i) Education	19.44	19.62	19.15
(ii) Health	9.37	8.64	10.51
(iii) Welfare	6.53	5.47	7.45
4. Non-Developmental Expenditure	16.89	20.55	17.88

Note : Development Expenditure and Non-Development Expenditure will not add to the total revenue expenditure because some items under non-development categories are excluded.

Sources : Computed

Interest liability recorded a high growth of 22.15 per cent per annum during 1978-91 period. After almost doubling its claim on Gujarat's total expenditures, interest liability continued to grow at 16.85 per cent per annum during 1991-98 (Table 3.9). It came to claim 13.70 per cent of the state's total expenditure and 2.99 per cent of NSDP in 1997-98 (RE) as against 9.98 per cent and 2.18 per cent respectively in 1990-91. This share, though rising as compared to its own past, is not high by itself. But a part of this burden has arisen for financing revenue deficit. To that extent, it is the reflection of poor management of the state finances.

Establishment, which essentially comprises wages and salaries, is the other major item of expenditure claiming all throughout more than one-tenth of the state's total expenditure. It has further increased subsequent to the recent pay revision in the wake of Fifth Pay Commission Report implemented by the Central Government. The charge on revenue in terms of wages and salaries shot up by Rs.15.00 billion as arrears of pay between January1, 1996 and March 31, 1998 and annually by another Rs.11.00

billion. To that extent, there will be a jump in establishment charges. The rise in establishment expenditure, which has increased at the rate of 15.43 per cent per annum, is largely due to rising emolument per employee rather than employment growth (Table 3.11). The fact remains, however, that the state government is faced with the problem of overstaffing. The GFC has examined this issue very closely and recommended a two-pronged strategy to reduce number of employees and improve productivity (Box Nos. 2 and 3). A high powered Expenditure Priorities Committee (EPC) should operationalize this strategy in an integrated manner while defining the role of government in the new context. At the same time the GoG should consider introducing an attractive VRS. The state government should strictly adhere to the policy of non-recruitment against natural attrition and filling posts through deputation rather than post creation. The GoG has indeed taken an important step by creating a Surplus Staff Cell out of the surplus employees of SOEs under the PSRP.[12]

Box No. 2

Initiatives to reduce staff redundancy

A GoG resolution enforced from 1990-91 required prior permission before filling any vacancy, new recruitment and promotion. Similarly, prior permission was required for travels abroad and in India by government employees for certain specified purposes, for purchase of new vehicles or disposing of the old ones.

Such measures while positive will make difference only on the margin.

Box No. 3

GFC Recommendations for Expenditure Reduction on Establishment

The GFC recommended the following two pronged strategy to reduce expenditure on establishment:

"On the one hand, a time-bound comprehensive programme of administrative reforms should be undertaken at all levels of government in order to streamline procedures and improve productivity…..The other part of the strategy should be aimed at reducing the number of government employees by hiving off organizations and activities which are no longer relevant to the basic objectives of the government or have become totally redundant in the present environment." (p.6)

Table 3.11 : Growth of Public Sector Employment and Salary Bill

Sr.No	Employment (000)	1980	1985	1990	1993	1994	1995
1.	State Government	187	204	217	215	217	215
2.	Local Bodies	234	266	290	300	311	309
3.	Public Enterprises	189	244	293	302	306	302
4.	Total	610	714	800	817	834	826
	State Salary Bill	1661.40	3227.20	6114.90	8702.20	9788.60	11617.90
	Per Employee (Rs.)	8884.49	15819.61	28179.26	40475.35	45108.76	54036.74

Source : GoG, DOES, Socio Economic Review, Economic & Functional Classification.

Subsidy

Explicit budgetary subsidies' share in total expenditure shots up to almost one-tenth (14.30 per cent in 1996-97) of Gujarat's revenue expenditure in 1997-98 from 6.40 per cent in 1990-91. Total subsidies inclusive of the implicit component will obviously be much higher. No estimate of this is available for any recent year. The volume on non-tax revenue has estimated the total implicit subsidy for Gujarat at Rs. 80.2 billion or Rs. 1790 per capita in 1995-96 and the per capita implicit subsidies for economic and social services at Rs. 402 and Rs. 934 respectively. The corresponding per capita implicit subsidies were worked out at Rs. 261.27 and Rs. 266.22 for 1987-88[13]. These budgetary subsidies have essentially arisen because of non-recovery of cost of public services. The state government has not yet recognized the unrecovered cost of non-merit public services as subsidies. To begin with, the state government should bring out an official estimate of the subsidies implicit in providing these services and present annually to the legislature for public debate as to the desirability of such large untargeted and indiscriminate subsidies. As for explicit subsidies, the minimal number of objective criteria-based targeted schemes will be more beneficial and cost effective.

Growing Inflexibility in Expenditure Allocation

Interest, wages and salaries, subsidies and transfers are four downward rigid items of expenditure. These items together accounted for 47.59 per cent of Gujarat's revenue expenditure in 1980-81. About a decade and a half-later (1997-98), they required as much as 64.82 per cent of its revenue expenditures. As a result, these four items alone demanded 84.3 per cent of the state's revenue receipt in 1997-98 as against 63.33 per cent in 1980-81 (Table 3.12). Its implication is that only 36.67 per cent of state's revenue receipts remained for other expenditures in 1980-81 and just about 15 per cent in 1997-98 (BE). This has set the limit of the allocative powers of the state government to allocate its non-debt receipts for any effective intervention elsewhere.

Table 3.12 : Claim of Downward Rigid Items on Revenue Receipts and Expenditure Gujarat Government

Sr. No.	% Claim on Revenue Expenditure	1980-81	1990-91	1996-97 R.E.	1997-98 B.E.
1.	Wages, Salaries and Pensions	13.49	15.23	14.00	18.02
2.	Interest	4.70	9.74	12.31	12.65
3.	Transfers	25.20	29.11	24.46	24.47
4.	Subsidies	4.20	6.40	14.30	9.68
5.	Total (1 to 4)	47.59	60.48	65.07	64.82
6.	% claim on Aggregate Revenue Receipt	63.33	95.85	85.09	84.43
7.	% of Aggregate Revenue Available for other Purpose	36.67	4.15	14.91	15.57

Source : GoG, DOES, An Economic and Purposè Classification of the Budget, Gujarat State, Relevant Issues

In a state of affairs such as this, maintenance of expenditure is treated as residual. This explains the reason for poor maintenance of roads, hospitals, administrative building, irrigation systems and other assets created. Poor maintenance of irrigation systems, power stations and other productive assets created has resulted in their gross under-utilization.

Declining Capital Formation

With the current expenditure crowding out capital expenditure, the gross capital formation in the state government sector as per cent of NSDP which was no more than 5 per cent in 1980-81 dropped gradually to less than 2 per cent in 1996-97. This is disproportionately low as compared to Gujarat's total expenditure income ratio of 20 plus per cent in the nineties.

Managing Debt Build-up

The outstanding debt as on March 31, 1986 as percentage of its NSDP was 20.19, which rose to 22.50 by March 31, 1998. The reasons for growing debt are obvious. The state had to borrow to meet the deficit arising from the current expenditure outpacing the state revenue while at the same time to finance an increasingly large plan. On the other hand, the net availability of loans (after taking care of interest and repayment) sharply declined to 37.70 per cent in 1997-98 (RE) from 51.19 per cent just two years before.

The growing debit of the state viewed in the context of falling capital formation suggests poor management of borrowed fund. Revamping investment policy, which explicitly considers rate of return together with terms of loan, has become unavoidable. It is more so when the Gujarat government had to borrow at an increasingly higher interest rate following interest rate liberalization. The interest rate at which Gujarat borrowed from the centre moved up to 12.55 per cent in 1997-98 from only 6.85 per cent in. 1986-87. It is even higher for internal debt inclusive of market loans and those from Public Account (Table 3.13).

Gujarat like other states regularly used surplus on Public Accounts to finance a part of its fiscal deficit (Table 3.8A). An easy access to this source has not helped the state in prioritization of its expenditure programmes keeping within the limit of its affordability. On the other hand, the state government, which essentially functions as a banker in respect of this account, has failed to maximize the return on the surplus on Public Account. It is, therefore, appropriate to establish a separate Pension and Gratuity Fund for Gujarat government employees out of annual contributions of the government. The state government should entrust public sector financial institutions/mutual funds with impeccable track record to manage it professionally. This institutional mechanism will serve the interest of the state better particularly after it comes out of the current imbalance on the revenue account.

Table 3.13 : Gujarat's Debt-NSDP Ratio and Average Interest Rate

Year	Outstanding Debt-NSDP Ratio (%)			Average Interest Rate (%)		
As on March 31, 1986, 1991, 97 & 98	Aggregate debt	Central loans	Internal debt	Aggregate debt	Central loans	Internal debt
1985-86	20.19	16.92	3.27	6.81	6.55	7.87
1990-91	24.31	21.23	3.09	8.43	8.39	8.67
1996-97	21.06	17.51	3.55	12.20	11.93	13.68
1997-98 (RE)	22.50	18.65	3.85	12.78	12.43	14.51

Source: Computed on the basis of data supplied by Finance Department, GoG.

Major Weaknesses of Budgetary and Expenditure Policy

Budgetary policy of the state has led to certain features of Gujarat finances that are not in conformity with the sound principles of public finance:

— current expenditures are outpacing revenue growth;

— non-development expenditures are growing faster than development expenditures;

— current expenditure is crowding out capital expenditure;

— the fast growing downward sticky items—some of them are uncontrollable — have drastically curbed the state's allocative flexibility and thus the state government has lost its control over expenditure priorities and its effectiveness;

— the method of loan financing even a part of revenue expenditure has imparted a feedback process in:

(a) revenue expenditure growth via rising interest liability, and

(b) debt build-up via shrinking net availability of fresh loan.

All these explain why the state has failed to realize the modest target of containing its fiscal deficit at 3.5 per cent of NSDP for 1997-98.

Reform Strategy

The state should adopt a three-fold strategy for restructuring its expenditure :

- restrict the role of the government to the areas of market failures inclusive of the provsion of merit goods and the activities and institutions that flourish private initiatives and investment;
- offload the activities outside the above domain.
- modernize the state machinery by (a) updating the existing rules, procedures and norms; (b) restructuring organizational structure eliminating multi-layer decision making process and updating the skill of staff; (c) introducing computerization and building MIS; and (d) removing staff redundancy.

Streamlining Budgetary and Expenditure Management

Expenditure inefficiencies of GoG have arisen from four major sources:

- continuing interface with the institutions, conventions and practices evolved in another regime;
- divergence between of policy goals/expenditure targeting and affordability;
- antiquated budgetary planning, monitoring and control; and
- procedure-driven but not delivery-driven functioning of implementing agencies.

A. Continuing Interface with the existing institution

Some of the weaknesses in budgetary and expenditure management have arisen from the existing system of intergovernmental transfers, practices and conventions evolved in the earlier regime that placed the public sector at the commanding height.

State's dependence on fiscal transfers is generally high. Though much lower than many states, Gujarat receives more than one-fifth of its total revenue receipts from the centre in the form of tax-share and grants in addition to almost similar size in terms of loans. As is widely recognized, the method of determining inter-governmental transfers has not promoted efficiency in expenditure management by states. On the contrary, Finance Commission transfers based on gap filling appoach together with its loan forgiveness had given wrong messages to states. This could be also one of the reasons for imprudence in the management of state finances.

Similarly, Planning Commission assistance in the ration of 30:70 between grants and loans for the major states which is invariant between types of activities has not encouraged states to base their investment decisions on the basis of rate of return and terms of finance.

Following the acceptance of planning for economic development, both the central and state governments have developed a compulsive obsession/urge to continually enlarge the size of their respective five-year plans without any reference to resource availability. This has eventually led to a number of adverse consequences on budgetary and expenditure policies at the level of both the centre and states.

The dichotomy that has arisen between plan and non-plan has resulted in compression of non-plan expenditure even if these relate to highly desirable public services and neglect of maintenance of assets. The separation has also discouraged proper attention to the affordability of the overall budget as well as total delivery of public services. This has eventually led to widening gap between the resource availability and expenditure level planned.

Balance from Current Revenue (BCR), Additional Resource Mobilization (ARM), contributions of SOEs, market borrowing, share in small savings, loans from financial institutions and loans from public accounts are the main sources in addition to plan assistance for financing a state plan. With the BCR turning negative since 1985 and the shrinking scope for raising non-debt resources, loan emerged as the major source of financing Gujarat's plan expenditure. This, in turn, has contributed to debt build-up, on the one hand, and growing interest liability under revenue account, on the other.

Mobilizing additional resources year after year to support increasingly larger plans resulted in adhoc measures that contributed to complexity in the tax system, thus making it less amenable to efficient tax administration and compliance and hence to improving tax buoyancy. Budgetary policy has paid little attention to tap the potential on non-tax sources such as water rates, power tariff and cost recovery of public provided services for enlarging plan investment.

To convention of adding committed and maintenance expenditure of plan scheme to non-plan expenditure at the end of every plan has the effect of expanding non-plan expenditure in bulk every five years. This practice together with rising interest liability from debt build-up for plan financing has contributed in no small measure to worsening revenue balance.

With increasingly larger plan size but sluggish revenue growth and laxity in expenditure management, states have experienced a secular deterioration in their fiscal balances. There has, now, been a drastic shift to a regime relying more on market forces. But the approach to planning or the role of a state in the new regime has not been appropriately altered even almost a decade after. There is, however, a growing awareness among the policy makers of the crippling effects on budget and expenditure management of these past development paradigm as well as practices and conventions.

In the new regime the state has to be a facilitator rather than a direct provider of growth. Planning should essentially focus on the areas of market failures and identifying the constraints of dynamic growth and instruments of strategic intervention for removing them.

Future reforms will involve

(i) doing away with plan and non-plan dichotomy in revenue expenditure and maintaining the distinction between revenue/current and capital expenditure;
(ii) redefining the role of planning with focus on the areas of market failures and strategic interventions;
(iii) abolishing the fixed loan component of central assistance to state plans and replacing this with specific purpose loans on the basis of bank-ability of investment programme;
(iv) substituting the current system of providing resources for numerous central schemes by a package of well-targeted schemes; and
(v) redistributive transfers with particular reference to poorer states.

These measures will inevitably entail extensive discussions and agreement among states and the centre in fora like National Development Council and Inter-State Council prior to their implementation.

B. Divergence Between Policy Goals/Expenditure Targeting and Affordability

Gujarat, like any other states, attempted to set an increasingly higher expenditure target from one plan to another but not within its affordability to achieve multiple objectives. In pursuit of too many objectives with limited resource availability, the state has ended up spreading resources too thinly across a wide variety of expenditure programme. The high powered committee, EPC as recommended earlier, should fix priorities in alignment with macro objectives and resources affordability.

Table 3.14 : An Illustrative List of Overlapping Activities/Schemes in Some Departments

Sr. No.	Name of the Department	Overlapping activities being prepared by various agencies/offices
1.	Tribal Department	Multiple agencies – Tribal Development Corporation, Tribal Development Commissioner, Project Administrator, Director of Tribal Department, Tribal Areas Sub-plan (TSAP), Tribal Advisory Board
2.	Welfare of Scheduled Castes	(i) S.C. Economic Development Corporation (ii) Scheduled Castes Welfare Plan as a part of the budget
3.	Rural Development	District Rural Development Authority (DRDA) District Panchayat Officers State Government's Rural Development Department
4.	Land Development	Some overlapping schemes which relate to agricultural development under agencies such as: (i) Agricultural Development Corporation (ii) Gujarat Land Development Corporation (iii) Waste Land Development Board (iv) Khar Land Development Board (DRDA also allocates for some of the activities looked after by the above agencies)
5.	Agriculture	Within Agriculture Department (i) District Agricultural Officer under District Panchayat (ii) Agro Industries Corporations (iii) Seed Development Corporation (iv) Seed Farms under various District Panchayats (v) Gujarat Agriculture University Schemes

Adding plan schemes irrespective of its resource affordability has contributed to the accumulation of ongoing projects that are rolled over from plan to plan without resulting in any assets or income therefrom. Implementing departments' preference to add new programmes to completing the existing ones has also contributed to the proliferation of incomplete projects. This has resulted in cost and time overrun. Again, different departments formulated expenditure programmes independent of one another to achieve almost identical objectives (Table 3.14). Such fragmented decision making yielded less than optimal results.

A high level committee of secretaries should:

(i) identify the programmes which require fast-tracking and those which deserve closing down, and
(ii) redesign overlapping schemes within and between departments for cost effectiveness and enhancing impact. The committee should function in close collaboration with the State Public Finance Reforms Committee (SPFRC).

For easy access to central government fund, the state undertook a large number of centrally sponsored schemes committing some of its own resources. Many a time this has distorted priorities. Worse still, the state has continued without proper evaluation in the schemes deploying its own resources even after the withdrawal of central funding.

Similarly, the state government has implemented a large number of externally aided projects. But the state had to absorb the project staff even after the completion of the projects for legal obligation or other extraneous considerations.

In situations such as above, apart from unintended resource commitment, government decisions work at cross-purpose. For example, Gujarat government took a policy decision not to recruit automatically against vacancies arising from natural attrition. But the absorption of staff employed on the centrally sponsored schemes/externally aided projects as above has acted counter to the objective of staff reduction.

The government should constitute a sub-committee with Chief Secretary as Chairman and Finance Secretary and Secretary of the concerned departments as members to decide as to the desirability of continuation of such schemes.

C. Antiquated Budgetary Planning, Monitoring and Control

Gujarat's budget based on 'procedural rationality' is essentially incremental with a near-term focus. This traditional budgeting accepts last year's expenditure as the base. Added to it, are the provisions for inflation, increase in salary, etc. The new schemes while being admitted allow for some reasonable increase. Thus this budgeting assumes:

(i) schemes sanctioned in the past need to be continued, and
(ii) the methods adopted for achieving a task are the best and there is no superior cost-effective method.

Such budgeting does not permit weeding out the schemes and programmes that have outlived their relevance. It is in this process that the government expenditure system has lost much of its effectiveness.

Zero-base budgeting, if used as a management tool, will improve expenditure effectiveness. This method entails defining objectives, mission and key-result areas under a decision unit. The process involves:

— identification and sharpening of objectives;
— examination of different alternatives to achieve them;
— selecting the most cost effective method among the available alternatives;
— prioritization and ranking of objectives and programmes; and
— switching of resources from low to high priority programmes.

It is clear that zero-base budgeting will weed out the activities that have outlived their utility and merge those which are overlapping. It will also establish a closer alignment between objectives and expenditure programmes. All this will eventually lead to ensuring expenditure effectiveness: getting more out of every rupee government spends. Gujarat should not postpone further this important budgetary reform.

Box No. 4

Attempts to introduce zero-base budgeting

Gujarat introduced zero-base budgeting in 1987-88 for agriculture and rural development and health and family planning along the recommendations of the Baveja Committee. The government made preparations to cover all departments but abandoned the method in 1988-89.

GoG is once again considering adopting this method of budgeting.

Maharashtra introduced zero-base budgeting from 1987-88 due to political and administrative resistance.

The budget formulation passes through multi-level bureaucratic scrutiny. This process does build into programmes some rationality based on elaborate procedures/forms but suffers from one serious weakness. The expenditure programmes thus incorporated in the budget have but only vaguely defined links with macro goals or even micro objectives at the department level. This leads to poor prioritization as well as weak budget monitoring and controls and thus to expenditure inefficiency. Priority-based ceiling for each department in alignment with set goals prior to budget preparation as recommended earlier, will encourage prioritization of expenditure programmes in departmental budgets.

D. Procedure-driven but not Delivery-driven Functioning of Implementing Agencies

Implementing agencies, in their monitoring and controls, are more oriented to meeting accounting requirements and seeking larger funds rather than improving the efficiency and quality of expenditures. The government should consider giving more autonomy and accountability to the line agencies, and fixing performance norms to encourage better service delivery.

Gujarat government introduced the practice of preparing annually 'Performance Budget' for strengthening monitoring physical performance of expenditure programmes. But this document relating to most departments does not provide even the basic parameters like unit cost and physical target. As a result, the whole exercise has become perfunctory and degenerated into an annual ritual. The government should consider integrating the basic parameters of performance budget into zero-base budgeting and in respective expenditure programmes while computerizing its budget operations.

To conclude, the analysis of Gujarat finances has clearly shown both the sources of inefficiencies as well as the areas for policy reforms. The paper has also suggested both the directions and strategy for fiscal reforms that would contribute to enhance effectiveness of budgetary policy. It is only with such fiscal reforms that the state will be better positioned to sustain higher industrial growth and meet the challenges of faster urbanization.

NOTES AND REFERENCES

1. See Report of the Tenth Finance Commission, December 1994, p.5.
2. State's own tax revenue-income ratio was exceptionally high in 1990-91. A closer examination of these ratios before and after this year as shown in appendix table bears this out.
3. Parekh, K.M., "Resource mobilization by Indian Status: A structural analysis with special reference to Gujarat", in Yoginder K. Alagh *et. al* (ed.) (1993) *Stability and Development,* Har Anand Publications.
4. The volume on Directions of Sales Tax Reform and Proposal of Value Added Tax Introduction of ADB Project on Gujarat's Reform of Public Finances.
5. See Report of the Tenth Finance Commission, December, 1994, p.9.
6. Report of the Comptroller and Auditor General of India for the year ended 31 March 1996, No.2 (Commercial) GoG, pp.121-124 and 132-133.
7. See Report of the Tenth Finance Commission, op. cit. p.10.
8. Report of the Gujarat State Finance Commission, April 1994, p.45.
9. For further details, see Report of the GFC, p.42.
10. For detailed discussion on growth performance, see Archana R. Dholakia, *Changes in the Trend and Structure of Fiscal Expenditure in Gujarat,* Anvesak, 1998.
11. CMIE, Economic Intelligence Service, *Profiles of States,* March 1997.
12. The surplus staff has been given three alternatives: (i) continue under a new management; (ii) accept voluntary retirement; and (iii) get registered under the Surplus Staff Cell.
13. Rao, M.G. and Mundle, S., *An Analysis of Changes in Government at State level*: *1977-78 to 1987-88* as reproduced in GFC, *Op.cit.* pp.43 and 44.

APPENDIX

Table 1A : Balances from Current Revenues (BCR) and Revenue Balance (1980-97) (Rs. in Billion)

Year	Revenue Receipt	Revenue Expenditure			BCR	Revenue
		Revenue Expenditure	Non—Plan Revenue Expenditure	Plan Revenue Expenditure		Surplus Deficit
1	2	3	4	5	6	7
1980-81	10.25	9.03	7.15	1.88	3.10	1.22
1981-82	11.59	10.39	8.38	2.01	3.21	1.20
1982-83	13.49	12.83	10.55	2.28	2.94	0.66
1983-84	15.65	14.26	11.65	2.62	4.01	1.39
1984-85	17.69	17.01	14.24	2.77	3.46	0.68
1985-86	19.02	19.72	16.77	2.95	2.25	-0.70
1986-87	21.60	24.69	19.48	5.22	2.12	-3.10
1987-88	28.06	30.93	22.43	8.50	5.64	-2.87
1988-89	32.36	33.62	27.40	6.22	4.95	-1.27
1989-90	36.01	37.27	31.11	6.17	4.91	-1.26
1990-91	33.79	40.82	34.00	6.81	-0.21	-7.03
1991-92	46.63	52.38	42.42	9.96	4.20	-5.76
1992-93	59.11	62.11	47.28	14.82	11.83	-3.00
1993-94	70.30	69.34	62.71	6.62	7.59	0.96
1994-95	78.06	75.44	67.19	8.25	10.88	2.62
1995-96	85.44	87.66	76.32	11.34	9.12	-2.22
1996-97	96.68	102.59	91.14	11.46	5.54	-5.91

Sources : Budget in Brief: NPRE figures have been supplied by Finance Department, Government of Gujarat.
Government of Gujarat, Directorate of Economics and Statistics.

Table 2A : Major Deficit Indicators (1980-98) As % of NSDP

Year	Budget	Revenue	Fiscal	Fiscal	Primary	Interest
1980-81	-0.62	-1.86	3.77	4.34	2.72	-0.81
1981-82	0.48	-1.47	3.07	3.76	2.07	-0.47
1982-83	-0.39	-0.76	4.33	5.12	3.18	-0.39
1983-84	-0.10	-1.23	3.61	4.00	2.57	-0.19
1984-85	-0.29	-0.58	4.43	4.87	3.18	-0.66
1985-86	0.16	0.58	4.23	4.61	2.68	-2.13
1986-87	-0.08	2.21	6.42	6.97	4.68	-3.95
1987-88	-0.12	2.06	7.02	7.74	4.81	-4.28
1988-89	0.23	0.65	3.76	4.66	1.77	-2.65
1989-90	-0.93	0.59	4.53	4.81	2.36	-2.76
1990-91	0.56	2.90	7.37	7.91	5.19	-5.07
1991-92	0.06	2.20	6.86	7.55	4.13	-4.93
1992-93	0.12	0.86	3.31	4.65	0.64	-3.54
1993-94	-0.02	0.25	1.34	2.50	-1.32	-2.41
1994-95	-0.02	-0.55	2.70	2.95	0.22	-1.93
1995-96	-0.13	0.45	3.53	3.94	0.84	-3.13
1996-97	-0.01	-1.04	4.15	2.41	1.32	-1.79
1997-98 (RE)	0.32	1.01	4.44	4.61	1.45	-4.00

Note: (-) sign Indicates Surplus.

Source: Directorate of Economics and Statistics, Budget in Brief, Gujarat State various issues.

Table 3A: Revenue Deficit as percentage of Gross Fiscal Deficit (Major States)

States	Revenue Deficit/GFD(%)			
	1985-90 Average	1990-95 Average	1996-97 (R.E)	1997-98 (B.E)
1. Andhra Pradesh	7.7	11.5	25.0	37.2
2. Bihar	-47.6	51.3	67.4	27.8
3. Goa	0.6	-38.3	-4.7	14.1
4. Gujarat	21.5	11.3	13.4	1.9
5. Haryana	-25.0	14.1	64.3	42.2
6. Karnataka	10.5	11.2	34.8	25.5
7. Kerala	36.4	44.0	49.7	51.9
8. Madhya Pradesh	-1.7	10.1	69.1	33.1
9. Maharashtra	11.5	8.8	28.6	11.0
10. Orissa	15.3	22.4	46.4	40.0
11. Punjab	9.9	45.9	51.3	45.1
12. Rajasthan	17.6	3.4	22.5	1.8
13. Tamil Nadu	12.5	72.3	52.7	49.8
14. Uttar Pradesh	9.3	34.2	56.8	69.8
15. West Bengal	18.0	52.0	52.9	42.3

Source: Reserve Bank of India Bulletin, February 1998, Supplement: Finance of State Government 1997-98.

Table 4.A : Gujarat: Revenue and Expenditure Total and Broad Components as % of NSDF

Year	Revenue Receipts	Total Tax Trans. from centre	States' Own Tax Revenue	States' Own Non Tax Revenue	Revenue Expenditure	Total Expenditure inclusive Repayment	Total Expenditure excluding Repayment
1980-81	15.66	2.90	8.11	2.83	13.80	22.90	20.00
1981-82	14.13	2.54	8.05	2.30	12.66	20.57	17.89
1982-83	15.55	2.43	8.80	2.83	14.79	23.49	20.68
1983-84	13.87	2.01	7.79	2.59	12.64	21.59	17.88
1984-85	15.07	2.61	8.35	2.83	14.49	21.41	19.94
1985-86	15.72	2.31	8.88	2.70	16.30	23.25	20.32
1986-87	15.40	0.88	9.02	3.97	17.61	27.11	22.38
1987-88	20.18	2.59	10.97	3.27	22.24	32.25	27.92
1988-89	16.60	2.04	9.60	2.94	17.25	26.18	21.25
1989-90	16.81	2.00	10.08	3.79	17.40	23.24	21.63
1990-91	13.92	1.15	9.89	1.66	16.82	23.54	21.83
1991-92	17.85	1.18	11.08	4.35	20.05	29.80	25.40
1992-93	17.03	2.34	9.96	3.34	17.89	25.03	21.68
1993-94	17.92	2.51	10.05	3.57	17.68	23.70	20.43
1994-95	16.31	2.04	9.91	3.11	15.76	20.08	19.26
1995-96	17.28	2.30	11.18	3.24	17.73	21.86	21.21
1996-97	17.00	2.07	10.67	2.77	18.04	22.89	21.46
1997-98	17.26	2.46	10.75	2.66	18.26	22.09	21.82

Note: Estimates for 1996-97, 1997-98,1998-99 are by us.

Table 5A : Composition of State Taxes

Year	Sales Tax	Profession Tax	Land Revenue Tax	Stamp & Registration Duty	State Excise Duty	Motor Vehicle Tax	Goods Passenger Tax	Electricity Duty	Entertainment Tax	Miscellaneous Tax/Duty	States' own Tax
1980-81	66.64	1.49	2.43	5.55	0.65	4.19	6.40	6.82	3.96	1.86	100.00
1981-82	69.99	1.38	2.20	5.70	0.60	4.01	2.44	7.76	4.24	1.67	100.00
1982-83	66.05	1.43	1.78	5.03	0.64	4.08	7.06	8.18	4.18	1.55	100.00
1983-84	63.12	1.49	1.85	4.54	0.60	4.03	9.61	9.15	4.34	1.27	100.00
1984-85	62.18	1.63	1.74	4.48	0.46	3.99	6.86	11.04	4.15	3.47	100.00
1985-86	64.25	1.73	1.60	4.41	0.53	3.85	5.47	11.01	3.73	3.42	100.00
1986-87	68.38	1.70	1.67	4.18	0.51	4.22	4.27	9.01	2.99	3.06	100.00
1987-88	66.88	1.75	1.23	4.44	0.55	6.68	5.79	8.78	2.48	1.42	100.00
1988-89	69.19	1.63	1.37	4.62	0.56	3.75	5.39	10.13	1.86	1.49	100.00
1989-90	71.05	2.07	1.42	5.10	0.62	4.03	4.32	8.38	1.64	1.37	100.00
1990-91	72.50	1.59	1.42	5.22	0.50	3.99	4.40	7.81	1.30	1.27	100.00
1991-92	69.49	1.35	1.27	5.77	0.45	3.91	2.61	13.01	1.11	1.04	100.00
1992-93	66.56	1.18	1.33	5.34	0.43	4.20	3.52	15.74	0.85	0.86	100.00
1993-94	70.30	1.13	1.50	5.35	0.47	4.43	2.98	11.81	0.87	1.16	100.00
1994-95	67.17	0.93	1.28	5.71	0.44	4.39	1.38	16.68	0.86	1.15	100.00
1995-96	67.51	0.86	1.46	6.68	0.40	5.74	2.02	13.07	1.07	1.20	100.00
1996-97	66.37	0.80	1.44	6.58	0.40	5.51	1.59	14.85	0.97	1.50	100.00
1997-98	67.90	0.82	1.07	5.96	0.42	5.78	0.91	14.89	0.89	1.37	100.00

Table 6A : Progress of Restructuring and Privatization of Gujarat's SOEs

Sr. No.	Name of SOE	ADB Condition	Present Status
1	GSTC	Closure	Done
2	GFDC	Closure	Under Implementation
3	GSRDC	Closure	Under Consideration
4	GWRDC	Closure	
5	GCCL	Closure	To be decided
6	GDDC	Closure	To be decided
7	GTCL	Transfer > 51% control	Under Implementation
8	GCEL	Transfer > 51% control	Under Implementation
9	GSEC	Transfer > 51% control	Under Implementation
10	APL (Agrocel)	Transfer > 51% control	Done
11	GIL (Insecticides)	Transfer > 51% control	Done
12	TCGL	Transfer > 51% control	
13	**GSFC**	Disinvestment 26% to 51%	26% done
14	**GMDC**	Disinvestment 26% to 51%	26% done
15	**GIIC**	Disinvestment 26% to 51%	Under Implementation
16	**GIDC**	Disinvestment 26% to 51%	
17	**GAIC**	Disinvestment 26% to 51%	
18	**GHB**	Merger	
19	GSCB	Merger	
20	GSLIDC	Merger	
21	GRIMCO	Merger	
22	GSHC(Handloom)	Merger	
23	GSHC(Handloom)	Merger	
24	**GMB**	Restructuring	
25	**GSIC**	Restructuring	
26	**GSRTC**	Restructuring	
27	**GWSSB**	Restructuring	
28	**FDCG**	Closure	

Last 4 SOEs are indirectly part of ADB conditions.

PW reports available for SOEs, which are in bold letter.

Source: Technical Secretariat to advise on restructuring of the SOEs under PSRP.

Table 7A : Composition of Expenditure

Year	Total Revenue and Capital Expenditure						Revenue Expenditure					
	Development Expenditure As % of		Social Service As % of		Economic Service As % of		Non Development Rev. Expenditure As % of		Interest As % of		Establishment As % of	
	NSDP	Total	NSDP	Total	NSDP	Total	NSDP	Total	NSDP	Total Exp.	NSDP	Total
1980-81	15.35	76.76	6.08	30.42	9.27	46.34	3.64	18.19	1.05	5.24	2.59	12.95
1981-82	14.08	78.73	5.55	31.04	8.53	47.69	3.06	17.11	1.00	5.57	2.06	11.54
1982-83	16.72	80.88	7.25	35.06	9.47	45.82	3.31	16.03	1.15	5.56	2.17	10.47
1983-84	14.57	81.52	5.85	32.75	8.72	48.77	2.82	15.75	1.04	5.81	1.78	9.94
1984-85	16.09	80.65	7.08	35.52	9.00	45.14	3.35	16.79	1.24	6.24	2.10	10.55
1985-86	15.77	77.59	7.81	38.42	7.96	39.17	3.99	19.63	1.55	7.63	2.44	12.00
1986-87	17.68	79.01	7.77	34.73	9.91	44.29	4.08	18.23	1.74	7.78	2.34	10.46
1987-88	22.11	79.19	9.67	34.64	12.44	44.55	4.99	17.86	2.22	7.94	2.77	9.92
1988-89	16.21	76.24	7.09	33.37	9.11	42.87	4.54	21.35	2.00	9.40	2.54	11.95
1989-90	16.30	75.37	7.10	32.83	9.20	42.53	4.86	22.45	2.17	10.04	2.68	12.41
1990-91	16.25	74.45	6.95	31.82	9.31	42.64	4.87	22.33	2.18	9.98	2.70	12.35
1991-92	19.17	75.49	7.70	30.32	11.47	45.17	5.49	21.61	2.73	10.74	2.76	10.87
1992-93	16.23	74.88	6.16	28.41	10.07	46.47	5.08	23.43	2.67	12.33	2.41	11.10
1994-94	15.09	73.86	6.39	31.27	8.70	42.59	4.93	24.13	2.66	13.01	2.27	11.11
1995-95	13.80	71.65	6.06	31.46	7.74	40.20	4.76	24.71	2.48	12.88	2.28	11.83
1995-96	15.50	73.07	6.61	31.15	8.89	41.92	5.23	24.67	2.69	12.66	2.55	12.01
1996-97	14.72	68.58	6.28	29.28	8.43	39.30	5.80	27.03	2.83	13.19	2.97	13.84

Source: GoG, **Budget in Brief.**

Table 8A : Debt Burden of Gujarat Government (Rs. in Million)

Fin. Year	Opening	Receipts	Discharge	Closing Balance	Interest Payment	NSDP	Outstanding
1985-86	20516.20	7019.70	3096.60	24439.30	1396.90	121030.00	20%
1986-87	24439.30	6863.20	2285.80	29016.70	1794.20	140220.00	21%
1987-88	29016.70	11790.20	5020.90	35786.00	2338.30	139080.00	26%
1988-89	35786.00	15423.00	9602.90	41606.10	3008.70	194960.00	21%
1989-90	41606.10	10645.90	3313.10	48938.90	3546.90	214230.00	23%
1990-91	48938.90	15863.00	5800.10	59001.80	4124.30	242690.00	24%
1991-92	59001.80	21708.20	11511.90	69198.10	5765.60	261240.00	26%
1992-93	69198.10	18337.90	11384.70	76151.30	7556.90	347140.00	22%
1993-94	77537.80	17722.30	12857.20	82402.90	8341.10	392260.00	21%
1994-95	82402.90	13370.10	3941.50	91831.50	9375.80	478690.00	19%
1995-96	91831.50	16199.60	3181.10	104850.00	10435.60	494470.00	21%
1996-97	104850.00	18441.90	3531.80	119760.10	12791.20	568640.00	21%
1997-98	119760.10	30124.40	7513.00	142371.50	15305.40	632900.00	22%

Note : Increased by Rs.1,38,84 crores due to proforma correction (Please see page 254 of Finance Accounts 1993-94).

Source : Finance Accounts 1985-86 to 1995-96.

4

Urbanisation, Employment Generation and Poverty Under the Shadow of Globalisation
The Case of Gujarat, India

AMITABH KUNDU

Introduction

Structural reform and the associated development strategy launched in India since the early nineties are expected to link the country, particularly its urban centres, with the global economy. Proponents of the strategy argue that the reform would accelerate rural-urban migration and give a boost to urban growth (Expert Group on Commercialisation 1996) and Planning Commission 1998). The expectation is based on the assumption that there will be massive inflow of capital, both from within and outside the country, resulting in rapid development of infrastructure and industries. This is likely to give impetus to the process of urbanisation since much of the industrial growth and consequent increase in employment would be either within or around the existing urban centres. Even when the industrial units get located in rural settlements, in a few years, the latter would acquire urban characteristics. All this would lead to high income and employment growth, alleviation of poverty and general improvement in the quality of life.

Critics of the new development strategy, however, point out that employment generation through industrialisation may not be high. A low rate of infrastructural investment, necessary for keeping budgetary deficits low, would slow down even agricultural growth. This, coupled with open trade policy, is likely to destabilise the agrarian economy, causing high unemployment and exodus from rural areas. This would lead to rapid growth in urban population. Thus, the protagonists as also the critics of economic reform seem to converge on the proposition that urban growth in the post-liberalisation phase would be very high. However, the critics hold that this will be associated with growth of low productive employment and poverty and its impact on the quality of life in the cities would be negative.

Given the alternate perspectives, it would be important to assess empirically the impact of economic liberalisation on the nature and pattern of urban growth in the country, focusing on some of the regions experiencing rapid economic growth. The present paper attempts to do this, taking Gujarat, one of the rapidly industrialising states, as a case study. The paper analyses the trends and pattern of urbanisation in the state and examines the interdependencies with the process of economic development, keeping the processes at the macro level in the background. This has been done by taking into consideration the changes in labour market along with those in the system of urban governance, land management development practices, commercialisation of infrastructure and basic services.

The second section, following the present introductory section, discusses the urbanisation trends in Gujarat in the context of those in the country. In the third section, the types of employment generated for males and females, changes in sectoral distribution of the workforce, etc. have been analysed both in rural and urban areas. The possible implications of these changes for the well-being of the workers have also been discussed here. These two sections are based on the secondary data, available from Population Census and National Sample Survey. The recent changes in the macro policies concerning urban development and their impact on rural-urban migration and the rate of urbanisation in future years have been examined in the fourth section. The final section puts forward a perspective of urbanisation in the state and the country.

Trends and Pattern of Urbanisation in Gujarat: An Analysis in a Comparative Framework

The state of Gujarat has experienced a rapid growth of population, much above that of the country since the beginning of the present century. This could be attributed to, besides a lower death rate particularly of children, to high rate of immigration. The latest census decade, however, reports a substantial decline in population growth rate during eighties, bringing it down to below the national level for the first time. The pace of urbanisation in the state, on the other hand, has apparently been less than that in the country, except in a couple of decades. The urban population in the state during 1981-91, for example, has grown at 2.90 per cent which is less than that of the previous decade, viz. 3.47 per cent. Importantly, the corresponding rates for the country are higher, 3.09 and 3.83 respectively (Table 4.1).

One may infer from the above discussion that the present rate of urbanisation in Gujarat is low and decelerating over time. It must, however, be pointed out that the population in the rural areas of the state has grown at a rate much below that of the country, going down further in recent decades. The annual exponential growth rate in the sixties was 1.96 per cent, which has come down to 1.80 per cent in the subsequent decades. As a consequence, the urban rural growth differential for Gujarat during 1981-91 works out as much larger than that of the country and in fact most of the other (large) states. The urban rural growth differential was 1.46 per cent in the state compared to 2.05 per cent in the country during seventies. The figure for the state has gone up to 1.51 per cent in the eighties, which is much above that of the country, viz. 1.29 per cent. It would, therefore, legitimate to argue that Gujarat is one of the rapidly urbanising states in the country in recent years.

Gujarat has registered a reasonably high rate of interstate (male) net immigration both in rural as well as urban areas during 1981-91 (Kundu and Gupta, 1996). It is next only to Maharashtra. More importantly, Gujarat is the only state where the rate of net immigration from outside the state has gone up significantly during the eighties, both in rural as well as urban areas. The only other state, which shows an increase in the rate, is Haryana but here the increment is negligible. It is, thus, evident that arrival of workers from outside the state is an important factor responsible for the pace of urbanisation in the state.

The distribution of population in different size-class of urban centres in the state is similar to that of the country (Table 4.1). About sixty-six per cent of the total urban population is in class I cities having population of one lakh or more. Another 24 per cent live in class II and III towns in the size-class between 20,000 and 100,000. A similar pattern is observed in other developed states like Karnataka and Tamil Nadu, as also at the national level. Some of the other developed states like Maharashtra and West Bengal have much higher share of populaton in class I cities. The less developed states like Bihar, Himachal Pradesh, Madhya Pradesh, Orissa, Rajasthan and Uttar Pradesh, on the other hand, have lower share of population in this size-class. One would, therefore, argue that the

Table 4.1 : Population Distribution and Growth Rates of Population in Different Size Class of Urban Settlements

Class Size	Percentage share to the total Urban Population						Decadal Growth Rate			
	Gujarat			India			Gujarat		India	
	1971	**1981**	**1991**	**1971**	**1981**	**1991**	**1971-81**	**1981-91**	**1971-81**	**1981-91**
Class I 1,00,000+	49.1	58.0	66.4	57.2	60.4	65.2	50.8	36.7	41.4	34.5
Class II 50000-100000	15.4	14.5	12.7	10.9	11.6	11	30.7	30.5	36.1	31.6
Class III 20000-50000	15.7	13.3	10.5	16.0	14.3	13.2	32.2	23.9	39.5	29.6
Class IV 10000-20000	12.8	10.2	7.7	10.9	9.5	7.8	26.3	20.0	35.0	28.4
Class V 5000-10000	6.7	3.7	2.4	4.4	3.6	2.6	26.1	23.8	37.0	30.0
Class VI <5000	0.2	0.2	0.2	0.4	0.5	0.3	13.2	22.1	47.7	43.9
All Common Towns	100	100	100	100	100	100	40.0	32.1	39.7	32.8
Decadal Growth Rate	—	—	—	—	—	—	41.2	33.6	46.2	36.1
Annual compound Growth Rate	—	—	—	—	—	—	(3.5)	(2.6)	(3.8)	(3.1)

Note: Growth rates of population in different size-class of towns (also all common towns) have been computed by considering only those towns that belonged to the category in the base year (and taking only their population at both the time points). Urban growth rates in the last two rows, however, are obtained by using the population figures as reported in the respective censuses.

structure of urban population in the state of Gujarat is similar to that of the developed states in the country.

The demographic growth profile for different size class of urban centres, computed by considering only those towns that belong to a class in the base year, reveals an interesting pattern (Table 4.1). The growth rates in class I cities work out to be higher than that in the lower order towns in the country. This was the case not only in the nineties but also in the eighties (Kundu, 1994). The only exception to this is the class VI towns that record growth rates higher than even the class I cities at the national level as also in several states. This is because many of these towns have been established through some public or private sector projects, administrative or military decisions and some other special consideration. Consequently, they do not fall in line with other towns in terms of socio-economic characteristics.

Importantly, the class I cities in Gujarat exhibit a higher growth rate than the smaller order towns, as noted at the national level. A similar pattern emerges in case of a few other developed states like Karnataka, Maharashtra, Punjab and Tamil Nadu (Kundu, 1983). In most of the less developed states, however, the class I cities are not having an edge over other categories in terms of demographic growth. Furthermore, the class I cities in Gujarat have grown at a rate faster than those in the country during the seventies. The gap between the two has, however, narrowed down in the eighties. Also, the class VI towns in the state have not grown at a faster rate than the class I cities, as is the case for several other states. This is because there are not many special purpose towns among them in Gujarat.

Another significant point is the deceleration of urban growth in Gujarat in all size categories during the eighties compared to the previous decade. This, however, is a national phenomenon since the decline is observed in all the states. Importantly, the ratio of the growth rate for class I cities to that of overall urban growth rate is higher in Gujarat than that the country in 1981 as well as 1991. This highlights the primacy of these cities, not merely in terms of their share in urban population but also a relatively higher growth rate. This is despite significant deceleration in the growth rate of these cities in Gujarat compared to smaller towns during the eighties.[1]

The pace of urbanisation varies across the districts in Gujarat but the disparity is not as high as in some of the backward states in the country like Orissa, Rajasthan and Bihar. The growth is fairly stable, ranging between 18 and 38 per cent except for three districts. Of these, two viz.

Gandhinagar and Banaskantha, register high growth due to special reasons like creation of state capital and low urban population in the base year. The growth rates, in general, are somewhat high in the developed districts like Surat, Rajkot and Vadodara with the sole exception of Ahmedabad. The pattern can be contrasted with that in less developed states that exhibit phenomenal urban growth in less developed districts.

Changing Employment Scenario and Workforce Structure in Gujarat

Work participation rate (WPR), defined as the percentage of workers to total population, comes out as higher for Gujarat than the country for the males, both in rural and urban areas. The data from Population Census as well as National Sample Survey (NSS) support this proposition (Table 4.2). The Census figures for WPR (main workers) among males work out as 54.4 per cent in rural and 50.8 in urban areas in the state in the year 1991. The corresponding figures for the country are 51.9 per cent and 48.6 per cent. For females, however, the gap is the other way around; the state level figures, viz. 17.7 per cent and 6.0 per cent in rural and urban areas, are below those for the country, viz. 18.8 per cent and 8.2 per cent. Importantly, the marginal workers among rural females in Gujarat are very high — much higher than that of the country. These constitute 17.9 per cent of the (rural) female population as opposed to 8.0 per cent in the country.

The NSS reports higher WPR by usual (principal) status than the Census (main workers) for all the four groups of workers, viz. males and females, rural as well as urban areas, considered in the study. This is so not only for Gujarat but also for the country. This pattern is observed even when we include the subsidiary workers in the workforce and consider them as comparable with the marginal workers of the Census. The figure for males in the state, by considering principal status only, comes to 56.5 per cent and 52.8 per cent for rural and urban areas respectively (Table 4.2). These are higher than those of the country. Based on Census and NSS data one would, therefore, argue that Gujarat enjoys high employment rates — much more than the country. In fact, male WPR in the state is higher than that of most of the large states, excepting a few like Andhra Pradesh, Karnataka, Tamil Nadu and Punjab. For females, too, Census and NSS report show higher figures for Gujarat in rural areas compared to that of the country and most of the states, when the total workers (main + marginal or principal + subsidiary) are taken into consideration. This is because a high proportion of women in Gujarat work on part-time or non-

Table 4.2 : Workforce Participation Rates by population Census and National Sample Survey

Category		Gujarat				India			
		1981		1991		1981		1991	
		Rural	Urban	Rural	Urban	Rural	Urban	Rural	Urban
Main Workers	Male	53.3	49.8	54.4	50.8	52.6	48.5	51.9	48.6
(Census)	Female	13.5	5.3	17.7	6.0	16.1	7.3	18.6	8.2
Marginal Workers	Male	0.9	0.3	0.5	0.2	1.2	0.5	0.7	0.3
(Census)	Female	13.4	1.0	17.9	1.2	7.0	1.0	8.0	1.0
		1987-88		1993-94		1987-88		1993-94	
Usual Status Principal	Male	53	50.4	56.5	52.8	51.7	49.6	53.8	51.3
(NSS)	Female	28.7	8.8	25.4	9.8	24.5	11.8	23.4	12.1
Usual Status Subsidiary	Male	2.9	0.6	0.9	0.7	2.2	1.0	1.5	0.8
(NSS)	Female	9.3	3.4	14.2	4.4	7.8	3.4	9.4	3.4

Note: The raw data for this table have been obtained from Population Census of different years. The data for India as whole, pertain to the country excluding Assam and Jammu and Kashmir, for which Census could not be conducted in 1981 and 1991 respectively.

regular basis — much larger than the country. It is only for urban females that the rates for Gujarat are less than those for the country, by both the sources of the data. This can only partly be explained in terms of socio-cultural prejudices, norms, traditional values etc. that restrict entry of women into urban labour market. A higher rate of female literacy in urban areas of the state and a higher unemployment rate therein could be yet another factor.

The annual growth rates in the number of male workers as per NSS in rural and urban areas of Gujarat work out as significantly higher than those of population. As a consequence, there has been an increase in male WPR (principal) during the period from 1987-88 to 1993-94. This is so, both in rural and urban areas. A similar pattern may be noted in the country as well. The increase in WPR, however, is larger for the state. By Population Census, too, Gujarat reports a distinct rise in male WPR. But that is not so in the country. The other significant phenomenon is the decline in the percentage of usual principal (status) workers among females in rural Gujarat as also in rural India during this period. There is, however, a sharp increase in the share of marginal or subsidiary status workers among females in rural Gujarat, more than compensating for the decline in the share of principal status workers. This could possibly be explained in terms of growth in demand for short duration jobs in informal activities where women are preferred. This has happened in urban areas as well but to a lesser extent. The corresponding increase in case of the country is modest.

Table 4.3 presents the age specific participation rates for males and females as per the NSS in 1993-94. The WPRs for the males in the state of Gujarat are expectedly higher than those in the country, both in rural and urban areas. The same holds for rural females. For urban females, on the other hand, the rates for Gujarat are less than those in the country in all the age groups. Further, the unemployment rates have been reported from NSS for the year 1993-94 in Table 4.4. These rates work out as higher in urban areas compared to rural areas in Gujarat as well as in the country, both for males and females. What is, however, more important is that the usual status rates, both unadjusted and adjusted, as well as the weekly rates in the state of Gujarat are much below the national average. This is also true both for males and females. Importantly, the gap between the rates of the state and the country works out very high in case of educated persons. The usual status unemployment rate for the educated persons above 15 years of age in Gujarat is only half that of the country. One may argue that employment opportunities for educated, both males and females, are significantly higher than in the rest of the country.

Table 4.3 : Age Specific Participation Workforce Rates (Percentage) by Usual (Principal) Status in 1993-94

Age Group	Rural Males		Urban Males		Rural Females		Urban Females	
	Gujarat	India	Gujarat	India	Gujarat	India	Gujarat	India
15-19	59.1	52.3	36.0	33.7	34.1	26.4	6.0	9.4
20-24	86.8	82.4	76.1	65.4	36.3	31.8	9.6	13.6
25-29	97.1	94.7	94.6	89.2	40.5	35.4	10.5	17.5
30-34	97.2	98.0	98.7	96.1	43.6	40.7	18.1	20.8
35-39	99.6	98.8	98.1	98.2	50.9	43.5	22.9	23.3
40-44	98.8	98.5	98.7	98.0	49.6	44.0	21.2	25.7
45-49	97.1	98.0	95.7	97.1	41.0	43.8	19.7	25.3
50-54	98.6	96.5	92.9	94.1	33.4	40.7	20.1	24.0
55-59	95.4	93.6	76.0	84.5	27.3	33.7	26.8	18.5
All	**56.5**	**53.8**	**52.8**	**51.3**	**25.4**	**23.4**	**9.8**	**12.1**

Source: National Sample Survey Organisation (1997).

Table 4.4 : Unemployment Rates by Different Concepts as Per NSS in 1993-94

Age Groups	Rural Males		Urban Males		Rural Females		Urban Females	
	Gujarat	India	Gujarat	India	Gujarat	India	Gujarat	India
1. a. Usual Status (Unadjusted)	1.5	2.0	3.3	4.5	0.5	1.4	6.2	8.2
1. b. Usual Status (Adjusted)	1.3	1.4	3.0	4	0.3	0.8	4.4	6.2
2. Weekly Status	2.7	3.0	3.9	5.2	1.6	3.0	5.9	8.4
3. Educated 15 + Usual Status (Principal)	4.5	8.5	3.2	6.9	8.6	24.9	13.2	20.6
4. Educated 15 + Usual Status (Principal+Subsidiary)	4.1	6.5	2.8	7.5	5.6	16.0	11.9	18.2

Source: National Sample Survey Organisation (1997).

In Table 4.5, we have the trend in unemployment rates by different concepts adopted by NSS for different groups of workers, viz. males, females cross-classified by rural and urban. At the national level, a decline in the rate may generally be observed during 1983-93, despite some increase in it in some of the categories in the drought year of 1987-88. Unfortunately, this has not happened in Gujarat. The incidence of unemployment in the state increased — much more than in the country — in 1987-88, which is understandable, since the impact of the drought here was more severe. However, when we consider the decade 1983-93, the rates may be noted as going up for some groups, particularly among urban females.

Table 4.5 : Unemployment Rates by Different Concepts

Usual Status (subsidiary workers are considered as employed)	1983		1987-88		1993-94	
	Gujarat	India	Gujarat	India	Gujarat	India
Rural Males	0.67	1.4	1.2	1.8	1.3	1.4
Rural Females	0.21	0.7	1.0	2.4	0.3	0.9
Urban Males	4.45	5.1	4.1	5.2	3.0	4.1
Urban Females	2.89	4.9	1.8	6.2	4.4	6.1
Current Daily Status						
Rural Males	5.15	7.5	4.7	4.6	6.0	5.6
Rural Females	4.77	9.0	7.1	9.0	4.7	5.6
Urban Males	7.72	9.2	7.1	8.8	5.7	6.7
Urban Females	5.22	11.0	6.0	12.0	7.8	10.4

Note: Usual status unemployment rates are the percentage of persons seeking or available for work to the total labour force, viz. workers unemployed. Similarly by current daily status, the rates have been computed by taking the unemployed person days as percentage to the total labour days, employed or available for work.

Source: National Sample Survey Organisation (1990 and 1997).

The percentages of regular workers among all female (usual status) workers in the state are below that of the country, both in rural and urban areas during the eighties and early nineties (Table 4.6). For males, however, the state level figure works out higher than the national figure. Further, the degree of casualisation is noted to be higher in the state than in the country for all the four groups. Importantly, the higher incidence of casual employment has come about at the cost of self-employed and not the regular workers, both in rural and urban areas.

Table 4.6 : Percentage of Usually Employed Persons by Principal and Subsidiary Status by Type of Employment

	Self Employed		Regular/Salaried		Casual	
	Gujarat	India	Gujarat	India	Gujarat	India
Rural Males						
1983	59.0	60.5	8.3	10.3	32.7	29.2
1987-88	47.9	58.6	12.3	10.0	39.8	31.4
1993-94	46.9	57.9	9.9	8.3	43.2	33.8
Rural Females						
1983	60.8	61.9	1.8	2.8	37.4	35.3
1987-88	47.8	60.8	3.4	3.7	48.8	35.5
1993-94	55.4	58.5	1.5	2.8	43.1	38.7
Urban Males						
1983	40.3	40.9	44.1	43.7	15.6	15.4
1987-88	38.6	41.7	44.8	43.7	16.6	14.6
1993-94	37.3	41.7	44.9	42.1	17.8	16.2
Urban Females						
1983	47.7	45.8	22.3	25.8	30	28.4
1987-88	40.2	47.1	28.6	27.5	31.2	25.4
1993-94	42.6	45.4	24.1	28.6	33.3	26.0

Source: National Sample Survey Organisation (1986, 1990 and 1997).

The distribution of workers across nine industrial categories in Gujarat is very similar to that of the country in 1991, as reported in Population Census (Tables 7a and 7b). This is so for all the groups of workers (Kundu, 1997). The shifts in the percentage distribution, taking place during the eighties, are also similar. Significantly, a decline is noted in the share of workers in agriculture and manufacturing. The fall is sharper in case of household manufacturing activities. Within the tertiary sector, transport and storage is the only sector whose share has gone down in all the groups except for rural males. An increase, on the other hand, is recorded

Table 4.7a : Percentage Distribution of Main Workers Across Industrial Categories in Rural Areas as per Population Census

Category	Males				Females			
	1981		1991		1981		1991	
	Gujarat	India	Gujarat	India	Gujarat	India	Gujarat	India
1. Cultivators	54.2	55.2	49.5	51.4	34.6	36.9	35.2	38.6
2. Agricultural Labours	23.7	24	24.5	26.4	54.0	50.4	50.6	49.3
3. Livestock & Forestry	2.6	2.5	2.7	2.1	2.8	1.8	6.4	1.6
4. Mining & Quarrying	0.3	0.5	0.4	0.5	0.3	0.3	0.3	0.3
5. Household Manufacturing	2.4	2.9	1.5	2.0	1.8	3.8	1.2	2.9
6. Non-Household Manufacturing	6.0	3.8	8.9	4.0	1.8	2.1	1.7	2.3
7. Construction	1.0	1.2	1.2	1.3	0.6	0.6	0.3	0.3
8. Trade & Commerce	3.4	3.3	3.9	4.0	0.9	1.1	0.9	1.1
9. Transport	1.8	1.4	2.2	1.6	0.2	0.1	0.1	0.1
10. Other Services	4.7	5.3	5.3	6.7	3.0	2.9	3.4	3.5

Table 4.7b : Percentage Distribution of Main Workers Across Industrial Categories in Urban Areas as per Population Census

Category	Males				Females			
	1981		1991		1981		1991	
	Gujarat	India	Gujarat	India	Gujarat	India	Gujarat	India
1. Cultivators	4.0	5.2	3.4	5.0	4.3	4.6	4.3	5.1
2. Agricultural Labours	3.5	4.7	3.7	5.4	15.1	16.6	13.8	15.6
3. Livestock & Forestry	1.7	1.8	1.8	1.7	1.8	1.8	2.0	1.5
4. Mining & Quarrying	0.4	1.1	0.6	1.2	0.4	0.7	0.5	0.7
5. Household Manufacturing	2.4	4.2	1.0	2.5	6.2	10.4	4.2	7.5
6. Non-Household Manufacturing	35.2	26.0	33.6	23.2	12.6	14.6	12.6	14.1
7. Construction	3.2	4.3	4.6	5.3	3.5	3.1	3.7	3.3
8. Trade & Commerce	21.0	21.3	23.5	23.7	9.3	8.9	10.7	10.0
9. Transport	10.4	10.0	9.4	9.2	4.1	2.2	2.6	1.9
10. Other Services	18.2	21.4	18.6	22.8	42.8	37.0	45.7	40.1

Source: Census of India 1981 and 1991.

in trade and commerce, other services and, of course, the total tertiary sector. This trend is observed in case of construction as well, except for rural females. Interestingly, the shifts within agriculture have a gender dimension. The share of cultivators has gone down but that of agricultural labourers has gone up among males, both in rural and urban areas. The trend for the females is just the opposite — it has increased in case of cultivators but declined for the labourers. These phenomena are common both to the state of Gujarat and the country.

One significant difference, however, is that the proportion of male workers in non-household (NH) manufacturing is much higher in the state compared to the country. About 6 per cent of the male workers in rural Gujarat are in NH manufacturing in 1981 which has gone up to 8.9 per cent in 1991. The corresponding figures for the country are 3.8 per cent and 4.0 per cent only. In urban Gujarat, however, the figure was 35.2 per cent in 1981, which has declined to 33.6 per cent in 1991. The decline in the figure for the country is sharper — from 26.0 per cent in 1981 to 23.2 per cent in 1991.

The other important difference is the high percentage of female workers in livestock, forestry, etc. in rural Gujarat — 2.8 compared to 1.8 in the country in 1981. The figure is higher than that for household industries in the state while for the country, it is the other way around. Further, the figure for the state has moved up to 6.4 per cent in 1991 while that for rural India has declined to 1.6 per cent. In urban Gujarat, too, the figure has increased in contrast to the declining trend at all India level. The other sectors wherein the growth in the number of female workers is larger than that of the workforce are cultivation, construction, trade and commerce and other services. These sectors, in general, report low productivity and a high incidence of poverty.

The data from the various rounds of NSS confirm most of the propositions arrived at through the Census data, discussed above. Furthermore, they give a few new insights (Tables 4.8a and 4.8b). The following conclusions may be derived based on the analysis of the NSS data. One, withdrawal of workforce from agriculture is a significant phenomenon in Gujarat, both in its rural and urban areas during 1983-93. Understandably, the workforce share of agriculture had fallen drastically in 1987-88 due to the drought factor. The figures nonetheless did not recover from the slump and are at a much lower levels in 1993-94 than in 1983. This contrasts sharply with the all India scenario. Two, the percentage of workers dependent on mining and quarrying in the state is low but has gone up significantly for all groups. This possibly corroborates the argument with regard to increasing exploitation of natural resources in the state, much more than in the country. A large number of NGOs and researchers have pleaded that this is creating environmental strains and ecological degradation in some of the regions. Three, growth of workers in manufacturing is phenomenal in rural areas of the state. In urban areas, too, the growth is high — much higher than that in the country — but slightly less than that of urban population. Four, construction and trade are the two other sectors that have seen a substantial increase in the share of workers in all the categories. Finally, the most significant change for the female workers is the dramatic rise in the share of employment in community and other services in urban areas. Based on the general understanding of the sectors and studies on their productivity, carried out through micro level studies, one would argue that this constitutes the "residual service sector", which is absorbing a large segment of the incremental female workforce, has very low labour productivity. The increase in its share of workforce may, therefore, be described as supply induced growth of employment during the eighties and early nineties.

Temporal and Spatial Profile of Poverty: Implications for Urbanisation

It would be worthwhile to analyse the changing pattern of poverty in the state in relation to that in the country and discuss its possible implications for urbanisation. Importantly, the head-count ratio of the poor in rural areas of Gujarat have been significantly below that of the country in the seventies and eighties — generally by over 10 percentage points. This is so irrespective of the poverty line and price index used by the experts in their calculation (Planning Commission 1993, Dubey and Gangopadhyay, 1998). One would like to explain this in terms of high per capita income in the state, particularly reasonably high labour productivity in agriculture and growth therein (Bhalla and Singh, 1998). Surprisingly, however, urban poverty in the state has been similar to the national average but always above the corresponding rural figures in all the years in the seventies and eighties, for which poverty could be computed, using the NSS data.

The phenomenon of urban poverty being higher than rural poverty occurs mostly in less developed states like Andhra Pradesh, Kerala, Madhya Pradesh, Uttar Pradesh and Rajasthan. Among the developed ones, Karnataka is the only other state where this is observed. One may explain the massive urban poverty in Gujarat in terms of high rate of immigration from other states, particularly in urban centres and their absorption in low paid casual jobs. Migration from within the state, from the drought prone areas, to the large urban centres is also substantial, although this is declining over the years.

Table 4.8a : Percentage of Rural Workers (Principal and Subsidiary Status) by Industrial Categories

	1983		1987-88		1993-94	
	Gujarat	India	Gujarat	India	Gujarat	Inida
Males						
Agriculture (0)	78.9	77.8	68.6	74.6	71.1	74.0
Mining and Quarrying (1)	0.2	0.6	0.5	0.7	0.7	0.7
Manufacturing (2&3)	7.1	7.0	9.2	7.4	12.3	7.0
Electricity (4)	0.2	0.2	0.1	0.3	0.2	0.3
Construction (5)	2.4	2.2	9.5	3.7	3.0	3.2
Trade (6)	3.5	4.4	3.6	5.1	4.2	5.5
Transport & Storage (7)	1.5	1.7	2.4	2.0	2.5	2.2
Finance & Insurance Service (8)	6.2	0.3	0.2	0.4	6.0	0.4
Communication & Services (9)	***	5.8	6.1	5.8	***	6.6
Females						
Agriculture (0)	92.0	87.8	75.9	84.8	90.6	86.1
Mining and Quarrying (1)	0.04	0.3	0.2	0.4	0.1	0.4
Manufacturing (2&3)	3.2	6.4	3.6	6.9	4.1	7.1
Electricity (4)	—	—	—	—	0.1	0.1
Construction (5)	0.8	0.7	16.9	2.7	1.4	0.9
Trade (6)	1.2	1.9	0.8	2.1	1.0	2.1
Transport & Storage (7)	0.1	0.1	0.1	0.1	—	0.1
Finance & Insurance Service (8)	2.8	—	2.6	—	2.6	0.1
Communication & Services (9)	***	2.8	***	3.0	***	3.3

Table 4.8b : Percentage of Urban Workers (Principal and Subsidiary Status) by Industrial Categories

	1983		1987-88		1993-94	
	Gujarat	India	Gujarat	India	Gujarat	India
Males						
Agriculture (0)	13.4	10.3	6.3	9.1	4.9	9.0
Mining and Quarrying (1)	0.1	1.3	0.5	1.3	0.6	1.3
Manufacturing (2&3)	35.6	27	33.3	25.7	33.7	23.5
Electricity (4)	0.5	1.1	0.8	1.2	0.9	1.2
Construction (5)	1.7	5.2	4.2	5.8	6.9	6.9
Trade (6)	16.7	20.2	22.8	22.0	19.9	21.9
Transport & Storage (7)	8.2	9.9	9.7	9.7	9.5	9.7
Finance & Insurance Service (8)	24.1	3.5	3.4	3.5	23.5	3.8
Community & Services (9)	***	21.4	19.0	21.7	***	22.6
Females						
Agriculture (0)	37.2	32	22.6	29.4	20.9	24.7
Mining and Quarrying (1)	—	0.8	—	0.8	0.7	0.6
Manufacturing (2&3)	18.8	27.1	23.8	27	20.2	24.1
Electricity (4)	0.1	—	0.3	0.2	—	0.3
Construction (5)	2.8	3.3	6.2	3.7	4.8	4.1
Trade (6)	8.1	9.0	12	10.0	10.0	10.0
Transport & Storage (7)	4.2	1.6	1.2	0.9	1.1	1.3
Finance & Insurance Service (8)	28.9	0.4	0.8	1.2	42.3	1.9
Community & Services (9)	***	25.8	33.2	26.6	***	33.1

Notes: Separate figure for Community and Other Services are not available in the cell marked by ***.
The figures for financial services, given just above, include the figures for Community Service as well.

Source: National Sample Survey Organisation (1990 and 1997).

The most significant development in the poverty scenario is the substantial decline in urban poverty in the state during 1987-93, after remaining almost stable at 40 per cent in the preceding decade. The percentage of the poor has gone down from 37.3 in 1987-88 to 27.9 in

1993-94. Rural poverty, too, has gone down — much more sharply than that in the country — but less than urban poverty; the figures being 28.7 per cent and 22.2 per cent at the two points of time. As a consequence, poverty ratios in Gujarat in 1993-94, are lower than the all India figures both in rural and urban areas. The developments within the state, altering significantly the poverty scenario, merit an in-depth empirical investigation. One would have to conduct micro level studies to determine whether this can be attributed to growth of income and employment opportunities or to decline in the rate of immigration in the urban centres in recent years.

Table 4.9 : Macro Economic Profile of Gujarat

Sectors	Percentage share in NSDP (1980-81 prices)	
	1980-81	1994-95 (Q)
1. Agriculture	37.2	23.2
2. Forestry	1.9	0.9
3. Fishing	0.8	1.3
4. Mining and Quarrying	0.9	0.7
5. Manufacturing (Registered)	15.1	23.3
6. Manufacturing (Unregistered)	5.6	6.4
7. Construction	5.5	3.4
8. Electricity, Gas	1.1	2.2
9. Transport, Storage	3.2	4.9
10. Trade	10.4	10.7
11. Banking	3.9	10.1
12. Real Estate	6.4	4.4
13. Public Administration	2.6	3.0
14. Other Services	5.4	5.6
NSDP (Rs. Crore)	6547.42	14167.37
Per capita NSDP (Rs.)	1940	3217

The level.of poverty varies significantly across the NSS regions within the state. The percentage of poor in rural areas is as low as 19 in Saurashtra while it is as high as 47 in Kutch in 1987-88. In central and southern Gujarat, the figures are around 24 per cent while in eastern region it is about 8 points higher. The spatial pattern of urban poverty, however, is quite different from that noted above. High figures are recorded for both Saurashtra and Kutch, viz. 54 per cent, much above the rural poverty ratios in the region. Further, eastern, central and southern Gujarat, too, show pretty high poverty figures — about five percentage points higher than that in their rural areas. One would hypothesise that urban areas in these regions of Gujarat are absorbing a large number of poor migrants from rural areas, despite general reduction of poverty in the state and the slight deceleration in urban growth in recent years.

Poverty estimates show very low disparity in rural areas of Gujarat in 1993-94. These are around 22 per cent except for Saurastra where it is as low as 10 per cent only. One would argue that there is not much of difference between rural areas of developed and backward regions. The disparity has gone down in urban Gujarat as well, yet it is higher than that of rural areas. The lowest level of urban poverty is reported in the central region, viz. around 30 per cent in 1987-88, followed by the northern region. This is understandable as a large part of the two regions fall within the "golden corridor" of industrial development. The regional scenario of urban poverty remains similar in 1993-94, the central and northern regions reporting low poverty levels, viz. 20 per cent and 30 per cent respectively. The reduction in case of Kutch and Saurashtra is by a huge margin — 20 percentage points.

The most significant point emerging from the analysis is that the spatial patterns of rural and urban poverty have no correlation. These do not get linked up through the dynamics of development in the region. Indeed, urban poverty happens to be low in the regions experiencing rapid industrialisation. This, however, does not make a dent on the wellbeing of the rural poor in the region. Rural poverty is low in the state but works out to be about the same in all the regions.

The high incidence of poverty in urban areas in Gujarat, much higher than in rural areas, has been an enigma for development economists (Alagh, 1995). Why, despite the poor performance in agriculture in large parts of the state, continuous decline in the area under cultivation since early seventies etc., poverty should be less here than in the country? What is more important, why should it decline significantly during 1987-93? These questions defy an explanation in the present format of empirical investigation. One can only hypothesise a few possible reasons. One, sectoral diversification in rural Gujarat, reflected in an increase in the share of non-household manufacturing as also livestock, fishing and forestry might have had an impact on the income levels of rural poor. Two, the anti-poverty programmes may be more successful in generating income in rural than urban areas of Gujarat. It needs to be pointed out that despite criticism with regard to formulation and implementation of anti-poverty programmes, the decline in poverty in the drought year of 1987-88 has been substantial. A part of the credit must go to the massive construction work undertaken largely in the rural areas. Gujarat, being generally the worst affected of the states during such crisis, has been receiving a large part of the funds under the programmes. These might have brought in some structural improvements in the rural economy to make a dent on poverty in the long run. Three, a large segment of the rural poor are migrating to urban areas in search of jobs in the organised sector. These jobs, however, prove to be elusive and most of the migrants get absorbed in low productive tertiary activities wherein employment has swelled in urban Gujarat during recent years.

The incidence of poverty among casual and self-employed workers in urban areas has generally been noted to be extremely high — much higher than among the regular workers. Similarly, construction and trade are the two sectors that report much higher levels of poverty than the average (Kundu, 1993). Significantly, these are the categories and production sectors in Gujarat that have gained in terms of share in total employment, as discussed in the previous section. The incremental workforce getting absorbed largely as casual and self-employed workers in low productive sectors certainly cannot be taken as healthy development from the viewpoint of workers' welfare or future urban development.

The inter-state analysis by Dutt (1997), however, gives a slightly different picture of poverty scenario in the state of Gujarat, which may be helpful in explaining the enigma. The study comes out with the striking result that rural poverty in Gujarat has always been at par or higher than that in the country. This is observed in all the years for which quinquennial data are available from the NSS, including the 50th round for the year 1993-94. Further, there is no drastic decline in poverty in rural or urban areas in the late eighties and early nineties. The annual data used by the scholars, on the other hand, shows that (rural) poverty percentage has gone up significantly from 42.9 in 1987-88 to 46.8 in 1992-93, but came down to 35.4 in 1993-94.

Poverty estimates for urban Gujarat, however, have fluctuated over the years — sometimes being above and sometimes below the national figure. Dutt's study reports a decline in urban poverty during 1987-93 not faster than that in rural areas. At the national level, there has been a faster decline in urban areas compared to rural areas.[2] This and other differences in the results of Dutt with those of Planning Commission can be attributed to the procedures of price adjustment. Dutt has converted the consumption expenditure data to constant prices using state level price indices, taking the consumption pattern of households around the poverty line, which may be more appropriate.

Pattern of Sectoral Growth of Income and its Impact on Urbanisation

There are serious problems in analysing the growth pattern at the state level, using the data from the State Statistical Departments or the Directorate of Economics and Statistics (DES) and comparing it with the national level scenario, based on the information from the Central Statistical Organisation (CSO). This is because there are discrepancies in the coverage in different states which vitiates the results, specially when one is analysing the income estimates at the sectoral level. CSO, however, makes an attempt to retabulate the data within a somewhat standardised framework but several anomalies still remain. Gujarat, despite its high level of economic development and fairly good statistical system, is not free from this problem. In fact, here, it is so serious that researchers have disagreed not only on the magnitudes of sectoral growth but also the directions of change. In addition, there is the general problem of the growth estimates varying widely due to the choice of the base and terminal years. For Gujarat, the problem is more serious since year to year fluctuations for value added in primary, secondary and tertiary sectors are high. Unfortunately, it is not possible to sort out the discrepancies and build up comparable estimates that would be acceptable to all official agencies. It would, nonetheless, be useful to be aware of the problems and the divergence of views regarding the sectoral growth scenario.

Gujarat, right after its formation — by carving it out from the state of Bombay in 1960 — had experienced rapid industrial growth. The growth of value added in industries has been very high — higher than that of the country. As a consequence, the overall growth of Net State Domestic Product (NSDP) has also been reasonably high. The growth rates during sixties and seventies were 3.3 per cent and 5.0 per cent respectively which compares favourably with those of the country that are less, viz. 3.1 per cent and 3.7 per cent respectively.

Computation of growth rates for the eighties and nineties is fraught with problems due to choice of the data source as also the base/ terminal years. The growth of NSDP from agriculture at 1980-81 prices obtained from the DES for the period from 1980-81 to 1989-90 has been estimated to be negative — over one per cent per year. The physical indicators pertaining to this sector like cropping intensity, area under different crops, etc. also show negative trends. Increase in irrigation has been marginal, much less than at the national level (Iyengar, 1996). The information available from the Ministry of Agriculture at the central level, however, points to a somewhat different scenario. Using this data set, Bhalla and Singh (1998) show that the annual growth in output during the period 1980-83 to 1992-95 has been about 2 per cent. They further demonstrate that the growth in agricultural productivity has been fairly high during their total study period — from early sixties to mid-nineties — slightly higher than that in the country. The state did much better than the country in this respect during 1962-73 and 1970-83. It is only during 1980-95 that the productivity increase in Gujarat works out as less than that in the country. The major problem in the state, however, is the decrease in gross cropped area during the entire study period except during 1962-65 to 1970-73. Using the CSO data, the annual exponential growth in the NSDP from agriculture during eighties works out as less than 1 per cent per annum. However, manufacturing and tertiary sectors have grown at over 7.5 per cent as per the DES statistics, which helps the annual growth of NSDP stabilise at about 5 per cent (Iyengar, 1996). In case of the latter two sectors, the growth estimates based on CSO data are about 10 per cent.

The growth rates in the nineties, too, vary significantly depending on the choice of the base and terminal year since the NSDP in Gujarat had gone down in the years 1989-90, 1991-92 and 1993-94 compared to their preceding years. Considering the period from 1990-91 to 1994-95, one would estimate an annual exponential growth rate to be about 7 per cent using the CSO data. The DES data from the state, however, gives a higher rate, viz. 10 per cent, if we include the year 1995-96 as well. In terms of total industrial investment, Gujarat has been at the top among the states — even above Maharashtra — for a couple of years during this period. This is reflected in an increasing share of the state in the total value of output or value added in the industrial sector of the country. The percentage share was 9.7 in 1970-71, which went up to 11.7 in 1980-81. Subsequently, it came down to 10.2 in 1990-91 to go up again to 11.2 in 1992-93.

Importantly, the growth of manufacturing sector during eighties and early nineties has come about mostly from the registered sector. Its percentage share at constant prices has gone up from 15.1 in 1980-81 to 23.3 in 1994-95. The share for unregistered manufacturing has gone up only marginally from 5.6 per cent to 6.4 per cent. The other sector reporting a very high growth is banking and insurance. The increase in the share of this sector from meager 3.9 per cent to 10.1 per cent is a major achievement. This reflects that the state is emerging as the commercially vibrant region in the country. All these sectoral shifts have come about at the cost of the primary sector. The share of agriculture in Gujarat has gone down from 37.2 per cent to 23.2 and that of forestry has declined from 1.9 to half of that figure during 1980-94. These are much sharper than that noted at the national level.

The rapid growth of manufacturing sector in the state can at least partially be explained in terms of growth of chemical and chemical products industry. The share of this industrial group has gone up from 16.4 per cent in 1980-81 to 36.2 per cent in 1992-93 in terms of capital employed in the factory sector, as per the information from Annual Survey of Industries. The increase in its share of net value added (NVA) is equally sharp — from 17.2 per cent to 39.6 per cent. The share in employment has also increased but much less — from 9.3 per cent to 16.5 per cent. The other industry, whose share is also very high, viz. 23.1 per cent, is rubber, plastic and petroleum. Importantly, the state claims about 26 per cent of the total NVA in chemicals in the country, the corresponding figure for rubber etc. is over 30 per cent in 1992-93. The share of cotton textile industry, on the other hand, has declined sharply over the years, the figure being less than 12 per cent in early nineties. The growth rates in net value added for several other sectors, viz. agro-processing, engineering and metal-based industries have also been less than that in the country, resulting in a decline in the state's share in national totals.

The scenario in the nineties seems to be somewhat different from that of the previous decade. Importantly, investment in textiles has, after a long period of decline and stagnation, started picking up since the liberalisation of the economy in 1991. The share of textiles in early eighties was less than 1 per cent of the total investment in mining and manufacturing. The average figure for three years in mid-nineties, viz. 1994, 1995 and 1996, however, is as high as 10 per cent. Similarly, the investment in cement has jumped up after 1991. Its share has increased from 0.4 per cent to 4.4 per cent during the above-mentioned period. Gujarat, however, lacks in investment in power sector, which is surfacing as its major bottleneck. The annual average growth rate in investment in the state has been 10.4 per cent during 1982-96, which is much less than that in the country, viz. 23.2 per cent.

The growth of enterprises outside the organised sector in the state has, however, been modest. The annual growth rates for agricultural and non-agricultural enterprises during 1980-90 are 3.8 per cent and 2.0 per cent respectively. These are below the corresponding growth rates of 6.1 per cent and 2.8 per cent at the national level. Even the growth of hired workers in the state in these enterprises is low – 2.4 per cent compared to 2.9 per cent at the national level. The share of the state in small-scale industrial (registered) units of the country in 1971 was 6.6 per cent. This was much less than that of registered units. Furthermore, the figure has declined during the nineties — touching a level as low as 5.9 per cent in 1993. Further, employment in khadi and village industries in the state has gone down in absolute terms from 1,24,000 in 1982-83 to 91,000 in 1992-93. All these have adversely affected the process of sectoral diversification, particularly in Saurashtra and Kutch regions (Iyengar, 1998).

Importantly, the investments in Gujarat during eighties and nineties have been capital intensive. The gross block in Central Government (non-departmental) Undertakings has increased by about 20 per cent per annum. The growth in employment in these undertakings has, however, been less than 0.2 per cent. The corresponding figures for the country are 17 per cent and 0.9 per cent. The adoption of this labour saving model of growth is a bit surprising because the number of industrial disputes and man-days lost in the state is negligible. The state's share in national total of man-days lost is less than 0.2 per cent which is much below Gujarat's share in industrial labour. Further, the number of industries reporting as sick or having outstanding credit is less than 0.3 per cent of the total in the country which is a reflection of a healthy investment climate in the state. All these should normally attract private entrepreneurs in to the state, specially those that are labour intensive in nature. This unfortunately has not happened in Gujarat.

The sectoral shift in industrial growth has significant spatial implications. Most of the petro-chemical industries are located in the southern districts of Bharuch, Surat and Jamnagar while cement industry has come up in Saurastra. The three districts noted above account for 58 per cent of the investments envisaged in the state in the year 1995-96. Further, the golden corridor districts comprising Mehsana, Ahmedabad, Kheda, Vadodara, Bhrauch, Surat and Valsad exhibit high occupational diversification during 1981-91. This process is conspicuous by its absence in the Kutch and Saurashtra (Iyengar, 1998).

Globalisation of Gujarat's Economy and the Pattern of Urbanisation

Gujarat presents a unique case of globalisation among the Indian states. It has historically been linked with the international market through migration of businessmen and their family-based interactions with the local entrepreneurial class. The exposure of the state's economy to American as also European market can, therefore, be traced back to pre-Independence period. The rapid growth of manufacturing sector in the state, export oriented growth of the economy etc. can be attributed to no small measure to the exogenous factors and the capital brought in by the non-resident business community and their linked enterprises. The growth of the economy was, however, centred around the city of Ahmedabad which emerged as a major city in Western India, next only to Bombay, the latter having an additional advantage of being a sea port.

The city of Ahmedabad, and more generally the economy of Western India, underwent some sort of crisis due to the collapse of textile industry in the post-Independence period. This can be attributed to indigenous industrialists' incapacity to keep pace with technological development and market trend. The impact was disastrous for the local economy. The number of industrial units in the Census Sector as per ASI declined by over 4 per cent a year during the period 1981-82 to 1992-93. Correspondingly, employment fell by over 2.5 per cent. Total investment in these industries came down by more than half per cent annually while value added declined by 2 per cent. The retrenchment due to closure of textile mills was alarming; this was about 6,500 in 1982 which went up to over 55,000 in 1992.

Employment share of the total industrial sector in the city economy has also been coming down during the eighties. The percentage of male workers in NH manufacturing was 46, which came down to 38 in 1991. Even for the females, the figure came down from 17 per cent to 14 per cent only. The employment share of household industries was in any case very low in Ahmedabad compared to urban Gujarat or other metro cities. Unfortunately, the number of workers came down in absolute terms during 1981-91 — it declined by over 9 per cent for males and 0.2 per cent for females.

The story of Ahmedabad in Gujarat would have been as tragic as many of the capital cities in African and Latin American countries that have been plunged into crisis after the economic base of the traditional industries have been rendered non-viable due to globalisation of the market. The long historical linkages of the city/state economy with the national and international system and the entrepreneurship of the local community, however, came in between and averted an impending disaster. As far as Gujarat is concerned, there was a structural shift in the economic base, moving to petrochemicals, cement, etc., as discussed above. The entrepreneurs took advantage of the proximity of the region to Bombay and the connectivity of the latter with Ahmedabad. The growth of industrial activities, thus, occurred in the corridor joining the two major cities of Western India. However, despite some industries coming up in Ahmedabad, which lies at one corner of what has been described as the "golden corridor", there has been a decline in the share of industries of Ahmedabad agglomeration as also the district. This has led to a low demographic growth in the agglomeration in recent years. Among the 23 metro cities in 1991, Ahmedabad ranks 7th from below in terms of population growth during 1951-91.[3] This, to a large extent, explains the deceleration in urban growth in Gujarat in recent years. This, nonetheless, could not destroy the growth potential of the agglomeration although it gave a massive shock to its economic base.

The structural shift in the state economy not merely led to high industrial growth in Gujarat in the post-Independence phase but also transformed the economic base of Ahmedabad city and its surrounding region. The latter not only managed to survive a catastrophe but also experienced a reasonable economic growth. Employment in the urban areas of Ahmedabad district or Ahmedabad Urban Agglomeration (AUA) grew at a much higher pace than in urban Gujarat. As a consequence, the WPR for the males in the agglomeration went up from 49.6 per cent in 1981 to 55.7 per cent in 1991. The corresponding increase for urban Gujarat is marginal – from 49.8 to 50.8 per cent only.

The share of manufacturing employment in AUA was significantly higher than in urban Gujarat or many other metro cities on the eve of Independence, for the reasons discussed above. The figure for the males was as high as 46.1 per cent even in 1981. The de-industrialisation in AUA is reflected in a drastic fall in this figure to 37.8 per cent in 1991. The corresponding decline for the state (urban segment) has been nominal — from 35.2 to 33.6 per cent in 1991. Further, there has been a sharp rise in the share of male as well as female workers in trade and commerce and other services within the agglomeration, much more than in the state. All these suggest that Ahmedabad is emerging as a commercial capital of Western India and the loss in the industrial base is being compensated by the growth of tertiary activities.

Is this growth of employment in AUA due mostly to the growth of low productive activities driven by excess supply of labour, as suggested in case of the state, due largely to migration from within and outside the state? An analysis of the nature of workforce raises reasonable doubts on such quick generalisations. One would note that the percentage of regular/

salaried workers among males has gone up during the period 1987-88 to 1993-94. Correspondingly, the share of casual workers has declined from 20 per cent to 13 per cent. For females, too, the share of casual workers has declined. The only difference between males and females here is that there has been a significant increase in the percentage of self-employed workers among females. Further, the unemployment rates in AUA, although, higher in urban Gujarat both for males and females, have gone down sharply during the early nineties. All these would serious discount the thesis of supply induced growth of employment in AUA under a globalised regime.

Another important feature of employment growth in the city and the agglomeration deserves special mention. The WPR for males in AUA has increased by six percentage points, as discussed above. The figure for AMC, however, has gone up marginally by about half a percentage point — from 49.1 to 49.6 only. This implies that much of the growth in male employment has been restricted to the towns falling within the agglomeration but located outside the corporation boundary. The employment growth for females, on the other hand, is quite different — it increased faster within the AMC compared to the other towns in AUA. This employment growth, mostly in self-employed category, may partly be attributed to women taking up hawking and other retail marketing activities, thanks to the strong NGO movement in the city. The high growth of male employment in the towns in the agglomeration and a rise in the share of regular workers can be viewed as a positive development.

The thesis of casualisation of workforce stands discounted, as far as AUA is concerned. Employment growth for males has taken place in regular category, as noted above. The wage rate in this category is likely to be higher than casual and self-employed categories. One may consider this also as a positive phenomenon in terms of the wellbeing of the labour force. Further, the share of employment in own account enterprises, viz. those not employing any hired labour in the city is slightly less than in urban Gujarat. The growth rate of employment in OAE in the city is about the same as in urban Gujarat. This would also question the proposition that the economy of the city of Ahmedabad is getting informalised at an alarming rate.

Importantly, the household level data generated through annual surveys by Natarajan (1998) reveals that income growth in Ahmedabad during the decade 1985-95 is rather low compared to other metro cities in the country. This is understandable in view of the collapse of its traditional industrial base and process of adjustment that took place, as discussed above. Nonetheless, the households at the bottom income category, viz.

up to Rs. 25,000 in 1995-96 prices, have done reasonably well and their percentage share in the total households have declined from 35.22 to 11.35 due to their upward mobility. Income distribution in the city has, thus, become more equal during late eighties and early nineties. Indeed, if percentage of households below the annual income of 18,000 is taken as an index of poverty, one would argue that poverty has declined in the capital city at a much faster rate than in urban Gujarat during the early nineties (Rao and Natarajan, 1996).

The positive trends in employment and income structure in Ahmedabad city, on the face of a collapse of textile industry, raises many more questions than it answers. Can the improvements in the overall economic conditions of the city, decline in poverty, etc. be attributed to planned slowing down of the rate of immigration in the agglomeration during the last ten to fifteen years? Do the rural poor find it much more difficult to get a foothold in the city now than before a decade or so? Are the soaring land prices, anti-encroachment drive by the local governments, changes in urban management, seeking to pass on the cost of basic amenities to the poor etc. responsible for slowing down their immigration.

Questions would arise also about the poverty in urban areas of Gujarat, which remains higher than rural poverty even in the nineties. Is it a healthy phenomenon that Ahmedabad, whose growth in recent years is propelled by commercial and business interests, reports a significant decline in poverty while that in the NSS region, where the city is located, works out as modest ? Tragically, the emergence of Ahmedabad as a global city has left even its immediate hinterland untouched. One may, therefore, ask whether the industrial growth in the "golden corridor" not making a dent on rural poverty in the region reflecting polarisation of growth. Is the high regional inequality in the state, as also in the levels of urban poverty, a necessary concomitant of globalisation ? It would be necessary to undertake in-depth studies using primary data to find satisfactory answers to some of these questions.

Perspectives on Future Urbanisation

An analysis of the workforce structure apparently presents an optimistic scenario for the state of Gujarat. The participation rates (WPR) for the males in the state have generally been much higher than in the country. This is valid for the females as well, if one takes the subsidiary employment into consideration. Further, the state has experienced a high growth of employment during the past decade or so — much more than in the country. Consequently, the rates of unemployment are low, both for males and females, in rural as well as in urban areas.

The high and increasing WPR (including the subsidiary employment) for men and women, lower unemployment rate, etc., in the state compared to the country etc., however, may not be matter of great satisfaction. This is because, firstly, there is a high incidence of casual employment in the state, among which a larger percentage is likely to be poor. The figure has gone up further in recent years. These reflect absorption of labour on temporary and part-time basis in various low productive activities. Secondly, employment growth is higher in sectors that, in general, have low productivity, low wage rate and a high incidence of poverty[4]. Thirdly, the WPR for females, considering only the main workers (of the Census) are less in Gujarat than those of the country, both in rural and urban areas. As per NSS, too, the women WPR, considering only the principal workers, are lower than the country in urban areas. Importantly, the WPR by principal status for rural females has gone down significantly during 1987-93. Also, female unemployment rates in Gujarat have gone up during 1983-93 by all the definitions, quite contrary to the trend at the national level. These suggest that a large part of the female employment is subsidiary or marginal in nature. Finally, there has been a phenomenal growth of female employment in low productive community-based services during 1983-93. This too reflects a slow but distinct process of immiserisation and feminisation of poverty in the state.

Undoubtedly, this high growth in employment has sustained the process of urbanisation in the state. The rural urban differential in population growth has been high and gone up slightly in the eighties. This has further been reinforced through inter-state migration, which has been maintained at a high level. One would, thus, stipulate that the impetus for urbanisation has come from the supply side. It can be attributed to high rate of rural urban migration — basically due to the incapacity of the rural hinterland to provide productive employment. This is supported by the fact that despite a decline in poverty in the state, urban poverty has been maintained at five to eight percentage points above rural poverty.

Importantly, industrial development has been highly uneven across the regions, Kutch and Saurashtra getting a very small share of the investments in the years following liberalisation. These two regions report high levels of urban poverty of 54 per cent in 1987-88, which is comparable to that in Bihar and Madhya Pradesh. Also, urban poverty in Ahmedabad region, which has not received much of industrial investment during late eighties and early nineties, works out as quite high.

It is reasonable to argue that the process of urbanisation cannot be sustained in the long run since poverty induced expansion in informal sector in urban areas seems to be reaching an upper limit. In the large cities, business and industrial interests are usurping urban land. In medium and small towns, the inadequacy of basic amenities, reflected in a low coverage of households through toilet facilities, wouid place a limit on their labour absorptive capacity. Given this macro scenario, slowing down in the rate of urbanisation in the state and growth of a few global centres in the nineties and subsequent decades emerge as a strong possibility.

Often the question is raised whether interventions by the state or central government can change this process and pattern of urban growth in Gujarat emerging through the market? Could that promote the growth of small and medium towns, particularly in Saurastra and Kutch regions and reduce the regional imbalances in development as well as poverty. The analysis of the trends in labour market and changing policy perspective make it clear that posing the issue as state *versus* market does not give much analytical mileage. One must ask what are the tools of intervention available to the Indian state in future years and with what objectives these are likely to be used.

The changes in the system of governance and urban planning, brought about through structural adjustment, as recommended by international agencies like the World Bank, USAID, etc. and broadly accepted by the Indian planners, envisage state's role only as a facilitator. If indeed the public agencies intervene as a facilitator in the market — removing its deficiencies and saving the actors from market failures — the above scenario would emerge, possibly with greater ease.

It is argued, even by the proponents of liberalisation, that given the socio-economic reality in India, it is difficult for private sector to bring about the desirable changes in urban land market, land use pattern, investment levels in infrastructure, etc. The development of global cities would necessitate "structural" changes in land and capital market that would be difficult to achieve without state becoming an active partner in the process. The message, however, comes loud and clear from the India Infrastructure Report and Ninth Plan that such changes are possible and are forthcoming. More specifically, the state of Gujarat has responded quite favourably in the past few years by ushering in the necessary changes in legislations and system of governance. It has, at the same time, opened up urban land and capital market. If the state continues to adopt the facilitator's role, it would have a couple of global cities with massive infrastructural and industrial investment around them within the next decade or so. The spatial structure of development would, then, be characterised by accentuation of regional imbalances, high poverty and a low quality of life in urban centres, excepting the few cities linked to the national and world market.

NOTES

1. The annual exponential growth rate of population in these cities in Gujarat has gone down from 4.1 per cent in the seventies to 3.1 per cent in the eighties. The decline is somewhat less sharp in the country, the figure going down from 3.5 to 3.0 per cent.
2. Yet another study by Rao and Natarajan (1996) suggests that urban poverty in Gujarat can be taken to have increased during 1990-93 as the percentage of households having annual income of Rs. 18,000 or less has gone up from 29.4 per cent to 32.9 per cent.
3. The tribal districts like Banaskantha, Sabarkantha, Panchmahals in the north and the Dangs in the south have got some marginal benefits through dispersal of small scale industries in the state.
4. A sectoral analysis of changing employment scenario for women at the all India level corroborates the proposition (Kundu 1994). The study further reveals that in several urban sectors, regular female workers were paid the same as the male casual workers and even less.

REFERENCES

Alagh, Y.K. (1995), "A Note on Measurement and Use of Poverty Estimates", *The Indian Journal of Labour Economics*, 38 (1).

Bhalla, G.S. and Singh, G. (1997), "Recent Development in Indian Agriculture : A State Level Analysis", *Economic and Political Weekly*, March 29.

Dubey, A. and Gangopadhyay, S. (1998), *Counting the Poor*, Department of Statistics, Government of India, New Delhi.

Dutt, G. (1997), India: Achievements and Challenges in Reducing Poverty, Report. No. 16483-IN, World Bank, Washington.

Expert Group on the Commercialisation (1996), The India Infrastructure Report: Policy Imperatives for Growth and Welfare, Ministry of Finance, Government of India, New Delhi.

Iyengar, Sudershan (1996): "Level and Pattern of Economic growth in Gujarat: 1980-94", Working Paper no. 72, Gujarat Institute of Development Research, Gota (Ahmedabad).

——— (1998), "Gujarat : A Development Profile, Report on the Project on Regional Development in India, in Sharriff, A. (ed.), A Dutch Government Project.

Kundu, A. (1993), "Employment Growth, Changing Workforce Structure and Poverty Employment Linkages in Urban Areas", International Labour Organisation, New Delhi.

Kundu, A., (1994), *Urban Development and Urban Research in India*, Khama Publications, New Delhi.

——— (1983), "Theories of City Size Distribution and the Indian Urban Structure – A Reappraisal", *Economic and Political Weekly*, July, 1983.

——— and Gupta, S. (1996), "Migration Urbanisation and Regional Inequality", *Economic and Political Weekly,* 31(52), December 26.

——— (1997), "Trends and Structure of Employment in the 1990s — Implications for Urban Growth", *Economic and Political Weekly,* 32 (24), June 14.

Natarajan, I. (1998), *India Market Demographic*, National Council of Applied Economic Research, New Delhi.

National Sample Survey Organisation (1986), "Key Results of Last Three Quinquennial NSS Enquiries on Employment and Unemployment", *Sarvekshana,* 9(4), Department of Statistics, Government of India, New Delhi.

National Sample Survey Organisation (1990), "Results of the Fourth Quinquennial NSS Survey on Employment and Unemployment", *Sarvekshana,* 9(4), Department of Statistics, Government of India, New Delhi.

National Sample Survey Organisation (1997), "Employment and Unemployment in India", 1993-94, Fiftieth Round, Department of Statistics, New Delhi.

Planning Commission (1993), "Report of the Expert Group on Estimation of Proportion and Number of Poor", Government of India, New Delhi.

Planning Commission (1998), *Ninth Five Year Plan*, Government of India, New Delhi.

Rao, S. L. and Natarajan, I. (1996), *India Market Demographic*, National Council of Applied Economic Research, New Delhi.

5

Non-Tax Revenue and Subsidies in Gujarat

ARCHANA R. DHOLAKIA

I. Introduction

Gujarat started facing the problem of fiscal imbalance on revenue account from the year 1984-85 onwards, prior to which it generally enjoyed surplus on the account which was diverted for capital formation in the government sector. In fact, the phenomenon of fiscal deterioration was observed for most the states including some of those who were otherwise known to be better fiscal performers after 1984-85 (Report of the Tenth Finance Commission, 1994; Dholakia Archana; 1999). The Tenth Finance Commission (TFC) also mentioned that the phenomenon of simultaneous fiscal deterioration in all the states may be due to some systematic factors but it did not go into the details of this issue. As argued by the author in another study, one of the important factors at the root for the fiscal crisis in Gujarat and similar better performing states was devolution policy of the Centre adopted in 1984-85 which has not only failed to give sufficient incentives for the fiscal performance, but has encouraged them to be indisciplined (Dholakia, Archana, 1999). Though these are very important factors that determine the fiscal discipline, the state has to accept them as given at least in the short-run. Hence, in the present analysis, which aims at considering the role and issues regarding the non-tax revenue and subsidies in Gujarat, the above factors would be treated as exogenous. Thus, we would consider the fiscal instrument of the non-tax revenue (NTR) of the state in relation to only those aspects and instruments over which the state has sufficient control and it can, if it so desires, try to achieve the constrained maxima in terms of reduction of revenue deficit as well as fiscal deficit through them. In the next section, therefore, we discuss the importance and role of the non-tax revenue (NTR), especially in the current context of fiscal crisis and new economic policy reforms at the state level. Section III discusses the status, scope as well as theoretical and practical parameters determining the NTR in Gujarat. Section IV is devoted to the methodology for measurement of total subsidies (i.e. explicit plus implicit), given to various social and economic sectors through the populist measures and/or low revenue receipts from these services. Section V presents the empirical estimates of subsidies given to various sectors and sub-sectors in the state. Section VI is finally devoted to summary and policy implications of the above.

II. Status, Scope and Determinants of Non-Tax Revenue in Gujarat

The share of NTR in the total own revenue receipts in the state has remained one fourth for all the years since 1978. (Dholakia, Archana, 1998a). The states like Punjab and Haryana, on the other hand, generate 40 per cent of their own revenue through this source. Even in absolute terms the amount collected by Gujarat was Rs. 357 per capita in 1995-96, which was less than the one third of that collected by Haryana and one half of what was collected by Punjab (Table 5.1). Of course, the performance of NTR was found to be dissatisfactory in majority of the states as observed by the TFC. It considered this to be a major cause for the yawning fiscal gaps and erosion of revenue resources of the states which crippled their efforts at providing reasonable services in many vital sectors like power, transport, irrigation and water supply (TFC, 1994 p.9).

Gujarat, like many other states, has experienced the deceleration in the growth rate of the tax as well as non-tax revenue during the reform period, coupled with accelerating growth of non-development expenditure (Dholakia, Archana, 1998). During 1981-91 (Pre-reform period) the tax revenue grew at the average compound rate of 16 per cent per annum which declined to 13 per cent during 1991-98 (ADB Report, 1999). The non-tax growth during similar sub-periods decelerated from 16 per cent per annum to 9 per cent per annum (ADB Report, 1999). Due to populist policies of the government, increase in the rate of interest on borrowing from the RBI, increasing debt of the state causing greater interest and debt servicing burden, the non-development expenditure during the reform period accelerated to 18 per cent from 12 per cent growth during 1981-91, (ADB Report, 1999). For implementation of the New Economic Policy reforms, the government of Gujarat also required additional resources for the infrastructural development and restructuring for which over and above the internal avenues, the state also depended on the external sources like the World Bank and Asian Development Bank (ADB). The latter, as a part of the conditionality of the loan, emphasised the restructuring of departmental and non-departmental enterprises and thereby reduction in fiscal deficit to about 2.5 per cent of NSDP from the then prevailing 4 to 4.5 per cent level. All these factors have built up the pressure on the state government to reduce the expenditure and/or enhance the own revenue resources. The option of reducing the expenditure is politically as well as administratively tough and in the volatile political situations no government would take chances by using such options. The second alternative with the state government is to generate larger resources through taxation either through changing the rates, base or both, but this also has quite limited scope given the tax laws and tax administration. Increasing the resources through taxation is also likely to be quite difficult because as the Gujarat State Finance Commission (GFC, 1994) had observed, the per capita tax collection in the state is already quite high in comparison to many other states. In spite of prohibition on liquor, the state ranks third in terms of per capita tax collection (Table 5.1).

If we exclude the excise revenue from tax collection of all states for comparison, Gujarat's per capita tax collection stands at the highest of all (Table 5.1). This also implies that burden of tax borne by non-liquor commodities in Gujarat is high compared to other states. This is not to say that it is impossible to increase tax revenue or tax-NSDP ratio. But the concern is more regarding its desirability, the cost at which this can be achieved and the time span required to achieve the objective. It may be argued that there is a considerable scope for raising larger tax revenue through appropriate administrative, civil and legal reforms. However, the state government requires technical capabilities, willingness and incentives from the Centre to initiate such reforms, the fruits of which can be enjoyed only in the long run. In the short run therefore by the *deductio-absurdom* principle the state will have to depend on the non-tax avenues which are inadequately tapped at present (GFC, 1994; and TFC, 1994; ADB Report, 1999). As we know, the NTR consists of interest receipts, dividend, royalty on mines and minerals, forest revenue, amount collected through fees and users charges on social services like health, education, housing, etc. and economic services like irrigation, power and transport. Unlike general taxes, it is possible to establish one-to-one correspondence between the users of the public services and payers from the same. The excess burden or dead weight loss on the society is likely to be less if the principle of benefit

Table 5.1 : Tax and Non-Tax Revenue of States — 1995-96

State	Tax Revenue			Non-Tax Revenue		State's Own Revenue		
	Per Capita Without Excise	Per Capita With Excise	As % of NSDP (With Excise)	Per Capita (Rs.)	As % of NSDP	Per Capita (Rs.)	As % of NSDP	Non-tax Revenue's % of Tax Revenue
(1)	(2)	(3)	(4)	(5)	(6)	(7)	(8)	(9)
1. Andhra Pradesh	917	928	11.90	223	2.86	1151	14.76	24.02
2. Bihar	553	572	15.00	96	2.51	668	17.51	16.75
3. Gujarat	1437	1442	13.27	357	3.29	1800	16.56	24.78
4. Haryana	1089	1393	11.38	1204	9.84	2597	21.21	86.45
5. Karnataka	1223	1393	16.91	256	3.11	1649	20.02	18.39
6. Kerala	1281	1426	19.80	173	2.40	1599	22.20	12.12
7. Madhya Pradesh	671	752	12.70	234	3.95	987	16.65	31.13
8. Maharashtra	1337	1461	11.24	322	2.47	1783	13.72	22.01
9. Orissa	680	701	13.16	183	3.43	883	16.59	26.04
10. Punjab	971	1398	9.68	804	5.56	2202	15.25	57.47
11. Rajasthan	724	870	13.48	466	7.22	1336	20.70	53.56
12. Tamil Nadu	1373	1533	16.70	147	1.60	1680	18.30	9.58
13. Uttar Pradesh	620	697	12.98	159	2.96	856	15.94	22.85
14. West Bengal	800	836	11.77	45	0.63	881	12.39	5.32

Source: RBI Bulletin, February, 1998.

taxation through 'pay and use' is applied through appropriate pricing of the public services. Hence, on a priority consideration it is better to generate revenue through levying appropriate prices for the public goods rather than increasing other kinds of indirect taxes like sales tax which the state has been practising.

There is also another and perhaps stronger justification for generating larger resources through NTR in Gujarat. The composition of the NTR by some major items evinces that if we disregard the revenue from the royalty on non-ferrous, minerals and other similar items, the revenue receipts from social and economic services in the state turn out to be less than 12 per cent of the total NTR compared to 34 per cent in Maharashtra (Table 5.2). Even if we include the receipts from the general services the figure for Gujarat rises to at the most 19 per cent against 46 per cent in Maharashtra. Now given the cost of production of these services, low revenue receipts (RR) from them indicate higher implicit subsidies which are non-targeted and non-transparent in nature (NIPFP Discussion Paper, 1997). They may also be termed as negative implicit taxes which have larger distortionary effects on resource allocation of the scarce resources as compared to explicit subsidies (GFC, 1994; Discussion paper of NIPFP 1997; ADB Report, 1999).

Table 5.2 : Composition of Non-Tax Revenue Receipts

Particulars	Gujarat			Maharashtra		
	1996-97 Accounts	1997-98 R.E.	1998-99 M.B.E.	1996-97 Accounts	1997-98 R.E.	1998-99 M.B.E.
1. Interest Receipts	53.34	47.06	31.97	54.55	43.42	43.87
2. General Services	6.92	13.66	8.19	7.69	12.24	10.95
3. Social Services	4.92	5.10	5.54	4.65	5.23	5.39
4. Economic Services	34.82	34.17	54.29	33.11	39.11	39.79
4. (a) Non-Ferrous Mining & Metallurgical Industries	(28.09)	(27.06)	(38.32)	(6.88)	(10.31)	(10.69)
Total Non-Tax Revenue (in Rs. crores)	1572.74	1681.39	1772.57	3746.80	3476.41	3463.44

Source : Budget Documents of Government of Gujarat and Government of Maharashtra, 1998.

Low and obsolete rate of users fees for public services coupled with their poor recovery, low rate of return on investment in the state owned public enterprises, poor recovery rate of interest on the loans given to public sector units, poor administration of the departmental and non-departmental undertakings leading to high cost of production and poor quality of services are all the reasons identified as the causes for the low revenue resource generation from the publicly provided services (GFC, 1994; ADB Report, 1999). Conceptually we may summarise all these factors and their relationship with the revenue receipts (RR) of public services as follows:

$$RR = F(P, Q, E)$$

Where, RR = Revenue Receipts from a public service.

P = Absolute price/charge fixed per unit of a public service.

Q = Quantity demanded of a public service.

E = Efficiency and Effectiveness of administration in terms of fixing up of a price and recovery of it from the users of a public service.

It can be seen that unlike private sector model where we consider total revenue as a function of only P and Q, here we have to explicitly consider one more factor E which stands for the efficiency and effectiveness in price determination and recovery in the model. This is because in case of the former once the goods are sold the prices are by and large recovered either on the spot or with some time lag. Moreover, since the price is determined by the interaction of demand and supply, the aspects of quality and efficiency are taken care of in the price itself. Absolute prices (P) of the public services, on the other hand, are fixed by the government, sometimes on the basis of the cost of production and/or several times arbitrarily. Hence more often than not, they ignore the transaction costs involved in terms of time, transport, tips, etc. incurred for the consumption of public services. Thus the effective price (P^*), at which the public goods/services are available to people differs substantially from the actually announced price (P). Moreover, if the quality of the public goods/service is inferior to what was guaranteed, which is again a common phenomenon, the price charged per unit of quality goes up implying that effective price

P* becomes larger than *P*, i.e. $P^* > P$. If this gap widens, it reduces the demand (Q) for a public service and encourages people to turn to private sector. This is commonly observed in the case of health and education services (ADB Report, 1999). In several cases this leads to under-utilisation of the capacity, which in turn enhances the burden of overhead costs per unit. Even the variable cost of manpower also does not decrease due to rigidities in the government rules including the labour laws. This leads to dwindling of operations and maintenance (O & M) cost causing further deterioration in the quality of a service. This further widens the gap between *P** and *P*. A vicious circle of low price, low-demand, low revenue perpetuates in this way.

There is another set of public goods/services where the situation is totally different. In this case, the absolute price fixed by the government (P) is so low in comparison to both the marginal cost as well as privately charged price that even with high transaction costs and quality problem the effective price to public P* turns out to be lower than the absolute price fixed by the government. i.e. $P^* < P$. Moreover, quite often even these low prices are not fully recovered hence the gap between *P** and *P* further widens leading to disproportionately larger demand than the production capacity. In such cases there occur the problems of over-crowding, over-utilisation and unwarranted exploitation of the scarce economic resources. Low water and electricity charges for agriculture sector are the cases in point (GFC, 1994). For instance, between 1981 and 1999 (January) the water rates charged to agriculture sector in Gujarat did not change at all. In 1994-95 they were found to be so low that even if fully recovered they could fetch the revenue of only Rs. 12 crores which could hardly meet one-third of the O & M expenditure for that year. With only seventy per cent recovery of this assessed revenue, the effective price of water to agriculture sector was still lower. Even with the recently revised prices of water, therefore, the state might at the most recover O&M expenditure plus less than one per cent rate of return on the capital employed in the past.

Another startling illustration of $P^* < P$ is the fees for medical students in government colleges in Gujarat which were not revised for more than 35 years or so until August 1998. In the year 1998-99, therefore, a medical student in the state spent less than one-tenth (Rs. 1200 per annum) of the amount spent by a student in Maharashtra (Rs. 13000) and contributed less than one per cent of the cost incurred by the government on his education. Interestingly, the fees are almost the same for the rich and poor students. The potential demand (Q) for this service is bound to be high due to wide gap between P^* and P, but there is a quantitative restriction on Q through the fixed number of seats, i.e. $Q = Q$. This implies that one of the objectives behind the subsidy given to a service, namely to encourage the consumption of a public goods, is simply not achieved (or allowed to be achieved). Moreover, due to almost the same price charged from the poor and the non-poor groups the benefits become general and untargeted in nature. Hence, such a pricing policy neither increases revenue, nor does it achieve the goals of a subsidy, namely increased consumption and equitable distribution of publicly provided services. It is largely because of the above-mentioned reasons that in Gujarat the contribution made by the government supplied social and economic services turns out to be less than 12 per cent of the total NTR (excluding non-ferrous mineral income). All publicly provided services together, namely, social, economic and general fetch hardly 20 per cent of the total NTR as against 40 per cent in Maharashtra (Table 5.2). And it is because of the meagre share of these items that the share of interest receipts dominates the other components. Otherwise, in terms of recovery rate of interest the performance is quite poor (0.17 per cent) (Finance Account, 1997), i.e. on the outstanding balance of loan of Rs. 100, government recovers only 17 paise per annum by way of interest. This reminds us of a saying that sometimes facts are more fascinating than the fantasies!

Several such illustrations of irrational pricing in the state can be given. What we, therefore, say is that in case of public services, role of the '*E*' factor, i.e. efficient pricing and effective recovery becomes quite important for generating the revenue. Hence, steps to improve E factors would be required to increase RR.

To look at the existing situation more positively, the cases similar to the ones discussed above provide tremendous scope for the government to raise additional revenue resources and wipe off its fiscal deficit partly or wholly. The GFC (1994) had meticulously worked out the potential rise in revenue through rationalisation of tariff rates in Gujarat. As per their estimates, through revision in water and power prices alone the state can generate Rs.600-700 crores (1993-94) per annum. Following some of these suggestions of the GFC and the ADB (1997-98) the Government of Gujarat (GoG) conducted some meetings and workshops in February, 1998, in which the possibility of raising additional resources through revision of the users charges of public services along with the problems of low interest and loan recovery rates were discussed. Consequential to that, some changes in the recovery policy and users charges have also been made recently through which the state envisages the increase in the total non-tax revenue (NTR) by Rs.483 crores in 1998-99 (RE) and Rs.352 crores in 1999-2000 (BE), from the 1996-97 (Rs. 1573 crores) level. As per the GFC (1994) and our calculations, which will be shown later, there is a much greater potential of this so-called insignificant source for increasing the total revenue than the state has tapped so far and it envisages to tap in 1999-2000.

It should be remembered even at the cost of repetition that fixing up of the right price is a necessary condition for increasing the revenue, the sufficient condition is provided by the efficient recovery of prices through administrative machinery and improvement in the quality of public services for which the people may like to pay such prices. This will reduce the implicit subsidies provided by the government. As the magnitude and rate of subsidies are extremely important to estimate the potential revenue generation in the state and also reduce distortions, we would give their estimates in Section IV, before which we would like to briefly discuss the methodology used for generating such estimates. This is attempted in Section III.

III. Methodology for Measuring the Government Subsidies

We have already noted in Section II that difference between the cost and the price of a public good/service (goods and services are used synomeously here) may be interpreted as subsidy or indirect negative tax. Hence, we can make use of the data on expenditure on a service and revenue receipts (RR) earned through fees/users charges through which are available from the budget documents, to estimate the subsidy flowing to a given service or a sector. As will be seen later, this will give the estimate of a total subsidy (i.e. explicit + implicit) flowing to a service or a sector. The sum of the subsidies of all services then gives the total subsidies given by a state. This is known as the Budget Based Approach of measuring subsidies. Using this approach we have estimated the social sector subsidies and economic sector subsidies separately for the years 1995-2000[1]. The concept of Total Cost (TC) includes the fixed cost component and does not necessarily include all revenue expenditures. Similarly, not all receipts of the department can be attributed to the sale of the public service. Hence, we have to make appropriate assumptions and adjustments to arrive at the estimate of of Total Costs (TC) and Revenue Receipts (RR) of a service, as would be discussed below. Moreover, we should also remember that the Budget Based Approach by its very name excludes out-of-budget subsidies given through tax exemption, deferment, etc. (NIPFP Discussion Paper, 1997). Thus the word total here implies summation of both implicit and explicit subsidies and excludes out of budget subsidies. Explicit subsidies, by their very nature, appear as expenditure items in the budget documents hence their estimation does not pose great problems. Implicit subsidies, on the other hand, arise due to low revenue receipts in comparison to the total cost of a service and can only be indirectly measured by subtracting explicit subsidies from the total subsidies estimated on the basis of the budget figures. Thus, estimation of indirect subsidies (and total subsidies) is more difficult and gives rise to various conceptual and methodological problems. Despite this, it is important to estimate their magnitude, since unlike explicit subsidies their beneficiaries are dispersed and difficult to identify; their impact is diffused and uncertain; creates greater excess burden in terms of misallocation of scarce resources reduction in quality of publicly provided services; and poor demand management (ADB Report 1999; NIPFP, Discussion Paper, 1997). Above all, the magnitude of implicit subsidies is much larger than the explicit ones hence reduction in them can have direct and significant impact on the fiscal deficit. This explains the importance given to their estimates produced by the various studies including the white paper on subsidies in India, published by Government of India (GoI) in May, 1997.

We should also note that not all publicly provided services should be included for subsidy estimation. Conventionally the goods and services provided by the government may be divided into (a) pure public goods (b) merit goods and (c) non-merit goods. Goods/Services belonging to first category (a) have to be excluded while estimating the subsidies, as these goods, namely, defence, administration, direction, justice, etc. are provided on the ground of 'externality' as well as 'non-excludability' criteria. The benefits generated from these goods are general and difficult to be evaluated in the absence of market mechanism and hence the provision of these goods has to be necessarily made through general taxes. While merit goods, i.e. category (b) are those goods which also create strong externalities but are possible to be provided by the private sector on price. However, they are so crucial for the welfare of the people at large that the government treats them as 'merit' goods and provide them for wider consumption. In the Indian context, elementary education, public health, etc. may be considered as merit goods. The remaining category (c) covers all those goods (non-merit) which do not have high externality nor their supply is crucial for consumption production in the economy, but are provided on the ground that they may be helpful to increase efficiency and productivity (As the government would like to think about them).

The merit and non-merit goods may be further classified into social and economic categories for estimating separately the subsidies flowing to social sector and economic sector. Though the classification of goods into social and economic categories is fairly clear and well defined than that of merit and non-merit used in the discussion paper of NIPFP, 1997 may be found to be somewhat arbitrary and subjective. However, to arrive at temporaly consistent figures with other studies and also to generate the estimates for Gujarat for the years 1995-2000, which are comparable with the cross-section estimates of different states (1993-94), we have retained the classification used by them[2]. In nutshell, the estimates of subsidies produced for merit and non-merit public goods also cross classification by social and economic categories are made for 1995-2000 on the lines of the Discussion paper on subsidy (NIPFP, Discussion Paper, 1997), we may put some important things discussed above in the form of equation as follows:

$$S_T = S_E + S_I \quad \ldots \quad (1)$$

Where S_T is total subsidies; S_E is explicit subsidies and S_I is implicit subsidies given to a sector. The equation to measure the subsidies given to a sector/service is:

$$S_T = TC - RR \quad \ldots \quad (2)$$

Where S_T = total subsidies; TC = total cost; RR = revenue receipts of a given sector/service.

We may remember that *TC* also includes some revenue expenditure component and explicit subsidies being shown as expenditures in the budget are therefore included in the *TC*. Hence in order to obtain the estimates of implicit subsidies S_I, we have to subtract S_E from the S_T. The estimates of S_E are available from the CSO as well as the state government's bureaux. The total cost (TC) of a service appearing in equation (2) consists of two components viz. variable cost (VC) and fixed cost (FC). As far as the former is concerned, it is estimated by deducting general expenditure on administration, direction, etc. from the revenue expenditure on a service for the year, which are published in the budget and other document. As far as FC[3], i.e. fixed cost is concerned, it is the annualized cost of capital, which is measured through the sum of depreciation rate and interest cost of capital estimated through making appropriate assumptions (ADB Report, 1999). RR, on the other hand, includes receipts from the fees/users charges of the service and the amount of dividend or interest received by the government from the public sector undertakings providing that service. By summing up the subsidies estimated for different publicly provided services arrived at in the above manner, total subsidies (S_T) given to a sector are obtained. It may be mentioned that the S_T includes subsidies given to non-departmental public enterprises operating in that particular service or sector. However, like the Discussion Paper (NIPFP Discussion Paper, 1997) subsidies given to non-departmental undertakings are also separately estimated by us by taking the difference between the annual cost of the government's capital (Equity + Loans) locked up in PSUs and the receipts (actual) on account of dividend and interest on that fund estimates presented in the Section V, where we have also presented the estimates of total subsidies by economic and social categories as well as merit-non-merit categories for some years for Gujarat.

For comparison purpose, inter-state estimates for 1993-94 are also provided.

IV. Empirical Estimates of Subsidies for Gujarat

The inter-state study conducted by the NIPFP gives the estimates of subsidies flowing to various sectors and sub-sectors for fifteen major states of India for the year 1993-94 (Table 5.3) (NIPFP, Discussion Paper, 1997). The inter-state estimates for earlier periods are also available from other sources but are not strictly comparable with the 1993-94 estimates, hence are not analysed here (Rao and Mundle, 1992). Following the same methodology as used by NIPFP, we have generated the temporal estimate for Gujarat for the five different years from 1995 to 2000.

Gujarat, in comparison to other states, very clearly emerges as the major distributor of bounties giving highest per capita subsidy of Rs. 1402 per annum, when the average subsidy given by all states is Rs. 850 per head (Table 5.3). Of course, there appears to be a general tendency on the part of all the richer states to give higher subsidies. Thus in terms of per capita subsidy, Punjab ranks next to Gujarat followed by Haryana and Maharashtra. However, the absolute difference in per capita subsidy given by Gujarat and Punjab is more than Rs.200, whereas between the other three states it is less than Rs. 30 (Table 5.3). The above estimates also

Table 5.3 : Government_Subsidies in Different States — 1993-94

State	Total Cost of Public Services (Rs. crores)	Total Receipts from public services (Rs. crores)	Subsidies (Rs. crores)	Per Capita Subsidy (In Rs.)	Cost Recovery (%)	Subsidies as % of NSDP
(1)	(2)	(3)	(4)	(5)	(6)	(7)
1. Andhra Pradesh	6566	544	6022	859	8.29	12.44
2. Bihar	5445	129	5316	576	2.38	17.11
3. Goa	447	120	327	2519	10.48	13.15
4. Gujarat	6294	139	6155	1402	2.21	16.03
5. Haryana	2338	332	2006	1159	14.19	10.88
6. Karnataka	5104	265	4839	1030	5.18	14.44
7. Kerala	3091	77	3014	1002	2.49	15.96
8. Madhya Pradesh	6099	331	5768	821	5.41	15.02
9. Maharashtra	10680	108	9602	1150	10.09	10.17
10. Orissa	2842	47	2795	847	1.65	18.14
11. Punjab	2928	233	2695	1177	7.96	9.21
12. Rajasthan	4891	518	4373	934	10.59	18.01
13. Tamil Nadu	6598	265	6333	1098	4.02	14.18
14. Uttar Pradesh	9597	310	9287	630	3.23	13.32
15. West Bengal	4770	164	4606	640	3.43	10.01
All 15 states listed above (Total)	77454	8119	69335	833	10.48	13.15
Average of 15 states	931	98	833	833	10.48	13.15

Source : Government Subsidies in India, A Discussion paper submitted to Finance Department, GOI by NIPFP, March, 1997.

imply that Gujarat is a state with the highest positive tax burden (on non-liquor commodities) as well as the highest negative tax burden (subsidies). Interestingly, this large absolute amount of per capita subsidy given by the state is not the result of higher per capita cost incurred by the state, but largely arises on account of poor revenue receipts from publicly provided services. This is evident from the poor cost recovery rate (RR divided by TC) of 2.21 per cent on government supplied services, which is the second lowest of all the states (Table 5.3). .When the average cost recovery rate (CRR) of the states is more than 10 per cent and that of the richer state like Haryana is more than 14 per cent,

Gujarat's performance of 2.21 per cent provides the cause for concern. The situation seems to have further worsened in the later years with per capita subsidies increasing by almost hundred per cent between 1993-1998 (RE) (Table 5.4). Already megre cost recovery rate of 1993-94 has thus further declined to 2.10 per cent in 1998-99. The budgeted figure for 1999-2000 does envisage some improvement in this respect (2.91 per cent), but that is quite marginal if at all achieved. It is so surprising, and even shocking, that the New Economic Policy Reforms, so fondly discussed by

Table 5.4 : Total Government Subsidies in Gujarat 1993-94 to 1999-2000

(In Rs. Crores)

Items	1993-94	1995-96	1996-97	1997-98	1998-99	1999-2000
(1)	(2)	(3)	(4)	(5)	(6)	(7)
Total Costs	6294	8216	9313	11192	13483	13629
Total Receipts	139	179	152	236	282	397
Total Subsidies	6155	8037	9161	10956	13201	13232
Per Capita Subsidies	1422[a]	1794	2013	2354	2784	2739
Cost Recovery rate (%)	2.21	2.18	1.63	2.11	2.10	2.91
As % of NSDP (16.03)	15.69[b]	13.89	13.70	15.54	15.21	13.26
% of social sector subsidy to total subsidies	39.38	41.63	39.35	39.24	45.22	46.03
% of economics sector subsidy to total subsidy	60.62	58.37	60.65	60.76	54.78	53.97

Notes : RE = Revised Estimates, BE = Budget Estimates

[a] = Per capita subsidy for Gujarat for 1993-94 is different from that in earlier Table due to different estimate of population considered by them.

[b] = Figure in the bracket in column (2) is based on unrevised estimates for NSDP.

Sources : 1. For column (2), same as Table 5.3.

2. Figures for 1995-96 are from ADB Report on Gujarat's Reform of Public Finances, 1999.

3. Figures in remaining columns are estimated by us by using Finance Accounts — 1995-96 of Government of Gujarat and various issues of Budget in Brief, GoG.

the centre and the state, show absolutely no impact on these variables. It is only in 1998 (four years after the GFC report!) that the state government has awakened and has started considering these issues little more seriously, which gets reflected in the 1999-2000 budget. We are using the word 'little' because although the direction of efforts is right, the required pace and the rigour are too inadequate to mobilize the resources for meeting even the reasonable targets of revenue generation and reduction in fiscal deficits. Considering the suggested rise of Rs. 600-700 crores by GFC (1994) only through the tariff revisions, the likely level of Rs. 397crores in 1999-2000 over Rs. 139 crores in 1993-94 is quite disappointing.

Let us now consider the sectoral allocation of subsidies. To start with, we will consider only two broad sectors, viz. social and economic. It may be argued on a *priori* ground that in the state economy belonging to a developing nation, the proportion of social sector subsidies should be larger than that of economic sector subsidies. This is because the former includes the services like education, health, housing, etc. which directly affect the consumption of basic commodities, so essential for the good quality of life of the people. Hence, the government is expected to play the larger role in the provision of social services than in the supply of economic services which largely affect the production aspects and can also be handled (perhaps more efficiently) by the private sector. But like many other states the situation in Gujarat is quite contrary to this expectation (Table 5.4). Until 1997-98, by and large, more than sixty per cent of the total subsidies have flown to economic sector goods/services. Incidentally, this figure excludes the subsidy by way of tax exemption and tax deferment, otherwise the figure would still be higher. It is only in last two years that due to some policy changes undertaken by the state government there is a shift towards the social sector subsidies, whose proportion rose from 40 per cent in earlier years to 45-46 per cent for 1998-99 and 1999-2000 (Table 5.4).

Let us now look at the distribution of subsidies by components of social and economic services. The major items in the former are education, health, water and sanitation, and in the latter agriculture, irrigation, power, industries and transport may be considered as the important ones. The data reveal that more than 60 per cent of the social sector subsidies in the state flow to education sector. But the cost recovery rate, i.e. CRR is as poor as 1.32 per cent. In 1993-94 this was marginally higher than that in Maharashtra and Punjab, who gave almost similar amount (around Rs. 300) of absolute subsidy on education per head of population. But during the

Table 5.5 : Subsidies Given to Major Social Sectors in Selected States 1993-94

Subsidies in different Sectors	Gujarat	Maharashtra	Haryana	Punjab
(1)	(2)	(3)	(4)	(5)
Education				
Total (Rs. Crores)	1360	2622	460	706
Per Capita (Rs.)	314	316	264	331
Cost Recovery Rate (%)	1.31	0.88	2.56	0.81
% of Total Social Subsidy	58.07	58.24	57.00	62.87
Health				
Total (Rs. Crores)	323	662	128	229
Per Capita (Rs.)	75	80	74	107
Cost Recovery Rate (%)	2.05	2.27	1.32	1.27
% of Total Social Subsidy	13.79	14.70	15.86	20.39
Water & Sanitation				
Total (Rs. Crores)	185	273	77	53
Per Capita (Rs.)	43	33	44	25
Cost Recovery Rate (%)	0.31	15.55	9.57	10.48
% of Total Social Subsidy	7.90	6.06	9.54	4.72
Welfare of SC/ST/OBC				
Total (Rs. Crores)	186	267	212	28
Per Capita (Rs.)	43	32	122	13
Cost Recovery Rate (%)	0.00	0.00	1.05	0.04
% of Total Social Subsidy	7.94	5.93	26.27	2.49
All Social Services				
Total (Rs. Crores)	2342	4502	807	1123
Per Capita (Rs.)	541	542	463	527
Cost Recovery Rate (%)	1.76	2.97	3.79	2.49

Source : Government Subsidies in India, A Discussion paper submitted to Finance Department, GOI by NIPFP, March, 1997.

later years it further fell in Gujarat (Table 5.6). For 1998-99, the estimated CRR of education in the state is 0.69 per cent implying that out of the cost of Rs. 100 incurred, only 69 paise is recovered through fees/users charges. The same is true for the health sector where the CRR has remained around 2.4 per cent or less in the state for all the years under the study (Table 5.6). Also, the situation in other states is no better (Table 5.6). As far as water and sanitation services are concerned, the relative subsidies given by Gujarat are quite high compared to Maharashtra, Punjab and Haryana (Table 5.5). To get an idea, we may say that when Punjab and Maharashtra recovered more than Rs.10 out of the cost of Rs.100 on this item, Gujarat recovered only 31 paise out of the same in 1993-94 (Table 5.5). Later on there is some improvement. But the CRR of this sector in Gujarat has remained around two per cent or so during the entire period under the study (Table 5.6). This, in fact, indicates the extent of potential of these sectors to either generate greater revenue or transferring them partly to private sector who should be allowed to charge higher with improved quality of these services.

Table 5.7 presents the estimates of subsidies given to different economic sub-sectors by some states. Even here the state of Gujarat ranks highest in terms of per capita subsidy (Rs. 859), followed by Punjab (Rs. 738) and the lowest in terms of cost recovery rate out of all major states. When the recovery rate on economic sectors in Maharashtra and Haryana are 16 per cent and 20 per cent respectively the 2.6 per cent rate in Gujarat is just pathetic and unjustified. This happened because the two major services, viz. irrigation and power, where Gujarat spends more than 60 per cent of its fiscal economic resources, earn the recovery rates of 2.5 per cent and less than one half respectively (Table 5.7). The temporal data on irrigation subsidies in Gujarat, however, reveal that the situation is improving due to some policy changes introduced during the last 2-3 years. Hence the CRR of irrigation has increased from 2.5 per cent to 5.9 per cent in 1998-99 and might still increase to 9.58 per cent in 1999-2000. In the power sector, however, not major break through has been achieved so far. On the instance of ADB the state has introduced some reforms to affect the revenue on one hand and decrease the costs on the other. The subsidies given to agriculture sector, which are borne by the government, are likely to be frozen at that level. Reduction in revenue expenditure is also implemented due to which the total cost of this service is envisaged to reduce by Rs. 300 crores in the year 1999-2000. Beyond this no major effect is seen on the government budget. Let us now look at the third important sector of economic infrastructure, namely, transport. It is a sector where again the state has to learn from other states. Haryana, for instance recovers more than Rs. 60 out of Rs. 100 spent, whereas Gujarat does not cover even 60 paise out of the same (Table 5.7). For industries also the per capita subsidy given by Gujarat is the highest and the CRR on that lowest. Even with all revisions made in the recent years the state is

Table 5.6 : Estimates of Subsidies Flowing to Major Social Sectors in Gujarat — 1993-2000

(In Rs. Crores)

Sector	1993-94*	1995-96	1996-97	1997-98	1998-99(RE)	1999-2000(BE)
(1)	(2)	(3)	(4)	(5)	(6)	(7)
Education						
Total Cost	1378	1878	2053	2293	3186	2969
Total Receipts	18	20	21	23	22	24
Subsidy	1360	1858	2032	2270	3164	2945
Cost Recovery Rate (%)	1.32	1.06	1.01	1.02	0.69	0.81
Health						
Total Cost	3296	469	516	625	925	936
Total Receipts	6.76	9	8	15	14	19
Subsidy	3289	460	508	610	911	917
Cost Recovery Rate (%)	2.05	1.93	1.58	2.36	1.56	2.07
Water & Sanitation						
Total Cost	185	546	545	801	1109	1313
Total Receipts	0.57	10	11	11.36	9.25	11.50
Subsidy	184.43	535	534	789	1100	1302
Cost Recovery Rate (%)	0.31	1.91	1.99	1.42	0.83	0.88

(Contd.)

Table 5.6 *(Contd.)*

Sector	1993-94*	1995-96	1996-97	1997-98	1998-99(RE)	1999-2000(BE)
(1)	(2)	(3)	(4)	(5)	(6)	(7)
Welfare of ST/ST/OBC						
Total Cost	185	232	265	307	395	480
Total Receipts	0.00	0.00	0.00	0.00	0.00	0.00
Subsidy	185	232	265	307	395	480
Cost Recovery Rate (%)	0.00	0.00	0.00	0.00	0.00	0.00
All Social Services						
Total Cost	2384	3398	3665	4367	6037	6168
Total Receipts	41.95	52	60	68	67	77
Subsidy	2342	3346	3605	4299	5970	6091
Cost Recovery Rate (%)	1.76	1.53	1.64	1.56	1.11	1.25

Note : RE = Revised Estimates BE = Budget Estimates.

Source : 1. For column (2), same as Table 5.3.

2. Figures for 1995-96 are from ADB Report on Gujarat's Reform of Public Finances, 1999.
3. Figures in remaining columns are estimated by us using Finance Accounts - 1995-96 of Government of Gujarat and various issues of Budget in Brief, GoG.

Table 5.7: Estimated Subsidies Given to Major Economic Sectors in Selected States — 1993-94

Sector	Gujarat	Maharashtra	Haryana	Punjab
(1)	(2)	(3)	(4)	(5)
Agriculture				
Total (Rs. Crores)	263	875	128	222
Per Capita (Rs.)	61	105	74	104
Cost Recovery Rate (%)	2.93	40.46	4.49	7.23
As % of Total Economic Subsidies	7.08	17.15	10.68	14.12
Irrigation				
Total (Rs. Crores)	1275	2253	444	417
Per Capita (Rs.)	295	271	255	196
Cost Recovery Rate (%)	2.53	3.82	4.40	3.82
As % of Total Economic Subsidies	34.31	44.17	37.06	26.53
Power				
Total (Rs. Crores)	1100	643	278	486
Per Capita (Rs.)	254	77	159	228
Cost Recovery Rate (%)	0.09	7.50	0.001	0.04
As % of Total Economic Subsidies	29.60	12.61	23.21	30.92
Industries				
Total (Rs. Crores)	176	85	31	116
Per Capita (Rs.)	41	10	18	54
Cost Recovery Rate (%)	1.21	3.61	5.04	1.52
As % of Total Economic Subsidies	4.74	1.67	2.59	7.38
Transport				
Total (Rs. Crores)	454	779	149	176
Per Capita (Rs.)	105	94	85	83
Cost Recovery Rate (%)	0.47	0.71	63.01	47.17
As % of Total Economic Subsidies	12.22	15.27	12.44	11.20
All Economic Services				
Total (Rs. Crores)	3716	5101	1198	1572
Per Capita (Rs.)	859	514	688	738
Cost Recovery Rate (%)	2.60	15.56	20.11	11.51

Source : Government Subsidies in India, A Discussion paper submitted to Finance Department, GOI by NIPFP, March, 1997.

Table 5.8 : Estimated Subsidies to Major Economic Sectors in Gujarat — 1993-2000

(Rs. in Crores)

Sector	1993-94	1995-96	1996-97	1997-98	1998-99(RE)	1999-2000(BE)
Agriculture						
Total Cost	332	515	571	610	806	795
Total Receipts	23	44	35	48	41	45
Subsidy	309	471	536	562	765	750
Cost Recovery Rate (%)	6.93	8.49	6.06	7.88	5.12	5.67
Irrigation						
Total Cost	1308	2227	2439	2890	2608	2650
Total Receipts	33	41	41	94	154	254
Subsidy	1275	2186	2398	2796	2454	2396
Cost Recovery Rate (%)	2.52	1.84	1.67	3.26	5.91	9.58
Power						
Total Cost	1101	1130	1658	2255	2736	2448
Total Receipts	1.04	2	1.3	2.67	2.00	2.00
Subsidy	1100	1128	1657	2252	2734	2446
Cost Recovery Rate (%)	0.09	0.22	0.07	0.12	0.07	0.08
Industries						
Total Cost	177	204	157	163	316	314
Total Receipts	2	19	4	5	4.39	4.33

(Contd.)

Table 5.8 *(Contd.)*

Sector	1993-94	1995-96	1996-97	1997-98	1998-99(RE)	1999-2000(BE)
Subsidy	175	185	153	158	312	310
Cost Recovery Rate (%)	1.21	9.31	2.54	3.14	1.39	1.38
Transport						
Total Cost	456	615	674	773	836	804
Total Receipts	2.13	3	3	3.07	3.20	4.20
Subsidy	454	612	671	770	833	800
Cost Recovery Rate (%)	0.44	0.46	0.44	0.40	0.38	0.52
All Economic Services						
Total Cost	3815	4819	5648	6825	7446	7461
Total Receipts	99.20	127	92	168	215	320
Subsidy	3716	4691	5556	6657	7231	7141
Cost Recovery Rate (%)	2.60	2.64	1.63	2.47	2.89	4.29

Note: RE = Revised Estimates BE = Budget Estimates.

Source : 1. Estimates for 1994-95 are taken from the same source as given in Table 5.3.
2. Figures for 1995-96 are taken from the ADB Report on Gujarat's Reform of Public Finances, 1999.
3. Estimates for 1996-2000 are made by us using the budget data and Finance Accounts of Government of Gujarat 1995-96.

expected to achieve the average CRR of 4.29 per cent in 1999-2000 (Table 5.8) on all economic services taken together, which is less than one-third of what was already achieved by Maharashtra, Punjab and Haryana in 1993-94. In short, the sectors from where we expect higher returns are giving the least.

What is still worse is that similar anomaly arises in the distribution of subsidies between merit and non-merit goods, with more than 70 per cent share going to the latter categories of goods.

Even within social sectors, the share of non-merit subsidies has been by and large exceeding the merit ones (Table 5.8). Within the economic sectors the composition between merit and non-merit has remained around 10 : 90 with occasional exceptions (Table 5.9). Thus the government has been working most in the services (non-merit economic) where it should be working the least. The absolute amount of subsidies going to the mentioned category is so large that even with 10 per cent reduction in its amount the state can generate Rs.688 crores which can meet 5 per cent of the state's revenue expenditure of 1999-2000.

For the purpose of benefit incidence, it is also important to know the composition of subsidies in terms of explicit and implicit attribute. It was mentioned in the earlier section that explicit subsidies are targetted more transparent and hence relatively less distortionary (NIPFP Discussion Paper, 1997). We may consider CSO data of National Accounts based subsidies as an approximate figure for explicit subsidies and subtract them from the total subsidies to get the rough magnitude of the implicit subsidies (Table 5.10). The data for 1993-94 suggest that proportion of explicit subsides is less than one-fourth. This is true for both social as well as economic services provided by the government. If we consider the GoG data of subsidies inclusive of Grants-in Aid (GIA) to local bodies for this purpose, still the share of implicit subsidies turns out to be minimum 60 per cent in the total. Thus even with the most conservative estimates the burden of implicit, non-targetted and largely unintended subsidies is one and a half times larger than the explicit ones in Gujarat.

As mentioned earlier, the subsidy estimates presented earlier relate to both departmental and non-departmental undertakings together. The latter category of public sector units is expected to generate adequate surplus for the purpose of reinvestment or for the current use. Hence, like the Discussion Paper (1997) referred above, separate estimates of subsidies flowing to non-departmental undertakings are also made by us for 1995-96 (Table 5.11). For 1993-94, for which inter-state estimates are available, we

Table 5.9 : Merit and Non-Merit Subsidies in Gujarat — 1993-2000

Item	1993-94	1995-96	1996-97	1997-98	1998-99(RE)	1999-2000(BE)
(1)	(2)	(3)	(4)	(5)	(6)	(7)
Amount of Subsidies (Rs. Crores)						
Social Sector						
Merit	1209	1572	1666	2384	2589	2615
Non-Merit	1133	1819	1938	1915	3381	3475
Economic Sector						
Merit	446	506	558	632	702	666
Non-Merit	3270	4185	4999	6024	6528	6476
Total Subsidies						
Merit	1655	2033	2224	3016	3291	3281
Non-Merit	4403	6004	6937	7939	9909	9951
Composition of Subsidies (%)						
Social Sector						
Merit	51.64	45.64	46.23	55.45	43.37	42.94
Non-Merit	48.36	54.36	53.77	44.55	56.63	57.06
Economic Sector						
Merit	11.99	10.79	10.04	9.50	9.71	9.33
Non-Merit	88.01	89.21	89.96	90.50	90.29	90.67
Total Subsidies						
Merit	27.61	25.30	24.28	27.53	24.93	24.80
Non-Merit	72.39	74.70	75.72	72.47	75.07	75.20

(Contd.)

Table 5.9 *(Contd.)*

(1)	(2)	(3)	(4)	(5)	(6)	(7)
As a Share of Total Subsidies (%)						
Social Sector						
Merit	19.00	19.00	18.19	21.76	19.61	19.76
Non-Merit	18.70	22.63	21.15	17.48	25.61	26.26
Economic Sector						
Merit	7.36	6.30	6.09	5.77	5.32	5.03
Non-Merit	53.98	52.07	54.57	54.99	49.45	48.94
Total Subsidies						
Merit	27.32	25.30	24.28	27.53	24.93	24.80
Non-Merit	72.68	74.70	75.72	72.47	75.07	75.20
Total Subsidies	100	100	100	100	100	100

Note: RE : Revised Estimates BE= Budget Estimates.

Source : 1. Estimates for1994-95 are taken from the same source as given in Table 5.3.

2. Figures for 1995-96 are taken from the ADB Report on Gujarat's Reform of Public Finances, 1999.

3. Estimates for 1996-2000 are made by us using the budget data and Finance Accounts of Government of Gujarat 1995-96.

Table 5.10 : Explicit and Implicit Subsidies in Gujarat — 1993-94

Subsidies	Subsidies in Rs. Crores	Subsidies Per Capita	Composition of Subsidies	As a Share of Total Subsidies
Social Sector				
(i) Explicit	2.38	0.54	0.10	0.04
(ii) Implicit	2421.62	551.60	99.90	39.35
(iii) Combined	2424	552.14	100	39.39
Economic Sector				
(i) Explicit	1414.34	322.16	37.90	22.98
(ii) Implicit	2316.66	527.69	62.10	37.64
(iii) Combined	3731	849.85	100	60.62
Total Subsidies				
(i) Explicit	1416.72	322.79	23.02	23.02
(ii) Implicit	4738.28	1079.29	76.98	76.98
(iii) Combined	6155	1401.99	100	100

Note : CSO Data do not strictly estimate explicit subsidies.
Sources : 1. Government Subsidies in India, A Discussion paper submitted to Finance Department, GoI by NIPFP, March, 1997.
2. ADB Report on Gujarat's Reform of Public Finances, 1999.

have depended on the paper. As Gujarat's per capita investment in PSUs is the highest of all the states, which is almost one and a half times the second state in this respect, namely, Punjab, the challenges and opportunities are high for the state. On the suggestions of the GFC (1994) and ADB the state has undertaken several measures like close down, privatisation and cost-reduction to improve the overall efficiency of these units. In 1993-94 the CRR of these units was around 6.5 per cent in Gujarat, much higher than 2.21 per cent in Maharashtra and 4.44 per cent in Punjab (Table 5.11). Thus in relation to other states Gujarat's performance is better. But in absolute terms it is much lower than the opportunity cost of capital (10.85 per cent). In 1995-96 the situation appears to have improved with the CRR of 7 per cent if we take 12.5 as the opportunity cost of capital in 1995-96 and 8 per cent if we take old figure for the cost of capital (Table 5.12).

Table 5.11 : Estimated Subsidies Given to Non-Departmental Undertakings in Different States — 1993-94

State	Amount invested (Equity Loans (Rs. Crores)	Cost of Capital invested (Rs. Crores)	Dividend/ Interest received (Rs. Crores)	Implicit subsidy (Rs. Crores)	Recovery Rate (%)	PSUs subsidy as % of NSDP
(1)	(2)	(3)	(4)	(5)	(6)	(7)
1. Andhra Pradesh	1231	136	45.60	90.04	33.63	0.19
2. Bihar	578	54	0.09	53.91	0.17	0.16
3. Goa	92	61	0.39	60.61	0.64	4.19
4. Gujarat	3026	328	21.26	306.74	6.48	0.93
5. Haryana	1428	166	0.95	165.05	0.57	0.92
6. Karnataka	1475	165	4.67	160.33	2.82	0.49
7. Kerala	762	88	3.91	84.09	4.43	0.45
8. Madhya Pradesh	631	63	0.80	62.20	1.27	0.16
9. Maharashtra	1047	123	2.73	120.27	2.21	0.13
10. Orissa	1067	118	0.60	117.40	0.51	0.75
11. Punjab	628	71	3.14	67.86	4.44	0.26
12. Rajasthan	1154	129	5.44	123.56	4.23	0.51
13. Tamil Nadu	690	82	0.80	81.20	9.98	0.19
14. Uttar Pradesh	1692	158	2.66	155.34	1.68	0.22
15. W.Bengal	876	100	1.78	98.22	1.78	0.23
All 15 states	15767	1746	103.73	1642.27	5.94	0.33
Average of all 15 states	1051	116	6.92	109.08	5.94	0.33

Note : Exact totals may not be obtained due to rounding off.

Sources : 1. For column (2), same as Table 5.3.

2. Figures for 1995-96 are from ADB Report on Gujarat's Reform of Public Finances, 1999.
3. Figures in remaining columns are estimated by us, by using Finance Accounts - 1995-96 of Government of Gujarat and various issues of Budget in Brief, GoG.

The overall cost recovery rate of public services is quite poor in spite of the fact that the cost recovery rate of PSUs in Gujarat is much higher as compared to a national rate implies that the improvement of departmental undertakings on margin performance is considerably bad as compared to other states. Thus to come up to the level of at least national average, the state will have to make larger efforts for the improvement of departmental undertakings on margin.

It has been painfully realised at the international as well as national level that small governments are the best governments. The central and the state governments also theoretically accept the idea of the least government intervention which can be measured through the share of taxes in the NSDP. As subsidies are negative indirect taxes, we must also consider their share also to measure the degree of intervention by the government. If we add both these shares, viz. taxes (excluding central taxes) and negative taxes imposed by the state, we find that it turns out to be almost one-fourth of NSDP (Table 5.13). This indicates the degree of the state's intervention. There are some fluctuation between 1993-94 and 1998-99, but the share has remained more than 22 per cent always (If one considers the central taxes outside the budget subsidies the share will still go up). It is only in 1999-2000 (BE) that the state envisages reduction by 2 per cent points over the earlier years. This is certainly a movement in the right direction (Table 5.13).

V. Summary and Policy Implications

Gujarat is among the highest taxed states in India. Whereas in terms of non-tax revenue (NTR) per head of population it ranks among the lowest.

The share of NTR in the state's own revenue has remained about 25 per cent, which is lower than observed in other richer states. Growth and buoyancy of NTR also show deceleration between the pre-reform and reform periods. In Gujarat the lower proportion of NTR is attributed to less than 15 per cent contribution of revenue generated out of all publicly provided economic and social services (exclusive of income from non-ferrous minerals). This, in turn, is attributed to low and obsolete users charges, poor recovery of prices, widening gap between effective price (P*) to public and actual price P fixed by the government arising due to 'E' factor mentioned in the paper. Due to this the burden of implicit subsidies, which are more distortionary in nature is higher than explicit subsidies. Estimates of total subsidies (explicit + implicit) based on the Budget

Table 5.12 : Subsidies to Non-Departmental Undertakings in Gujarat by Economic and Social Sectors 1995-96

Item	Social Sector		Economic Sector		All Sectors		All sectors subsidies at the rate (10.85 used in 1993-94)*	
	Amount in Rs. Crores	As % of NSDP	Amount in Rs. Crores	As % of NSDP	Amount	As % of NSDP	Amount	As % of NSDP
(1)	(2)	(3)	(4)	(5)	(6)	(7)	(8)	(9)
A. Amount invested								
(Equity + Loans)	202.34	0.35	3924.54	6.78	4126.88	7.13	4126.88	7.13
B. Cost of Capital Invested	25.29	0.04	490.57	0.85	515.86	0.89	447.77	0.77
C. Dividend/Interest	2.16	0.004	34.46	0.06	36.62	0.06	36.62	0.06
D. Subsidy (B-C)	23.13	0.036	456.11	0.79	479.24	0.83	411.15	0.71
E. Cost Recovery Rate (%)	8.53	—	7.02	—	710	—	8.18	—

Note : (*) The estimates of PSUs and cost recovery rates are based on the cost of capital assumed to be 10.85 per cent on total stock of capital in NIPFP Discussion paper, 1997. Since the state's borrowing went up since then with a more difficult terms, i.e high interest rate the new rate (1995-96) turns out to be 12.49 per cent. Estimates in columns (1) to (7) are based on this rate.

Source : ADB's Report on Gujarat's Reform of Public Finances, 1999.

Table 5.13 : Degree of the State's Intervention

Items	1993-94	1995-96	1996-97	1997-98	1998-99	1999-2000
(1)	(2)	(3)	(4)	(5)	(6)	(7)
1. Own Tax Collection	10.05	9.20	9.07	8.75	9.44	9.31
2. Subsidies	15.69	13.89	13.70	15.54	15.21	13.26
Total	25.74	23.09	22.70	24.29	24.65	22.57

Note : RE = Revised Estimates BE = Budget Estimates

Sources : 1. Estimates for1994-95 are taken from the same source as given in Table 5.3.

2. Figures for 1995-96 are taken from the ADB Report on Gujarat's Reform of Public Finances, 1999.
3. Estimates for 1996-2000 are made by us using the budget data and Finance Accounts of Government of Gujarat 1995-96.

Approach show that per capita subsidies in Gujarat were highest (1993-94) and has grown to almost double in 1998-99. Out of these the proportion of merit subsidies is quite small as compared to non-merit subsidies. Between the two sectors, viz. social and economic, the subsidies flowing to the former are less than 50 per cent of the total subsidies. Subsidies given in Gujarat are comparatively high on account of lower revenue receipts for a given cost of capital. This is indicated by the low (2.21 per cent) and declining cost-recovery rate of almost all sectors except irrigation and transport. The low recovery rate of 2.21 per cent on all public services in the state is quite low compared to national average of 10 per cent and 14 per cent rate achieved by Haryana. The degree of intervention measured through the sum of positive tax NSDP ratio and negative tax (i.e. subsidies) NSDP was almost 25 per cent of NSDP in 1993-94, which has marginally declined during the later years but still higher than 20 per cent. Thus, the so-called New Economic Reforms initiated by the centre and the state show no impact on these fiscal parameters. The recovery rate of non-departmental undertakings in Gujarat is considerably higher (6.48 per cent) than the national average and still improving. This further proves that performance of departmental undertakings is pathetic in absolute sense as well as in relation to other states. To improve this situation upward revision in users charges, reduction of political interference, incentives to the departments by rechanneling a part of income earned by them as an incentive are called forth by giving priority.

The fact that Gujarat has poor recovery rate of almost all major social and economic services may also be viewed as a good future opportunities *inter alia* challenges, to mobilize considerable amount of revenue resources. In order to evince this we have generated the estimates of potential revenue at 1998-99 level (Table 5.14). We have generated two sets of estimates by selecting the most potent sub-sectors providing social and economic services. For the first set of estimates, we considered the states' average cost recovery rates for 1993-94 for the selected services and multiplied them with the corresponding total costs of these services of 1998-99. This would give us an idea that even if the state of Gujarat achieves only the average performance level of all the states in terms of cost recovery, by how much the revenue would increase at 1998-99 cost level. The second set of estimates, which we consider as optimum in relation to given circumstances, is prepared by taking the maximum cost recovery rates achieved by certain states in 1993-94. That is, we are not considering the theoretically best performance for the government supplied services but are considering those values which are already achieved by one or the other Indian states in 1993-94. To generate the best or optimum revenue estimates these rates are multiplied by the corresponding total costs of public services in 1998-99[4]. Columns 7 and 8 present the two sets of estimates of revenue receipts from these services for 1998-99. The results show that even if Gujarat reaches the level of average performance of the states in each service considered above, it can generate Rs.890 crores by way of revenue receipts from these services, the amount which is higher than the 1998-99 (RE) figure, i.e. actual performance by Rs.642 crores. This is close to what was also estimated by GFC (1994). If we consider the set of estimates (column 8 of Table 5.14) based on the best achieved recovery rates of different states the potential revenue comes to a startling figure of Rs.3371 crores. This is higher than the currently expected figure of revenue receipts from these services to the government by Rs.3122 crores for 1998-99. This can reduce the fiscal crisis of the state quite considerably because for 1998-99 the extent of revenue deficit and fiscal deficit is quite high (Budget in Brief, GoG, 1999-2000). The figure of fiscal deficit (based on RE) is as high as 5.5 per cent of NSDP, which is higher by about 3 percentage points than the targeted figure of the state and also prescribed by the ADB. This may be interpreted as the situation of severe fiscal imbalance, which can be corrected if the revenue potential shown in column 8 is achieved through

Table 5.14 : Cost Recovery Rates in Socio-Economic Services and Potential for Revenue Generation in Gujarat

(Rs. Crores)

Sector	Cost Recovery Rates (CRR) (in %)				Actual and Potential Revenue Receipt in Gujarat 1998-99 Based on		
	Existing Rates in Gujarat (1998-99(RE)	Average of 15 Major States (1993-94)	Maximum Achieved by States (1993-94)	Total Cost of Services in Gujarat 1998-99 (Rs. Crores)	Existing CRR	Average CRR of Fourteen States	Maximum CRR in States
Education	0.69	1.06	2.56 (Haryana)	3186	22	34	82
Health	1.56	1.55	2.86 (West Bengal)	925	14	14	26
Water & Sanitation	0.83	5.27	15.55 (Maharashtra)	1109	9	58	172
Agriculture	5.12	14.15	40.46 (Maharashtra)	806	41	114	326
Irrigation	5.91	4.02	9.47 (Uttar Pradesh)	2608	154	154*	247
Power	0.07	14.99	71.46 (Andhra Pradesh)	2736	2	410	1955

(Contd.)

Table 5.14 *(Contd.)*

Sector	Cost Recovery Rates (CRR) (in %)				Actual and Potential Revenue Receipt in Gujarat 1998-99 Based on		
	Existing Rates in Gujarat (1998-99(RE)	Average of 15 Major States (1993-94)	Maximum Achieved by States (1993-94)	Total Cost of Services in Gujarat 1998-99 (Rs. Crores)	Existing CRR	Average CRR of Fourteen States	Maximum CRR in States
Industries	1.39	5.85	11.45 (Karnataka)	316	4	27	36
Transport	0.38	9.60	63.01 (Haryana)	836	3	80	527
Total of above sectors	—	—	—	12522	249	891	3371

Notes : * Since CRR of irrigation in Gujarat for 1998-99 is higher than the individual performance of all states in 1993-94, we have taken that as an ideal or best achieved CRR for calculating the potential revenue.

The cost recovery rate of power in Goa is still high (96%) but we have not considered as it is a small state whose population is less than 10 per cent of the total population.

Sources 1. Estimates for1994-95 are taken from the same source as given in Table 5.2.

2. Figures for 1995-96 are taken from the ADB Report on Gujarat is Reform of Public Finances, 1999.

3. Estimates for 1996-2000 are made by us using the budget data and Finance Accounts of Government of Gujarat 1995-96.

revision of tariff rates and/or incentives to state undertakings. The estimates suggest that the state can bring down its fiscal deficit to only 1.9 per cent of NSDP from 5.5 per cent by setting and achieving the targets of cost recovery rates shown in column 6 of Table 5.14. Putting it in an alternative way the state can keep the target of reducing the fiscal deficit to 2.5 per cent level as it desires and still be left with the revenue of about Rs.1000 crores which increases its manoeuvr ability with respect to other instruments and steps like tax restructuring and rationalisation to reduce the distortions. Even with the achievement of the average rates the state can reduce its fiscal deficit (1998-99 level) by 0.75 percentage points. This is the significance of the so-called insignificance non-tax revenue in Gujarat.

NOTES

1. Social services include education, health, housing, water supply and sanitation, nutrition, etc. Economic services include agriculture and allied services, transport,industries, power, irrigation, civil supplies, soil and water conservation, road and birdges and so on (NIPFP Discussion Paper, 1997).
2. Elementary education, public health, sewerage and sanitation, welfare of SC and ST, nutrition are all defined as merit social goods. Thus higher education, family welfare, water supply, etc. are put into non-merit, social goods category. Similarly, economic expenditure on social and water conservation, environment, flood, roads and bridges are taken as merit-economic goods and rest as non-merit economic goods.
3. FC = Nominal depreciation rate considered here is long-term average rate of inflation plus 2 per cent real rate of depreciation (7.39 per cent + 2 per cent).

   Rate of interest on locked up capital is the average rate of interest paid by the government in the last few years.

   RR here includes receipts from the fees and users charges from various social and economic services only, hence is lower than entire NTR which also includes other items including those relating to general services.
4. Though Budget estimate for 1999-2000 are available, we would like to use revised estimates for 1998-99 as the former are showing the intensions and the latter the most likely achievements.

REFERENCES

Dholakia, Archana (1998a), "Growth and Structure of Tax and Non-Tax Revenue of Gujarat", *Indian Journal of Regional Science*, Vol. 30, No.1.

Dholakia, Archana (1999), "Role of the Centre in Fiscal Balance of States - A Case of Gujarat", appearing in *Journal of the Indian School of Political Economy*, April-June, 1999.

Dholakia, Archana, (1998), "Changes in the Trends and Structure of Fiscal Expenditure in Gujarat", *Anvesak*, Vol. 28, No.1, January-June.

Government of Gujarat (1994), Report of the Gujarat State Finance Commission, (Chairman: Shri Sanat Mehta), April.

Government of Gujarat, An Economic and Purpose Classification of the Budget, Annual Publication.

Government of Gujarat, Budget in Brief - Gujarat State: Budget Publication, Annual Publication.

Government of Gujarat, February (1997), Finance Accounts, 1995-96.

Government of India (1997), Government Subsidies in India, Discussion paper, Ministry of Finance, May.

Government of India (1994), Report of the Tenth Finance Commission, (Chairman: K.C. Pant) December.

NIPFP (1997), Government Subsidies in India, a Discussion paper submitted to Department of Economic Affairs, Ministry of Finance, GOI, March.

Rao, G. and Mundle, S. (1992), *An analysis of Changes in State Government Subsidies : 1977-87*, in Bagdri, A., *et al.* (ed), NIPFP, Delhi.

Report of the Asian Development Bank on "Gujarat's Reform of Public Finances, Vol. I, Parts B and C., February, 1999.

Reserve Bank of India (1998), *Reserve Bank of India Bulletin*, Supplement on Finances of State Governments, 1997-98.

6

Recent Changes in Industrial Economy of Gujarat

Issues and Evidences

DINESH N. AWASTHI

Introduction

Gujarat, the second most industrialised state in the country, has also emerged as the second most import investment destination, only next to Maharashtra.[1] It is claimed that Gujarat has achieved this spectacular success because of its entrepreneurial endowment, progressive policies and political will of the government (irrespective of the political party in power), proactive and efficient bureaucracy, conducive industrial relations, relatively well-developed infrastructure and its industrial structure. The state has responded well to the economic reforms sweeping the country. Consistent with the policies of the government of India, it also undertook a serious exercise in economic reforms by setting up State Finance Commission in 1992, which gave an 'Agenda for Reform' to the government. Its recommendations were accepted not only by the government, but also by all the political parties cutting across the party lines.[2] This kind of stability in policy formulation and execution has helped Gujarat a great deal in generating confidence among investors. Several changes have taken place in the policy framework as well as industrial environment, especially after 1991, in Gujarat. It is, therefore, only prudent to have a closer look at the trends and pattern of industrialisation in the state in the last 10 years.

How the Gujarat Economy has Performed in Response to Economic Liberalisation

In the decade before liberalisation, the economy of Gujarat grew at a rate lower than the national average. The average annual growth rate of net state domestic product (NSDP) of Gujarat in the post-liberalisation period (1990-91 to 1995-96) was around 6.0 per cent compared to the corresponding rate of 5.6 per cent between 1985-86 and 1990-91. It was the case with the per capita NSDP also. It may also be noted that per capita NSDP in Gujarat was almost 20 per cent higher than the national average during 1995-96. As a result, with Rs.3172 per capita NSDP, it improved its position from 9th in 1990-91 to 5th in 1995-96 at all India level (Table 6.1).

Manufacturing Sector—The Engine of Growth

The share of manufacturing sector in NSDP has continued to grow over time, compared to agriculture or other sectors of the state economy. Its share in NSDP increased from 20.68 per cent in 1980-81 to 33.81 per cent in 1995-96. It has grown at an annual average rate of 11.56 per cent during the decade 1985-95, compared to 1.55 per cent in the case of agriculture and 8.26 per cent in the case of other sectors. The overall state economy grew at an average annual rate of 7.30 per cent (Table 6.2).

Compared to all India average, the manufacturing sector in Gujarat has grown at a faster pace. The share of manufacturing sector (33.8 per cent) in Gujarat's NSDP is also higher than its share (27.7 per cent) in the NNDP at all India level. The state has also improved its relative rank from 4th in 1980-81 to 1st in 1990-91 at all India level. Since 1990-91, it is number one in terms of contribution of manufacturing sector to NSDP among various states. During the post-liberalisation period (1990-91 to 1995-96) also, it registered a 10.70 per cent average annual rate of growth, compared to 6.90 per cent for all India (Table 6.3).

Gujarat has a significant share in the factory sector also at the national level. With only about five per cent population of the country, Gujarat accounts for 9.8 per cent of employment and 11.40 per cent value added generated in the factory sector at all India level (Table 6.4). This puts Gujarat as industrially second most developed state, next to Maharashtra.

It tops the other states in terms of its share in gross output of gas and steam (51.6 per cent of all India) and wool, silk and synthetic fibres (19.5 per cent). It has improved its share in chemical products and accounts

Table 6.1 : Share of the State Domestic Product of Gujarat in all India Net Domestic Product (At Factor Cost)

(Rs. Crore at 1980-81 Prices)

			Gujarat			All India	
Sr. No.	Years	UNIT	NSDP	NSDP: PC	Rank	NDP	NDP-PC
1.	**1980-81**						
	NSDP	Rs. crore	6541	1940	8	110340	1625
	State Share in NDP	%	5.9				
2.	**1985-86**						
	NSDP	Rs. crore	8124	2186	8	140226	1857
	State Share in NDP	%	5.9	NA		NA	NA
	Change over1980-81	%	5.1	2.5		5.4	2.9
3.	**1990-91**						
	NSDP	Rs. crore	10915	2659	9	190218	2267
	State Share in NDP	%	5.7	NA		NA	NA
	Change over1985-86	%	6.9	4.3		7.1	4.4
4.	**1995-96**						
	NSDP	Rs. crore	14211	3172	5	243617	2648
	State Share in NDP	%	5.8	NA		NA	NA
	Change over1990-91	%	6.0	3.8		5.6	3.4

Source : Based on *EPW* Research Foundation, National Accounts Statistics of India : 1950-51 to 1995-96 (Revised Edition), Bombay, Sameeksha Trust, October 1997.

Table 6.2 : Shift in Sectoral Composition of the NSDP in Gujarat

(Value in Rs. Crore)

Years	Agriculture		Manufacturing		Others		All Sectors	
	Values	% Share	Values	% Share	Values	% Share	Values	% Share
1980 - 81								
NSDP Values	2434	37.18	1354	20.68	2759	42.14	6547	100.00
1985 - 86								
NSDP Values	2277	27.72	2228	27.12	3709	45.15	8214	100.00
% change over 80-81	(-)1.30		12.90		6.90		5.10	
1990 -91								
NSDP Values	2715	24.88	3128	28.66	5071	46.46	10914	100.00
% change over 85-86	3.80		8.10		7.30		6.60	
1995 - 96								
NSDP Values	2630	18.51	4804	33.81	6776	47.68	14210	100.00
% change over 90-91	(-)0.60		9.90		6.00		6.04	
Annual Avg.Gr.Rate (1985-86 to 1995-96)	1.55		11.56		8.26		7.30	

Source : Based on *EPW* Research Foundation, National Accounts Statistics of India : 1950-51 to 1995-96 (Revised Edition), Bombay, Sameeksha Trust, October, 1997.

Table 6.3 : The Share of Manufacturing Sector in the Net State Domestic Product of Gujarat and in All India Net Domestic Product (At Factor Cost)

(Rs. Crore at 1980-81 Prices)

Sr. No.	Years	UNIT	Gujarat Mfg. NSDP	Gujarat Share*	Rank	All India Mfg. NDP	All India Share
1	**1980-81**						
	NSDP from Manufacturing	Rs. crore	1354	20.7	4	18698	16.9
	State Share in NDP	%	7.2				
2	**1985-86**						
	NSDP from Manufacturing	Rs. crore	2228	27.1	3	26413	18.8
	Change over1980-81	%	12.9			8.3	
	State Share in NDP	%	8.4				
3	**1990-91**						
	NSDP from Manufacturing	Rs. crore	3128	28.1	1	39408	20.7
	Change over1985-86	%	8.1			9.8	
	State Share in NDP	%	7.9				
4	**1995-96**						
	NSDP from Manufacturing	Rs. crore	4804	33.81	1	52969	21.7
	Change over1990-91	%	10.7			6.9	
	State Share in NDP	%	9.1				

*Share of manufacturing in NSDP/NDP.

Source : Based on *EPW* Research Foundation, National Accounts Statistics of India: 1950-51 to 1995-96 (Revised Edition), Bombay, Sameeksha Trust, October, 1997.

Table 6.4: Relative Position of Gujarat in Factory Sector at All India Level from 1980-81 to 1994-95

Sr.	Variable	Gujarat		Andhra Pradesh		Karnataka		Maharashtra		Tamil Nadu		All India	
No.	Year	Value	%	Value	%	Value	%	Value	%	Value	%	Value	%
1.	**Number of Factories**												
	1980-81	10208	10.6	11155	11.6	5381	5.6	15576	16.1	10292	10.7	96563	100.00
	1985-86	10305	10.2	12746	12.6	5456	5.4	14970	14.8	12429	12.3	101016	100.00
	1990-91	10943	9.9	15205	13.8	5911	5.4	15595	14.2	14617	13.3	110179	100.00
	1994-95	12034	9.8 (4)*	16616	13.5(3)	6184	5.0(8)	17763	14.4(2)	18755	15.2(1)	123010	100.00
2.	**Invested Capital (Rs. crore)**												
	1980-81	4398	9.4	27246	5.9	2064	4.4	8318	17.2	3864	8.3	46881	100.00
	1985-86	8257	9.4	5517	6.3	3694	4.2	14782	16.8	8335	9.5	88112	100.00
	1990-91	18696	9.6	20361	10.4	7862	4	35399	18.2	17700	9.1	194913	100.00
	1994-95	38578	10	33489	8.6(5)	15633	4.0(9)	66837	17.2(1)	40005	10.3	387535	100.00
3.	**Number of Employees**												
	1980-81	699427	9.1	666150	8.6	396236	5.1	1337718	17.3	794993	10.3	7714679	100.00
	1985-86	665746	8.9	660482	8.8	376197	5	1199825	16	856217	11.5	7471515	100.00
	1990-91	675448	8.3	832120	10.2	418955	5.1	1239152	15.2	962589	11.8	8162504	100.00
	1994-95	782908	8.5(4)	1070762	11.5(2)	473134	5.1(7)	133187	14.5(1)	1166330	12.6(2)	9227097	100.00
4.	**Net Value Added**												
	1980-81	1139	9.5	584	4.9	603	5.1	2986	25	1229	10.3	11930	100.00
	1985-86	2152	9.2	1262	5.4	1172	5	6022	25.8	2402	10.3	23266	100.00
	1990-91	4468	8.67	2981	5.8	2769	5.4	12004	23.3	5793	11.2	51515	100.00
	1994-95	12359	11.4(2)	7609	7.0(5)	5906	5.4(7)	23881	22	11698	10.8	108517	100.00

* Figures within the parenthesis are the rank of Gujarat in all India.

Source: Government of India, Annual Survey of Industries: Summary Results for Factory Sector (Various Volumes), New Delhi, Central Statistical Organisation.

for almost a quarter of the country's gross output. The other sectors, where it is one of the three major contributing states, are cotton textiles (11.91 per cent) rubber, plastic, petroleum and coal products (12.90 per cent), metal products (10.1 per cent) and non-metallic mineral products (11.2 per cent).[3] It has, however, lost its position to other states as far as machinery and machine tools, other industries, electricity, food products and repair services are concerned. It held third place till 1985-86 in machinery and machine tools (9.30 per cent), other industries (9.7 per cent) and electricity (8.9 per cent). In repair services, Gujarat was the top most contributor with about 15.20 per cent gross output. However, within a span of five years, it lost its position to other states (Table 6.5).

Table 6.5 : Share of Gujarat in Industries in which its Contribution in Gross Output is Among the Top Three States in the Country*

Sr. No.	Industry Sectors	1985-86		1990-91		1994-95	
		Share	Rank	Share	Rank	Share	Rank
1.	Cotton Textiles	21.60	2	16.60	2	11.90	3
2.	Wool, Silk & Synthetic Fibers	25.00	2	21.60	1	19.50	1
3.	Rubber, Plastic, Petroleum & Coal	11.80	3	0.00	NA	12.90	3
4.	Chemical Products	22.40	2	21.50	2	24.70	2
5.	Metal Products	9.00	2	10.60	2	10.10	2
6.	Machinery and Machine Tools	9.30	3	0.00	NA	0.00	NA
7.	Other Industries	9.70	3	0.00	NA	0.00	NA
8.	Electricity	8.90	3	0.00	NA	0.00	NA
9.	Repair Services	11.50	3	15.20	1	0.00	NA
10.	Food Products	0.00	NA	0.00	3	0.00	NA
11.	Non-Metallic Mineral Products	0.00	NA	0.00	3	11.20	3
12.	Gas and Steam	0.00	NA	0.00	1	51.60	1

* Zero values of gross output indicate that Gujarat is not among the top three producers of that particular product. It does not mean that this industry sector does not exist in Gujarat.

Industrial Composition

Gujarat's industrial structure is dominated by 10 major groups which account for over 80 per cent of the number of factories, about 97 per cent of fixed capital investment, 92 per cent of gross output and 86 per cent employment in factory sector. Among these top ten sectors, chemical sector with almost 30 per cent share dominates in terms of output (factory sector in 1994-95, the latest year for which data are available from Annual Survey of Industries). It is followed by food-products (10.84 per cent); rubber, plastic, petroleum and coal (10.48 per cent); electricity (9.01 per cent); machinery and machine tools (8.45 per cent), wool, synthetic fibres (6.76 per cent); cotton textiles (6.11 per cent); basic metal and alloys (5.01 per cent); non-metallic mineral products (3.33 per cent); and paper and papers products (2.09 per cent). The textile sector, which dominated during the sixties, no more holds the sway in terms of either output or investment or number of factories. Nevertheless, it still remains the second most important sector in terms of employment, followed by machinery and machine tools (11.20 per cent); and wool, silk and synthetic fibres (9.83 per cent). In terms of number of factories, machinery and machine tools dominate the scene with almost 16 per cent share indicating a major share of small-scale firms in this sector. It is closely followed by non-metallic mineral products (12.02 per cent) and only then comes chemical and chemical products with about 11.87 per cent share (Table 6.6).

There has, however, been a significant shift in the industrial structure of Gujarat during the decade 1985-95 in favour of chemical and chemical products sector. Its share in gross output increased by about 3 per cent (from 26.75 per cent to 29.79 per cent) during the decade. On the other hand, textiles lost their share heavily, which shrank from 12.04 per cent in 1985-86 to 6.11 per cent in 1994-95. Major gainers were food products (from 9.80 per cent to 10.84 per cent), electricity (6.47 per cent to 9.01 per cent), machinery and machine tools (7.52 per cent to 8.45 per cent) paper and paper products (1.81 per cent to 2.09 per cent) and non-metallic mineral products (Table 6.6). Main losers in terms of gross output, besides textiles, were rubber, plastic, petroleum and coal products (13.12 per cent to 10.48 per cent), wool, silk and synthetic fibres (8.15 per cent to 6.76 per cent) and basic metal and alloys (5.28 per cent to 5.01 per cent).

Trends in Industrial Investments in Medium and Large Industries

Another indicator of Gujarat's vibrant response to new economic environment is that investments in its medium and large-scale sector grew at a much higher rate during the first five years of post-liberalisation (1990-91 to 1995-96) compared to the five years of pre-liberalisation period

Table 6.6 : Contribution of Top Ten Industry Sectors to the Industrial Sector of Gujarat from (1985-86 to 1994-95)

Industry Group	Number of Units			Fixed Capital Investment			Gross Output			Employment		
	1985-86	1990-91	1994-95	1985-86	1990-91	1994-95	1985-86	1990-91	1994-95	1985-86	1990-91	1994-95
1. Chemical & chemical prod.	1036	1163	1429	1939.37	5104.69	9840.38	3590.91	7127.64	16824.58	84651	95976	136678
2. Rubber,plastic,petro.&coal	516	662	701	130.09	662.06	1742.2	1760.64	2708.98	5916.13	14820	21408	28256
3. Cotton textiles	1037	964	770	462.77	580.77	1264.96	1616.27	2354.01	3452.98	159784	132667	105218
4. Food products	942	1036	1051	185.31	361.26	853.56	1315.51	3509.79	6121.43	64953	69918	70343
5. Wool, silk,syṇhetic fibres	526	667	1005	333.96	807.89	1541.21	1093.51	2211.71	3815.83	55504	64757	76998
6. Basic metal and alloys	692	730	830	156.85	189.32	1319.59	708.84	1490.99	2828.97	33217	25516	30665
7. Electricity	5	2	5	1338.73	3768.73	6915.4	868.78	3163.77	5085.6	37373	41642	50491
8. Machinery & machine tools	1646	1750	1917	236.94	614.71	1499.81	1008.82	2617.82	4770.83	71179	77449	87666
9. Non-metallic mineral products	1337	1316	1446	280.17	588.81	1583.38	434.25	914.88	1879.94	58757	53574	53075
10. Paper and paper products	401	505	500	79.37	190.12	423.94	242.31	646.33	1180.79	17595	19088	23243
TOTAL OF THE TOP TEN	8138	8795	9654	5143.56	12868.36	26984.43	12639.84	26745.92	51877.08	597833	601995	672633
ALL INDUSTRIES	10305	10943	12034	5310.47	13098.68	27912.47	13423.74	27592.27	56469.26	678965	688734	732905
PERCENTAGE SHARES OF DIFFERENT SECTORS												
1. Chemical and chemical prod.	10.05	10.63	11.87	36.52	38.97	35.25	26.75	25.83	29.79	12.47	13.94	17.46
2. Rubber, plastic, petro. & coal	5.01	6.05	5.83	2.45	5.05	6.24	13.12	9.82	10.48	2.18	3.11	3.61
3. Cotton textiles	10.06	8.81	6.40	8.71	4.43	4.53	12.04	8.53	6.11	23.53	19.26	13.44
4. Food products	9.14	9.47	8.73	3.49	2.76	3.06	9.80	12.72	10.84	9.57	10.15	8.98

(Contd.)

Table 6.6 *(Contd.)*

Industry Group	Number of Units			Fixed Capital Investment			Gross Output			Employment		
	1985-86	1990-91	1994-95	1985-86	1990-91	1994-95	1985-86	1990-91	1994-95	1985-86	1990-91	1994-95
5. Wool, silk,synhetic fibres	5.10	6.10	8.35	6.29	6.17	5.52	8.15	8.02	6.76	8.17	9.40	9.83
6. Basic metal and alloys	6.72	6.67	6.90	2.95	1.45	4.73	5.28	5.40	5.01	4.89	3.70	3.92
7. Electricity	0.05	0.02	0.04	25.21	28.77	24.78	6.47	11.47	9.01	5.50	6.05	6.45
8. Machinery & machine tools	15.97	15.99	15.93	4.46	4.69	5.37	7.52	9.49	8.45	10.48	11.25	11.20
9. Non-metallic mineral products	12.97	12.03	12.02	5.28	4.50	5.67	3.23	3.32	3.33	8.65	7.78	8.06
10. Paper and paper products	3.89	4.61	4.15	1.49	1.45	1.52	1.81	2.34	2.09	2.59	2.77	2.97
TOTAL OF THE TOP TEN	78.97	80.37	80.22	96.86	98.24	96.68	94.16	96.93	91.87	88.05	87.41	85.92
ALL INDUSTRIES	100.00	100.00	100.00	100.00	100.00	100.00	100.00	100.00	100.00	100.00	100.00	100.00

(1985-90). Within the manufacturing sector, major contribution to growth has come from medium and large industries during the post-liberalisation period. On the basis of data collected from District Industries Centres (DICs), we worked out rates of growth of industries in Gujarat for number of factories, employment and investment, separately for small, medium and large as well as the factory sectors. Table 6.7 presents the annual compound rates of growth for these sectors for the years 1985-86 to 1990-91, 1990-91 to 1995-96 and 1985-86 to 1995-96. As can be seen from the Table, the overall industrial growth (factory sector) in Gujarat, in terms of investment, employment and number of factories, was significantly higher during the five years of post-liberalisation (1991-96) compared to the corresponding period before liberalisation. Another important point to note is that medium and large industry sector grew at a significantly high rate (23.38 per cent) than the small industries sector, which registered only 13.22 per cent rate of growth per annum during the post-liberalisation period. Before 1991, investments in both the segments grew almost at the same rate at around 14.50 per cent.

Table 6.7 : Inter-Scalar Growth of Industrial Sectors in Gujarat

(Annual Compound Rate of Growth in %)

Sr. No.	Sectors	Years 1985-86 to 1990-91	1990-91 to 1995-96	1985-86 to 1995-96
		Growth in Number of Factories		
1.	Small-Scale Sector	9.48	8.26	8.87
2.	Medium & Large Sector	10.55	14.45	12.48
3.	Factory Sector (1+2)	9.49	8.32	8.9
		Growth in Investment		
1.	Small-Scale Sector	14.15	13.22	13.68
2.	Medium & Large Sector	14.58	23.38	18.90
3.	Factory Sector (1+2)	14.52	22.08	18.24
		Growth in Employment		
1.	Small-Scale Sector	7.79	7.32	7.55
2.	Medium & Large Sector	10.31	12.14	11.22
3.	Factory Sector (1+2)	8.40	8.61	8.50

Note: Based on Data collected from DICs.

This is also reflected in the trend observed in medium and large projects being executed in Gujarat. The post-liberalisation period witnessed five-fold growth in the number of projects sanctioned and over three and half times increase in the projects commissioned, compared to 1983-90. Similar trends were witnessed in investment and employment (Table 6.8). Same trend is observed from the data on investment proposals filed for setting up ventures in Gujarat. Both in terms of the number of IEMs and investment, Gujarat had a significant share at all India level, touching even 26 per cent of the total national investment in 1995 (Table 6.9).

Table 6.8 : Industrial Investments in Gujarat in Medium and Large Industries

Status	From 1-1-83 to 31-12-90	From 1-1-91 to 30-4-96	Percentage Increase
A. Projects Sanctioned			
1. Number of Projects	886	4423	
2. Annual Average No. of Projects	110.75	829.83	649.25
3. Investment (Rs. crore)	21378	170169	
4. Average Annual Investment	2672.25	31926.64	1094.85
5. Employment Potential	141637	843673	
6. Average Annual Employment	17704	158287.61	794.07
B. Projects Commissioned			
1. Number of Projects	328	1182	
2. Annual Average No. of Projects	41	221.76	440.87
3. Investment (Rs. crore)	4760	14923	
4. Average Annual Investment	595	2799.8	470.55
5. Employment Potential	47788	199353	
6. Average Annual Employment	5973.5	37402.1	426.18
C. Projects Under Implementation			
1. Number of Projects	52	2852	
2. Annual Average No. of Projects	6.51	535.08	6130.2
3. Investment (Rs. crore)	5260	124903	
4. Average Annual Investment	670	23433.9	3497.46
5. Employment Potential	9044	418160	
6. Average Annual Employment	1130.5	78454.1	694.28

Source : INDEXTb.

Table 6.9 : Progress of Investment Proposals Filed Through IEMS for Gujarat (August 1991 to January, 1998)

Year	Gujarat		India		% Share of Gujarat	
	Projects (Nos.)	Investment (Rs. cr)	Projects (Nos.)	Investment (Rs. cr.)	Projects (Nos.)	Investment (Rs. cr)
1991	292	8224	3084	76310	9.46	10.78
1992	809	20545	4860	115872	16.64	10.73
1993	589	10627	4456	63976	13.32	16.61
1994	756	20311	4664	88771	16.21	22.89
1995	1113	33784	6502	125509	17.12	26.92
1996	694	16228	4825	73278	14.38	22.15
1997	116	1625	1016	10645	11.42	15.27
1998	322	122194	3329	1241419	9.67	9.84
TOTAL	4691	233538	32736	1795780	14.33	13.00

Sources : 1. Upto 1997, Industries Commissionerate, Gandhinagar, 1997.
2. For 1998, CMIE, Survey of Investment Projects - Overview, Mumbai, Centre for Monitoring Indian Economy, February, 1998.

Tables 6.10 and 6.11 present relative share of Gujarat in investments in the projects under implementation and already commissioned during 1996-98. During all the years Gujarat has maintained its lead over other states in terms of investments in pipeline as reflected by projects under implementation. However, it lost to Orissa, Maharashtra and Tamil Nadu by a very narrow margin in 1998, when compared with the commissioned projects (Gujarat, 9.84 per cent; Tamil Nadu, 10.01 per cent; Maharashtra, 10.22 per cent and Orissa 10.44 per cent). Nevertheless, if one looks at the distribution of IEMs and investment sanctioned during the months of March and November 1997, it is clear that it still maintains the lead with about 20 per cent share in investment (Table 6.12).

Sectoral Allocation of Investments

It is worth noticing that investments are primarily coming in the manufacturing sector in Gujarat with a share of over 51 per cent, followed by infrastructure (46.70 per cent). The corresponding figures for Maharashtra are 39.36 per cent and 68.34 per cent; and for Karnataka the percentages are 38.67 and 60.50 (Table 6.13). In a way, it is encouraging that it is the manufacturing sector investment in Gujarat, which could lead to growth in a shorter duration than the infrastructural investments that have longer gestation period. But from the point of long term sustainability of economic growth, and in particular industrial growth, it may be pragmatic to attract more investments in infrastructure.

Table 6.10 : Trends in Investment by States
(Projects Under Implementation)

(Value Rs.in Crore)

Sr. No.	States	Nov. 1995		Nov. 1996		Nov. 1997	
		Value	%	Value	%	Value	%
1.	Gujarat	65151	17.17	73273	16.51	76253	14.26
2.	Maharashtra	43195	11.39	50936	11.47	57966	10.84
3.	Uttar Pradesh	37366	9.85	38973	8.78	35897	6.71
4.	Karnataka	25369	6.69	35717	8.05	44561	8.33
5.	Orissa	19018	5.04	16121	3.63	34991	6.54
6.	Tamil Nadu	17712	4.67	21418	4.82	26909	5.03
7.	Other States	171443	45.19	207470	46.74	258228	48.29
	ALL INDIA	379,344	100	443,908	100	534,805	100

Source: CMIE, Survey of Investment Projects—Overview, Bombay, Centre for Monitoring Indian Economy, November 1997.

Table 6.11 : Trends in Investment by States
(Total Investment in Projects Commissioned)

(Value Rs. in Crore)

Sr. No.	States	Oct. 1996		Oct. 1997		Jan. 1998	
		Value	%	Value	%	Value	%
1.	Gujarat (3)	121,802	10.24	127,318	10.17	122,194	9.84
2.	Maharashtra (2)	111,178	9.9	128,737	10.28	126,840	10.22
3.	Uttar Pradesh (6)	83,698	7.45	73,713	5.89	71,764	5.78
4.	Karnataka (5)	113,575	10.11	119,470	9.54	116,974	9.42
5.	Orissa (1)	104,821	9.33	130,078	10.39	129,662	10.44
6.	Tamil Nadu (4)	89,842	8	125,643	10.04	124,210	10.01
7.	Other States	498,533	44.37	546,795	43.69	549,775	44.29
	ALL STATES	1,123,449	100	1,251,756	100	1,241,419	100.00

(Numbers within parantheses are the ranks of the states in 1997).
Source: CMIE, Survey of Investment Projects—Overview, Mumbai, Centre for Monitoring Indian Economy, November 1997.

Table 6.12 : State-wise Distribution of IEMs and Investment
(In the months of March and November, 1997)

Sr.No.	Names of the States	March, 1997				November, 1997			
		IEMs	% Share	Investment	% Share	IEMs	% Share	Investment	% Share
1.	Gujarat	4369	14.86	111396	20.09	4670	14.60	115842	19.62
2.	Maharashtra	5238	17.81	100119	18.06	5583	17.46	104174	17.65
3.	Uttar Pradesh	2897	9.85	53542	9.66	3187	9.97	57861	9.80
4.	Tamil Nadu	2690	9.15	33258	6.00	2933	9.17	38233	6.48
5.	Andhra Pradesh	1904	6.47	43932	7.92	2081	6.51	48512	8.22
6.	Madhya Pradesh	1722	5.86	46494	8.39	1851	5.79	48381	8.19
7.	Karnataka	1050	3.57	26677	4.81	1133	3.54	28990	4.91
8.	West Bengal	1196	4.07	17434	3.14	1344	4.20	18804	3.19
9.	Other States	8341	28.36	121509	21.92	9199	28.76	129587	21.95
	Total	29407	100.00	554361	100.00	31981	100.00	590384	100.00

Source: CMIE, Survey of Investment Projects—Overview, Mumbai, Centre for Monitoring Indian Economy, November, 1997.

Table 6.13 : State-wise Distribution of Total Investment by Major Industry Sub-Groups

(Value in Rs.Crore)

Sr.	States	Manufacturing		Mining		Infrastructure		Total
No.		Value	% & Rank	Value	% & Rank	Value	% & Rank	Percentage
1.	Gujarat	65017	51.06 (1)	2890	2.27 (4)	59411	46.70 (3)	100.00
2.	Maharashtra	37802	39.36 (3)	2959	2.30 (3)	87987	68.34 (1)	100.00
3.	Uttar Pradesh	32667	26.00 (5)	53281	42.41 (1)	39695	31.59 (5)	100.00
4.	Karnataka	46201	38.67 (4)	990	0.83 (5)	72279	60.50 (2)	100.00
5.	Orissa	62757	48.25 (2)	13069	10.05 (2)	54252	41.70 (4)	100.00

Note : Numbers within parentheses are the ranks of the states.

Source : CMIE, Survey of Investment Projects—Overview, Bombay, Centre for Monitoring Indian Economy, November 1997.

Within the manufacturing sector, the investments in Gujarat continue to be heavily concentrated in chemical and petrochemical sector (40.15 per cent), followed by engineering (10.75 per cent), textiles (8.84 per cent) and glass and ceramics (8.33 per cent). A few other important sectors attracting investment are food processing, drugs and pharmaceuticals, electrical and electronics (Table 6.14). Another encouraging fact here is that almost 82 per cent of the investments are committed to those sectors which have high export potential and account for over 45 per cent share of the national export target.

Table 6.14 : Product Group-wise Status of LOI/LOP/IEM for Projects (UI & NIA) as on October 31, 1997

Sr. No.	Product Group	Projects No.	Projects %	Investment Rs. Cr.	Investment %	Employment No.	Employment %
1.	Chemicals & Petrochem.	692	29.70	44904	40.15	111738	28.11
2.	Engineering	320	13.73	12029	10.75	63897	16.08
3.	Textiles	399	17.12	9887	8.84	81811	20.58
4.	Glass & Ceramics	115	4.94	9319	8.33	26175	6.59
5.	Food Processing	195	8.37	2036	1.82	30200	7.60
6.	Drugs & Pharmaceuticals	214	7.18	1515	1.35	23358	5.88
7.	Electrical & Electronics	94	4.03	1322	1.18	13321	3.35
8.	Others	301	12.92	30839	27.57	46933	11.81
	TOTAL	2330	100.00	111851	100.00	397433	100.00

Source: INDEXTb, Monitoring Division, Udyog Bhavan Gandhinagar Gujarat.

Structure of Industrial Growth

Industrial investment in Gujarat, as mentioned earlier, grew at an annual compound rate of 18.24 per cent during 1986-96. However, the growth during 1991-96 (post-liberalisation era) with 22.08 per cent was much higher than 14.52 per cent recorded during 1986-91 (pre-liberalisation period). However, the growth was not evenly spread across various regions of Gujarat, and was rather concentrated in some regions within the state. Since the government of Gujarat has been offering fiscal and financial incentives to divert industrial investments to backward areas, one would expect that such efforts would help in channeling investment into backward talukas.[4] To understand the directional change in investments across 184 talukas comprising Gujarat[5], we worked out the concentration ratios of talukas in investment in Gujarat across sectors over 1986-96.[6]

Table 6.15 provides concentration ratios for the share of 25 top talukas (pooled in groups of five talukas each in serial order beginning from the top) in investment. These talukas account for over three quarters of the share of investment in small-scale sector, 89.02 per cent of medium and large industry sector and about 86 per cent of overall industrial investment in Gujarat even now (in 1996). In 1986, the corresponding figures were 78.69 per cent, 97.67 per cent and 93.41 per cent. The residual investment was spread across all the 159 talukas. Though there appears to be a modest decline in the concentration ratios between 1986 and 1996, even now the first (top) five talukas account for 44.36 per cent of investment in small-scale sector, 61.11 per cent in medium and large and 58.89 per cent of the factory sector. Albeit, a few new (backward) talukas have replaced a few old ones, but only at the margins.

Trends in New Investment Flows Among Talukas in Gujarat

To assess the pattern and trend of new investments flow, we worked out concentration ratios of the new investments for the top 40 talukas in four groups comprising 10 talukas each for the period 1986-91 and 1991-96, for small, medium and large, and factory sectors. These top 40 talukas account for over 97 per cent of the investment in small-scale sector and about 99 per cent of the investments flowing into medium and large-scale sector; irrespective of the periods.[7] The ratios are presented in Table 6.16. The pattern is almost that of the earlier concentration ratios, but with higher intensity. In this case, investments instead of getting dispersed over space have got further concentrated (from 94.25 per cent in 1986-91 to 95.70 per cent between 1991-96, in factory sector). The first 10 talukas account for almost 58 per cent of the investment during the first incentive block and 59.41 per cent in 1991-96, in small-scale sector. The corresponding figures for medium and large sector were 80.42 per cent and 76.53 per cent; and for factory sector the figures were 74.42 per cent and 73.93 per cent. Nevertheless, investments have flown to 13 backward talukas also. However, the magnitude of this shift is almost negligible. The first 40 talukas of 1986-91 continued to have their sway by garnering over 86 per cent of the new investments. The remaining 13 new entrants could get only 9.87 per cent of investment. The balance 3.82 per cent new investment was shared by the remaining 131 talukas. The situation, even in the case of small-scale industries has deteriorated where the spread of new

Table 6.15 : Concentration Ratio of Total Investment for Top 25 Talukas of Gujarat

(Percentage Investment)

Sr. No.	Sectoral and Temporal Classification	In 1st 5 Talukas	In 1st 10 Talukas	In 1st 15 Talukas	In 1st 20 Talukas	In 1st 25 Talukas	Others	Total
1.	Small Scale Sector							
	1986	48.70	61.15	69.03	74.41	78.69	21.31	100.00
	1991	45.59	57.03	65.39	70.83	74.84	25.16	100.00
	1996	44.36	56.43	63.67	69.62	74.11	25.89	100.00
2.	Medium & Large Industry Sector							
	1986	69.98	82.70	91.25	96.01	97.67	2.33	100.00
	1991	61.87	78.60	84.81	89.51	93.18	6.82	100.00
	1996	61.11	73.45	80.73	85.47	89.02	10.98	100.00
3.	Total (Factory Sector)							
	1986	65.80	78.03	86.04	90.86	93.41	6.59	100.00
	1991	57.92	73.87	80.28	85.22	89.09	10.91	100.00
	1996	58.89	71.01	77.80	82.45	86.13	13.87	100.00

Source: Based on data collected from DICs and Commissionerate of Industries, Government of Gujarat.

investments have become more skewed. The top 40 talukas, continued to hold prime position in attracting new investments even during 1991-96 period, with about 86.53 per cent share against 84.43 per cent during 1986-91.[8]

Table 6.16 : Concentration Ratio of New Investment in Talukas of Gujarat

Sr. No.	New Sectoral Investment	In 1st 10 Talukas	In 1st 20 Talukas	In 1st 30 Talukas	In 1st 40 Talukas	Remaining Talukas	Total
1.	Small Scale Sector						
	1986-91	57.85	71.67	78.71	84.43	15.57	100.00
	1991-96	59.41	75.15	81.68	86.53	13.47	100.00
2.	Medium & Large Industry Sector						
	1986-91	80.42	91.60	95.96	98.06	1.94	100.00
	1991-96	76.53	88.26	94.00	97.02	2.98	100.00
3.	Total (Factory Sector)						
	1986-91	74.42	86.67	91.66	94.52	5.48	100.00
	1991-96	73.93	86.13	92.38	95.70	4.30	100.00

Source : As in Table 6.15.

The above analysis suggests that the investments have flown mostly to talukas that have proximity to some major industrial concentrations, with the advantage of forward and backward linkages, or are on major trunk route or near the ports. Most of the talukas in the periphery could hardly get any significant investment in medium and large industries. As a matter of fact, 111 talukas during 1986-91 incentive period and 88 talukas during 1990-95 incentive period did not receive even a rupee of investment in medium and large industries. If one puts up Rs.10 crore as cut-off point, only 42 talukas during 1986-91 and 47 talukas during 1991-96 qualified this condition. In fact, none of the districts of Banaskantha, Surendranagar and Dangs receive any major investment in medium and large industries during the decade, and if one takes out Anjar from Kutch and Prantij from Sabarkantha, even these districts will fall in the category of 'No Investment in M&L Industries'.

Polarity in Investments

This led us to evolve a hypothesis that there is an element of polarity in the investment flows. The investments, therefore, will get centred round industrial magnets (poles) irrespective of the quantum of subsidies or tax holidays. To see if the polarity syndrome holds good in the present context, we identified eight major industrial poles, viz., Ahmedabad, Vadodara, Bharuch, Surat, Valsad, Rajkot, Jamnagar and Bhavnagar depending upon their share in the factory sector investments in 1996. Having identified the poles we plotted the talukas adjacent to these poles and added investment of those talukas to the investments in the poles in a particular year. This provided us the polar concentration of investments in the total factory sector in 1986, 1991 and 1996.

Table 6.17 provides the shares of various poles. As could be seen from the Table, almost 76 per cent of the investment was concentrated in and around the industrial magnets or poles in 1996, which is marginally higher than 1986. One would have expected a more decentralised pattern of investments to take place, if the incentives worked. The polarity would have given way to a more even spread of investments. But, contrary to the expectations, concentration has increased. The loss of Ahmedabad and Bharuch poles over a period of time has been the gain of Vadodara and Surat poles. Another argument, often put forth, is that the investments are concentrated on Ahmedabad-Bombay corridor in the state. We just remove the share of Saurashtra poles, viz. Rajkot, Jamnagar and Bhavnagar (which in any case are mini-poles), the share of the corridor works out to 73.38 per cent in 1986, 66.92 per cent in 1991 and 74.35 per cent in 1996. All these facts, put together, indicate that industrial development in Gujarat has been regionally lopsided.

The Cluster-Based Growth of Small-Scale Industries in Gujarat

A recent study that listed 138 clusters states that "there exist about 350 SME clusters in India" (Gulati, 1996). However, there might not be more than 50 major clusters in the country, if we consider only those spatial concentrations of small and medium (SME) industries manufacturing homogenous or related products that contribute at least 25 per cent of the country's production.[9] Otherwise, any industrial centre could be classified as one or the other variant of a cluster. Keeping this definition in view, one could legitimately argue that the pattern of industrial development has been cluster-based in Gujarat as a large number of spatial and sectoral clusters of small firms have historically existed in the state, specially in Saurashtra region of Gujarat. Brass-parts and components in Jamnagar, diesel engines and components in Rajkot, wall-clocks and flooring tiles in Morbi, weights and measures in Savarkundala, textile printing in Jetpur and salt industry in coastal Saurashtra testify this pattern. Besides these clusters in Saurashtra, other notable clusters of SMEs in Gujarat are chemicals in Vapi and Ankleshwar, plastic spectacle frames and other plastic products in Vadodara, jari and diamond cutting industries in Surat, dyes and intermediates, detergent soap, pharmaceuticals and textile machine parts in Ahmedabad.

Table 6.17 : Polarity of Investments in Factory Sector Across Talukas Surrounding the Growth Poles in Gujarat (in 1986,1991 & 1996)

Sr. No.	Pole	1986 Investment	1986 Share in State	1991 Investment	1991 Share in State	1996 Investment	1996 Share in State
1.	Ahmedabad	181947	24.43	247578	16.88	494021	12.42
2.	Vadodara	24539	3.29	69128	4.71	609700	15.33
3.	Bharuch	92090	12.36	119113	8.12	412074	10.36
4.	Surat	220943	29.66	492639	33.58	1311106	32.96
5.	Valsad	27057	3.63	53389	3.64	130528	3.28
6.	Rajkot	16967	2.28	25064	1.71	37562	0.94
7.	Jamnagar	1276	0.17	11962	0.82	19563	0.49
8.	Bhavnagar	1141	0.15	2847	0.19	22069	0.55
	Pole Total	565960	75.98	1021720	69.64	3036623	76.33
	Gujarat Total	744834	100.00	1467117	100.00	3978275	100.00

1. Ahmedabad-Gandhinagar Pole (Ahmedabad, Gandhinagar, Kadi, Kalol, Dascroi, Dholka, Sanand, Dehgam, Mehmedabad and Matar)
2. Vadodara Pole (Vadodara, Dabhoi, Padra, Vaghodia, Savli, Sinor, Anand, Borsad, Karjan and Petlad)
3. Bharuch Pole (Bharuch, Ankleshwar, Jhagadia, Vagra and Amod)
4. Surat Pole (Choryasi, Olpad, Kamrej, Palsana, Navsari)
5. Valsad Pole (Valsad, Pardi, Ganadevi, Chikli, Dharampur)
6. Rajkot Pole (Rajkot, Kotda Sangani, Lodhika, Paddhari, Wankaner, Jasdan, Chotila)
7. Jamnagar Pole (Jamnagar, Lalpur, Jodia, Dhrol, Kalavad)
8. Bhavnagar Pole (Bhavnagar, Sihor, Umrala, Ghogha, Vallabhipur, Dhandhuka)

Table 6.18 : Status of Medium and Large Industry Investments in Gujarat

A. DISTRICT-WISE ANALYSIS OF LOI/LOP/IEM STATUS
(AS ON 31-10-1997)
PROJECTS U.I. & N.I.A.* (Rs. crore)

Districts	Projects	% Share	Investment	% Share	Employment	% Share
Bharuch	320	13.73	21533	19.27	50467	12.7
Surat	257	11.03	20931	18.72	24622	6.2
Vadodara	378	16.22	6377	5.7	56484	14.21
Jamnagar	56	2.4	31154	27.85	32825	8.26
Kutch	35	1.51	9061	8.1	13225	3.33
Other Distts.	1284	55.11	22775	20.36	219780	55.3
TOTAL	2330	100	111851	100	397443	100

B. DISTRICT-WISE ANALYSIS OF LOI/LOP/IEM STATUS
AS ON 31-10-1997
(Projects Commissioned)

Districts	Projects	% Share	Investment	% Share	Employment	% Share
Bharuch	222	11.09	4614	13.15	31569	8.97
Surat	415	20.73	15979	47.04	95632	27.18
Vadodara	262	13.09	4852	14.28	39688	11.28
Jamnagar	23	1.15	364	1.07	7139	20.29
Kutch	43	2.15	130	0.38	3691	1.05
Other Distts.	1037	51.79	8029	23.64	174233	49.51
TOTAL	2002	100	33968	100	351942	100

C. DISTRICT WITH INVESTMENT EXCEEDING RS.5000 CRORES IN GUJARAT

Bharuch	S.Sarovar, Petrochem, Power	38111	29.93	—	—
Surat	Fertilizer, Petrochem, Power	11354	8.92	—	—
Vadodara	Refinery, Chemicals	5451	4.28	—	—
Jamnagar	Refinery, Petrochemicals	30078	23.62	—	—
Kutch	Alumina, Cement, Fertilizer	8213	6.45	—	—
Amreli	Power, Copper, Cement	14635	11.49	—	—
TOTAL		127318	10.17**	—	
ALL INDIA		1251756		—	

* UI (Under Implementation), NIA (No Information Available), LOI (Letter of Intent), LOP (Letter of Permission), IEM (Industrial Entrepreneurs Memorandum)

** Percentage of all India.

Sources: For A & B, Industrial Extension Bureau (Monitoring Division), Govt. of Gujarat.

For C, CMIE, Survey of Investment Projects — Overview, Bombay, Nov. 1997.

The brass-part and component cluster in Jamnagar accounts for almost 90 per cent of the output of the product in the country (Awasthi, 1997); and, diesel engine cluster accounts for about 80 per cent of the production of Lister and Peter type of diesel engines in the country (Basant, 1997). Almost 50 per cent of the SMEs in dyes and intermediates are located in Ahmedabad (Awasthi, 1993). The textile printing industry in Jetpur is one of the biggest centre of its kind (Dupont, 1995), and Morbi has emerged as a major cluster of flooring tiles in India (Das, 1996a). Similarly, diamond cutting and polishing in Surat is the biggest cluster in this industry in the country (Kashyap and Tewari, 1986). Almost similar are the cases of other clusters mentioned above.

There are, however, a few striking differences between most of the Saurashtra clusters and the clusters in south Gujarat. The Saurashtra clusters are autonomous in their origin. The emergence of clusters in Saurashtra owes to availability of artisan skills, be it brass-parts cluster in Jamnagar or textile printing in Jetpur. Moreover, these clusters are also quite old, while the clusters in south Gujarat are of recent origin (except the diamond cluster in Surat, which is of the Saurashtra clusters variety). The technology in the Saurashtra clusters has become rather obsolete like in diesel engine cluster in Rajkot that is using almost 100 years old technology (Basant, 1997). On the other hand, the south Gujarat clusters, that are induced, belong to modern product lines, like chemicals in Vapi and Ankleshwar.[10] Though these clusters are likely to have relatively weaker community linkages, which otherwise is considered to be an important feature of a classical cluster, such linkages might develop over a period of time.

What is so special about clusters? Why at all one needs to highlight their existence? The reason is not far to seek. The experience across the countries indicates that the clusters give rise to various kinds of economic and non-economic inter-firm linkages that improve efficiency and international competitiveness of small and medium enterprises (SMEs), because of the economies of scale and scope. The clustering leads to collective efficiency gains which individual firms can hardly achieve. Argument is that because of the backward and forward linkages, networking, joint action (external and agglomeration economies), the transaction costs in a cluster are reduced. As a result, small firms operating in a cluster enjoy collective efficiency, which individual firms do not (Nadvi and Schmitz: 1994, Schmitz, 1995). This leads to better and more efficient use of factors of production, on the one hand, and provides a competitive edge to SMEs, on the other. A few studies undertaken to understand the dynamics of industrial clusters in Gujarat indicate that the firms operating in industrial clusters have much better resilience to policy changes than those operating in isolation do (Awasthi, 1997, Basant, 1997). It is probably because of this phenomenon, the industrial sector in Gujarat has been able to withstand the competition emanating from the recent sweep of economic liberalisation. Whether it is textile printing in Jetpur (Dupont, 1995) or brass-parts and components industry in Jamnagar (Awasthi, 1997) or flooring tiles industry in Morbi (Das, 1996a) or garment cluster in Ahmedabad (Das, 1996b), all of them have prospered and continued to grow, despite high competition – external and internal. International experiences on clusters also indicate that it is much better to support clusters of SMEs than supporting individual units (Humphrey and Schmitz, 1995).

It may, however, be noted that the policy framework for promoting small industries still stipulates support to individual units rather than to a group of related units or industrial clusters in India. The liberalisation process, the country is currently passing through, necessitates a policy shift in favour of clusters (Awasthi, Krishna and Sebastian, 1993). For, it might be more cost effective in a resource scarce economy like ours. Realising that (i) the clusters offer tremendous potential for enhancing the competitiveness of small industries sector; (ii) they have certain inherent strengths due to collectivism which individual, stand alone units do not have (as units operating clusters have shown more resilience to policy changes than stand alone units; and (iii) it is more cost effective to offer support at the cluster level rather than at unit level, even the government of India is contemplating a significant policy shift in favour of clusters. For example, Abid Hussain Committee set up by the Government of India, which submitted its report in July 1997, also lays due stress on promotion of cluster of small industries. The Report states that:

> *"A fundamental flaw in the policy for small cluster development in India has been that it has ignored the clusters that have taken roots as a result of entrepreneurial effort. Worldwide experience suggests that such clusters can stagnate in their late stages of developed unless they are supported by institutions. These clusters are appropriate units for focused development of a large number of enterprises in a way that lower the cost of administration of development programmes. Since these clusters usually specialise*

> *in a single activity, it is possible to design composite programmes meeting their inter-related needs. It will also be possible to forge government private sector partnership for effective implementation of region development programmes....".*[11]

The Future Trends

With emerging global competition, establishment of WTO and the like, it will no more be possible to safeguard the interests of small industries through protectionist policies. The better alternative will be to help these units become internationally competitive on the basis of quality, technology and niche markets, wherever possible. This adds to the rationale for supporting and strengthening clusters of units which, by and large, have emerged autonomously and have successfully faced the policy-led turbulence. They have survived because of the strengths they draw from their operating together. Government will need to be proactive in strengthening these clusters, so that they become more dynamic. Therefore, the government should device a two pronged strategy under which it should strengthen the existing clusters and at the same time try to identify potential for promoting new clusters. For example, one could think of promoting an engineering industry or foundry cluster in Bhavnagar, given the availability of iron scrap from Alang Ship Breaking Yard.

However, at this stage, it will be prudent to mention that a few clusters have started showing negative externalities, irrespective of their age. The examples of this variety are the chemical clusters in Vapi and Ankleshwar, dyes and intermediate cluster in Ahmedabad and textile printing in Jetpur. The negative externalities, in terms of water pollution, are glaring in all these clusters. Even the courts had to intervene to restrict their operations to safeguard the 'public interest'. Given this experience, the government's plan to set up chemical industrial estates in south Gujarat, especially for chemical industries, needs a careful scrutiny. Unless adequate precautions are taken, the emergence of such clusters could turn out to be counter productive and a retrograde step.

As far as large scale industries are concerned, recent information on large projects under implementation indicates that as on 31-10-1997, Gujarat accounts for Rs.1,27,318 crore, which is about 10.17 per cent of the total national investment of Rs.12,51,756 crore. The data also indicate that, the way Gujarat is poised to play a major role in the country's industrial future, with its major share in the industrial investment at all India level,

Bharuch, Surat and Vadodara in south Gujarat and Amreli, Jamnagar and Kutch in Saurashtra and Kutch regions with about 84.69 per cent of the state share are poised to play a critical role in the future. Within Gujarat, only five districts are likely to corner about 45 per cent (1046 of the 2330) of the number of projects and employment in Gujarat. The investment appears to be even more concentrated as the share of these five districts works out to almost 20 per cent. Of the five, at least three districts, viz. Bharuch, Surat and Vadodara are in any case highly industrialised and Jamnagar is an emerging industrial giant. However, of the 2002 projects, which were already commissioned by 30-10-1997 with an investment of Rs. 33, 968 crore and employment of 3,51,942 workers, only Bharuch, Surat and Vadodara together claimed about 45 per cent of projects, 75 per cent investment and about 47.50 per cent of employment. The other two districts, viz. Jamnagar and Kutch accounted for over three per cent projects (Table 6.18). These were the ones, which also emerged as districts with investment exceeding Rs. 5000 crore in Gujarat in November 1997. Another important feature that emerges is the sectoral composition of industries with a focus on chemical, petrochemical, fertilizer, power and cement projects in these districts, influencing the industrial structure of the state as a whole.

One must emphasise that in terms of regional spread it may not be the most ideal state of affairs. Nevertheless, given the priority for overall industrial development of the state, it may be more pragmatic to let the investment flow to a region which may be more ideal location but may not be most backward keeping its long term spin off in view. After all, the investments have also flown to areas like Amreli or Kutch or Jamnagar, which were (are) also industrially backward. These are the regions which are most ideal for cement industry and access to sea route gives a clear locational and strategic advantage to Jamnagar for refinery and petrochemicals for obvious reasons, besides fiscal incentives. Surat, Baroda and Bharuch in any case have been the major centres of chemical and petrochemical products.

The existing high share of chemical and petrochemical industries and the pattern of new investment flows, especially in central and south Gujarat, deserve a word of caution. While it could lead to faster industrial growth, the state may have to pay a very heavy price in future because of the attendant pollution problems, which could cause serious environmental damages. The government should take precautionary measures from now itself than doing fire fighting at a latter date.

The government of Gujarat has been offering an impressive array of fiscal and financial incentives to attract industries. However, a critical bottleneck, that could dampen the flow of industrial investments in Gujarat, is that of infrastructure. Gujarat does not compare favourably with its competing states like Maharashtra, Karnataka, Tamil Nadu or Andhra Pradesh in terms of quality of infrastructure — both social and physical. A recent review of infrastructure, therefore, observes that:

> "......*various parameters of infrastructure development of Gujarat are not in concurrence with its higher status in terms of level of industrialisation. It is probably because of some historical factors or because of being the 'second best option', Gujarat is getting investments. However, it must be clearly understood that unless major investments are made in infrastructure, the state will not be able to retain its dominant position in the investment flows in the days to come. After all, capital especially large and foreign has become very mobile during the last decade and a half. Merely fiscal incentives will not be able to attract industries to the state. They will, at best, remain only auxiliary and not the primary attraction for investments. The government of Gujarat must take note of this fact, while formulating its policies for industrial development.*" (Awasthi, 1998, p. 125).

NOTES

1. Parthasarathy (1998), in a very interesting article on competitive advantage of different states in India observed that Gujarat remains the second most sought after state for investors.
2. It is often argued that a stable government is necessary for attracting investment. For, it is also taken as an indicator of the stability of the policies. However, Gujarat, in this context, has a unique characteristic that long term policies related to industrial development have never been adversely affected because of the change in government. Despite six Chief Ministers and a Governor's rule, the industry has never suffered, so is the process of economic reforms. As a matter of fact, Asian Development Bank (ADB) decided to collaborate and support Gujarat by giving US $ 250 million worth loan for Public Sector Resource Management Programme directly to the state. This is first time for the ADB to have directly sanctioned any assistance to a state in India.

3. It may be noted that it lost almost half of its share in textiles within 10 years (from 21.6 per cent to 11.90 per cent in 1994-95).
4. This section is based on the data on registration of units as reported by various District Industries Centres of Gujarat. Therefore, it may not perfectly match with Annual Survey of Industries data in some cases, as that is as per the reporting of the factories in operation. To that extent, the ASI data is more up-to-date and accurate. Here, the term Factory sector connotes the aggregate values of all the small, medium and large factories in Gujarat, registered with the District Industries Centres and the Commissionerate of Industries, government of Gujarat.
5. Recently, the government of Gujarat has created a number of new talukas. Now the number of total talukas in Gujarat stands at 223.
6. Concentration ratio means the sum of shares of top 25 talukas in industries in Gujarat in 1986, 1991 and 1996; and of the top 40 talukas in terms of net investment flows during 1986-91 and 1991-96. We arrived at these numbers as they, together, account for over 85 per cent share of investments in the state.
7. It should, however, be noted that these are not the same talukas over time and across sector. Quite a few new talukas have entered replacing the old ones. Nor are they same talukas across the sectors. But by and large, about 75 per cent of the same talukas continue to have the concentration with about 20 per cent to 25 per cent new talukas making their presence felt.
8. See Awasthi (1998), p.63, for details.
9. The main attributes of industrial clusters are "geographical proximity, sectoral specialisation, predominance of small and medium-sized firms, close inter-firm collaboration, inter-firm competition based on innovations, a socio-cultural identity which facilitates trust, active self-help organisation and supportive regional and municipal governments". Product specific cluster of small enterprises in the West have proved the efficiency of such clustering, where a few product specific firms get concentrated and create a niche for themselves. The fate of a firm in a cluster gets linked with the fate of other firms operating in the cluster, leading to inter-firm dependence and thus co-operation. The industrial clusters provide ample opportunity for such a networking, leading to increased collective efficiency despite intense inter-firm competition. Such clusters have also been observed to lead to flexible specialisation resulting into a number of process innovations in developed countries like Italy, Germany, Denmark and Japan.
10. For the concept of autonomous and induced clusters, see Kashyap and Shah (1995).
11. A committee was appointed by the government of India to review the policies to promote small-scale enterprises under the Chairmanship of Shri Abid Husain in 1997. The committee also favoured promotion of small-

scale enterprises through promoting and strengthening clusters. The quote is from the Report, p.80.

REFERENCES

Awasthi, Dinesh N. (1992), "Growth of Firms: A Study of Dyes and Intermediates Industry in Ahmedabad", in *Journal of Entrepreneurship*, No.1, Vol. 1.

Awasthi, Dinesh N., Krishna, K.V.S.M. and Sebastian, Jose (1993), A Report on the Impact of New Economic Policies on Small Scale and Tiny Sector, Mimeograph, Ahmedabad, Entrepreneurship Development Institute of India, November.

Awasthi, Dinesh N. (1997), The Brass-parts and Components Industry Cluster: Jamnagar, A Research Report (unpublished), Ahmedabad, Entrepreneurship Development Institute of India.

Awasthi, Dinesh N. (1998), A Study on Impact of Incentive Schemes on Industrialisation of Gujarat, Research Report (Unpublished), Industrial Extension Bureau, Government of Gujarat.

Basant, R. (1997), The Diesel Engine Industry Cluster: Rajkot, A Research Report (unpublished), Ahmedabad, Indian Institute of Management.

Das, K. (1996a), Collective Dynamism and Firm Strategy: The Flooring Tile Cluster in Gujarat, India, Working Paper Series, No.76, March, Ahmedabad: Gujarat Institute of Development Research.

Das, K. (1996b), Flexibility Together: Surviving and Growing in a Garment Cluster, Ahmedabad, India, Working Paper Series, No.79, June, Ahmedabad: Gujarat Institute of Development Research.

Dupont, V. (1995), *Decentralised Industrialisation and Urban Dynamics: The case of Jetpur in West India*, New Delhi: Sage Publications.

Government of India (1997), Report of the Expert Committee on Small Enterprises, New Delhi, Ministry of Industries, July.

Gulati, M. (1996), *Restructuring and Modernisation of SME Clusters in India*, Vienna, United Nations Industrial Development Organisation.

Humphrey, J. and Schmitz (1995), Principles for promoting clusters and networks of SMEs, Paper Commissioned by the Small and Medium Enterprises Branch, No.1, October, Sussex: Institute of Development Studies.

Kashyap, S.P. and Tiwari, R.S. (1986), *Shaping of Diamonds in Surat: Some Passas (Facets)*, Monograph Series 12, Ahmedabad: Sardar Patel Institute of Economic and Social Research.

Kashyap, S.P. and Shah, A. (1995), "Induced Industrial Clustering and Efficiency: An Exploratory Study of Gujarat's Industrial Estates", *The Journal of Entrepreneurship*, Vol. 4, No. 1, Jan.-June.

Nadvi, Khalid and Schmitz Hubert (1994), "Industrial Clusters in Less Developed Countries: Review of Experiences and Research Agenda", Discussion Paper 339, Institute of Development Studies, January.

Parthasarathy, Rukmini (1998), "Best States to Invest in", *Business Today,* December 22, 1997 - January 6, 1998.

Schmitz, Hubert (1995), "Collective Efficiency: Growth Path for Small-Scale Industry", *The Journal of Development Studies,* Vol. 31, No. 4, April.

7

Institutional Change and Entrepreneurial Development in the SSI Sector of Gujarat

TAKASHI SHINODA

Introduction

The economic development of India and each of its states is greatly determined by the growth in the manufacturing industry. It is no exaggeration to say that the mode and historical development of manufacturing has controlled the level of development of each state.

This paper is aimed at examining the mode and process of entrepreneurial development in Gujarat, particularly among the entrepreneurs in Small Scale Industries (hereafter referred to as SSIs). The state of Gujarat came into existence in 1960 as the result of the bifurcation of Bombay State. Industrial production of the state at that time ranked eighth among the Indian states. There were around 2000 SSIs and around 3000 factories, mainly related to cotton and food production. As to location, most of these industries were concentrated in the industrial pockets of Ahmedabad, Vadodara, Surat, Rajkot and Bhavnagar.

At present, Gujarat has a steady base of SSIs in the field of machinery and parts, basic metal industries, rubber and plastic products, and chemical and chemical products, which function as a driving force for upgrading the industrial structure of the state. In the course of economic development of the state, the importance of food products and cotton textiles has declined drastically since 1980s. The present economic structure in Gujarat shows a fairly balanced picture with the development of both capital intensive and high-tech units, as also labour intensive units.

Although it is widely recognized that entrepreneurs play a very important role in economic development, the research on entrepreneurial development has been mainly confined to the study of large business firms[1], highly mobile business communities such as Marwaris[2], and the managing agency system that moulded the business scene in India, while bypassing the large number of entrepreneurs in medium and small scale industries. Also, entrepreneurship among the backward classes has rarely been studied.

This paper is composed of three sections. The first deals with the industrial development of the modern sector, with special reference to SSIs[3], in light of industrial policy and the sector's actual performance. Section two analyses the social background of entrepreneurs according to religion and caste based on a directory of manufacturers compiled by the state government in 1989. We will also examine the correlation between social groups and the type and geographical distribution of industries. The majority of manufacturers in the directory belong to non-backward classes. Lastly, mode and characteristics of newly registered SSI units promoted by Scheduled Castes (SCs)[4], Scheduled Tribes (STs)[5] and Socially Educationally Backward Classes (SEBC)[6] will be examined. Thus, the paper is aimed at analysing the recent entrepreneurial development of both the middle upper classes and the backward classes in the SSI sector.

INDUSTRIAL DEVELOPMENT IN GUJARAT

Industrial Structure and the Modern Sector

It was in 1954 when the Small Industries Development Programme was introduced. At the initial stage, SSI had been defined by two criteria: fixed capital investment and employment, but the definition was changed in 1960, as investment in plant and equipment became the sole criterion. Since then, the ceiling for investment was revised upward in 1966, 75, 80, 85, 91 and 97 on account of inflation and technological development. The ceiling was set at Rs. 35 lakh for SSI and Rs. 45 lakh for ancillary units in 1985 then lifted to Rs. 60 lakh and Rs. 75 in 1991. In 1997 it was raised again drastically to Rs. 3 crore for SSI and Rs. 25 lakh for tiny industries.

For the purpose of administration and development programmes, SSIs are divided into seven industries: handicraft, handloom, khadi, village and cottage, coir, sericulture, power loom and residual SSIs. In terms of the type of equipment and production process, the first five are generally referred to as the "traditional sector," and the remaining two are called the "modern sector."[7] Administratively, each group has been overseen by supervisory bodies, the modern SSI units being supervised by the Small Industry Development Organization (SIDO).

There are three sources of information on the modern sector: Annual Survey of Industries (ASI), SIDO census of the registered SSIs, and surveys for the Directory and Non-Directory Manufacturing Establishment.[8] However, none of these data sets covers all the industrial units with the basic characteristics of SSI. Moreover, comparability among the above three sets of data is very limited due to differences in the coverage and definition of industrial units surveyed. Despite these difficulties, SIDO censuses provide us with some very useful information, since here we are concerned with the basic characteristics of the modern SSI unit. Apart from the above data, other sets of data compiled by the state government will also be examined to analyse entrepreneurial development among the different social groups in Gujarat.

Small Scale Industries in Gujarat

Turning to the characteristics of SSI units in Gujarat based on the second SIDO census conducted in 1987-88, to begin with, since registration with SIDO is on voluntary basis, the survey results are not comprehensive. However, it does give us a fairly representive picture of the general trends among SSI units. The second SIDO census targeted 58,328 SSI units, leaving 4898 units that could not be traced. Out of the remaining 53,430 units, as many as 18,977 units had been shut down, indicating that the mortality ratio among SSI units is very high.[9]

Table 7.1 presents the workforce, fixed capital, working capital, and production output of the 34,453 SSI units known to be in operation by two types of spatial distinction, A and B. A "metropolitan area" indicates a city with a population of over one million. Only Ahmedabad met this criteria in the reference year. A "backward area" is defined by the central and state governments separately in the light of administrative priority to correct regional disparities. Nearly 80 per cent of survey's SSI units were located either in metropolitan or urban areas, while only 21 per cent were located in rural areas. However, if we look at the figures for annual registration of SSI units in recent years, we notice that the share of units

Table 7.1: Workforces, Fixed Capital, Working Capital and Production of SSIs (1987-88)

(Unit/Person/Lakh/Rupees)

	Area	Working Units	Employment		Fixed Capital		Working Capital		Production	
			Total	Per Unit	Total	Per Unit	Total	Per Unit	Total	Per Unit
A	Rural	7248.00 (21.00)	57290.00 (20.70)	8.00	13734.00 (22.90)	1.89	12445.00 (15.30)	1.72	65647.00 (18.30)	9.00
	Urban	20105.00 (58.40)	160745.00 (58.00)	8.00	34716.00 (57.90)	1.73	47218.00 (57.90)	2.35	203048.00 (56.60)	10.00
	Metro-polis	7100.00 (20.60)	58920.00 (21.30)	8.00	11468.00 (19.10)	1.62	21854.00 (26.80)	3.08	89929.00 (25.10)	12.60
B	Backward Area	11588.00 (33.60)	93938.00 (33.90)	8.00	23838.00 (39.80)	2.06	24605.00 (30.20)	2.12	115823.00 (32.30)	10.00
	Non-Backward Area	22865.00 (66.40)	183017.00 (66.10)	8.00	36080.00 (60.20)	1.58	56913.00 (69.80)	2.49	242801.00 (67.70)	10.60
	Total	34453.00 (100.00)	276955.00	8.00	59918.00 (100.00)	1.74	81517.00 (100.00)	2.37	358624.00 (100.00)	10.40

Source: Govt. of Gujarat, Industries In Gujarat (Some Statistics), Industries Commissionerate, Gandhinagar, 1922, pp. 16-18.

located in rural area has been increasing due to a special package granted to them. The same is true of SSIs in backward areas.

Total number of persons employed by SSIs was approximately 2.77 lakh according to the SIDO census. Interestingly, there was no difference in terms of spatial distinction among units regarding the average number of workers employed per unit, which came to 8. Those units without the use of motor power made up only 5.9 per cent of all the operating SSIs (12.4 per cent in rural areas; 3.8 per cent in urban areas and 5.1 per cent in metropolitan areas). Thus, most of the SSI units were using motor power and also employing more than ten workers, making them factories under the Factory Act. The SIDO census reveals that 4,451 SSI units, or 13 per cent of the units in operation, were covered by Factory Act. This means that nearly 42 per cent of 10,655 reported factories fell within the SSI sector during the reference year.

Investment ceilings for plant and machinery during the reference year were Rs. 3 lakh for tiny industries, Rs. 35 lakh for SSIs and Rs. 45 lakh for ancillary industries. The number of tiny industry units has increased drastically from the late 1980s. The percentage share among newly registered SSI units has increased from 29 per cent in 1985-86 to 90 per cent in 1997-98, partly due to the revision of investment ceilings in 1991, and partly due to the entrepreneurial development among the middle and lower classes in Gujarat.

The data on capital investment per unit shows a clear tendency that fixed capital investment in rural areas appears slightly higher than units in urban and metropolitan areas, but working capital and production output are smallest among the three areas in the A category. A similar tendency is observed among the two areas in the B category. Units in backward areas surpassed those in non-backward areas in fixed capital investment and *vice versa* in working capital and production output.

As for the type of organisation, most of the units took the form of individual proprietorships or partnerships, with a share of 52 per cent and 44 per cent respectively, followed by limited companies (3.4 per cent) and co-operatives (0.2 per cent)[10]. The percentage share of units registered for utilization of reservation of products among newly registered units declined from 30 per cent in 1983-84 to 19 per cent in 1985-86[11]. The units registered for government purchase also declined from 640 units (14 per cent) in 1983-84 to 413 units (9 per cent) in 1985-86[12]. Thus, the units which are interested in government protection have tended to decline. It is reported that goods valued at Rs. 106 crore, or around 3 per cent of total production, were exported during the reference year.

ENTREPRENEURS AND SOCIAL GROUPS

Surname (Title) and Caste (Group)

The main source of data for this section is a directory of manufacturers in Gujarat compiled by the Industrial Extension Bureau (hereafter referred to as INDEXTB) of the government of Gujarat. The government has compiled this type of directory five times in 1969, 1980, 1983 (supplementary version), 1989 and 1992. The analysis presented here is based on the 1989 version (reference period is 1987)[13]. This version compiled basic information on about 31,000 running units of SSI, medium and large-scale sector. Though break-up figures of units among these sectors are not given, the SSI units may share at least two-thirds of the total surveyed units since the number of working factories in Gujarat was about 13,000 only during the reference period.

The directory compiled such information as (1) enterprise name, (2) name of entrepreneur, (3) type of industry, according to the National Industrial Classification (NIC:four digits), and (4) address. For cross sectional analysis, we fed into a computer the above sets of data of those units classified in four digit NIC codes which had more than 100 entries only[14] resulting in a sample of 19,454 units. Regarding the name of entrepreneur, the given name is arranged to come first, followed by a middle name, if any, and then the surname (including title and name related to occupation, village etc) according to the judgment of INDEXTB.[15] The analysis in this section will be concentrated on those surnames that appear more than 50 times, accounting for 55 per cent of the total sample, and 73 per cent of all entrepreneurs who reported their surnames.

Table 7.2 shows the distribution of 41 surnames by group and frequency. These surnames have been divided into seven groups corresponding to the caste (group) or religion that is supposed to use such names[16]. Group 1 consists of those surnames common among the Brahmans[17]. Group 2 contains what are considered names originally used by the Rajputs (warrior and landlord class)[18]. These surnames have also been adopted by some segments of the backward classes in the course of their sanskritization, which tended to identify Kshatriya as their varna. Group 3 is made up of surnames commonly used by the Baniyas (Hindu Baniyas and the Jains)[19], with some exceptions, since some Parsis and Muslims[20] use these names (but their number is small in Gujarat). Group 4 consists of surnames used commonly by upper castes like the Baniyas, Brahmans and Patidars. Group 5 is made up of the single surname (title)

'Patel', which denotes a village head, a governmental functionary before independence. This title was used by any village head irrespective of his religion or caste. However, since this title has become widely accepted among the populous and powerful Patidars (previously known as the Kanbis) since the 1930s, we may assume safely that the majority of users of this title belong to Patidars, as far as the directory is concerned. Group 6 contains surnames used only by the artisan castes and Group 7 consists of surnames exclusively used by Muslims. Based upon these correlations, we regard the entrepreneurs of Group 1 to be Brahmans, Group 2 Kshatriyas (a combination between the Rajputs and the backward classes), Group 3 Baniyas, Group 5 Patidars (though they are not the overwhelming majority in this group), Group 6 artisan castes, and Group 7 Muslims[21].

Table 7.2 : Distribution of Major Surnames by Group and Frequency

	Group 1	Group 2	Group 3	Group 4	Group 5	Group 6	Group 7
Frequency							
2000+	0.00	0.00	0.00	0.00	Patel	0.00	0.00
1000~1999	0.00	0.00	Shah	0.00	0.00	Panchal	0.00
300~999	0.00	0.00	0.00	0.00	0.00	Mistri	0.00
100~299		Parmar	Gandhi Jariwala Modi	Mehta Desai	0.00	Gajjar Luhar Prajapati	Momin
50~99	Bhatt Dave Joshi Pandya Sharma Trivedi Vyas	Chauhan Chaudhri Makvana Rathod Solanki Dodiya	Agraval Doshi Jain Kapadiya	Vora	0.00	Soni	Mansuri Shekh Basmiya Panara

Source: Govt. of Gujarat, The Gujarat Directory of Manufacturers, Industrial Extension Bureau, Ahmedabad, 1989.

Social Group and Type of Industry

Here the aim is to examine the correlation between social group and type of industry. The first step is to classify related industries into two types, which we will call "concentrated" and "dispersed", based on the degree of correlation with social group. Secondly, we examine the distribution of industries for each social group to see if patterns of entrepreneurial development differ among different social groups.

Distribution of Social Group by Type of Industry

Table 7.3 presents the distribution of the top five reoccurring surnames by type of industry. To confirm an actual dominance of individual surnames, the percentages of their distribution are shown against the total sample amount of 19,453. Also, the percentages of those surname groups which occurred over 50 times against the total sample amount are used as a criterion to discover the degree of concentration.

We may regard the food products (81.7 per cent), wood products (77.2 per cent), and non-metallic mineral products (65.7 per cent) industries as highly concentrated in terms of surname group percentages, followed by the leather products (34.6 per cent), wool, silk and synthetic textiles (34.7 per cent), hosiery and garments (36.1 per cent), repair services (42.6 per cent), and electrical machinery and parts (46.0 per cent) industries.

Now, examining the distribution of major surnames in the list, the name Patel occupies the top position in all the above-mentioned industries, except hosiery and garments. The dominance of Patel is overwhelming. Shah follows Patel, occupying either second or third place in most of the industries. Panchal is not only very frequent in eight industries, but also is ranked second just following Patel in metal and machinery-related industries. Most of the other surnames in the list belong to Baniya and the artisan castes. Interestingly, artisan surnames such as Mistri, Suthar, Prajapati and Luhar are found in the type of industry in which they have some traditional base and network. Momin and Basmiya, Muslim surnames, appear in the cotton textile industry only. We do not find industries with a high concentration of Brahman or Kshatriya surnames, with the exception of the leather industry, but the sample is very small.

The name Patel accounts for 22.3 per cent of all manufactured products in the sample. Its share is particularly high in food product (I) (53.6 per cent), food product (II) (33.8 per cent), wood products (45.4 per cent), and non-metallic mineral products (34.1 per cent). The agro-based and rural-based industries have played a very important role in the entrepreneurial development of the Patidars. Wood products and non-metallic mineral products are closely linked to the construction industry, which the Patidars have dominated in recent years.

Table 7.3 : Distribution of the Top Five Surnames by Type of Industry

(Frequency/ %)

Industry Group	Ist	2nd	3rd	4th	5th	Total (% of 50+Group)
Food Products (1)	Patel	Shah	Thakkar	Modi	Sheth	399.00
	(53.60)	(13.50)	(3.00)	(2.00)	(1.80)	(81.70)
Food Products (2)	Patel	Shah	Thakkar	Modi	0.00	139.00
	(33.80)	(6.50)	(2.90)	(2.90)	0.00	(54.00)
Cotton Textiles	Patel	Momin	Shah	Panara	Basmiya	2272.00
	(20.7)	(10.40)	(5.00)	(3.00)	(2.30)	(50.00)
Wool, Silk &	Patel	Jarivala	Shah	Kapadiya	0.00	2152.00
Synthetic Fibre	(15.30)	(4.60)	(4.20)	(1.50)	0.00	(34.70)
Hosiery	Shah	Patel	Mehta	Jain	Sheth	249.00
Garments	(13.70)	(8.80)	(1.60)	(1.60)	(1.20)	(36.10)
Wood Products	Patel	Mistri	Suthar	Panchal	Shah	1043.00
	(45.40)	(13.80)	(5.50)	(2.90)	(2.10)	(77.20)
Paper Products &	Patel	Shah	Mehta	Sheth	0.00	764.00
Printing	(20.40)	(16.00)	(2.70)	(2.10)	0.00	(58.80)
Leather Products	Patel	Parmar	0.00	0.00	0.00	26.00
	(7.70)	(7.70)	0.00	0.00	0.00	(34.60)
Rubber & Plastic	Patel	Shah	Mehta	Desai	Panchal	1169.00
Products	(19.20)	(13.90)	(1.90)	(1.60)	(1.30)	(54.70)

(Contd.)

Table 7.3 *(Contd.)*

Industry Group	Ist	2nd	3rd	4th	5th	Total (% of 50+Group)
Chemical & Product	Patel (26.50)	Shah (12.60)	Desai (1.90)	Modi (1.60)	Mehta (1.50)	1893.00 (58.10)
Non-Metallic Mineral Product	Patel (34.10)	Shah (10.80)	Prajapati (3.30)	Doshi (1.40)	0.00 0.00	659.00 (65.70)
Basic Metal Industries	Patel (23.80)	Panchal (13.50)	Shah (7.90)	Mistri (2.40)	Luthar (1.60)	1219.00 (61.90)
Metal Product	Patel (12.90)	Panchal (12.20)	Shah (7.40)	Luthar (5.10)	Mehta (1.50)	2115.00 (56.10)
Machinery & Parts	Patel (20.30)	Panchal (13.40)	Shah (6.00)	Mistri (2.70)	Gajjar (1.50)	3507.00 (59.10)
Electrical Machinery	Patel (18.00)	Shah (9.20)	Panchal (2.40)	Mehta (2.30)	Desai (1.20)	884.00 (46.00)
Transport Equipments	Patel (22.90)	Panchal (7.50)	Shah (6.20)	Mistri (2.60)	Sharma (1.50)	611.00 (57.90)
Misc.Manufacturing Equipments	Patel (30.50)	Shah (7.20)	Prajapat (4.00)	Mistri (3.60)	0.00 0.00	223.00 (59.60)
Repair Service	Patel (16.30)	Panchal (6.20)	Mistri (3.90)	Shekh (2.30)	0.00 0.00	129.00 (42.60)
Total	Patel (22.30)	Shah (7.80)	Panchal (5.30)	Mistri (1.90)	Momin (1.40)	19453.00 (55.40)

Source: Govt. of Gujarat, The Gujarat Directory of Manufacturers, Industrial Extension Bureau, Ahmedabad, 1989.

Among the dispersed type of industry, in which there are no dominant surnames, wool, silk and synthetic textiles as well as hosiery and garments are similar to cotton textiles, which have attracted many entrepreneurs irrespective of religion and caste. This is because in these industries, traditional technology and modern technology are able to coexist. In contrast, the electrical machinery and parts industry belongs to the modern sector, together with rubber and plastic products and chemical products, which are not bound by any caste occupational tradition.

Table 7.4 shows the distribution of surname groups by type of industry. Since we consulted only those surname groups whose frequency came to more than 50, the percentage share of each group does not represent that of the total sample. Still, we can identify the dominance of Groups 5, 3 and 6, as a whole. An industry-wise examination reveals that Group 5 dominates in food product (I), wood products, non-metallic mineral products, and miscellaneous manufacturing. Group 3 shares high percentages in wool, silk and synthetic textiles, hosiery and garments, paper products and printing, rubber and plastic products, and chemical and chemical products. The percentage share occupied by Group 6 varies considerably among industry types. Its share is high only in those industries somehow linked to the traditional technology of artisan castes. Likewise, the dominance by Group 7 is seen only in cotton textiles, with which Muslims have long been associated as entrepreneurs.

If we consider the total sample including those surnames whose frequencies of occurrence are less than 50, the percentage share of the Patidars would appear somewhat smaller, while that of the Baniyas would increase considerably[22]. As a result, the percentage differentials between the two groups would shrink considerably. The percentage share of Group 1 would slightly increase, while those of Groups 2 and 6 would decline.

Distribution of Industries by Social Group

Table 7.5 presents the distribution of industries by surname group. It is interesting to note that this distribution pattern varies considerably among the surname groups. Broadly, these surname groups can be divided into concentrated and dispersed types based on their distribution pattern among industries. We may regard Groups 1, 3, 4 and 5 as dispersed, and Groups 2, 6 and 7 as concentrated. Among the latter, Group 6 shows a higher concentration in machinery and parts, except apparatus (35.6 per cent), metal products (23.2 per cent), wood products (13.0 per cent), and basic metal industries (12.1 per cent), while Group 7 is especially

Table 7.4 : Distribution of Surname Groups by Type of Industry

(Frequency/ %)

Type of Industry	Group 1	Group 2	Group 3	Group 4	Group 5	Group 6	Group 7	Total
Food Products (1)	4.00	0.00	88.00	10.00	214.00	8.00	2.00	326.00
	(1.20)	0.00	(27.00)	(3.10)	(65.60)	(2.50)	(0.60)	(100.00)
Food Products (2)	2.00	2.00	21.00	1.00	47.00	2.00	0.00	75.00
	(2.70)	(2.70)	(28.00)	(1.30)	(62.70)	(2.70)	0.00	(100.00)
Cotton Textiles	21.00	30.00	158.00	17.00	470.00	10.00	429.00	1135.00
	(1.90)	(2.60)	(13.90)	(1.50)	(41.40)	(0.90)	(37.80)	(100.00)
Wool, Silk &	21.00	17.00	325.00	41.00	330.00	12.00	1.00	747.00
Synthetic Fibre	(2.80)	(2.30)	(43.50)	(5.50)	(44.20)	(1.60)	(0.10)	(100.00)
Hosiery	6.00	2.00	53.00	7.00	22.00	0.00	0.00	90.00
Garments	(6.70)	(2.20)	(58.90)	(7.80)	(24.40)	0.00	0.00	(100.00)
Wood Products	13.00	14.00	37.00	9.00	474.00	252.00	6.00	805.00
	(1.60)	(1.70)	(4.60)	(1.10)	(58.90)	(31.30)	(0.70)	(100.00)
Paper Products &	39.00	20.00	179.00	34.00	156.00	18.00	3.00	449.00
Printing	(8.70)	(4.50)	(39.90)	(7.60)	(34.70)	(4.00)	(0.70)	(100.00)
Leather Products	1.00	3.00	2.00	0.00	2.00	0.00	1.00	9.00
	(11.10)	(33.30)	(22.20)	0.00	(22.20)	0.00	(11.10)	(100.00)
Rubber & Plastic	47.00	30.00	249.00	48.00	225.00	35.00	6.00	640.00
Products	(7.30)	(4.70)	(38.90)	(7.50)	(35.20)	(5.50)	(0.90)	(100.00)

(Contd.)

Table 7.4 *(Contd.)*

(Frequency/ %)

Type of Industry	Group 1	Group 2	Group 3	Group 4	Group 5	Group 6	Group 7	Total
Chemical &	53.00	38.00	390.00	73.00	502.00	36.00	8.00	1100.00
Product	(4.80)	(3.50)	(35.50)	(6.60)	(45.60)	(3.30)	(0.70)	(100.00)
Non-Metallic	25.00	29.00	105.00	11.00	225.00	38.00	0.00	433.00
Mineral Product	(5.80)	(6.70)	(24.20)	(2.50)	(52.00)	(8.80)	0.00	(100.00)
Basic Metal	42.00	25.00	131.00	20.00	290.00	233.00	13.00	754.00
Industries	(5.60)	(3.30)	(17.40)	(2.70)	(38.50)	(30.90)	(1.70)	(100.00)
Metal Product	44.00	115.00	232.00	59.00	273.00	451.00	13.00	1187.00
	(3.70)	(9.70)	(19.50)	(5.00)	(23.00)	(38.00)	(1.10)	(100.00)
Machinery & Parts	90.00	150.00	321.00	84.00	713.00	688.00	25.00	2071.00
	(4.30)	(7.20)	(15.50)	(4.10)	(34.40)	(33.20)	(1.20)	(100.00)
Electrical Machinery	22.00	39.00	106.00	38.00	159.00	39.00	4.00	407.00
	(5.40)	(9.60)	(26.00)	(9.30)	(39.10)	(9.60)	(1.00)	(100.00)
Transport	32.00	24.00	64.00	16.00	140.00	75.00	3.00	354.00
Equipments	(9.00)	(6.80)	(18.10)	(4.50)	(39.50)	(21.20)	(0.80)	(100.00)

(Contd.)

Table 7.4 *(Contd.)*

(Frequency/ %)

Type of Industry	Group 1	Group 2	Group 3	Group 4	Group 5	Group 6	Group 7	Total
Misc. Manufacturing Equipments	5.00	7.00	23.00	8.00	68.00	21.00	1.00	133.00
	(3.80)	(5.30)	(17.30)	(6.00)	(51.10)	(15.80)	(0.80)	(100.00)
Repair Service	4.00	6.00	4.00	1.00	21.00	14.00	5.00	55.00
	(7.30)	(10.90)	(7.30)	(1.80)	(38.20)	(25.50)	(9.10)	(100.00)
Total	471.00	551.00	2488.00	477.00	4331.00	1932.00	520.00	10770.00
	(4.40)	(5.10)	(23.10)	(4.40)	(40.20)	(17.90)	(4.80)	(100.00)

Source: Govt. of Gujarat, The Gujarat Directory of Manufacturers, Industrial Extension Bureau, Ahmedabad, 1989.

Table 7.5 : Distribution of Industries by Surname Group

(Frequency/ %)

Type of Industry	Group 1	Group 2	Group 3	Group 4	Group 5	Group 6	Group 7	Total
Food Products (1)	4.00	0.00	88.00	10.00	214.00	8.00	2.00	326.00
	(0.80)	0.00	(3.50)	(2.10)	(4.90)	(0.40)	(0.40)	(3.00)
Food Products (2)	2.00	2.00	21.00	1.00	47.00	2.00	0.00	75.00
	(0.40)	(0.40)	(0.80)	(0.20)	(1.10)	(0.10)	0.00	(0.70)
Cotton Textiles	21.00	30.00	158.00	17.00	470.00	10.00	429.00	1135.00
	(4.50)	(5.40)	(6.40)	(3.60)	(10.90)	(0.50)	(82.50)	(10.50)
Wool, Silk &	21.00	17.00	325.00	41.00	330.00	12.00	1.00	747.00
Synthetic Fibre	(4.50)	(3.10)	(13.10)	(8.60)	(7.60)	(0.60)	(0.20)	(6.90)
Hosiery	6.00	2.00	53.00	7.00	22.00	0.00	0.00	90.00
Garments	(1.30)	(0.40)	(2.10)	(1.50)	(0.50)	0.00	0.00	(0.80)
Wood Products	13.00	14.00	37.00	9.00	474.00	252.00	6.00	805.00
	(2.80)	(2.50)	(1.50)	(1.90)	(10.90)	(13.00)	(1.20)	(7.50)
Paper Products &	39.00	20.00	179.00	34.00	156.00	18.00	3.00	449.00
Printing	(8.30)	(3.60)	(7.20)	(7.10)	(3.60)	(0.90)	(0.60)	(4.20)
Leather Products	1.00	3.00	2.00	0.00	2.00	0.00	1.00	9.00
	(0.20)	(0.50)	(0.10)	0.00	0.00	0.00	(0.20)	(0.10)

(Contd.)

Table 7.5 *(Contd.)*

(Frequency/ %)

Type of Industry	Group 1	Group 2	Group 3	Group 4	Group 5	Group 6	Group 7	Total
Rubber & Plastic Products	47.00 (10.00)	30.00 (5.40)	249.00 (10.00)	48.00 (10.10)	225.00 (5.20)	35.00 (1.80)	6.00 (1.20)	640.00 (5.90)
Chemical & Product	53.00 (11.30)	38.00 (6.90)	390.00 15.70	73.00 (15.30)	502.00 (11.60)	36.00 (1.90)	8.00 (1.50)	1100.00 (10.20)
Non-Metalic Mineral Product	25.00 (5.30)	29.00 (5.30)	105.00 (4.20)	11.00 (2.30)	225.00 (5.20)	38.00 (2.00)	0.00 0.00	433.00 (4.00)
Basic Metal Industries	42.00 (8.90)	25.00 (4.50)	131.00 (5.30)	20.00 (4.20)	290.00 (6.70)	233.00 (12.10)	13.00 (2.50)	754.00 (7.00)
Metal Product	44.00 (9.30)	115.00 (20.90)	232.00 (9.30)	59.00 (12.40)	273.00 (6.30)	451.00 (23.30)	13.00 (2.50)	1187.00 (11.00)
Machinery & Parts	90.00 (19.10)	150.00 (27.20)	321.00 (12.90)	84.00 (17.60)	713.00 (16.50)	688.00 (35.60)	25.00 (4.80)	2071.00 (19.20)
Electrical Machinery	22.00 (4.70)	39.00 (7.10)	106.00 (4.30)	38.00 (8.00)	159.00 (3.70)	39.00 (2.00)	4.00 (0.80)	407.00 (3.80)
Transport Equipments	32.00 (6.80)	24.00 (4.40)	64.00 (2.60)	16.00 (3.40)	140.00 (3.20)	75.00 (3.90)	3.00 (0.60)	354.00 (3.30)

(Contd.)

Table 7.5 *(Contd.)*

(Frequency/ %)

Type of Industry	Group 1	Group 2	Group 3	Group 4	Group 5	Group 6	Group 7	Total
Misc.Manufacturing Equipments	5.00 (1.10)	7.00 (1.30)	23.00 (0.90)	8.00 (1.70)	68.00 (1.60)	21.00 (1.10)	1.00 (0.20)	133.00 (1.20)
Repair Service	4.00 (0.80)	6.00 (1.10)	4.00 (0.20)	1.00 (0.20)	21.00 (0.50)	14.00 (0.70)	5.00 (1.00)	55.00 (0.50)
Total	471.00 (100.00)	551.00 (100.00)	2488.00 (100.00)	477.00 (100.00)	4331.00 (100.00)	1932.00 (100.00)	520.00 (100.00)	10770.00 (100.00)

Source: Govt. of Gujarat, The Gujarat Directory of Manufacturers, Industrial Extension Bureau, Ahmedabad, 1989.

concentrated in cotton textiles (82.5 per cent). The distribution pattern of Group 2 also shows relatively a higher concentration in machinery and parts, except apparatus (27.2 per cent), and metal products (20.9 per cent). Notably, these highly concentrated industries tend not only to have some traditional linkages with the surname group in question, but are also labour intensive, while the dispersed groups show reasonably high percentages among capital intensive industries, such as chemical products, rubber and plastic products, and wool, silk and synthetic textiles.

So far, the correlation between industry and surname group has been considered without any inquiry into tendencies among individual surnames. It is interesting to note that each group contains several surnames that are closely associated with particular industries even among the dispersed surname groups. For example, Jarivala and Kapadiya in Group 3 are highly concentrated in silk and synthetic textiles, with as many as 91.5 per cent of the Jarivala and 60 per cent of the Kapadiya names being listed in that industry. Among Group 2, all the surnames except Chaudhri show high concentration in machinery and parts, except apparatus, and in metal products. Among Group 7, Basmiya, Panara, Momin and Mansuri show extremely high concentrations in cotton textiles, with shares of 96.3 per cent, 95.8 per cent, 90.1 per cent, and 83.6 per cent, respectively.

The artisan caste surnames attract special attention. As Table 7.6 shows, Panchal, classified as an "advanced" caste in pre-independence censuses and constituting the most frequently occurring surname in Group 6, is concentrated in machinery and metal-related industries, with a smaller number of entries in cotton textiles and chemical products. On the contrary, Soni, again classified as an advanced caste in pre-independent censuses, is associated with cotton textiles and chemical products. Its distribution pattern by industry has a lot of similarity with that of Group 3. Soni households may have thus enjoyed many more opportunities for capital accumulation through trade and business than through manufacturing gold products. Both Suthar and Mistri are highly concentrated in wood products, their traditional occupation. Luhar is concentrated in machinery and metal industries, in which it has some advantages in technology and networks. Adversely, Prajapati shows dispersed pattern like that of Soni, though it still maintains an association with the non-metallic mineral products industry.

Table 7.6 : Distribution of Artisan Castes by Type of Industry

(Frequency/ %)

Type of Industry	Gajjar	Luhar	Mistri	Panchal	Prajapathi	Soni	Suthar	Total
Food Products (1)	1.00	0.00	1.00	4.00	1.00	1.00	0.00	8.00
	(0.80)	0.00	(0.30)	(0.40)	(1.00)	(1.70)	0.00	(0.40)
Food Products (2)	1.00	0.00	0.00	1.00	0.00	0.00	0.00	2.00
	(0.80)	0.00	0.00	(0.10)	0.00	0.00	0.00	(0.10)
Cotton Textiles	1.00	0.00	0.00	1.00	4.00	4.00	0.00	10.00
	(0.80)	0.00	0.00	(0.10)	(4.00)	(6.90)	0.00	(0.50)
Wool, Silk &	6.00	0.00	1.00	3.00	1.00	1.00	0.00	12.00
Synthetic Fibre	(5.10)	0.00	(0.30)	(0.30)	(1.00)	(1.70)	0.00	(0.60)
Hosiery	0.00	0.00	0.00	0.00	0.00	0.00	0.00	0.00
Garments	0.00	0.00	0.00	0.00	0.00	0.00	0.00	0.00
Wood Products	16.00	4.00	144.00	30.00	1.00	0.00	57.00	252.00
	(13.60)	(2.70)	(38.70)	(2.90)	(1.00)	0.00	(57.00)	(13.00)
Paper Products &	0.00	0.00	3.00	2.00	2.00	9.00	2.00	18.00
Printing	0.00	0.00	(0.80)	(0.20)	(2.00)	(15.50)	(2.00)	(0.90)
Leather Products	0.00	0.00	0.00	0.00	0.00	0.00	0.00	0.00
	0.00	0.00	0.00	0.00	0.00	0.00	0.00	0.00
Rubber & Plastic	2.00	0.00	10.00	15.00	1.00	4.00	3.00	35.00
Products	(1.70)	0.00	(2.70)	(1.50)	(1.00)	(6.90)	(3.00)	(1.80)

(Contd.)

Table 7.6 : Distribution of Artisan Castes by Type of Industry

(Frequency/ %)

Type of Industry	Gajjar	Luhar	Mistri	Panchal	Prajapati	Soni	Suthar	Total
Chemical &	5.00	1.00	4.00	2.00	17.00	6.00	1.00	36.00
Product	(4.20)	(0.70)	(1.10)	(0.20)	(17.00)	(10.30)	(1.00)	(1.90)
Non-Metallic	1.00	0.00	7.00	6.00	22.00	1.00	1.00	38.00
Mineral Product	(0.80)	0.00	(1.90)	(0.60)	(22.00)	(1.70)	(1.00)	(2.00)
Basic Metal	8.00	19.00	29.00	165.00	7.00	3.00	2.00	233.00
Industries	(6.80)	(12.70)	(7.80)	(16.00)	(7.00)	(5.20)	(2.00)	(12.10)
Metal Product	15.00	107.00	46.00	259.00	10.00	9.00	5.00	451.00
	(12.70)	(71.30)	(12.40)	(25.00)	(10.00)	(15.50)	(5.00)	(23.30)
Machinery & Parts	53.00	13.00	93.00	469.00	20.00	13.00	27.00	688.00
	(44.90)	(8.70)	(25.00)	(45.40)	(20.00)	(22.40)	(27.00)	(35.60)
Electrical Machinery	9.00	0.00	5.00	21.00	2.00	2.00	0.00	39.00
	(7.60)	0.00	(1.30)	(2.00)	(2.00)	(3.40)	0.00	(2.00)
Transport	0.00	5.00	16.00	46.00	2.00	4.00	2.00	75.00
Equipments	0.00	(3.30)	(4.30)	(4.40)	(2.00)	(6.90)	(2.00)	(3.90)
Misc.Manufacturing	0.00	1.00	8.00	2.00	9.00	1.00	0.00	21.00
Equipments	0.00	(0.70)	(2.20)	(0.20)	(9.00)	(1.70)	0.00	(1.10)
Repair Service	0.00	0.00	5.00	8.00	1.00	0.00	0.00	14.00
	0.00	0.00	(1.30)	(0.80)	(1.00)	0.00	0.00	(0.70)
Total	118.00	150.00	372.00	1034.00	100.00	58.00	100.00	1932.00
	(100.00)	(100.00)	(100.00)	(100.00)	(100.00)	(100.00)	(100.00)	(100.00)

Source: Govt. of Gujarat, The Gujarat Directory of Manufacturers, Industrial Extension Bureau, Ahmedabad, 1989.

Industrial Location and Social Group

The distribution of industry by caste is determined by the socio-economic mobility of each caste as a whole, embodied in level of education, enterprise, the existence of a information network, level of capital accumulation, etc., all of which have been shaped in the course of the historical development of the region. Patterns of investment and entry into industries have fairly been diversified among the highly mobile castes, while among the less mobile, we still find a close linkage with their traditional occupations. The distribution pattern of industries involved in by a given caste is also affected by its pattern of business location in Gujarat, particularly when the geographical distribution of that caste is limited to a small region. Of course, this can be compensated for to, some extent, by migration on the part of entrepreneurs in the case of highly mobile castes.

Table 7.7 shows that patterns of geographical distribution vary considerably among our surname sample groups. The dispersed pattern characterizes Groups 1, 3 and 5, among which nearly half of the sample's entrepreneurs are located in central Gujarat, while the rest are widely scattered over other regions. This dispersed pattern in geographical distribution seems to be positively related with the diversified distribution of industries in which these surname groups participate. On the contrary, a concentrated geographical distribution pattern marks Groups 2, 6 and 7. The main region of Group 2 is Saurashtra, while Group 6 is highly concentrated in central and northern Gujarat. These two groups also share a common feature in regard to their high concentration in the machinery and metal product industries. Group 7 is not only highly concentrated in central Gujarat, but also exclusively concentrated in cotton textiles.

As the result of differences in geographical distribution pattern among these surname groups, there is considerable variation in their distribution by region. Before going into detail, let us turn to the weight of those surnames who appear more than 50 times in the total sample, to point out any limitations before we proceed with the analysis. Their weight is as high as 84.2 per cent for northern Gujarat, followed by 65.3% for central Gujarat. However, their weight is relatively low for Saurashtra and southern Gujarat, 42.2 per cent and 41 per cent respectively. In northern Gujarat, Groups 5 and 6 dominate, while in central Gujarat, Groups 3, 5 and 6 appear most frequently, although all the groups have set down roots in the region. If we consider Saurashtra in terms of the total listing, the

Table 7.7 : Distribution of Surname Groups by Region

(Frequency/ %)

Surname Group	Kutch	Saurashtra	North Gujarat	Central Gujarat	South Gujarat	Total
Group 1	1.00	107.00	46.00	245.00	72.00	471.00
	(0.20)	(22.70)	(9.80)	(52.00)	(15.30)	(100.00)
	[2.0]	[4.7]	[3.1]	[4.5]	[4.9]	[4.4]
Group 2	3.00	336.00	74.00	105.00	33.00	551.00
	(0.50)	(61.00)	(13.40)	(19.10)	(6.00)	(100.00)
	[6.1]	[14.8]	[4.9]	[1.9]	[2.2]	[5.1]
Group 3	19.00	419.00	214.00	1264.00	572.00	2488.00
	(0.80)	(16.80)	(8.60)	(50.80)	(23.00)	(100.00)
	[38.8]	[18.4]	[14.3]	[23.1]	[38.7]	[23.1]
Group4	11.00	137.00	11.00	182.00	136.00	477.00
	(2.30)	(28.70)	(2.30)	(38.20)	(28.50)	(100.00)
	[22.4]	[6.0]	[0.7]	[3.3]	[9.2]	[4.4]
Group 5	11.00	1019.00	632.00	2158.00	511.00	4331.00
	(0.30)	(23.50)	(14.60)	(49.80)	(11.80)	(100.00)
	[22.4]	[44.8]	[42.2]	[39.5]	[34.6]	[40.2]
Group 6	4.00	191.00	507.00	1083.00	147.00	1932.00
	(0.20)	(9.90)	(26.20)	(56.10)	(7.60)	(100.00)
	[8.2]	[8.4]	[33.8]	[19.8]	[9.9]	[17.9]
Group 7	0.00	68.00	14.00	429.00	9.00	520.00
	0.00	(13.10)	(2.70)	(82.50)	(1.70)	(100.00)
	0.00	[3.0]	[0.9]	[7.8]	[0.6]	[4.8]
Total	49.00	2277.00	1498.00	5466.00	1479.00	10770.00
	(0.50)	(21.10)	(13.90)	(50.80)	(13.70)	(100.00)
	[100.0]	[100.0]	(100.00)	[100.0]	[100.0]	[100.0]

Source : Govt. of Gujarat, The Gujarat Directory of Manufacturers, Industrial Extension Bureau, Ahmedabad, 1989.

distribution concentration of Groups 2 and 3 would definitely increase, while that of Group 5 would decrease. The picture posed by southern Gujarat is quite different from the other regions studied that Group 5 does not predominate there like in the other regions. Instead, it is Group 3 that plays the leading role in southern Gujarat. If we consider the total listing, we find the largest number of surnames in south Gujarat to be of Baniya and non-Gujarati, but to a slightly less extent . It is well known to students of the region's economy that it has been attracting massive investment and many entrepreneurs from outside states, resulting in the most diversified region in terms of the composition of entrepreneurs among the regions in Gujarat.

SSI ENTREPRENEURS AMONG THE BACKWARD CLASSES

The SSI sector plays a very essential role in the industrial structure of India. It includes many industrial units of modern sector, and is partly overlapped with factory sector too. Thus, SSI is important to encourage the growth of industrial entrepreneurship among various communities throughout the country. The basic framework of SSI policies, since its inception, has long been characterised by various protective measures, including a special package for the weaker sections such as SCs, STs, OBCs and women. However, a lot of changes in the policy framework for SSIs are being taken place since the introduction of new economic policy in 1991.

The purpose of this section is to analyse the mode and particularity of SSI units promoted by SCs, STs, SEBCs and women in Gujarat in recent years after the new economic policy. The reference period in this section is from 1992 to 1997, which is comparable to some extent with the Gujarat Directory of Manufacturers.

Salient Features

Table 7.8 presents the yearly number of units registered in Gujarat from 1992/93 to 1997/98 according to area, type and community. Before going into analysis, it may be useful to explain several terms used in the table. All units are classified into three areas, metropolitan, urban and rural, according to the census classification. Any units located in the industrially backward area, as defined by the central and state governments, are eligible for aforementioned package concerning finance, subsidies and concessions. This special package is also applicable to the units promoted by SC, ST, SEBC and female entrepreneurs upon application and subsequent approval. There may be some eligible entrepreneurs who have not applied for this package, though their number should be very small, particularly among SCs and STs, since the package is probably the most attractive for them. However, failure to apply would be more frequent among SEBCs, because the package has become available to them only recently. Women constitute another such category, but they cannot be

Table 7.8 : Distribution of Units by District and by Category of Entrepreneurs During 1992-93 — 1997-98

(No. of Units/Workers)

	A: No.of Units				B: Employment			
	All	SC	ST	SEBC	All	SC	ST	SEBC
1. Ahmedabad	17583	268	14	272	74726	696	39	864
	[21.4]	[7.4]	[1.7]	[23.0]	(4.20)	(2.60)	(2.80)	(3.20)
2. Amreli	1517.00	268.00	1.00	27.00	3699.00	478.00	2.00	169.00
	[1.8]	[7.4]	[0.1]	[2.3]	(2.40)	(1.80)	(2.00)	(6.30)
3. Banaskantha	1945.00	308.00	46.00	87.00	6044.00	600.00	60.00	318.00
	[2.4]	[8.5]	[5.6]	[7.4]	(3.10)	(1.90)	(1.30)	(3.70)
4. Bharuch	4358.00	84.00	124.00	45.00	14133.00	205.00	238.00	142.00
	[5.3]	[2.3]	[15.1]	[3.8]	(3.20)	(2.40)	(1.90)	(3.20)
5. Bhavnagar	3563.00	496.00	29.00	167.00	16419.00	1560.00	53.00	749.00
	[4.3]	[13.7]	[3.5]	[14.1]	(4.60)	(3.10)	(1.80)	(4.50)
6. Dangs	10.00	0.00	0.00	0.00	14.00	0.00	0.00	0.00
	[0.0]	[0.0]	[0.0]	[0.0]	(1.40)	0.00	0.00	0.00
7. Gandhinagar	1126.00	32.00	1.00	0.00	3863.00	150.00	1.00	0.00
	[1.4]	[0.9]	[0.1]	[0.0]	(3.40)	(4.70)	(1.00)	0.00
8. Jamnagar	3208.00	193.00	4.00	57.00	8787.00	302.00	14.00	119.00
	[3.9]	[5.3]	[0.5]	[4.8]	(2.70)	(1.60)	(3.50)	(2.10)

(Contd.)

Table 7.8 *(Contd.)*

(No. of Units/Workers)

	A: No.of Units				B: Employment			
	All	SC	ST	SEBC	All	SC	ST	SEBC
9. Junagarh	2226.00	34.00	4.00	58.00	9736.00	97.00	9.00	241.00
	[2.7]	[0.9]	[0.5]	[4.9]	(4.40)	(2.9)	(2.30)	(4.20)
10. Kheda	3766.00	56.00	10.00	0.00	10524.00	257.00	12.00	0.00
	[4.6]	[1.6]	[1.2]	[0.0]	(2.80)	(4.60)	(1.20)	0.00
11. Kutch	1774.00	368.00	12.00	75.00	7228.00	736.00	36.00	458.00
	[2.2]	[10.2]	[1.5]	[6.4]	(4.10)	(2.00)	(3.00)	(6.10)
12. Mehsana	4647.00	196.00	21.00	8.00	23951.00	516.00	63.00	18.00
	[5.7]	[5.4]	[2.6]	[0.7]	(5.20)	(2.60)	(3.00)	(2.30)
13. Panchmahals	2228.00	30.00	87.00	6.00	8491.00	43.00	420.00	54.00
	[2.7]	[0.8]	[10.6]	[0.5]	(3.80)	(1.40)	((4.8)	(9.00)
14. Rajkot	8251.00	68.00	14.00	41.00	28724.00	230.00	37.00	151.00
	[10.0]	[1.9]	[1.7]	[3.5]	(3.50)	(3.40)	(2.60)	(3.70)
15. Sabarkantha	2497.00	232.00	166.00	145.00	6498.00	263.00	196.00	213.00
	[3.0]	[6.4]	[20.2]	[12.3]	(2.60)	(1.10)	(1.20)	(1.50)
16. Surat	11823.00	37.00	139.00	181.00	56955.00	95.00	306.00	597.00
	[14.4]	[1.0]	[16.9]	[15.3]	(4.80)	(2.60)	(2.20)	(3.30)

(Contd.)

Table 7.8 *(Contd.)*

(No. of Units/Workers)

	A: No.of Units				B: Employment			
	All	SC	ST	SEBC	All	SC	ST	SEBC
17. Surendranagar	2347.00	820.00	0.00	0.00	10168.00	1570.00	0.00	0.00
	[2.9]	[22.7]	[0.0]	[0.0]	(4.30)	(1.90)	0.00	0.00
18. Vadodara	4430.00	61.00	30.00	1.00	21638.00	215.00	76.00	6.00
	[5.4]	[1.7]	[3.6]	[0.1]	(4.90)	(3.5)	(2.50)	(6.00)
19. Valsad	4816.00	57.00	120.00	10.00	20993.00	209.00	290.00	39.00
	[5.9]	[1.6]	[14.6]	[0.8]	(4.40)	(3.70)	(2.40)	(3.90)
Total	82115.00	3608.00	822.00	1181.00	332618.00	8222.00	1861.00	4255.00
	[100.0]	[100.0]	[100.0]	[100.0]	(4.10)	(2.30)	(2.30)	(3.60)

Notes : (1) Asterisk indicates the backward district. (2) Brackets in the column A show the percentage distribution while brackets in the B column shows the employment per unit.

Source: Industries Commissionerate, Gandhinagar, computed by INDEXTB, Computer Centre, Ahmedabad.

considered any weaker as eligible candidates under this system. The demarcation between tiny and non-tiny units is based solely on fixed capital investment for plant and machinery. During our reference period, the investment limits for tiny industry was Rs. 5 lakh and for non-tiny industry Rs. 65 lakh. For anciliary units Rs. 75 lakh was the ceiling (however, the ceiling was revised to Rs. 25 lakh for tiny industry to Rs. 3 crores for non-tiny industry in 1997). The small-scale service business and enterprise (SSSBES) is a new category that was added to SSI in 1991. It includes various activities in service industries having nothing to do with manufacturing. Our major findings are as follows :

First, the number of registered units increased constantly during the reference period, but not to the extent expected in view of the new economic policy. Rather, the annual growth rate of SSI units slowed down during this period compared to the late 1980s.

Secondly, units in industrially backward areas occupied a high percentage share of around 40 per cent throughout the period, mainly due to a positive response by entrepreneurs towards the special subsidies and concessions offered to them. As a result, the initial motivation of the government to decrease regional imbalance in industrial development was achieved to some extent.

Thirdly, the number of those units run by SC, ST, and SEBC entrepreneurs fluctuated considerably during the reference period. Among these groups, SCs were entering the SSI sector most eagerly, achieving a share of 4.4 per cent during the period. However, the number of SC units declined steeply in 1996-97, but we do not know why. The number of ST units is still relatively less among the backward classes. This seems to be simply associated with their narrow base and limited network in SSI sector. While the number of SEBC units showed an increasing trend, which should continue for years to come. Their potential has yet to be tapped by legal and institutional support. Contrary to SC and ST units, female-led units recorded a constant increase during the period.

Fourthly, the weight of non-tiny units was declining both in terms of the numbers and its percentage share. Instead, tiny units showed a steady increase in numbers and percentage share, which is partly due to the newly set capital limits for this category of enterprise (Rs. 5 lakh) in 1991, and partly due to a drastic increase in the number of SSSBES units in recent years. With the creation of SSSBES category in 1991, structural changes in SSI units have begun to occur.

Distribution of SSI Units by District

In the course of the development of SSIs in Gujarat, the geographical distribution of SSI units has become more and more dispersed to cover even the backward districts of the state, particularly following the late 80s. Previously, SSI units were more concentrated in the three industrial centres of Ahmedabad, Rajkot and Surat. However, as Table 7.9 demonstrates, geographical distribution among newly registered units in our reference period gives us a changing pattern, though the three industrial centres still occupy a combined share of around 46 per cent of all SSIs. In contrast to this overall picture, geographical distribution of SSI units run by SC and ST entrepreneurs shows a distinct pattern in their concentration in particular regions as well as backward districts. The units owned by SCs are much more concentrated in Saurashtra and Kutch (however, very lightly in Rajkot), and those units owned by STs are heavily concentrated in such districts which constitute a tribal belt. The other characteristic shared by SC and ST-owned units is considerable annual fluctuation in terms of the number of newly registered units in each district. Distribution of units by district within their concentrated regions has changed drastically year after year. In contrast to SCs and STs, geographical distribution pattern of units owned by SEBCs is similar to that of the total units, with a geographically wider distribution and comparatively less percentage share of those units located in the backward districts.

Workforce data for SSI units in the Table is closely associated with type of industry and amount of investment, resulting in some differences in the number of employees by district irrespective of entrepreneurial category. Since the majority of SSI units falls into the category of tiny industry or SSSBES, the number of employees per unit appears small. However, we notice a not so insignificant gap among the units along entrepreneurial category lines. Among the backward classes, the number of employees per unit is highest in the units owned by SEBCs, and is positively related to their relative leadership in investment, as will be examined later.

Distribution of SSI Units by Group of Industry

As Table 7.10 shows, Gujarat has a steady base of SSIs at present in machinery and parts, basic metal industries, rubber and plastic products, and chemicals and chemical products, which functions as a driving force for upgrading the industrial structure of the state as a whole. Previously,

Table 7.9 : Distribution of Units and Investment by Group of Industry and by Category of Entrepreneurs During 1992-93 — 1997-98

Industry Group	A: No.of Units				B: Investment (Lakh Rupees)			
	All	SC	ST	SEBC	All	SC	ST	SEBC
1. Food Products	4703 [5.7]	51 [1.4]	253 [30.7]	71 [6.0]	9994.46 (2.13)	88.33 (1.73)	85.13 (0.34)	415.93 (5.86)
2. Beverages, Tobacco etc	508 [0.6]	4 [0.1]	0 [0.0]	14 [1.2]	254.51 (0.50)	0.66 (0.17)	0.00 0.00	2.61 (0.19)
3. Cotton Textiles	2829 [3.4]	1479 [41.0]	24 [2.9]	14 [1.2]	11524.19 (4.07)	154.73 (0.10)	8.90 (0.37)	75.75 (5.41)
4. Wool, Silk & Synthetic Fibre	4337 [5.3]	265 [7.3]	16 [1.9]	41 [3.5]	35898.37 (8.28)	70.65 (0.27)	68.05 (4.25)	191.08 (4.66)
5. Hosiery & Garments	12828 [15.6]	784 [21.7]	160 [19.5]	178 [15.1]	4956.41 (0.36)	93.21 (0.12)	29.59 (0.18)	55.92 (0.31)
6. Wood Products	2513 [3.1]	32 [0.9]	45 [5.5]	67 [5.7]	1711.60 (0.68)	6.01 (0.19)	4.67 (0.10)	13.78 (0.21)
7. Paper Products & Printing	1948 [2.4]	16 [0.4]	20 [2.4]	18 [1.5]	6819.99 (3.50)	7.54 (0.47)	16.73 (0.84)	58.18 (3.23)
8. Leather Products	766 [0.9]	239 [6.6]	38 [4.6]	12 [1.0]	171.56 (0.22)	13.64 (0.06)	2.85 (0.08)	1.02 (0.09)

(Contd.)

Table 7.9 *(Contd.)*

Industry Group	A: No. of Units				B: Investment (Lakh Rupees)			
	All	SC	ST	SEBC	All	SC	ST	SEBC
9. Rubber & Plastic Products	3091 [3.8]	60 [1.7]	8 [1.0]	41 [3.5]	16041.20 (5.19)	244.09 (4.07)	16.42 (2.05)	176.24 (4.30)
10. Chemical & Chemical Products	2424 [3.0]	15 [0.4]	4 [0.5]	19 [1.6]	15771.87 (6.510)	116.21 (7.75)	21.63 (5.41)	185.19 (9.75)
11. Non-Metallic Mineral Products	3175 [.39]	107 [3.0]	9 [1.1]	99 [8.4]	14169.01 (4.46)	198.91 (1.86)	22.95 (2.55)	248.31 (2.51)
12. Basic Metal Industries	2123 [2.6]	11 [0.3]	4 [0.5]	17 [1.4]	13647.99 (6.43)	40.16 (3.65)	3.56 (0.89)	137.17 (8.07)
13. Metal Products	4140 [5.0]	18 [0.5]	16 [1.9]	50 [4.2]	7687.21 (1.86)	12.36 (0.69)	18.70 (1.17)	43.49 (0.87)
14. Machinery Parts	6702 [8.2]	45 [1.2]	28 [3.4]	88 [7.5]	11638.80 (1.74)	87.19 (1.94)	34.78 (1.24)	105.75 (1.20)
15. Electrical Machinery	1386 `[1.7]	16 [0.4]	4 [0.5]	9 [0.8]	3886.52 92.77)	36.79 (2.30)	16.99 (4.25)	11.05 (1.23)
16. Transport Equipments	594 [0.7]	7 [0.2]	1 [[0.1]	14 [1.2]	1889.10 (3.20)	1.24 (0.18)	1.10 (1.10)	31.44 (2.25)
17. Misc.Manfucaturing Industries	4332 [5.3]	21 [0.6]	8 [1.0]	53 [4.5]	3954.43 (0.91)	28.96 (1.38)	1.98 (0.25)	76.61 (1.45)

(Contd.)

Table 7.9 *(Contd.)*

Industry Group	A: No.of Units				B: Investment (Laksh Rupees)			
	All	SC	ST	SEBC	All	SC	ST	SEBC
18. Repair Services	16546 [20.1]	365 [10.1]	137 [16.7]	270 [22.9]	2395.34 (0.14)	19.81 (0.05)	12.62 (0.09)	22.62 (0.08)
19. Others	6589 [8.0]	73 [2.0]	44 [5.4]	88 [7.5]	6501.51 (0.99)	63.03 (0.86)	22.90 (0.17)	179.81 (2.04)
Total	82115 [100.0]	3608 [100.0]	822 [100.0]	1181 [100.0]	176455.10 (2.15)	1283.27 (0.36)	389.56 (0.47)	2031.49 (1.72)

Note : Brackets in the column A shows the percentage to total, while brackets in the column B shows the investment per unit.
Source : Industries Commissionerate, Gandhinagar, computed by INDEXTB, Computer Centre, Ahmedabad.

Table 7.10 : Distribution of Units by Investment in P & M and by Category of Entrepreneurs During 1992-93 to 1997-98

(Number of Unit/%)

Category of Entrepreneurs	Investment in P & M (Lakh Rupees)						
	0 - 1	1-5	5-25	25-60	60-75	75+	Total
All Entrepreneurs	64315 (78.32)	10191 (12.41)	5807 (7.07)	1749 (2.13)	39 (0.05)	14 (0.02)	82115 (100.00)
SC Entrepreneurs	3485.00 (96.59)	73.00 (2.02)	40.00 (1.11)	10.00 (0.28)	0.00 0.00	0.00 0.00	3608.00 (100.00)
ST Entrepreneurs	780.00 (94.89)	25.00 (3.04)	16.00 (1.95)	1.00 (0.12)	0.00 0.00	0.00 0.00	822.00 (100.00)
SEBC Entrepreneurs	863.00 (82.90)	94.00 (9.03)	64.00 (6.15)	20.00 (1.92)	0.00 0.00	0.00 0.00	1041.00 (100.00)
Women Entrepreneurs	3415.00 (85.52)	359.00 (8.99)	179.00 (4.48)	40.00 (1.00)	0.00 0.00	0.00 0.00	3993.00 (100.00)

Note (1) : Data of SEBC for 1994/95, and of Women for 1993-94 is missing.
Note (2) : Figures in bracket indicate percentage to total.
Source : Industries Commissionerate, Gandhinagar, computed by INDEXTB, Computer Centre, Ahmedabad.

food products and cotton textiles were major industries among the SSIs, however, the importance of these industries has declined drastically since the 1980s. Thus, the structure of SSIs in Gujarat now shows a fairly balanced picture with the development of both capital intensive and high-tech units as well as labour intensive units.

Among the backward classes, only SEBC entrepreneurs have been able to diversify their businesses in either capital or labour intensive industries. Their industrial structure is very similar to that represented by all the units. On the contrary, the distribution of SSI units owned by either SC or ST entrepreneurs shows a clear concentration pattern. In the cotton textiles, hosiery and garments as well as leather products industries, SC unit shares are as high as 70 per cent. Furthermore, these three industries are directly linked with their traditional skills and knowledge. ST entrepreneurs control a 67 per cent share of the food products, hosiery, garments and repair services industries combined. The common feature among these industries is easiness of entry aided by the small amount of investment necessary to enter. However, it would be misleading not to point out that a segment of SC and ST entrepreneurs, though small in number, has already gained a foothold in non-traditional industries, such as machinery and parts, and rubber and plastic products.

Although we used to regard the tiny business sector as an entity with a monolithic structure, particularly when we compare it to non-tiny SSIs. Differences in the amount of fixed capital investment on plant and equipment among tiny units do have much relevance for assessing the economic base according to entrepreneurial category. That is to say, we find large differences in such investments among the categories of entrepreneurs, ranging from Rs 2.15 lakh for all units to Rs. 0.36 lakh for SC units. This gap is around 6 times. The per unit investment of ST units is almost the same as that of SC units. Thus, both SC and ST units constitute the marginal segment in terms of investment, even in the tiny business sector. Though SCs lead in the number of units among the backward classes, per unit investment in cotton textiles, their major industry, shows surprising smallness. SCs have been most conscious about the utilization of institutional measures among the backward classes in Gujarat. Accordingly, the scale of their entry into the SSI sector was larger in relation to their small population than STs and SEBCs. Thus, a very large segment of SC units has been promoted by economically not well-off entrepreneurs, a fact reflected in the smallness in their per unit investment figures. In terms of the relation between the utilization of institutional measures and entrepreneurial development, STs lag behind SCs. Their further entry into the SSI sector has been restrained by their geographical distribution pattern to a considerable extent.

Per unit investment by SEBCs is particularly high among the backward classes, and the difference with all units is marginal. In almost all categories of industry, SEBC units are ahead of SC and ST units in terms of per unit investment. In addition, the per unit investment of SEBC units exceeds that of all units in food products, cotton textiles, chemicals and chemical products, and basic metal industries. Thus, the economic basis of SEBC units are relatively sound and strong as far as their newly registered units during the reference period are concerned. However, since the promotional package for SEBCs started only recently, the scale of their entry into the SSI sector is still very small in relation to their large population size. It should not take long for them to become better familiar with this new institutional arrangement. So far, entry into the SSI sector seems to have been confined to the wealthy segment among the SEBCs. In the coming years, the entry of other segments among SEBCs may accelerate and their industrial development within the SSI sector will play a very important role in strengthening their economic as well as political power.

Our analysis would be incomplete without an examination of the highly mobile sections among the backward classes. Here, the tiny business sector (up to Rs. 5 lakh) is divided into two groups. The first are those units with investment of less than Rs. 1 lakh, or "very tiny" units, making up 78 per cent of all SSI units belonging the tine business sector. The percentage share of this group is much higher among the backward classes, particularly among SC and ST units, to the tune of around 95. Some units in the very tiny group and most of the second group of tiny units with Rs. 5 lakh and more investment are factories. These larger tiny units are generally managed by more motivated and aspirant entrepreneurs. Although their numbers are very small among the backward classes, they sometimes play a very important and essential role for the entrepreneurial development of their communities.

A good example of such a role can be observed in the activities of the modern SC entrepreneurs. The SC elite, which has been the major beneficiary of various institutional measures, including the reservation policy and other developmental programmes since independence, are now pointing their sights towards entry into business and industry. This tendency was initiated in 1980s, when the importance of reservation for government jobs came to a standstill due to an increasing gap between the number of SC candidates and the actual beneficiaries, and was further strengthened in the 1990s in the course of the new economic policy. In response to such conditions, members of the modern elite have taken the initiative in networking their elite fellows, creating their own media, and forming class-based organizations, in addition to caste associations. In this connection, the Scheduled Castes Chamber of Commerce and Industry was formed in Ahmedabad in 1993, with several leading SC entrepreneurs deeply involved, together with some members of parliament and high-ranking officials in their community. According to the most recent membership list of 1997, total membership was around 500 and included many SSI entrepreneurs, representatives of cooperatives and household manufacturers, in addition to politicians, bureaucrats, teachers, advocates and journalists. The Chamber has functioned not only as a pressure group for political and economic benefits, but also as a base for networking and education. Although the achievements of the Chamber to date has not met full expectations, it has contributed a lot towards demonstrating the aspirations of the scheduled castes for further development, both internally and externally.

In such a highly commercialized and industrialized state as Gujarat, it is crucial even for the backward classes to have a steady foothold in business and industry, not only for economic development, but also for letting their voices be heard properly in the process of regional as well as national integration.

Conclusion

This paper has aimed at analysing the pattern of entrepreneurial development among the middle and upper classes as well as the backward classes in contemporary Gujarat in order to paint a comprehensive picture of recent entrepreneurial development in one of the most commercialized and industrialized states in India. For the analysis of middle upper classes, we used a directory of manufacturers in Gujarat (1989). We tried to identify their social groups (religious, caste [group]) based on the title, surname, etc. used by the members themselves. In order to analyze the backward classes, recent data on the SSI sector (1992/93-97/98) was utilized in an attempt at a cross-sectional understanding.

The cross-sectional analysis on manufacturers in the modern sector reveals that some social groups are quite concentrated in particular types of industry. For example, artisan castes show a higher concentration in machinery and parts, metal products, wood products and basic metal industries, while the Muslims are heavily concentrated in cotton textiles. These social groups are still bound to the industries to which they have been linked traditionally. In contrast, the types of industry among the Baniyas, Brahmans and Patidars show fairly dispersed patterns, demonstrating steady footholds in such high-tech and capital intensive industries as chemicals and chemical products, rubber and plastic products, and wool, silk and synthetic textiles.

The distribution pattern of industry seems to be determined by the socio-economic mobility of each social group, embodied in levels of education, enterprise, network systems, capital accumulation, etc., all of which have been shaped in the course of historical development of the region as a whole. Among the more highly mobile social groups, the distribution pattern of industry has been fairly diversified, and among the less mobile social groups, we still find closer bonds to their traditional occupations. Entry barriar seems to have discouraged them to invest in "non-traditional industry".

The cross-sectional analysis on the SSI units, promoted by the backward classes, gives us a clear picture on the basic characteristics of their entrepreneurship. Among the backward classes, SC and ST units show a concentration pattern in their geographical and industrial distribution. Contrary, SEBC units show a pattern of dispersion. Since investment data is available regarding SSI units, we can check the correlation between investment pattern and industrial distribution pattern. In this connection, it is interesting to point out that the units of those social groups, which take a concentration pattern in their industrial distribution, are inferior in terms of per unit investment. In the case of SC and ST entrepreneurs, their poorness in capital and network seems to have pushed them to invest either in the type of industries with which they have some traditional linkage or in such industries which they can easily enter with low amount of capital. The same can be applied to the case of artisan castes and the Muslims, though the directory of manufacturers does not provide us with any investment data.

SCs have been most conscious about the utilization of institutional measures among the backward classes in Gujarat. The number of their SSI units exceeds those of ST and SEBC units. However, their per unit investment is lowest among the backward classes. STs still lag behind SCs in terms of utilization of institutional measures and development programmes. The entrepreneurial development of STs has been restrained by their geographical distribution pattern, to a considerable extent.

Although the units promoted by SEBC have a steady foothold in SSIs, the scale of their entry into SSI sector is very much limited in light of their population size. Since the promotional package for SEBC started recently, beneficiaries have not been much in number. But it will not take much time for them to be familiar with this institutional change. So far, the entry into SSI sector seems to have been confined to the wealthy segment among SEBCs. For the comming years, the entry of other segments among SEBCs may also accelerate and their performance in SSI sector will be essential for strengthening their economic as well as political power.

Acknowledgement

[This paper would not have been possible without the cooperation of Prof. Pravin Sheth and Prof. R.L. Raval for the analysis of surnames, and Dr. Anil Gumber, National Council of Applied Economic Research for data processing and analysis, and Prof. S.P. Kashyap, Sardar Patel Institute of Economic and Social Research, Mr. Achyut Yagnik, SETU, and Dr. Rakesh Basant, Indian Institute of Management for their useful comments and criticism. I would like to express my sincere gratitude to all of them. Of course, any errors that may be found and all interpretations of the data in this paper are solely those of the author.]

NOTES

1. There are a lot of good research works on business history and zaibatsu in India. For example, See, Ray, R.K. (ed.), *Entrepreneurship and Industry in India 1800-1947*, Delhi, Oxford Univ. Press, 1992; Nafziger, E.W., *Class, Caste and Entrepreneurship - A Study of Indian Industrialists*, Honolulu, East-West Centre, 1978; Singer, M.(ed.), *Entrepreneurship and Modernization of Occupational Cultures in South Asia*, Duke Univ.,1973; Tripathi, D. (ed.), *Business Communities of India*, New Delhi, Manohar, 1984; do., *State and Business in India*, New Delhi, Manohar, 1987; do., *Business and Politics in India*, New Delhi, Manohar,1991; do., The *Dynamics of A Tradition: Kasturbhai Lalbhai and His Entrepreneurship*, New Delhi, Manohar, 1981; Tripathi, D. & M. Mehta, *Business Houses in Western India: A Study in Entrepreneurial Response 1850-1956*, New Delhi, Manohar, 1990. Regarding entrepreneurs in Cotton textile industries in Ahmedabad, see, Mehta, M., *The Ahmedabad Cotton Textile Industry: Genesis and Growth*, Ahmedabad, New Order Book Co.,1982.

2. See, Timberg, Thomas A., *The Marwaries*, New Delhi, 1978; Taknet, D.K., *Industrial Entrepreneurship of Shekhawati Marwaris*, Jaipur, 1987 (First published 1986).
3. To understand the basic structure and controversial issues regarding SSIs, the following report is very handy and useful. Hussain, C.A., Report of the Expert on Small Enterprises, New Delhi, National Council of Applied Economic Research, 1997.
4. In Gujarat, SC population is smallest among the backward classes with a share of 7.41 per cent of state population in 1991. They are widely distributed in all regions of Gujarat, but their urban ratio is fairly high. They are also advanced in education compared to the other backward classes.
5. STs are mainly concentrated in hilly districts, with a share of 14.92 per cent of state population in 1991.Their concentration in hilly and backward districts makes them difficult to be upward mobile.
6. Regarding the reservation for SEBCs in Gujarat, the first commission was formed in 1972 to fix the beneficiary group. The commission identified beneficiaries on the basis of caste. It identified 82 castes and proposed 10 per cent reservation for colleges. After the anti-reservation agitation in 1981, the second commission was appointed. It recommended new criteria, income and occupation, for the identification of beneficiaries. But it was not accepted by the government. The reservation policy for SEBCs is very conservative in light of their population size.
7. Hussain, *op.cit,* p.52.
8. ASI covers all operating factories registered under the Factory Act that either employ 10 or more workers with the use of electrical power, or 20 or more workers without electricity. These factories are divided into two sectors: the census sector and the sample sector. Those factories with 100 or more workers are put into the census sector irrespective of the use of electricity, and are subject to yearly surveys. The other factories are put into the sample sector, and half of them are counted every other year according to stratified uni-stage sampling. Some SSI units meeting the above criteria are counted by the ASI; and since investment data is compiled by the survey, it is easy to sort out the data on those SSI units. Nearly 20 years after the implementation of the Small Scale Industries Development Programme, SIDO organized the first nationwide census of the registered SSIs in 1973- 74 in order to collect detailed information on the number of units, their work forces, fixed investment, loans outstanding, inputs, output and export activities. SIDO was able to collect information from only 1.4 lakh units out of around 2.6 lakh units expected. Thus, a considerable number of registered units were not traceable or already closed down. Since then, the data has been updated periodically based on the sample survey, but it still has many limitations in accuracy and coverage. So a second census was conducted in 1987-88 to obtain more accurate data on the major characteristics of registered SSIs.

The census was hoped to be useful not only in identifying SSI units eligible for further concessions, but also in estimating the mortality rate of SSIs. SIDO collected data from around 8 lakh units out of the one million units expected. These two SIDO censuses constitute a very important source of information on modern SSI units, though it is estimated that only about two-thirds of the eligible units are in fact registered with SIDO.

The third source of information on SSIs is made up of surveys for the Directory and Non-Directory Manufacturing Establishment. The first survey of this kind was conducted in 1977 by the Central Statistical Organization (CSO) in collaboration with the Department of Economics and Statistics, while the second survey was carried out in 1984-85 as part of the National Sample Surveys. Conducted on a sample basis, the first covered around 1.8 lakh enterprises and the second around 1.4 lakh. In the second survey, only the number of employees' criterion was adopted to distinguish between Directory and Non-Directory enterprises. Those units with workforces between 6 and 9 employees were classified as "directory manufacturing establishments" (DMEs), units with between 1 and 5 workers as "non-directory manufacturing establishments" (NDMEs), and units with no hired workers as own account establishments" (OAEs). Out of these three categories, part of the DMEs and NDMEs form a segment of the SSI modern units.

9. Govt. of Gujarat, Industries in Gujarat (Some Statistics), Industries Commissionerate, Gandhinagar, 1992, p.27.
10. Govt. of Gujarat, *op.cit.*, p.16.
11. Govt. of Gujarat, Industries in Gujarat (Some Statistics), Industrial Extension Bureau, Ahmedabad, 1987, p.3.
12. *Ibid.*
13. Govt. of Gujarat, The Gujarat Directory of Manufacturers, Industrial Extension Bureau, Ahmedabad, 1989. From 1969 version to 1983 version, the government compiled information on all the units registered with SSI and medium and large scale sector, available in the Statistical Cell of Industries Commissionerate. Initially, a unit-wise survey was thought to obtain accurate information, but it was not found feasible due to time constraints. However, with the progress of computerization at INDEXTB, it was decided to collect information directly from each unit registered in the state for the1989 version. Various government offices and associations of industries including Chambers of Commerce and local industries associations at estates extended their cooperation to locate the running units.
14. This was done for the convenience of cross sectional analysis based on four-digit classification, which will be examined in future. As the result, those industries with less number of entries are not considered in this paper except leather industry, in which I have a keen interest.
15. Of course, there are some exceptions: 4644 names being either with the

suffix, 'bhai' or with no mention. For the rest of the 14810 names, however, a surname was given. In all, as many as 1610 different surnames can be found in the sample, out of which surnames appearing more than 50 times come to 41, accounting for 10,770 entrepreneurs, and those appearing more than 5 but less than 49 times come to 219 kinds, accounting for 2546 entrepreneurs. Those appearing less than 4 time come to 1350, accounting for 1494 entrepreneurs.

16. In Gujarat there is still a close association between caste and one's major surname, particularly among middle and upper castes (groups), such as the Brahmans, Baniyas, Rajputs, Patidars and the artisan castes, although there are some exceptions. Major surnames used by Muslims are also identical. On the other hand, the situation is somewhat complicated among the backward classes (i.e., lower castes) because they have tended to adopt and change their surnames as one means of sanskritization. Yet, we can point to some specific tendencies among them. For example, the use of Rajput surnames is still common among SCs and SEBCs, though some segments of SCs such as the Garos/Garodas (the priest caste among SCs) use Brahman surnames, and the use of 'Patel' has also come to prevail in recent years. In any case, our analysis should not be disturbed much by this, because the entry of backward classes into the modern manufacturing sector is still small in scale compared to middle and upper castes.

17. Enthoven, R.E., *The Tribes and Castes of Bombay*, Vol. 1, Delhi, Cosmo Publications, 1975 (reprint of 1920) ,pp.213-254; Campbell, J.M., Hindu *Castes and Tribes of Gujarat*, Vol. 1, Gurgaon, Vintage, 1988 (reprint of 1901), pp.1-54; Rajgor, S., *Gujaratna Brahman no Itihas* (in Gujarati), Ahmedabad, Pratisthan, 1987.

18. Enthoven, R.E., *op.cit.*,Vol. 2, pp. 243-260 (Koli), Vol. 3, pp.269-297 (Rajput); Campbell, J.M., *op.cit.*, Vol. 1, pp. 123-151 (Rajputs), pp.237-251 (Kolis).

19. Enthoven, R.E., *op.cit.*,Vol. 2, pp.82-98 (Jains), Vol. 3, pp.412-442 (Vanias); Campbell, J.M., *op.cit.*, Vol. 1, pp. 69-122 (Traders).

20. Engineer, A.A., *The Muslim Communities of Gujarat: An Exploratory Study of Bohras, Khojas and Memons*, Delhi, Ajanta Publications,1989; Do.,The Bohras, Ghaziabad, 1980.

21. The correlation between the type of surname and caste and/or religion seemed to be very positive in the case of Groups 1, 3, 6 and 7, which correspond to the Brahmans, Baniyas, artisan castes and the Muslims; while the surnames of Groups 2, 4 and 5 are shared by several castes and communities. Nevertheless, we should point out some particular tendencies regarding the combination of castes. That is to say, the surnames of Group 2 are widely used by both the Rajputs and the backward classes, and the surnames of Group 4 are shared by various upper castes. Also, the Patidars are the core users of the surnames in Group 5, though they are also shared by many castes and communities.

22. Because we find many surnames used by the Baniyas (Choksi, Dani, Modi, Kothari, Kotecha, Parekh, Sanghvi, Nanavati, etc.), and to a lesser extent, Brahmans (Jani, Acharya, Goswamy, Shukla, Varma, etc.) among surnames appearing less than 49 times in the directory, while we find quite less number of surnames in the list for the Patidars, Kshatriyas and artisan castes.

8

Agriculture Development in Gujarat
Problems and Prospects

NITI MATHUR and S.P. KASHYAP

Introduction

Two distinct phases of pre-green revolution (1949-50 to 1964-65) and post-green revolution (1967-68 to 1996-97) characterize the post-independence agricultural scenario of our country. In the former phase land reforms and development of large-scale irrigation infrastructure were emphasized. This period was also marked by weather induced or otherwise severe food grains deficits and large scale imports of foodstuff. Agricultural breakthrough was attained in mid-sixties with intensive use of new seed-fertilizer technology. Even though this was initially confined to the irrigated north-western part of the country, it led to tremendous increases in wheat and later on, rice yields. Given the spread of irrigation, yield increase became the main source of agricultural growth during this period. The technology gradually spread to larger areas, more recently in the eastern India, thereby reducing the regional disparities. Later on intensity of fertilizer use and other inputs increased even in the rainfed areas with visible rise in output. However, in bad monsoon years the output suffered in rainfed areas leading to crop output fluctuations. Rainfed areas too witnessed increasing diversification in the cropping patterns and shifts from coarse cereals to oilseeds.

The regional differences in agricultural development on account of resource endowments and varying levels of investments in rural infrastructure have been assessed through inter-state analysis. Such studies have been also carried out across districts by categorizing similar performing districts (Bhalla & Tyagi, 1989; Bhalla & Alagh, 1979; Bhalla & Singh, 1998). It is also important to have an in-depth look at the changes in crop output levels and growth of agricultural inputs at district level for individual states to arrive at micro level strategies. It may be mentioned that Gujarat displays considerable heterogeneity in terms of agro-meteorological and climatic conditions as well as soil and water regimes. The cultivation of leading crops in each of the agro-climatic sub-region is conditioned by water availability and other natural phenomena.[1]

In order to identify region-specific strategies for development it is essential to view the pattern of growth of agriculture at the district level. In this paper, the discussion is focused on the period covering the years 1961-63 to 1991-93. It, thus, incorporates both the pre and post-green revolution periods of agriculture development.

The specific objectives are to analyze pattern of agricultural development for triennium 1961-63, 1971-73, 1981-83 and 1991-93; to analyze impact of technology on yield levels during these periods and to examine growth of agricultural productivity of workers engaged in agriculture sector.

The information on area and output for the crops used in this present study has been compiled from season and crops reports, published by the Department of Agriculture, State Government. The analysis has been conducted for 17 major crops and crop groups. Crops covered are rice, wheat, bajra, jowar, maize, other cereals, total cereals, tur, other pulses, total pulses, total foodgrains, groundnut, mustard, other oilseeds, total oilseeds, cotton and sugarcane. These crops together shared 88.58 per cent of the gross cropped area in TE 1963 and 77.49 per cent during TE 1993. While shifts in the cropping pattern are apparent from such an analysis, the study would have been far more comprehensive had information been included for other cash crops such as spices, condiments, tobacco, fruits, vegetables, etc. A few unpublished reports have also been important information sources.

In order to study changes in pattern of agricultural development and growth, triennium averages of area and output has been used for early 60s, 70s, 80s and 90s. The first triennium captures the picture prevailing before introduction of green revolution, while the subsequent periods depict the changes taking place with the advent of new technology and resulting crop diversification. The value of output for crops has been estimated at 1990-93 prices. Growth of output changes in districts and estimates of productivity level have been ascertained using this aggregate value of output for the selected crops only.

Overview

Agriculture in Gujarat is marked by erratic and uneven rainfall. The state receives only one rainfall (S.W. Monsoon) between the months June/July to September/October. Precarious and uneven nature of rainfall often results in scarcity conditions especially in Kutch and parts of Saurashtra.

Rainfall	NSA to State's Geographic Area (%)	Districts
More than 1150 mm	3	Dangs, Bulsar
Between 750 and 1150 mm	31	Surat, Bharuch, Baroda, Kheda, Panchmahals, Junagarh
Less than 750 mm	66	Gandhinagar, Ahmedabad, Mehsana, Sabarkantha, Banaskantha, Kutch, Amreli, Bhavnagar, Jamnagar, Rajkot, Surendranagar

Source : Agro-climatic Regional Planning at State Level, ARPU Working Paper No. 5.

The southern districts of the state generally receive high and assured rainfall, central districts medium and less assured rainfall, and northern districts, Saurashtra and Kutch receive scanty and more irregular rainfall. The C.V. of annual rainfall ranges from 20.9 to 73.2 per cent across the state (Joshi, 1996). The entire state can be divided into three-rainfall regimes—high, medium and low, as follows :

Of the total sown area, only about 3 per cent receive high rainfall of 1150 mm and above. Nearly 31 per cent and 66 percent of the net sown area are medium to low rainfall regions respectively. Nearly 40 per cent and 54 per cent of the population in the state resides in medium and low rainfall regions, while the high rainfall region accommodates only about 6 percent of the total population. The state faces a problem in water availability, which is also manifested in its irrigation development. Amongst all the inputs, increased availability of irrigation is an essential condition in raising productivity levels along with a shift in the cropping pattern from less to more remunerative crops, which are often water intensive. The net irrigated area as percentage of the net sown area for the whole state during 1984 was 27.2, which has reached to 31.2 during 1994. Over time irrigated farming is becoming important. Northern districts of Ahmedabad, Gandhinagar, Banaskantha, Sabarkantha and Mehsana boast of the largest developed irrigation potential. Irrigation through dug-wells and tube-wells account for as much as 79 per cent of all the sources combined. Surface irrigation, particularly canals, is common in the southern districts of Bharuch and Surat and also in Dangs and Bulsar comprising the southern hills sub-region. Since the available unexploited potential is largely for surface irrigation, the development of watersheds as well as major and medium irrigation facilities acquire a high priority.

During 1991, agriculture in Gujarat engaged 56 per cent of the total workforce and 27 per cent of the state domestic product originated from this sector. Thirty years ago, the corresponding shares were much higher at 64 and 48 per cent respectively.[2] This clearly indicates that the state is reducing its dependence on agriculture for income and employment generation and also suggests that the economy is witnessing structural transformation. This transformation is more rapid in Gujarat compared to that in India. This pace of structural transformation in the state has been cited to be the result of adoption of the "textiles first strategy". Such a strategy *vis-à-vis* "machine first strategy", apart from inducing agriculture and industry linkages, is also more labour intensive. This is manifested in the decline of the share of cereals and foodgrains, giving way to non-foodgrain crops as oilseeds, spices, horticultural, crops, etc. or non-traditional, non-food crops. Gujarat is predominantly a non-food crop economy with preponderance of groundnut, tobacco and cotton. Presently, the commercial orientation is more associated with oilseeds, paddy, wheat, sugarcane, pulses, vegetables, spices, etc. In the last 3 decades, the percentage share of area under these crops has increased, while that under cotton, tobacco and coarse cereals has decreased. The landslide decline in the area of coarse cereals of bajra and jowar is mainly responsible for reduction in cereal area. The rise in the share of superior cereals of rice and wheat has been only marginal in Gujarat. A notable feature of cropping pattern changes in the recent times is the significantly enhanced share of other crops, occupying almost a quarter of gross cropped area (GCA). However, the production of cereals has gone up during this period, due to doubling of yield. The large production increase is coming from wheat (about three-fold), rice and bajra (one and a half times) arising out of yield enhancement (Joshi, 1996). The agriculture in the state is on the whole diversified with cropping pattern that is quite suitable to agro-climatic conditions. Livestock farming and fisheries in the coastal districts are other important land-based activities in the state.

It is apparent that Gujarat requires a policy that encourages agro-processing industries and value addition of agriculture produce. Farm input industries also need attention as they enable technological transformation of agriculture. Such a transformation would stimulate rural and employment led economic growth which is conducive to reducing poverty ratio (Desai, 1997).

Area increase has the components of increase in the net sown area as well as rise in the intensity of cultivation. As most of the cultivable land has been brought under cultivation, the net sown area in the state has ceased to grow. The gross cropped area expanded, but at the very low rate of 0.21 per cent. In the past, between 1961-63 to 1971-73, the cropped area at state level grew marginally at 0.10 per cent largely due to the expansion of net sown area. In the next phase of 1971-73 to 1981-83, there was a slight acceleration in cropped area at 0.72 per cent per annum. The growth was high in the Saurashtra districts, namely, Bhavnagar, Jamnagar, Junagadh as well as in Kheda, Valsad and Mehsana. Expansion of net sown area as well as climatic conditions enabled the increase in the intensity of cultivation. During 1981-83 to 1991-93, as compared to the previous decade, there was a perceptible decline in the growth rate of cropped area from 0.72 to -0.17 per cent per annum. It is evident that growth in cropped area over time has ceased to be a major constituent of the increase in the crop output in the state.

Increase in cropping intensity contributes to the growth of cropped area, in addition to the spread of net sown area. At the state level, the cropping intensity increased from being 1.05 per cent in 1961-63 to 1.13 per cent during 1991-93. Up to the early eighties, the cropping intensity recorded an appreciable increase in all the districts. Cropping intensity in the eighties declined in certain districts due to weather and rainfall adversities, particularly in Amreli, Bhavnagar, Jamnagar, Junagadh and Rajkot—all the districts belonging to Saurashtra sub-regions.

The above indicates that at the state level the contribution of expansion of sown area to output growth is on the wane. Rising intensity of cultivation is a more important factor contributing to output.

Gujarat's agriculture, besides being weather dependent, is small scale on account of pressure of population and inadequate growth of off-farm employment opportunities. During 1990-91, the average size of operational farm holding was 2.93 hectares. Over time the share of small and marginal holdings in increasing. In 1990-91, 45 per cent of the farmers held land between 2 to 10 hectares and operated nearly 63 per cent of the total land under the plough.

HYVs for bajra, rice, wheat and maize are popular in the state. HYVs of cotton and oilseeds, mainly castor, rapeseed, mustard, groundnut and some pulses like tur and gram are also commonly grown. Fertilizer use in the state has continuously increased since the 80s.

Cropping Pattern at State Level and Changes

The area shares for major crops/crop groups for the triennium ending 1963, 1973, 1983 and 1993 are depicted in Table 8.1.

Table 8.1 : Cropping Pattern Changes for State

(Area share as % to GCA)

Crop/Crop Group	TE 1963	TE 1973	TE 1983	TE 1993
Rice	5.47	4.78	5.6	5.54
Wheat	4.03	4.75	6.08	4.72
Jowar	13.27	9.29	9.97	4.29
Bajra	14.21	13.09	13.55	11.38
Maize	2.75	2.49	3.41	3.38
Total Cereals	42.55	45.18	41.23	29.79
Tur	0.9	0.95	3.12	3.85
Total Pulses	5.14	4.67	9.28	8.38
Total Foodgrains	47.69	49.85	49.55	38.17
Groundnut	21.31	18.65	19.84	18.41
Mustard	0.14	0.57	1.88	3.42
Total Oilseeds	23.55	21.28	25.19	27.46
Sugarcane	0.22	0.48	1.07	1.18
Cotton	17.12	20.96	13.08	10.68
Other Crops	11.42	7.43	11.11	22.51
GCA (ha)	9982357	10085200	10838800	10646550

Source : Season and Crop Reports, Department of Agriculture, Government of Gujarat.

Area under cereals declined in the last 3 decades from 42.5 per cent to 29.8 per cent. Decline was the sharpest in the last decade and can be attributed to the fall in area under coarse cereals. Area under jowar and bajra went down remarkably. The total area under cereals declined by nearly 11.13 lakh hectares. Area under total foodgrains remained stagnant from 1963 to 1983, but declined dramatically in the last decade reaching 38 per cent of the cropped area. This happened despite the increase in area under pulses from 5 to 8.4 per cent during the last thirty years. In the last 3 decades area under oilseeds moved from 23.5 to 27.5 per cent. Increase in the share under mustard from 0.14 to 3.4 per cent was largely responsible for such an increase in oilseeds area. Irrigated cultivation of mustard is gaining importance in the state over the years. Groundnut on the other hand, is losing importance, its share falling from 21 to 18 per cent and is probably being replaced by other rabi oilseeds such as castor. Share of cotton in GCA has also declined. Share of sugarcane, although quite marginal, has increased steadily from 0.2 per cent in 1963 to 1.2 per cent in 1993. This is an outcome of spread of canal irrigated area.

It is evident that area under foodgrains in the state is being replaced by other crops. Cash crops are gaining in the state's agriculture, particularly oilseeds (mustard), pulses and sugarcane. While cotton area has shrunk, its output has by no means suffered, primarily because of technological developments which led to greater yields. In addition, "other crops" combined, including tobacco, spices, condiments, fruits and vegetables, are becoming more important in the agricultural economy of Gujarat. During the sixties with increase in area under foodgrains and sugarcane, the share under other crops declined from 11.4 to 7.4 per cent. Thereafter, their share increased quite steadily. The gain has been particularly dramatic in the last decade. In the eighties the share of such non-traditional non-food crops, including fruits/vegetables, recorded incredible increase. In TE 1993, 22.5 per cent of the gross cropped area in the state was accounted for by these crops. In respect of this category of crops, between 1961-63 to 1991-93, except in Amreli and Vadodara, the relative share increased in varying proportions across districts. The rise varied between 2 percentage points in Sabarkantha to 28 percentage points in Surat. The rise was quite low in Junagadh, Sabarkantha, Bhavnagar and Dangs, while it was substantially high in Surat, Mehsana, Banaskantha, Kutch and Kheda. It needs to be emphasized that these crops are amenable to processing and value addition. Efforts are needed for rapid expansion of post-harvest processing facilities which will pay the cultivators richly, besides creating possibilities for off farm employment and income generation.

Growth of Agricultural Output

Output growth is a function of increases in yield, area and changes in cropping patterns. Contribution of each of these components in the agricultural growth of the districts is being assessed. The effect of growth in male agricultural workers and other inputs on output and yield is also in the process of being estimated.[3]

Chart 1 depicts the level and growth of aggregate output at district level for the major crops. The districts have been grouped into categories of high, medium and low rainfall, as described earlier. The crops considered in the analysis are rice, wheat, jowar, bajra, maize and tur as the primary foodcrops; groundnut and mustard as the main oilseeds. Among the cash crops, sugarcane and cotton are used in the computations. Due to the exclusion of other important crops such as tobacco, oilseeds, castor, spices, horticultural crops, etc., the output and growth rates are, to some extent, understated particularly for 1991-93 over 1981-83. For the selected crops, the triennium ending average of output has been calculated for 1961-63, 1971-73, 1981-83, 1991-93 using the all India prices for triennium ending 1993. Growth rates are the compound annual growth rates.

For the entire duration of the study, Gujarat's agriculture grew at 1.21 per cent. The highest output growth was recorded in Banaskantha, Kutch, Mehsana and Bhavnagar districts (at rates between 2.25 to 3.6 per cent). This was largely on acount of switchover to non food crops in these districts. Growth rate was medium in Surendranagar, Vadodara, Valsad, Dangs, Kheda and Amreli (between 1.23 to 1.99 per cent).

During the sub-phases, several changes took place in the districts in the pattern of agricultural development. During the initial phase, that is between 1961-63 to 1971-73, high performance districts were Banaskantha, Kutch, Mehsana, Junagadh and Jamnagar. These districts had very low output to begin with on account of bad rainfall and poor irrigation development. By the seventies the output all but doubled here. After the sixties these districts made noteworthy progress in irrigation development which is reflected in the output increase. Medium growth was registered in Vadodara, Surendranagar, Amreli, Bhavnagar and Rajkot. Except for Vadodara, the remaining districts in this group fall in the poor rainfall region of Saurashtra. Growth here was again led by appreciable gains in irrigation development.

A view of the incremental output during 1971-73 over that in 1961-63 (Chart 2) corroborates the above findings. Nearly 60 per cent of the incremental output of Rs. 6315.2 million generated during this phase was

Chart 1: Districtwise Levels of Output for Major Crops

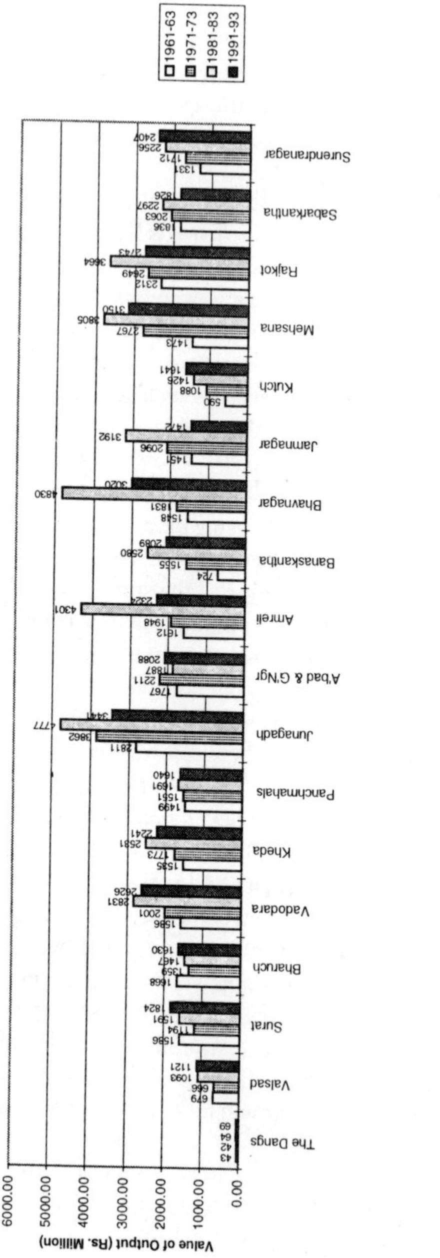

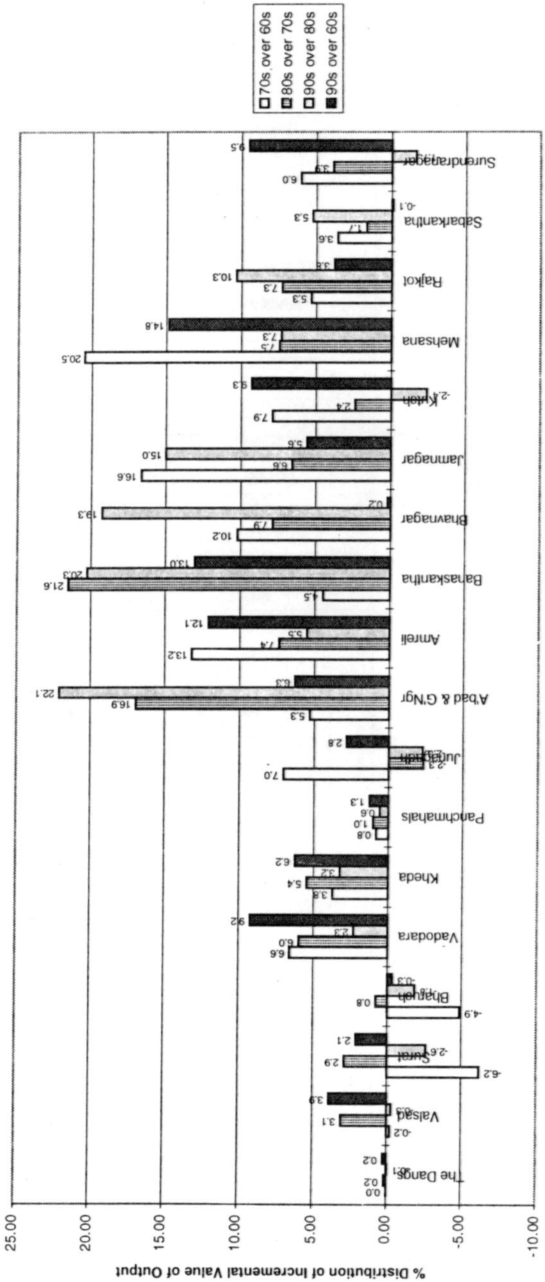
70s over 60s
80s over 70s
90s over 80s
90s over 60s
% Distribution of Incremental Value of Output
Surendranagar
Sabarkantha
Rajkot
Mehsana
Kutch
Jamnagar
Bhavnagar
Banaskantha
Amreli
A'bad & G'Ngr
Junagadh
Panchmahals
Kheda
Vadodara
Bharuch
Surat
Valsad
The Dangs

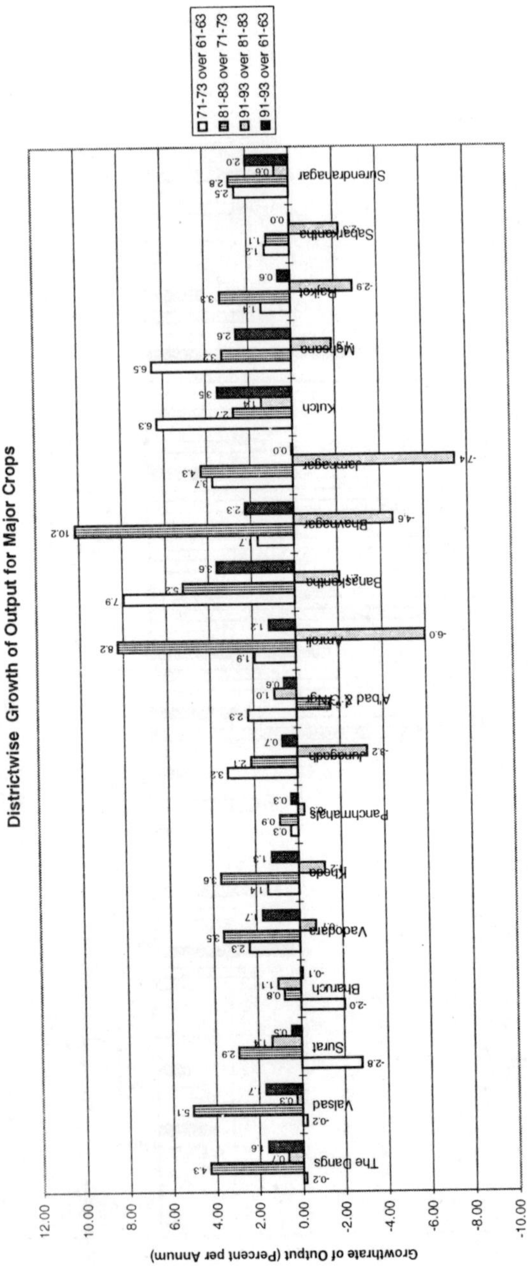
Districtwise Growth of Output for Major Crops
71-73 over 61-63
81-83 over 71-73
91-93 over 81-83
91-93 over 61-63
Growthrate of Output (Percent per Annum)
The Dangs
Valsad
Surat
Bharuch
Vadodara
Kheda
Panchmahals
Junagadh
A'bad & G'Ngr
Amreli
Banaskantha
Bhavnagar
Jamnagar
Kutch
Mehsana
Rajkot
Sabarkantha
Surendranagar

Chart 2: Incremental Value of Output by Districts

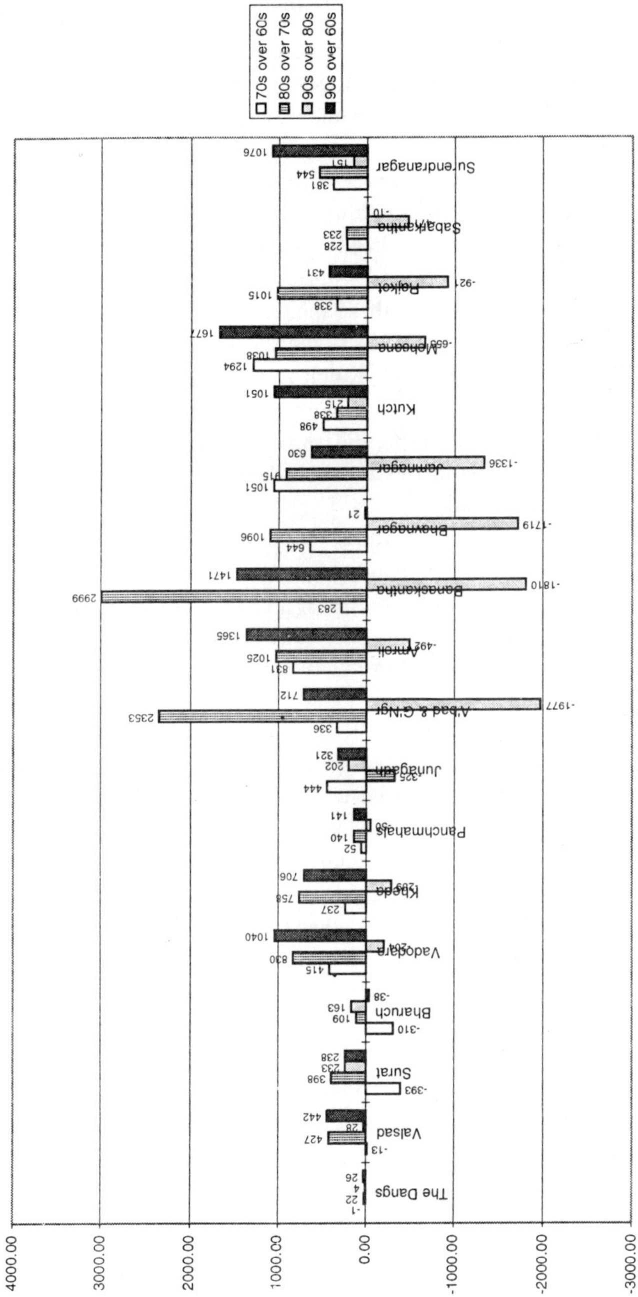

accounted for by the districts of Banaskantha, Jamnagar, Junagadh, Mehsana and Kutch, combined together. The contribution of Amreli, Bhavnagar, Kheda, Rajkot, Surendranagar and Vadodara to the increase in output during 1961-63 to 1971-73 was about 32 per cent.

The second phase from 1971-73 to 1981-83 was characterized by faster agricultural output growth in the state, the rate accelerating to 3.6 per cent. Districts that consolidated their position were Amreli, Bhavnagar, Kheda, Dangs, Vadodara and Valsad. On account of technological developments in agriculture these medium growth districts of the first phase became high growth areas in the subsequent period. On the other hand, Banaskantha, Junagadh, Kutch and Mehsana could not maintain their high rates of output growth and recorded significant deceleration. In absolute terms the output during 1981-83 over that during 1971-73 recorded an increase of Rs. 13914.5 million, more than double the increase recorded during the earlier period.

The growth of agricultural output for the crops selected in the period 1981-83 to 1991-93 marked a turn around. At the state level, the growth of output decelerated to reach -2.12 per cent from +3.64 per cent recorded in the previous phase. Negative growth was recorded in all the districts which had improved production in the second phase *vis-à-vis* the first phase. Most notably, output growth became negative in the districts of Amreli, Bhavnagar, Jamnagar, Rajkot, Vadodara and also in Kheda. The group of districts, where output growth was continuously decelerating from the first phase onwards, was Banaskantha, Junagadh, Kutch, Mehsana and Sabarkantha. However, there was a sharp increase in the contribution made to the incremental output between 1981-83 to 1991-93 by Amreli, Jamnagar, Junagadh, Sabarkantha and Rajkot. These were also the districts where the share of "other crops" in the gross cropped area rose between 3 to 10 percentage points.

It emerges that after the eighties crop output has stagnated or decelerated. Shift in the cropping pattern is taking place. Output growth and share in incremental output has been largest for a few districts in Saurashtra, Kutch, Amreli and Banaskantha. In Kutch, it must be noted that a large area is under wastelands. Possibly, in the limited cropped area, efforts are being made to maintain the output levels. In the remaining districts resource stress is probably becoming a serious issue. Overdrawal of ground water in the districts of north Gujarat and Saurashtra is a problem that demands urgent attention. Land and water management strategies suggested under ACRP thus are crucial in the coming decades to overcome the problems being encountered in these districts (ARPU, Working Paper No. 10, 1998, Chapter on Gujarat).

Changes in Crop Yields (kg/ha) and Land Productivity (Rs./ha)

Growth of yield is an important component of growth in value output. Before the advent of the new seed-fertilizer technology, the major source of output growth was area expansion. However, in subsequent decades the significant increases in yield levels of cereals and other crops became the major contributor to output growth.

Before we assess the value of yield for the districts, it is essential to see the changes taking place in the output in physical terms for the major crops (Table 8.2). Yield of crops per hectare is a direct reflection of the technical inputs added to the land resource. Nearly all the foodgrains witnessed remarkable strides in yield enhancement at least until the early eighties. Thereafter, output in physical terms started to either stagnate or decline. Yield of rice at state level had been increasing progressively from the early sixties till the eighties. No major breakthrough in rice yield was observed in the subsequent decade. Similarly in case of wheat, yield increase till the early eighties was remarkable—by nearly 157 per cent (from 902 to 2316 kg/ha). In the early nineties, however, a small decline was observed in yield of wheat. In case of coarse cereals from the sixties through the early eighties, appreciable yield gain was attained for bajra.

Table 8.2 : Yield Level for Major Crops

(Kgs/Ha.)

Crop/Crop Group	TE 1963	TE 1973	TE 1983	TE 1993
Rice	873	918	1335	1332
Wheat	902	1651	2316	2119
Jowar	298	377	566	597
Bajra	435	744	1194	891
Maize	1062	1222	1397	1193
Tur	497	696	719	780
Groundnut	611	605	817	586
Mustard	520	938	1399	1052
Sugarcane	5461	5215	7422	8337
Cotton	136	163	205	239

Source : Department of Agriculture, Government of Gujarat.

For jowar output enhancement has not been that noticeable. Yield of maize, on the other hand, has remained largely constant in the past three decades. Amongst pulses, yield per hectare has recorded a steady increase.

Mustard yield has more than doubled from 520 to 1399 kg/ha between TE 1963 to 1983, after that period a small decline was observed. Groundnut yield peaked in the early eighties. By early nineties it fell to reach an all time low. Amongst the other cash crops, sugarcane yield has increased steadily in the past thirty years to be 8337 kg/ha in the nineties. This is an increase by 53 per cent over the yield observed in early sixties. Cotton yield too has nearly doubled in the state during the period of study.

Chart 3 depicts the levels and changes that have taken place in the growth of aggregate land productivity during 1961-63 to 1991-93. Land productivity in the analysis constitutes the value of output of the major crops, viz., rice, wheat, jowar, bajra, maize, tur, groundnut, mustard, sugarcane and cotton divided by the cropped area under these crops. During this period, in Gujarat, while the value of output increased at 1.21 per cent per annum, value of yield per hectare registered growth rate of nearly 1.7 per cent per annum. This accounted for the entire growth of output, as area expansion recorded a negative growth at -0.4 per cent per annum. Highest increase was registered in Kutch, followed by Banaskantha, Mehsana, Surendranagar, and Bhavnagar at annual rates falling between 1.45 to 4.72 per cent per annum.

Between 1971-73 and 1961-63, at the state level the rate of increase in value of yield was at 2.6 per cent per annum. Within the districts, high growth rates of yield were recorded in Banaskantha, Kutch and Mehsana, significantly raising their output levels. Moderately high growth rate was observed in Jamnagar, Junagadh, Surendranagar and Vadodara districts.

Between 1971-73 to 1981-83, the growth rate of land productivity decelerated marginally at 2.52 per cent. However, by 1981-83 with the increased use of inputs and irrigation expansion, many districts recorded notable increases in crop productivity. The growth rate of productivity was quite high in Bhavnagar, Amreli and Banaskantha.

During 1981-83 to 1991-93, commensurate with the output performance, the performance of productivity at state level was also dismal. The rate of land productivity growth decelerated to -0.04 per cent from 2.52 per cent annual increase registered in the preceding period. Predictably, the yield levels in all these districts became considerably

Chart 3: Districtwise Land Productivity of Major Crops

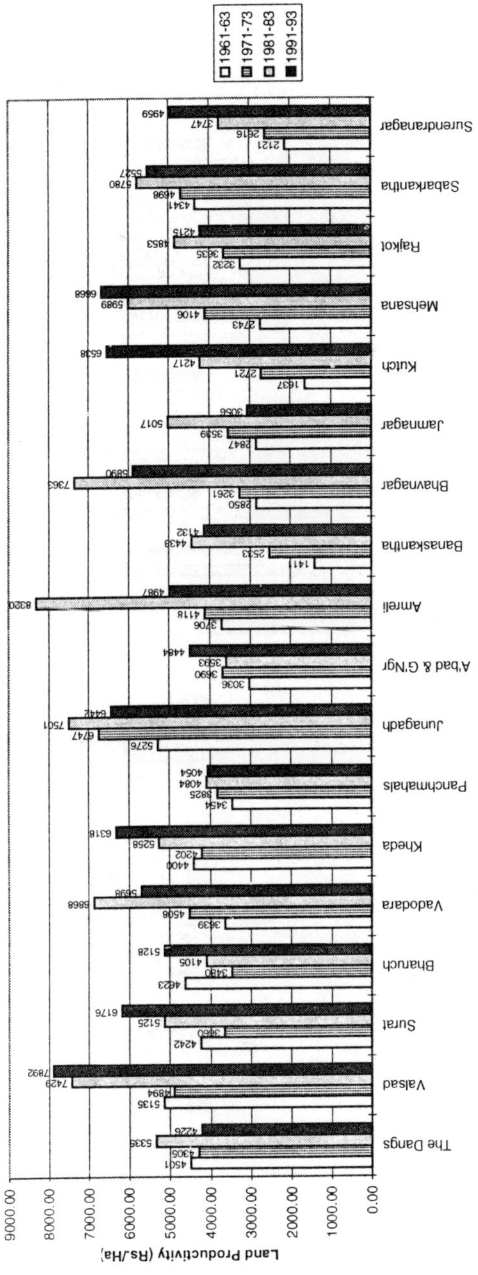

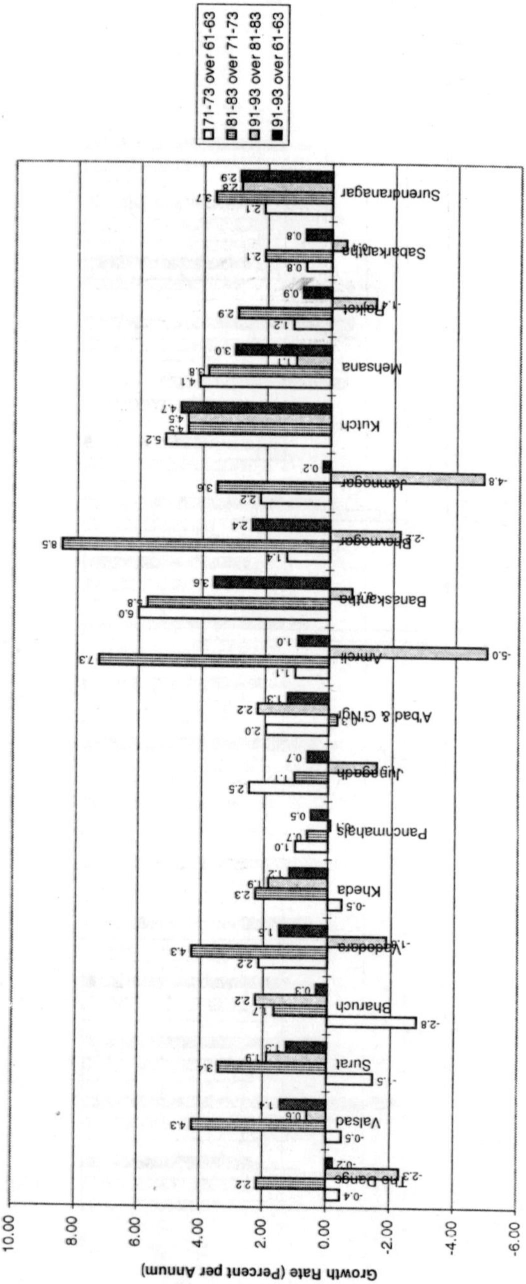
71-73 over 61-63
81-83 over 71-73
91-93 over 81-83
91-93 over 61-63
Growth Rate (Percent per Annum)
10.00
8.00
6.00
4.00
2.00
0.00
-2.00
-4.00
-6.00
The Dangs
Valsad
Surat
Bharuch
Vadodara
Kheda
Pancmahals
Junagadh
A'bad & G'Ngr
Amreli
Banaskantha
Bhavnagar
Jamnagar
Kutch
Mehsana
Rajkot
Sabarkantha
Surendranagar

lower than the previous period.

The coefficient of variation of land productivity has fallen in the state from 32 to 23 per cent between 1961-63 to 1991-93. Thus, while agriculture is stagnating, disparities amongst the districts are declining as far as the land productivity is concerned.

It emerges that productivity gains after the eighties have become unimportant. However, mention may be made of the fact that the year 1991-92 included in computing the triennium average for 1991-93 was a particularly bad year for Gujarat's agriculture. Moreover, labour productivity fall after all may not be as alarming as it appears when we consider that the labour is also engaged in "other crops", that constituted nearly 22 per cent of the GCA during 1991-93. Possibly more and more productive area is being diverted to such crops, which may be the answer to the falling productivity levels of the selected crops. We also cannot ignore the possibility that modern inputs are being increasingly diverted to consolidate the output of the "other crops", which have not been considered in our analysis. Nevertheless, the fact remains that nearly all the districts, as far as major crops are concerned, are attaining stagnancy in agriculture. It is apparent that in the future if agriculture has to absorb labour, it would be at falling productivity unless major technological breakthroughs are attained.

Input Use, Yield Levels and Output Growth

Districtwise details on area irrigated, number of tractors pump-sets and consumption of fertilizers are given in Table 8.3. The table reveals that the yield and growth of crop output are positively associated with the use of modern inputs. In 1991-93, the high productivity districts of Valsad, Mehsana, Kheda, Surat and Sabarkantha were characterised by high levels of area under irrigation. In Valsad, high rainfall may have been a causal factor in addition to high level of irrigation development. In most of the districts the consumption of fertilizers was also of the highest order. In Surat it was 173 kg/ha, followed by Kheda (132 kg/ha), Sabarkantha (99 kg/ha), Valsad (90 kg/ha) and Junagadh (71 kg/ha). Districts where the area under food grains is of less importance had slightly lower levels of fertilizer use, for instance in Jamnagar, Surendranagar and Kutch.

At the state level, there is a strong relationship between use of modern inputs and the magnitude of crop output. Between 1961-63 and 1981-83, the output nearly doubled.

Table 8.3 : Districtwise Level of Input Used

District	No. of Tractors (per 000 ha)			No. of Pumpsets (per 000 ha)			Consumption of Ferti. (Kgs/ha)			% of GCA Irrigated (Kgs/ha)			Cropping Intensity		
	1961-63	1981-83	1987	1961-63	1981-83	1987	1961-63	1981-83	1991-93	1961-63	1981-83	1991-93	1961-63	1981-83	1991-93
A'bad & G'Ngr	0.47	3.82	7.20	8.60	26.35	31.11	1.42	26.42	69.98	9.28	19.16	28.82	1.00	1.04	1.08
Amreli	0.55	3.56	4.66	17.40	93.79	112.45	4.35	56.67	51.86	6.32	13.89	10.84	1.01	1.13	1.05
Banaskantha	0.05	1.84	4.23	4.53	45.09	74.07	0.51	13.19	42.10	7.81	22.76	33.00	1.08	1.19	1.30
Bharuch	0.43	1.37	3.42	3.79	10.37	15.39	3.34	18.91	50.12	2.75	10.28	13.08	1.00	1.01	1.01
Bhavnagar	0.17	2.18	3.61	14.21	84.99	104.53	3.46	44.07	61.60	8.32	21.22	23.37	1.02	1.17	1.11
Jamnagar	0.17	1.64	1.97	23.69	100.93	113.23	1.86	36.20	30.91	5.40	23.97	22.91	1.03	1.22	1.10
Junagarh	0.24	2.49	4.12	38.55	145.62	185.26	6.18	63.03	71.39	14.28	20.45	17.91	1.06	1.17	1.12
Kutch	0.12	1.43	3.19	8.03	23.13	30.50	10.26	5.89	25.30	6.94	10.67	15.58	1.02	1.05	1.08
Kheda	1.07	7.60	12.23	10.94	28.11	43.73	10.15	66.62	131.74	9.41	46.25	52.77	1.06	1.18	1.21
Mehsana	0.36	5.09	6.95	18.89	35.38	19.38	1.34	33.50	59.89	19.29	40.38	49.97	1.07	1.32	1.29
Panchmahals	0.06	0.47	1.23	2.74	24.99	67.52	0.77	15.21	47.26	2.22	9.82	14.33	1.21	1.12	1.17
Rajkot	0.36	2.76	3.36	23.07	118.10	134.69	4.30	70.36	66.35	6.51	22.61	25.43	1.01	1.13	1.10
Sabarkantha	0.31	3.84	6.55	19.78	109.21	120.48	0.77	71.48	99.32	11.21	34.29	30.53	1.10	1.12	1.17
Surat	1.13	5.49	8.32	6.96	24.00	38.56	4.84	87.41	173.29	6.44	29.57	38.69	1.05	1.07	1.08
Surendranagar	0.21	2.08	3.11	6.26	44.59	39.96	0.16	12.42	33.02	4.04	13.06	16.91	1.01	1.02	1.04
The Dangs	1.00	0.07	0.04	0.37	0.81	2.06	0.00	0.81	0.34	0.10	0.22	0.18	1.00	1.00	1.00
Vadodara	0.47	2.14	3.36	5.61	17.91	24.89	7.88	49.42*	82.22	3.86	23.21	27.52	1.03	1.04	1.04
Valsad	0.60	3.90	8.08	12.55	40.95	71.55	3.66	33.72	90.34	4.41	17.84	29.55	1.11	1.10	1.10
Gujarat	0.38	2.93	4.81	13.55	58.74	73.17	3.64	39.55	66.17	7.85	22.76	27.30	1.05	1.13	1.13

Source : Bhalla and Singh, 1998; Fertilizer Statistics for Different Years.

Table 8.4 : Determinants of Per Hectare Productivity Regression Results : Districts of Gujarat

Model : log(Prod) = a + b1 log(x1) + b2 log(x2) + ... (Stepwise Regression)

Step	R-bar Square	Constant term	Fertilizer	Cropping Intensity	Male Agri. Workers	Irrigation	Pumpsets	Tractors
60s								
1.	0.40	3.67						0.29 (3.44)
2.	0.61	3.80			0.40* (3.01)			0.22 (3.11)
3.	0.67	3.65			0.47* (3.71)		0.15*** (1.89)	0.17 (2.51)
4.	0.79	3.73			0.47* (4.65)	–0.30** –(2.85)	0.31* (3.64)	0.17 (3.07)
80s								
1.	0.09	3.60	0.09** (1.67)					
2.	0.26	3.59	0.26** (2.74)			–0.20*** –(2.11)		
3.	0.38	3.58	0.27* (3.11)	1.62*** (2.03)		–0.26** –(2.88)		
4.	0.39	3.68	0.24** (2.68)	1.84** (2.25)		–0.36** –(2.83)		0.13 (1.06)

(Contd.)

Table 8.4 *(Contd.)*

Step	R-bar Square	Constant term	Fertilizer	Cropping Intensity	Male Agri. Workers	Irrigation	Pumpsets	Tractors
90s								
1.	0.16	3.67						0.09
								(2.06)
2.	0.30	3.86				–0.23***		0.31
						–(2.05)		(2.69)
3.	0.32	3.92				–0.20***	–0.07***	0.31
						–(1.65)	–(1.22)	(2.71)

Significance of T at * 1 per cent level
** 5 per cent level
***10 per cent level

During this period the per hectare consumption of fertilizers rose from 4 to 40 kg/ha. Substantial gains were also made in the use of pump-sets, from 13.5 to 59 per thousand hectares. Percentage of GCA under irrigation increased from 7.8 per cent during 1961-63 to 22.7 per cent during 1981-83. Consequently, the growth of output between 1971-73 to 1981-83 accelerated at 3.6 per cent.

The gain in input use continued during the next decade too. By nineties, the change in irrigated area was only by five percentage points. Most important increase was in the use of fertilizer. The consumption rose from 39 to 66 kg/ha. Between 1981-83 to 1991-93, in the districts of Bharuch, Surat and Kutch, output growth was high. Growth in the consumption of fertilizers too was quite large here, the jump being quite substantial from the consumption levels in 1981-83 in these districts.

Table 8.4 gives preliminary explorations about determinants of land productivity across districts for three points of time. It is seen that overall explanatory power of the model used declines with time. In the initial phase male agricultural worker productivity, pump-sets and rudiments of mechanization were crucial in determining land productivity. Fertilizer consumption emerged as a crucial determining factor during the eighties. The early nineties were marked by significant distortions in the fertilizer use pattern, arising from the introduction of policy changes and the resulting sudden rise in fertilizer prices. This may have led to fall in productivity levels in the state for most crops. Nonetheless, results are quite unsatisfactory for the nineties. Maybe there are excluded variables that are important. Also the fact that we are not taking into account "other crops", which are input intensive and had become quite important (22 per cent of GCA), also affects the performance of estimated equation.

Changes in Labour-force and Labour Productivity

The absorption of labour in agriculture is affected by factors such as output growth, increases in cropping intensity, crop composition, besides changes in the production process. In addition to this degree of mechanization, size of holdings and wage levels also play a crucial role in determining the labour absorption. Farm sector also serves as the parking place of the poor. It is, therefore, important to ascertain the variations at district level in the pattern of growth of agricultural workers productivity, particularly of the male workforce. The agriculture worker productivity in the study is based on the output of selected crops at 1990-93 prices (Table 8.5).

Between 1961-63 and 1971-73, the growth rate of agricultural output in the state at 2.19 per cent, exceeded that of male agricultural workers of 1.83 per cent per annum. Hence, the male worker productivity increased very slowly at annual rate of 0.41 per cent. During this period districts having high growth of output, were associated with high growth of male agriculture workers too, e.g. in Banaskantha, Jamnagar, Junagadh, Mehsana, Surendranagar and Kutch.

In the next decade of 1971-73 to 1981-83, growth rate of output increased from 2.2 to 3.6 per cent per annum. The growth rate of male agricultural workers in this phase decelerated to 1.56 per cent. Consequently, at the state level, due to the slow down of growth in male workers, MAWs productivity recorded an increase in the growth at 2.1 percent per annum. Among the districts, Amreli, Jamnagar, Surendranagar and Rajkot recorded medium to high growth and maintained their lead in workers productivity in the state. Amreli, Bhavnagar, Kheda, Dangs and Valsad recorded phenomenal growth ranging between 3.2 to 7.4 per cent annually in male worker productivity as compared to very low or negative rates in the preceding period. This was primarily owing to large acceleration in the rate of output growth in these districts between 1971-73 to 1981-83. On the other hand, in Banaskantha, Kutch and Mehsana, there was a decline in the rate of increase in MAWs productivity due to noticeable slow down in the agricultural output.

The eighties departed significantly regarding growth of output. Output coming from the selected crops declined quite remarkably. Despite a further deceleration in the engagement of male agricultural workers in the state, the fall in output led to landslide decline in the workers productivity. The worker productivity declined in nearly all the districts. The CV of male agricultural worker productivity increased between 1973 and 1983. Consequent to the deceleration in the productivity levels after eighties, the CV too declined from 58 to 54 per cent, indicating thereby that regional disparities existing earlier are reducing.

Table 8.6 depicts across districts the decadal direction of change in land and labour productivity. During the first decade there were 11 districts that witnessed the rise in both land and labour productivity. The number rose to 15 in the next decade. There is complete reversal in the directional change in 1991-93 over 1981-83. Only two districts occupy ++ cell, whereas 13 districts show decrease in both land and labour productivity. There cannot be more telling evidence of stagnancy and decline of state's agriculture in the more recent period. May be inclusion of "other crops" would soften the severity of conclusions. To a limited

Table 8.5 : Districtwise Level and Growth of Male Agricultural Workers Productivity

(Rs. Per Worker at 1990-93 prices)

District	Male Workers Productivity				Growth Rate (Per cent Per Annum)			
	1961-63	1971-73	1981-83	1991-93	71-73 over 61-63	81-83 over 71-73	91-93 over 81-83	91-93 over 61-63
A'bad & G'Ngr.	9233	9620	7539	7229	0.41	–2.41	–0.42	–0.81
Amreli	11956	12044	22275	12010	0.07	6.34	–5.99	0.02
Banaskantha	3049	5432	7407	4917	5.94	3.15	–4.01	1.61
Bharuch	8403	6013	5917	5876	–3.29	–0.16	–0.07	–1.19
Bhavnagar	8711	8456	17334	17259	–0.30	7.44	–0.04	2.31
Jamnagar	11282	12604	16265	7095	1.11	2.58	–7.96	–1.53
Junagadh	12695	13775	14415	8916	0.82	0.46	–4.69	–1.17
Kutch	5776	8304	9918	10486	3.70	1.79	0.56	2.01
Kheda	3772	3712	4569	3574	–0.16	2.10	–2.43	–0.18
Mehsana	4780	7305	8961	6647	4.33	2.06	–2.94	1.11
Panchmahals	3901	3469	3206	2645	–1.17	–0.79	–1.90	–1.29
Rajkot	12872	11786	13606	9566	–0.88	1.45	–3.46	–0.98
Sabarkantha	9019	8667	8054	5569	–0.40	–0.73	–3.62	–1.59
Surat	7476	4461	4972	5093	–5.03	1.09	0.24	–1.27
Surendranagar	11862	11946	13896	13160	0.07	1.52	–0.54	0.35
Dangs	2208	1807	2484	2154	–1.98	3.23	–1.41	–0.08
Vadodara	5272	5740	6913	5820	0.85	1.88	–1.71	0.33
Valsad	3149	2867	4164	3401	–0.93	3.80	–2.00	0.26
Gujarat	6975	7226	8849	6441	0.35	2.05	+3.13	–0.27
CV	48.42	48.44	58.09	54.49				

extent,. perhaps. The stagnancy argument also finds reflection in the reducing share of agriculture in the state's net state domestic product (NSDP) from the eighties onwards. In the beginning of the eighties, share of agriculture—the most dominant sub-sector, in the NSDP was 37.2 per cent. By 1990-91 the share declined to 24.8 per cent and further to 17.8 per cent in 1997-98. Clearly, manufacturing and service sectors are gaining importance in Gujarat's economy.

Summing Up

The following inferences are emerging from analysis in the preceding sections:

- The district level analysis of levels and growth of agriculture output during 1961-63 to 1991-93 has brought out the changing nature of agriculture development in Gujarat in the post-green revolution phase, and particularly during the eighties. These developments have led to the spread of new technological inputs on a wider scale. During the seventies, the output in the state doubled compared to that recorded in the sixties. Districts having greater input use experienced faster growth of output. Thus during 1970-71 to 1981-83, crop output recorded unprecedented annual growth rate of 3.6 per cent compared to 2.2 per cent of the previous decade.
- The analysis indicates to the fact that yield growth is the dominant source of output growth in the state and contribution of area to growth has declined in almost all the districts.
- The eighties decade was marked by crop diversification towards non-traditional non-food crops. There has been a visible decline in the share of food crops and crop diversification away from coarse cereals towards oilseeds, which are perhaps more remunerative. Increase in area under crops other than food crops and traditional non-food crops of sugarcane, cotton and oilseeds is becoming important. This is a positive development and would create opportunities for weaning away excess labour from agriculture. Occupational diversification arising from interdependence between farm and non-farm activities is crucial for employment generation and poverty alleviation.
- The land productivity coming from the selected crops has experienced significant deceleration after the eighties. Agriculture in the state is heading towards stagnancy. Declining productivity levels of the

selected crops perhaps indicate that increasingly productive and problem free lands are being allocated to "other crops". These crops perhaps also account for major portion of purchased inputs (fertilizers, water, tractors, etc.).

- The male agriculture worker productivity up to the early seventies registered a marked increase. Thereafter, labour productivity too has declined substantially.

The fall in the productivity levels indicates that the state requires a rethinking on its resource use pattern. Agriculture requires technological and scientific inputs in order to come out of the prevalent stagnancy. Higher investments in irrigation, rural infrastructure, research and extension would have a beneficial impact on agricultural output and are important determinants of total factor productivity. These non-price factors are important in inducing technical change in agriculture. Resource management strategies suggested under ACRP are thus important for sustainability and inter-generational equity considerations. ACRP lays emphasis on area-based resource endowments and technologies and suggests techno-economic exercises dealing with resources for different geographical entities. Adoption of sustainable technologies for resource management and evolving suitable cropping systems would hold centrestage in steering the state's farm sector to the desired growth path. The policy suggested for Saurashtra and Kutch under this approach as cited below serves as an illustrative example:[4]

> The Saurashtra and Kutch regions are largely arid to semi-arid and mainly suffer from scarcity of water. The kharif crops suffer from erratic rainfall. Due to heavy run off, the little rain that is received cannot be stored so as to be used in the lean periods.

With a view to overcoming the above problems, the following measures are suggested:

(i) Since bajra, groundnut and cotton are the main crops of this region on which its economy depends, certain minimum level of production needs to be sustained irrespective of the rainfall pattern during the kharif season. As distribution of rainfall during the season is natural and its occurrence beyond human control, hence this necessitates breeding of crop varieties suited to the likely rainfall pattern. With the advanced technology now available in genetic engineering, it may be possible to evolve tailor made varieties suited to each sub-region or district.

This approach requires study of rainfall patterns and working out probabilities of receiving rains during the various periods of the season. It also entails studying the lifecycle and critical periods of present day genotypes available in the gene pool. The lifecycle then needs to be superimposed on to the rainfall pattern studied, in an attempt to synchronize its critical periods with the highest probability of rainfall periods. This will ensure certain minimum production of crops during all years. A crash programme to evolve such tailor made crop varieties should be taken up by the State Agricultural Universities.

(ii) Harvesting and conservation of rain water is another aspect that needs attention for which —

(a) In conservation of rainwater in the fields through ridge formation on key line contours is a must. This will ensure greater withstanding of crops to intermittent drought which is common in many parts of Saurashtra-Kutch region.

(b) Harvesting of rainwater by undertaking massive programme of harnessing run off in small rivulets/nallas etc. through construction of check dams/percolation dams etc. This will at least help in recharging ground water that can be used in lean periods or as a life saving irrigation to crops as well as for domestic purposes.

Acknowledgement

The authors acknowledge the help and encouragement received from Dr. S.N. Joshi, Dr. R.D. Desai, Shri Kedar Mehta, Shri Shailesh Dave and Dr. Amita Shah for her comments and suggestions.

NOTES

1. The diversity in agro-climatic environment, temperature regime and resource endowment has resulted in inter and intra-state differences in agricultural development. To tackle this phenomena planning for agricultural development based on agro-climatic sutuations is essential. Agro Climatic Regional Planning approach (ACRP) lays emphasis on development of natural resources and their optimim utilisation in a sustainable manner within the existing regional

constraints and potentials. This approach considers an agro-climatic sub region, having a higher degree of commonlity of resource endowments as the more appropriate planning unit (GOI), Planning Commission, 1989, 1991, 1998). Based on these premises Gujarat has been delineated into seven sub regions, keeping the district boundaries intact.

2. The above is only an overall tendency. The contribution of farm sector to the state economy varies depending on level and pattern of rainfall each year.
3. The econometric work on this and some other aspects of Gujarat's agriculture has not taken the final shape as yet. We, however, report later some preliminary findings.
4. Courtesy Dr. S.N. Joshi.

REFERENCES

Bhalla, G.S. and Alagh, Y.K. (1979), *Performance of Indian Agriculture : A District-wise Study*, New Delhi, Sterling Publisher.

Bhalla, G.S. and Tyagi, D.S. (1989), *Patterns of Indian Agricultural Development-A District Level Study*, New Delhi, ISID.

Bhalla, G.S. and Singh, Gurmail (1998), *Recent Developments in Indian Agriculture-A District Level Study*, New Delhi, CSRD, JNU (mimeo).

Desai, B.M. and Namboodiri, N.V. (1997), "Developing Agriculture in Gujarat - A Strategies Perspective for Ninth Plan", *Economic and Political Weekly*, March 29.

Joshi, S.N. (1996), "Cropping Pattern Changes in Gujarat", *Anvesak*, Vol. 26, No. 2, July-December.

Joshi, S.N. (1995), "Agricultural Development Perspective - Gujarat", *Anvesak*, Vol. 25, No. 1, January-June.

Mathur, Niti (1997), "A Decadal Growth of Gujarat's Agriculture and Perspective", Technical Paper No. 28, Ahmedabad, ARPU.

Patel, A.S. (1996) "Development of Agriculture in Gujarat: Crop Pattern Aspects", presented at Dr. D.T. Lakdawala Memorial Seminar on the Economy of Gujarat - Performance and Prospects, Baroda. (mimeo)

Planning Commission (1991), "Agro-Climatic Regional Planning at State Level-Profiles, Issues, Strategies and Programmes", Working Paper No. 5, Ahmedabad, ARPU.

Planning Commission (1998), "Agro-Climatic Regional Planning - Recent Developments", Working Paper No. 10, Ahmedabad, ARPU.

Annexe 1 : Districtwise Levels and Growth of Area (GCA)

District	Area (in hectares)				Per cent Annual Compound Growth Rate			
	1961-63	1971-73	1981-83	1991-93	71-73 over 61-63	81-83 over 71-73	91-93 over 81-83	91-93 over 61-63
A'bad & G'Ngr	643958	641700	619330	574630	-0.04	-0.35	-0.75	-0.38
Amreli	501246	508200	559330	522100	0.14	0.96	-0.69	0.14
Banaskantha	859706	894800	982670	1056450	0.40	0.94	0.73	0.69
Bharuch	457593	425000	437670	425900	-0.74	0.29	-0.27	-0.24
Bhavnagar	629640	630000	727330	701450	0.01	1.45	-0.36	0.36
Jamnagar	555410	640100	723000	640250	1.43	1.23	-1.21	0.47
Junagadh	597520	643000	717330	643300	0.74	1.10	-1.08	0.25
Kutch	528522	636900	703000	622000	1.88	0.99	-1.22	0.54
Kheda	556683	516600	614000	616400	-0.74	1.74	0.04	0.34
Mehsana	752798	778400	900670	900620	0.33	1.47	0.00	0.60
Panchmahals	581918	534200	533000	551300	-0.85	-0.02	0.34	-0.18
Rajkot	738300	798200	805000	804250	0.78	0.08	-0.01	0.29
Sabarkantha	495309	485100	496670	506350	-0.21	0.24	0.19	0.07
Surat	473345	410200	425000	453350	-1.42	0.36	0.65	-0.14
Surendranagar	685138	690300	668670	675150	0.08	-0.32	0.10	-0.05
Dangs	40099	44800	44800	54200	1.11	0.00	1.92	1.01
Vadodara	558481	528600	554330	561450	-0.55	0.48	0.13	0.02
Valsad	326691	282100	327000	337400	-1.46	1.49	0.31	0.11
Gujarat	9982357	10088200	10838800	10646550	0.11	0.72	-0.18	0.21

Source : Bhalla and Singh, 1998.

Annexe 2 : Districtwise Levels and Growth of Net Sown Area (NSA)

District	Area (in hectares)				Per cent Annual Compound Growth Rate			
	1961-63	1971-73	1981-83	1991-93	71-73 over 61-63	81-83 over 71-73	91-93 over 81-83	91-93 over 61-63
A"bad & G"Ngr	641326	637000	593670	533550	-0.07	-0.70	-1.06	-0.61
Amreli	494894	478800	495000	495300	-0.33	0.33	0.01	0.00
Banaskantha	796905	819700	827670	811050	0.28	0.10	-0.20	0.06
Bharuch	456255	423700	432670	423450	-0.74	0.21	-0.22	-0.25
Bhavnagar	615561	599500	620000	630050	-0.26	0.34	0.16	0.08
Jamnagar	539916	607400	591330	584550	1.18	-0.27	-0.12	0.27
Junagadh	564574	593300	612670	573350	0.50	0.32	-0.66	0.05
Kutch	520425	627700	668670	575200	1.89	0.63	-1.49	0.33
Kheda	525752	488700	520000	511450	-0.73	0.62	-0.17	-0.09
Mehsana	705513	688700	684000	696450	-0.24	-0.07	0.18	-0.04
Panchmahals	482892	485100	477000	472250	0.05	-0.17	-0.10	-0.07
Rajkot	730254	731600	710670	731350	0.02	-0.29	0.29	0.00
Sabarkantha	450307	411500	443670	431300	-0.90	0.76	-0.28	-0.14
Surat	449894	390400	396670	420050	-1.41	0.16	0.57	-0.23
Surendranagar	679024	675100	657000	647450	-0.06	-0.27	-0.15	-0.16
Dangs	40086	44700	44700	54000	1.10	0.00	1.91	1.00
Vadodara	541587	521100	534000	539450	-0.38	0.24	0.10	-0.01
Valsad	294696	265600	297330	306750	-1.03	1.13	0.31	0.13
Gujarat	9529861	9489600	9606720	9437000	-0.04	0.12	-0.18	-0.03

Source : Bhalla and Singh, 1998.

9

The Participatory Irrigation Management Programme in Gujarat
Institutional and Financial Issues

R. PARTHASARATHY

Introduction

Most irrigation systems, whether large or small, are reported to have serious problems relating to the distribution of water and its use efficiency. The irrigation department, which is responsible for building, operating and maintaining the structures, has been found to be inadequate in keeping the systems in proper shape. Importantly, almost all governments experience a shortage of funds necessary to carry out the repair and maintenance work of the systems (Brewer *et al.*, 1997). The alternative to imposing demands on government funds is recovering the costs through user charges. The experience in many countries has been that so far, governments have neither been able to ensure timely payments from farmers nor charge an economic price for the water. Further, the necessity of dealing with individual farmers has made water charge collection a costly exercise. In India, it was during British rule that the irrigation and revenue departments assumed total responsibility for building and managing the systems. Since then it has been assumed that farmers in large systems could take up responsibility of construction of field channels and management below the outlet level (Stone 1984, Chambers 1988). However, the experience across different systems and across states in India disputes this assumption.

Studies suggest that some of the systems, that were managed traditionally by water users, had performed well both with respect to efficiency and distribution. Also, they were able to charge water rates that were significantly higher than the government rates (Sengupta, 1991; Datye and Patil, 1987; Maloney and Raju, 1994; Pant and Verma, 1983). The users associations reflect definite institutional arrangements in which rewards and sanctions were clearly defined in order for the systems to work. Therefore, one solution that has been tried in various places is to transfer the responsibility for the operation and maintenance (O&M) of the canal systems below a certain point to the local farmers. Presently, most of the state governments in India are encouraging the formation of water users' associations and want to eventually transfer irrigation management to irrigators. The July 1995 Government of Gujarat Resolution on participatory irrigation management (PIM) is also a step in this direction.

To stress the point that for improving the management of irrigation system, user involvement and institutional development are necessary to state the obvious. Organized irrigators' associations are expected to serve as channels for feedback and feed-forward information to improve the performance and services provided by O&M irrigation personnel (Ferrer and Lucero, 1988). There is also a view that institutional development should be matched by improvements in the physical infrastructure for management transfer to be effective (Bandaragoda, 1998). Together these points suggest that, though in the long run, irrigation management transfer (IMT) may bring down the government expenditure on maintaining the irrigation systems, in the short run, there has to be a committed outlay to have a genuine transfer of management. Further, the users associations also have to find ways and means of raising funds to ensure their viability.

This paper first reviews the experience of various countries that have attempted irrigation management transfer programmes to understand the range of issues involved (section 2). Section 3 discusses the state of irrigation in Gujarat and presents the details of the participatory irrigation management (PIM) programme. Against the background of over four years of programme implementation, section 4 critically examines the viability aspect of the water users association (WUA) formed under the PIM programme. The last section summarises the emerging lessons from the experiences of irrigation management transfer programmes with special reference to the PIM programme in Gujarat.

Review of the Irrigation Management Transfer Programmes

Management transfer is being implemented around the world but little information is available about its impact. Notable benefits of the different stakeholders managing the irrigation system in the Philippines (Ferrer & Lucero, 1988) are (a) in getting farmers assistance in water distribution, (b) in facilitating the maintenance of the farm level facilities and improvement or repair of canals, and (c) in resolving irrigation related conflicts or problems at lower levels which where previously dealt with the government authorities. Vermillion (1997) states that after management transfer in the Philippines, there has been a substantial increase of over 50 per cent in the water fee collection rate, improvements in operation and maintenance (O & M) and a rise in cropping intensity (which may not necessarily be only due to management transfer). Similar are results from the Nepal project (Ansari, 1989) which also show that after organising irrigation facilities, there are changes in cropping pattern and an increase in cropping intensity by 75 per cent. On the other hand, there is little evidence to suggest that irrigation management transfer has resulted in a reduction in the cost of irrigation management by the government.

Unlike the case of the Philippines, the IMT Programme in Mexico was a rapid top-down process that met with relatively little resistance from farmers (Kloezen *et al.*, 1998). This rapid top-down process was made possible because (a) IMT was part of a much wider set of agricultural and political liberalization policies; (b) it was accompanied by a new law that not only supported the transfer of authority and responsibility to the users but also provided them concessions to use the infrastructure and machinery; (c) it had a strong political commitment; (d) leaders and staff of WUAs were given professional training; (e) the WUAs agreed to jointly manage the system with the agency during a fixed and relatively short period of time; and (f) the programme's aim was not to maximize direct user participation in O & M, but to involve farmers in representative governance.

However, the IMT in the Alto Rio Lerma District, Mexico (Kloezen, 1998) had very little impact on surface water allocation and distribution and in the use of groundwater. Though the transfer had resulted in improvements in system maintenance, especially at lower system levels, there has been a moderate increase in the proportion of the total O&M budget spent on maintenance expenditures per hectare. Perhaps because of the increase, Johnson III (1997) suggests that the users need to establish an investment fund to cover emergencies and future development in order to sustain the transfer.

There is another angle to the Mexican case. With population growth and structural transformation from an agricultural society to an industrial nation, the demand for water has increased. Yet, Mexico's legal system does not clearly specify the rights for irrigated agriculture or state how these rights can be protected against increasing demands for water from municipal and industrial users. Further, the irrigation fee levels generally did not rise even to compensate the erosion of the value of the currency. Also, there was a high turnover of staff hired by the WUAs. Finally, there were observable difficulties in identifying the new roles that the (government) agency could take on.

Brewer and others (1997) argue that the problems at Tambraparani irrigation system in Tamil Nadu arise from fundamental issues that apply to all large irrigation schemes. It is essential to modify water distribution rules over time in tune with the increasing demands on irrigation systems from both farmers and other users. Further, the involvement of users in these changes is essential to ensure that the distribution rules serve their desires and that the users accept the limitations on uses imposed by water availability and other features of the system. If the users have direct influence over system management, they are more likely to force needed changes. Periodic reviews of the distribution rules should be made, but the processes involved in changing the rules should make it sufficiently difficult to ensure that only necessary changes are made. This calls for considering the water users institutions to be dynamic bodies and the process of transfer to be a long drawn affair rather than a one-time change in management.

Bandaragoda (1998) argues that improvements in the physical infrastructure should be matched with improvements in the institutional framework. While planning for modernization of existing irrigation systems, the design should consider the institutional implications of changing the existing design. Similar to Tambraparani, in Pakistan too the rigidity of a fixed schedule (of water distribution) was designed to prevent exploitation of water rights. But with increased cropping intensities and changes in the cropping pattern, the water allocation per unit of land became inadequate. Due to increasing demand for water, some users have started developing strategies to overcome supply inadequacy through flexibility in water turns, such as rotation, merging, substitution, exchange and trading of turns. Even the rotational water distribution system (*warabhandi*) was found to bring inequity in water use. Although the design-related discrepancy did not affect the operations of rotational water availability in individual watercourse commands, it was found to impose inequity in water distribution among different sets of water users within the larger system and to induce corresponding behavioural strategies to circumvent the individual disadvantages. In addition. availability of groundwater seems to have encouraged water users to disregard the discipline of rotation system.

Yet another concern among donors as well as project planners is the low returns on investment in infrastructure development in developing countries. Often the problem of implementation (especially post-construction O&M activities) is overlooked at the time of designing the physical infrastructure for an irrigation project. Identifying the roots of some of the implementation problems during project preparation stages and incorporating appropriate remedial action in the design itself escapes the attention of planners (Bandaragoda, 1998).

Summing up, the literature on IMT points out that farmers' involvement in water distribution and maintenance systems has led to an improvement in resolving irrigation-related conflicts, which were previously dealt with by government authorities. Though the IMT has led to an increase in the water fee collection rate and improvements in the O&M of the system, none of the studies shows that the cost of irrigation management by the government has been reduced. Importantly, there is little evidence to show that the per unit rate of water has been increased after the transfer. In fact, IIMI's study on irrigation service fees in five Asian countries concludes that irrigation agencies with a significant degree of financial autonomy have often been able to reduce the amount of direct payment required from farmers through institutional arrangements where the agencies earn secondary income from sources other than charges on water users (Small, 1987). On the other hand, the newly-created users organisations were also found to incur managerial expenses. Perhaps based on this evidence, Johnson III (1997) suggests a need for users to establish an investment fund to sustain the transfer.

The other dimension brought out by various studies is the increase in the demand for water for non-agricultural use. Yet, in most of the places the legal system does not seem to specify the rights for irrigated agriculture and also fails to state how these rights can be protected against increasing demands for water from municipal and industrial users. Therefore, it becomes imperative to codify water laws to protect agricultural water rights.

The success of IMT was evidently due to a much wider set of agricultural and political liberalization policies. It was not only accompanied by new laws that supported the transfer of authority and responsibility to the users, but also had high political commitment. Orientation and training of leaders of WUAs and governmental staff also emerge as one of the essential ingredient of the IMT (the Andhra Pradesh model has all these elements, see for details, Parthasarathy, 1998).

Evidently, the basic philosophy behind the IMT seems to transform the irrigators from being beneficiaries to partners in planning and implementing irrigation development programmes. The PIM programme of the government of Gujarat is also based on this premise. To understand the PIM programme in a proper perspective, first the irrigation scenario in Gujarat is discussed.

Irrigation in Gujarat: Imperatives for Reforms

The public investment on irrigation (excluding Narmada) in Gujarat shows a declining trend over the six plan periods up to the Eighth Plan (Table 9.1). However, the net area irrigated and the gross area irrigated show a steady rise over the period 1971-1996 (Table 9.2). Between 1980 and 1992, the average annual increase in net area irrigated is 2.47 per cent and that of the gross irrigated area is 2.90 per cent. Presently, the government canals form 20 per cent of the net irrigated area. There are areas of concern with respect to utilisation of the irrigable area, annual recovery of water charges and contribution of water charges to the total O&M expenditure in the state (Table 9.3). Further, there are problems related to water charges and availability of O&M funds. The water rates were last revised in 1981 and the revised norms (1998) for O&M expenditure leaves a large gap between the estimated expenses and the expenditure trend observed so far (Table 9.4). To study the patterns of O&M expenditure and to suggest suitable revisions in the norms for O&M grants, the government of Gujarat appointed a committee (Subba Rao Committee) in 1998.

The committee recommended that a grant should be made of Rs. 470 per hectare for projects with gated spillways and Rs. 440 per hectare for ungated spillways. For establishment expenditure, the grant comes to Rs. 650 per hectare (including a provision of 95 chowkidars for a division of 16000 hectares). Even these estimates do not appear to be very realistic. Assuming an annual average inflation rate of 10 per cent, the present O&M outlay appears to be roughly one-fourth of the amount required in the year 2003 (Table 9.4). These estimates, however, certainly do not take into account the expenditure for setting up the participatory irrigation management programme currently underway in Gujarat.

On the systems front, the irrigation facilities in Gujarat can be broadly grouped into two categories. First are the systems and their command area located in water scarce areas (WSA) like North Gujarat and Saurashtra; and second are the systems and the command areas of water

Table 9.1 : Public Investment in Irrigation during Five Year Plans

(Rs. in Crores)

Plan	Gujarat				India	
	Investment in Irrigation			Total Plan outlay	Outlay for Irrigation	Total Plan outlay
	Narmada	Others	Total			
III Plan			46 (19.2)	240	664 (7.7)	8577
IV Plan			131 (24.0)	545	1354 (8.6)	15779
V Plan			241 (24.0)	1005	3877 (9.8)	39426
VI Plan			136 (3.6)	3760	10930 (9.9)	110467
VII Plan	1064 (64.2)	593 (35.8)	1657 (27.6)	6000	16590 (7.5)	221436
VIII Plan	2000 (53.2)	1756 (46.8)	3756 (36.8)	10200 (provisional)	26548 (6.1)	434100

Notes: 1. For the sixth plan period public investment is provided under three heads; minor irrigation (88 crores), soil and water conservation (28.94 crores) and irrigation command area development (18.77 crores) for Gujarat.

2. Figures in parentheses are percentage to total outlay.

Sources: 1. Various volumes of the Five-Year Plan documents, Government of Gujarat, Gandhinagar.

2. Statistical Outline of India, 1997-98, pp. 219-220.

Table 9.2 : Gross and Net Irrigated Area: Gujarat

(in 000 Hectares)

Year	Net irrigated area	Gross irrigated area
88-89	2493	2904
89-90	2464	2907
90-91	2438	2911
91-92	2372	2880
92-93	2643	3227
93-94	2541	3087
94-95	3002	3655

Source: Directorate of Economics and Statistics, Government of Gujarat. Gandhinagar.

Table 9.3 : Basic Characteristics of Irrigation in Gujarat

1. Net cropped area (1994-95)	9665000 ha.
2. Gross cropped area (1994-95)	11245100 ha.
3. Net irrigated area (1994-95)	3002100 ha
4. Gross irrigated area (1994-95)	3654800 ha.
5. Gross irrigated area as % to GCA (94-95)	32.50
6. Net irrigated area as % to NCA (94-95)	31.24
7. Percentage distribution of NIA by source	
a. Govt. and panchayat canals	19.75
b. Wells and tubewells	78.80
c. Tanks	1.18
d. Others	0.27
8. Net irrigated area by canals	593000 ha.
9. Annual plan outlay on irrigation and flood control (1996-97)	Rs. 1233 crores
10. Average annual increase (in %) between 1980-81 and 1992-93 of	
a. Net area irrigated	2.47
b. Gross area irrigated	2.89
11. Potential irrigable area (June 1997 in lakh ha.)	64.88
12. Potential created (June 1997 in lakh ha.)	35.85
13. Utilisation of irrigable area (June 1997 in lakh ha.)	30.32
14. Capital investment in irrigation up to 1993 (Rs. in crores)	3220
15. Average water charges per ha. (1981 rates)	Rs. 165
16. Total annual assessment of O&M (April 94)	Rs. 12 crores
17. Recovery as water charges as % of total O&M expenditure	33.33
18. Average annual recovery from water users as % of total assessment	65

Sources : 1. Various volumes of Socio-Economic Review, Directorate of Economics and Statistics, Government of Gujarat, Gandhinagar.
2. Various Volumes of Five-Year Plan documents, Government of Gujarat, Gandhinagar.
3. Unpublished reports of the Department of Irrigation, Government of Gujarat.

abundant areas (WAA), as in the Central and South Gujarat regions. Besides the two categories, it is also important to note that the irrigation systems in WSA have lined canals whereas it is not uncommon to see unlined canals below the sub-minor and in many cases below the minor level in systems located in WAA. These differences appear to play a crucial role in the effectiveness of the PIM programme, as will be discussed later.

Table 9.4 : Amount Required for O & M of Existing Irrigation Schemes till 2003

Year	R&M costs for Works per hectare		Establishment costs per ha.	Assuming 1.5 million ha. of irrigated area amount needed		
	With gated spillway	without gated spillway		for Works	for Estb.	Total
1998	470	440 (455)	650	682	975	1657
1999	517	484 (500)	715	750	1072	1822
2000	568	532 (550)	786	825	1179	2004
2001	625	585 (605)	865	907	1297	2204
2002	688	644 (666)	951	999	1426	2425
2003	756	708 (732)	1046	1098	1569	2667

Note : Figures in parentheses are arithmetic averages of R&M cost.

Source : For columns 2 and 3, unpublished reports of the Department of Irrigation, Government of Gujarat, Gandhinagar.

PIM in Gujarat

With the objectives of improving agricultural productivity and building up the capacities of irrigation water users to manage efficiently, a participatory irrigation management (PIM) programme was launched in Gujarat in 1995. This programme, covering major and minor irrigation works, is also expected to significantly lower the O&M expenditure of the government on irrigation schemes. The PIM model is based on the experience in the Philippines. Recognising the initial condition differences between the two countries and changes called for in the management of irrigation systems, PIM programme was first introduced in thirteen selected pilot project areas. Given the experience of Indian NGOs in implementing participatory developmental projects, the government invited the active support of NGOs in setting up the PIM.

Under the PIM programme, prior to transferring the system to the users associations (*piyat mandalis*), were to be formed and registered,

R&R of the system below the outlet level to be completed, users share in the R&R costs to be collected, and training and orientation to be provided to WUA office-bearers to enable them to manage the WUA subsequently. Importantly, the implementation process has an explicit component of monitoring mechanisms, such as the High Level Working Group (HLWG), sub-committees and process documentation research (PDR). PDR results were envisaged to be an important source of feedback to the implementers and policy makers.

PDR on PIM

In order to deal with these concerns and objectives of the PIM, PDR was to document, analyse and facilitate the implementation process, including providing inputs for possible mid-course corrections. PDR was carried out in six of the thirteen pilot projects (Table 9.5). In each site, there was a Field Observer stationed and the researchers focused on the village as a unit rather than just the WUA. PDR adopted a combination of survey and observation methods and produced half-yearly reports, analytical papers, newsletters and oral presentations to the implementing agencies and to the HLWG constituted by the government of Gujarat. In addition, baseline surveys were also conducted, focusing on agriculture, irrigation and the WUAs (for details on PDR, see, Parthasarathy and Iyengar, 1988).

Progress of PIM

Besides the 13 pilot schemes, WUAs were formed and irrigation management 'turned over' in approximately 40,000 hectares of command area. Importantly, there have been significant changes in water allocation, distribution and management in almost all the WUAs. However, the completion of R&R work appears to be varied across the sites and the most notable feature determining the success of completing the R&R work is the presence of an NGO. Similarly, process components like people's participation, collection of contribution, fixing water rates higher than the government's, gender and equity concerns and conflict resolutions of the WUAs present mixed results. There are significant variations in the progress of PIM between areas that had lined canals prior to PIM and areas that have unlined canals. The progress seems to be better in areas that have unlined canals probably because the repair and rehabilitation work on the canals demonstrated the earnestness of the government to transfer the management of canals in good condition.

Table 9.5 : Basic Characteristics of the PIM Project Villages: Gujarat

Projects/Details	Thalota	Laksmipura	Chandrawadi	Tranol	Kunjrav	Digas
Name of the System	Daroi	Dantiwada	CMIP	Mahi Canal	Mahi Canal	Ukai
Project Location	Visnagar, Mahesana	Patan	Mahendrada, Junagadh	Anand	Anand	Hansot Bharuch
Presence of NGO	Yes	Yes	Yes	No	No	No
Number of Males	703	2145	1492	2261	3278	2004
Females	726	2236	1489	2227	3883	2001
Population	2331	7717	4198	6674	7161	6084
Workers Male	607	1858	1317	2046	1887	1845
Female	550	1597	1168	1712	1312	1548
Number of Households	456	1316	752	1358	1134	1213
Cultivator	347	748	549	694	601	582
WUA member	210	174	222	168	91	169
Date of WUA registration	Feb. 2, 1996	Dec. 18, 1995	Oct. 21, 1995	Nov.30, 1996	Jun.2, 1998	Nov. 29, 1995
Turnover	Dec.16, 1996	Oct.19, 1996	Not yet	Nov.30, 1996	Not yet	Jul.31, 1997 (part)
PIM command area (ha)	224	245.68	463	355.57	296	921.05
Cultivated area (ha)	759.38	3533.39	3293.56	1382.06	941	4841.14

Source: Household Survey, 1997-98, Gujarat Institute of Development Research, Ahmedabad.

Among the components of PIM, it appears that the user farmers have attached more significance to technical improvements than to non-technical matters in the initial phase. And, wherever the strategy of carrying out first the R&R work, followed by formation of the WUA and transferring the management, has been adopted, the performance of the WUA seems to be better.

In the formation of the WUAs, there seem to be some common problems across the pilot projects. For instance, the difficulty in convincing farmers to participate and contribute was a serious handicap. Apathy was also found to hamper the motivation work (for an analysis on the participatory model, see, Parthasarathy, 1998). Secondly, there were observable differences in the understanding of PIM policy at different levels of the bureaucracy. Thirdly, it has been observed that even in areas where there are successful milk and other cooperatives, the water users cooperatives seem to lack in support and enthusiasm; perhaps there are differences between sellers' and buyers' cooperative.

Implications on Time Schedule

Keeping in view the target of the department of irrigation, Government of Gujarat, to turn over 50 per cent of the existing command area to users' associations, the pace of PIM programme implementation appears to be slow. The pace of the programme is measured in terms of the extent of R&R work done, level of awareness about the PIM among the users and efforts made towards improving the skills needed by WUA members to manage the affairs of the association through training. Table 9.6, provides an estimate of R&R costs that have to be incurred to cover 50 per cent of the extant canal command. These estimates are based on the per hectare cost of R&R work incurred so far on the pilot projects.

It appears that in the programme, NGOs' support and their effectiveness have been assumed. Eventually, it became apparent that even after four years not many NGOs had taken to the PIM programme. In fact, the number of NGOs involved in the PIM programme has remained the same as it was in the beginning. Secondly, there are areas that are not amenable to forming a WUA, for example, areas covered through direct outlets on a main canal or a sub-minor. Similar is the case with the small number of benefiting households under some of the outlets.

There are other important lessons to be learned from the implementation of the PIM programme. The first is the question of

Table 9.6 : Estimated Cost and Expenditure on R&R Work and Cost Projections for Different Projects and Systems

Details	Thalota	Tranol	Kunjrav	L' Pura	Digas	C'wadi
Name of the irrigation system	Daroi	Mahi	Mahi	Dantiwada	Ukai-K	C'wadi
Total command area of the system	61,085	212,000	212,000	45,755	331,557	—
Total command area of the project	224	356	296	246	921	463
Total no. of benefiting households in the project area	216	334	425	151	432	222
Initial cost estimate for R&R (1995-96)	124,050 (dept) 259,000 (NGO)	10,01,817	398,240	9830	NA	22,53,839
Revised cost estimate for R&R (March 1999)	—	—	—	100,000	—	35,33,532
Actual expenditure up to March '99	332,546	7,48,475	343,100	10,000	30,07,379	14,88,134
Cost per ha. (as per estimate)	1156	2814	1345	407		7632
Cost per ha. (as per expenditure)	1485	2102	1159	41	3265	3214
Cost per household (estimate)	1199	2999	937	662		15917
Cost per household (Expd.)	1540	2241	807	66	6962	6703
% Difference between revised estimate and initial cost estimate				1017		157
% amount spent to initial cost estimate	128	75	86	102	—	66
Projected expenditure for R&R for 50 per cent of the command area (based on cost per ha) in Rs. '000	3530		220480	9311	541268	NA

Note: Projected expenditure for R&R work for 50 per cent of the command area (of 15 lakh hectares) i.e. 750,000 hectares at Rs. 1797 = Rs. 13477.5 lakhs.

Source: Unpublished reports of the Department of Irrigation, Government of Gujarat, Gandhinagar.

introducing suitable (financial?) incentives, especially for the department's staff at the field level for successfully implementing the programme. As is the case with many government departments, there are very few promotion avenues for field staff. This aspect assumes importance, especially when the programme implementation calls for changes in the method, attitude and style of functioning. Second, people's participation is found to vary over a wide spectrum, from leadership-centred management of the WUA to agency-influenced participation in the WUA. Presently, the concept of participation is interpreted merely in terms of the number of meetings held and the election of the WUAs' office-bearers.

Among the areas of concern, the lack of emphasis on federating the WUAs seems to be important. Presently, the WUAs are formed in isolated portions of the canal system and there is an obvious absence of linkage between any two WUAs in the same system. Consequently, the WUA not only look disjointed but also give an impression that forming the WUA is an end by itself. Evidently, the WUAs have to be interdependent to manage the supplies of water and only coordination between them can lead to an overall efficiency of the system. Progressively, water management has to address basin level issues along with local, i.e., below outlet level distribution and management of water. In this context, the irrigation management policy adopted by the Andhra Pradesh legislature and the Mexican experience offer useful insights (see for instance, Parthasarathy, 1998; Johnson III, 1997; Kloezen, 1998).

There are various components in the PIM programme and some of them have philosophical implications. As mentioned, one of the important expectations of IMT in general, and PIM in particular (though never stated explicitly in the policy), is the long-run aim of the government to reduce its expenditure. This presupposes that WUAs will be self-sufficient in maintaining and operating the irrigation system. One of the essential conditions for this to happen is the financial viability of the WUAs. The viability of the WUAs depends not only on the one time grant of Rs. 225 by the Government of India and a matching grant of the Government of Gujarat towards its O&M expenditure, but crucially on the WUAs' ability to ensure regular income. Obviously, the important source of regular income for a WUA is the water charges. In addition, the adequacy of this income depends on the WUAs' ability to charge higher rates for water than those of the government's. Most of the WUAs formed in the pilot phase of the PIM programme have recognised this aspect. There are, however, some issues in WUAs charging a rate higher than the government's and the lessons have wider applicability. The following section discusses this aspect.

Issues in Raising Water Rates

One of the features of the new WUAs being formed in Gujarat is the water charges levied by them which were higher than what the government charges. Some of the WUAs, like Thalota[1], Tranol[2] and Lakshmipura[3] have fixed new water charges. Among these WUAs, Thalota had initially fixed the highest rate, which was then two-and-half times higher than that of the government rates[4]. Around this time, Lakshmipura had fixed a water rate that was 30 per cent more than the government rate, while Tranol charged a flat one-time rate of 20 per cent of the water charges and created an operation and maintenance fund. Except in Tranol, there has been considerable discussion about the hike in water charges adopted by the WUAs.

Admittedly, the government water rates are abysmally low, however, the analytic of pricing of water appears to be complex (for a detailed discussion on this aspect, see, Parthasarathy, 1999). Partly, the complexity arises due to the existence of other sources of water like tubewells and partly due to the general attitude that water is a "free good" which the government supplies. In the case of the irrigation systems in north Gujarat like Dharoi and Dantiwada, the supply of water for irrigation purposes is only during winter season and occasionally one or two waterings are given during the monsoon seasons. Even during winter, full irrigation has been rarely possible, the number of waterings usually being two or three. It is pertinent, therefore, to determine the relative importance of the different sources of irrigation in the PIM project villages.

Water Pricing: Competing Sources

When the canal water charges are based on area and crops and the tubewell charges are higher than the canal water, as the number of waterings from the canal increases, the marginal utility of additional watering should be positive, while the average price (per watering) declines. However, in most of north Gujarat's villages, farmers do not view marginal utility only by the cost parameter. This is because water supply by the 'tubewell companies'[5] is considered not only to be reliable but also efficient in terms of revenue. Many studies have shown that output is higher with the use of ground water rather than canal water (Dhawan, 1990). For crop cultivation, when the timeliness criterion is not met, the marginal utility of additional waterings may sometimes be negative. For the supplier, however, as the number of canal watering increases, the incremental cost is zero while the average cost declines. In order to reduce the average cost of water, an increase in the number of waterings is only a necessary condition; the sufficient condition is the efficiency in water distribution.

Theoretically, the competition among the two sellers, WUA and the tubewell companies, in a community of irrigators will force competitive pricing of water. However, the community is likely to avoid this outcome for the following reason. In the north Gujarat context the two sources of water are not equally endowed. Further, the water users know very well that the underground aquifers might dry up or the cost of repairing the tubewell will be expensive. Further, when the reservoir is full it will increase the availability of canal water, making water from the two sources a substitutable product to some extent. Hypothetically, therefore, until the time they become near perfect substitutes, the more assured water source will command a higher price than the other. Perhaps it is this aspect that contributes to the resentment among the WUA members to the price hike of canal water. The other reason for the reported resentment is attitudinal.

Farmers' Response to Water Rates Hike

For some members of the WUA the logic of paying a higher rate to the WUA than what the government charges for water was not clear. It was also not clear as to why they should pay more to the WUA when improvement in the reliability of water supply is beyond its control. Importantly, there is a question regarding the possible uses of the profit the association makes. Under the Societies Act it seems that the WUA cannot distribute the surplus income over and above sharing some fixed portion (12 or 15 per cent) as dividend among its members. Therefore, some members question the very parameter that is commonly understood as the one that improves the financial viability of the association. This aspect indicates the need to think of alternatives to the present arrangement of registering the water users associations under the Societies Act or the need for suitable legislation with respect to incomes and disbursements of the water users associations (For a detailed discussion on the aspect of legal registration, see, Maloney and Raju, 1994).

As expected, the response to the hike in water charges was varied among the different community members and by size of land holdings. A majority of the landholders who use both canal and tubewell belong to the Patel community who also have higher than average size of land in the village[6]. Ninety per cent of the farmers who depend exclusively on the canal are from the Thakore community and the opposition to the hike is, by and large, from the members of this community. Other irrigators and the NGO that quoted the prevailing water rates of the tubewell and argued the case for raising the canal water charges apparently did not put forward a convincing argument. Even among the users of tubewell and canal not all are happy with the raise in the canal water charges. This is because not only the expected incremental returns to canal water are zero (unless the number of waterings increases), but the additional cost for tubewell irrigation[7] is also zero. So why incur additional cost for canal irrigation when marginal returns are asymptotic towards zero?

Shah (1993) points out, water prices charged by owners of "electric water extracting mechanisms" (including tubewells) are much higher even in Gujarat's water abundant areas and in the states like Uttar Pradesh, Haryana, Andhra Pradesh, Bihar and Tamil Nadu. Shah's analysis suggests the possibility of lowering tubewell water rates as and when the number of waterings from the canal improves. This is the possibility the farmers counted too.

In Thalota, the tubewell water rates fell when canal water rates increased. This was because as the number of canal waterings increased (to four against the usual one or two) during the 1997-1998 winter season, the farmers' dependence on tubewell water decreased. As a result, the tubewell command area declined by fifty per cent. There were also changes in the method of levying water charges by the tubewell 'companies'. For the wheat crop, for example, tubewell companies shifted the basis to the number of waterings actually used by the farmers. While the rate per watering remained the same, the total expense for the farmer declined sharply. The total income for the tubewell companies also declined. In fact, with the prospect of the canal supply and the required number of waterings increasing, there was an expectation that the tubewell water charge will further decline. However, the farmers do not want this to happen.

Farmers were also keen to evolve a reserve price for tubewell waters in order to protect the tubewell 'companies'. They have decided to use at least two to three waterings from the tubewell and use it in conjunction with canal waters[8]. This was intended to reduce the losses of the tubewell companies since the fixed costs (of the companies) have to be met in any case. "In many parts of north Gujarat, where tubewell depths can go up to 400 metres and investment per WEM up to Rs. 5 lakh, pressures to maintain high utilization rates and cover the fixed costs have resulted in various forms of price discrimination. These pressures have enormously increased after the introduction of progressive flat power charges in June 1987 which have rendered all the costs of tubewell operation into overheads. The standard practice has been to charge a lower price (Rs. 30-45 per hour for 75 hp motor) during kharif season when the water demand function is highly elastic and twice as much or more for rabi and summer (Rs. 60-75 per hour)" (Shah, 1993, p 64).

Summary

Since June 1995, the Government of Gujarat has been implementing a participatory irrigation management programme (PIM) with the ultimate objective of improving agricultural productivity. As water is one of the crucial inputs in agricultural production, the programme specifically aims at improving water distribution management by ensuring proper maintenance of irrigation canals and timely and adequate water supply to the farmers of a command area. To do this, the policy has envisaged active involvement of command area farmers in major, medium and minor irrigation schemes. The Government of Gujarat had initially launched 13 PIM projects in different regions of the state on a pilot basis and in six of these non-governmental organisations (NGOs) were to support the process. Evidently, the programme aims at addressing (irrigation) system-related issues as well as the operational issues of water distribution and management. In the first three-and-a-half year period, only the second set of issues could be addressed to. The larger issue of system management is expected to come up soon.

The significance of PIM lies in the fact that it aims at improving the performance and financial viability of irrigation structures through a system of cost recovery and turnover of operations and maintenance to local water users themselves. One of the important expectations of the PIM is the long-run benefit to the government through a reduction in its expenditure. This presupposes that WUAs will be self-sufficient in maintaining and operating the irrigation system. One of the essential conditions for this to happen is the financial viability of the WUAs. Further, at the policy level, the PIM projects mark an important shift from a top-down "blueprint" approach to a participatory "process approach".

Irrigation management transfers around the world and the

experience of the PIM programme in Gujarat point to the fact that farmers' involvement in water distribution and maintenance of systems has indeed led to an improvement in resolving irrigation related conflicts. However, given the fact that in the short run the government has to incur additional expenditure to set up the programme, even the revised norms for O&M expenditure by the government of Gujarat is found to leave a large gap between the provision made and the required funds.

On the system front, even in the early 1980s the average annual revenue from water rates covered only about 8 per cent of the annual operation and maintenance costs in Gujarat. Admittedly, the government water rates are abysmally low, however, the analytic of the pricing of water appears to be complex. Partly, the complexity arises due to the existence of other sources of water like tubewells which are more dependable.

Transfer of irrigation management responsibility from the governmental irrigation authority to local management demands both allocative and investment decisions by the WUAs. For these decisions to be effective, some assurance on the quantity and timing of water entitlement are needed. In fact, given the increasing competition for available water both within and across sectors, a clarification of legal rights is desirable. Essentially, the new policy has to mature into laws. The other advantage of this progression may be that water rights will also allow transfer of water from lower to higher value uses.

NOTES

1. Thalota pilot project is a part of the Dharoi Right Bank Canal Project. Since 1979-80, the Dharoi project has been irrigating 5,550 hectares of land in the five talukas of Kheralu, Visnagar, Mehsana, Sidhpur, and Vijapur in Mehsana district. Thalota pilot project encompasses the entire command area of the Branch Canal Number 2 (D2T) which is a distributory of Right Bank canal of Dharoi Dam on the Sabarmati River. A direct outlet from the D2T and its four sub-minors, DSM 1, DSM 2, DSM 3 and DSM1/1 irrigate a total of 267.43 hectares. During the years 1972-1976 the government constructed the canal network in Thalota. The canal started functioning in 1979-80; however, water was available only for two years after which canal fell into disuse.
2. The total command area of the Tranol Sub-Minor is 355 hectares but due to *kuchcha* watercourses, only 185 hectare being irrigated. The Sub-Minor has 14 outlets with each outlet having a committee. A representative from each outlet committee is a member of the 15-member executive committee. The fields of Kunjrav farmers are clustered together and can be irrigated from the same outlets. The main crops are tobacco (80%), rice (10%), and horticultural crops like bananas lemons, and chilies.

3. The pilot project covers the command area of Lakshmipura Minor, a minor of the distributory 13-L which branch out from the Gadh branch canal which is a part of the Dantiwada Irrigation project. The Minor is 2,347 metres long and eight outlets. It aims to irrigate 245.28 hectares of land, about 75 per cent of which falls in Lakshmipura village, and the remaining 25 per cent in the adjoining village of Vagdod. Whereas Lakshmipura residents own most fields lying in the head-reach area of minor, fields located at the tail-end belong mostly to Vagdod farmers.
4. The upward revision of water charges took place after a PRA exercise undertaken by the NGO working on this project during the monsoon season of 1997. Subsequently, the water rates have been brought down and for the kharif season of 1997 the rates were only 50 per cent higher than the government rates.
5. The joint ownership of tubewells is locally referred to as 'tubewell companies' in north Gujarat. These companies varying numbers of partners, who contribute to the equity capital in different proportions. Water is transported through underground pipelines. Importantly, there is no difference in the price charged for water to all categories of users. The shareholding members, however, have a preferential claim to water over other buyers of water in years of scarcity (for details, Shah, 1993).
6. It was reported that historically the land ownership in the village had been fairly even. However, among the crops other than Patels, the family size had always been higher, which eventually led to fragmentation of lands. Also, marriage related expenses which are high led these community members to sell or pledge lands, mostly to Patels. This, presently and holding appears unequally distributed and with the advent of irrigation in the village, the income inequality also widens.
7. The additional cost is zero because the tubewell companies charge on the basis of crops, area cultivated and for particular season, irrespective of the number of watering.
8. This process of blending water from the two sources is also expected to help improve the quality of water (since canal water is reported to be too cold); help improve the taste of wheat, and reduce the salinity of the soil.

REFERENCES

Andhra Pradesh Farmers Management of Irrigation Systems Act (1997), *Act and Rules* (Act 11 of 1997), Department of Irrigation and Command Area Development, Governmnt of Andhra Pradesh.

Ansari, Nasiruddin (1989), Rehabilitation of Communal Irrigation Schemes in Nepal, ODI-IIMI Irrigation Management Network Paper 89/1C June.

Bandaragoda, D.J. (1998), Need for Institutional Impact Assessment in Planning Irrigation System Modernization, IWMI Research Report 21, May 1998.

Bandaragoda, D.J. (1998), Design and Practice of Water Allocation Rules : Lessons from Warabandi in Pakistan's Punjab, IIMI Research Report 17, May.

Brewer, Jeffery D.; Sakthivadivel R.; Raju K.V. (1997), Water Distribution Rules and Performance: A Case Study in the Tambraparani Irrigation System, India, IIMI, December.

Brewer, J., Kolavalli, S., Kalro, A.H., Naik, G., Ramanarayan, S., Raju, K. V. and Sakthivadivel, R. (1997) Irrigation Management Transfer In India: Policies, Processes and Performance, (unpublished report), Indian Institute of Management, Ahmedabad and International Irrigation Management Institute, Colombo, December.

Chambers, R. (1988), *Managing Canal Irrigation: Practical Analysis from South Asia*, Oxford and IBH Publishing, New Delhi.

Datye, K.R. and Patil, R.K. (1987), Farmer Managed Irrigation Systems: Indian Experiences, Centre for Applied Systems Analysis in Development, Bombay.

Ferrer, A.M.; Lucero L.C., (1998), Developing Partnership in the Management of Irrigation System, ODI-IIMI Irrigation Management Network Paper 88/1c. June.

Johnson III, Sam H. (1997), Irrigation Management Transfer in Mexico: A Strategy to Achieve Irrigation District Sustainability, IIMI Research Report.

Kloezen, Wim H. Carlos Garces - Restrepo and Sam H. Johnson III, (1998), Impact Assessment of Irrigation Management Transfer in the Alto Rio District, Mexico, IIMI Research Report 15 March.

Maloney, C. and Raju, K.V. (1994), The Role of Farmers' Organisations in Environmentally Beneficial Water Management, in M. V. K. Sivamohan and C.A. Scott (eds), *India: Irrigation Management Partnerships*, Booklinks Corporation, Hyderabad.

Pant, N. and Patil, R.K. (1983), *Farmers' Organisation and Irrigation Management,* Ashish Publishing House, New Delhi.

Parthasarathy, R. (1998), Water Users Association in Irrigation Management Programme: Participation Strategies in a Game Theoretic Framework, in Vishwa Ballabh (ed.) *Proceeding of the International Workshop on Shared Resource Management in South Asia: The Next Step*, Institute of Rural Management, Anand, February 17-19, 1998.

Parthasarathy, R. and Iyengar, S., (1998), Participatory Water Resources Development in Western India: Influencing Policy And Practice Through Process Documentation Research, jointly with Sudarshan Iyengar, in David Mosse, John Farrington and Alan Rew (ed.) *Development As Process: Concepts and Methods for Working with Complexity*, Routledge, London.

Parthasarathy, R. (1998), Reforms in Irrigation Management: Bottoms-up Versus Top-Down Models, Gujarat Institute of Development Research Working Paper 104, November.

Parthasarathy, R. (1999), Political Economy of Irrigation Water Pricing, Gujarat Institute of Development Research Working Paper 109, February.

Sengupta, N. (1991), *Managing Common Property: Irrigation In India and the Philippines*, Sage Publications, New Delhi.

Shah, Tushaar (1993), *Groundwater Markets and Irrigation Development: Political Economy and Practical Policy*, Oxford University Press, Bombay.

Small, Leslie (1987), Irrigation Service Fees in Asia, ODI - IIMI Irrigation Management Network Paper 87/1C. April.

Stone, I. (1984), *Canal Irrigation in British India: Perspectives on Technological Change in a Peasant Economy*, Cambridge University Press.

Vermillion, Douglas (1997), Impacts of Irrigation Management Transfer, IIMI, Research Report 11, April.

Veneracion, Cynthia (ed.) (1989), A Decade of Process Documentation Research: Reflections and Synthesis, Institute of Philippine Culture, Anteneo de Manila University, Quezon City, Philippines.

10

Watershed Programmes in Gujarat
A Long Way to Go !

AMITA SHAH

Introduction

The recent spurt in watershed development programmes (WDPs) is a policy response to the increasing environmental crisis and non-sustainability of agriculture, especially in the dryland/semi-arid regions. Starting from the scattered measures for soil and water conservation, undertaken mainly as relief works on adhoc basis, WDPs have traversed through a fairly long way to its present status of a well conceived integrated approach for watershed based development within a micro region. *Prima facie*, the integrated approach focuses on conservation and development of the three natural resources, i.e. land, water and vegetation in consonance with the symbiotic relationship among them. This approach, when interfaces with the socio-economic structures, brings into its fold various other dimensions of integration (Shah, 1998), namely, economic, social, financial and administrative (Table 10.1). Conceptually therefore, the integrated approach has gone much beyond the scientifically determined methods of soil-water conservation on a watershed basis. In its more recent form, i.e. the "watershed plus" approach, it incorporates a large number of activities that promotes (a) farming systems based development in agriculture and allied sectors; and (b) non-farm employment as well as local institutions so as to ensure sustainability of life systems, especially people's livelihood. In a way, this approach indicates a new paradigm, within which specific programmes or policy measures get identified and designed.

Table 10.1: Typology of Linkages in an Integrated Approach for Watershed Development

Type of Linkage	Main Features
1. Ecological Environmental	Symbiotic relationship between land, water and vegetation. All the three resources should be developed and utilised in a mutually reinforcing manner. Conservation alone is not sufficient. Development of one may lead to regeneration of the other.
2. Economic	Farming systems approach based on interdependence between crops, livestock and trees. Output of one activity becomes input for another in a closed-knit cycle.
3. Social	Congruence between various stakeholders, viz. cultivators, landless labourers, herders; across social groups and across owners of land at different altitude in watershed.
4. Financial	Complimentarily between public and private investments, pooling of resources; and cross subsidisation across socio-economic groups and watershed activities.
5. Administrative	Co-ordination between the line departments, viz. agriculture, irrigation, horticulture, soil and water conservation, animal husbandry, forestry, rural development, etc.

Given the holistic approach, WDPs become more complex to implement as compared to some of the individual component-based schemes like irrigation, animal husbandry or afforestation. Some of the features that make the implementation of WDPs more complicated are: (a) emphasis on conservation rather than mainly on promoting the use of a particular natural resource/input; (b) the scientific treatment measures cut across the boundaries of individually owned farms as well as revenue villages; (c) it involves trade-offs across resources as well as individual stakeholders; (d) the resultant impact is often slow and at times non-tangible; and (e) the process is interactive and continuous, hence, requires fine tuning between physical and social engineering.

Keeping these challenges in view, WDPs, of late, have laid increasing emphasis on flexibility, participatory processes and institutional building. NGOs, with their presumably better skills in these aspects, are being involved more than ever before. For instance, in the two major national level schemes, namely, National Watershed Development Programme for Rainfed Plains Region (NWDPRA) and Watershed Development Project (WPR) involve NGOs as partners and as project implementing agencies respectively[1]. It is hoped that with this kind of *modus operandi,* it will be able to tap the full potential of watershed-based integrated development in the region.

By now, a large number of watershed projects have been launched by the central as well as state governments, NGOs and bilateral developmental agencies. The experiences, as of now, are quite varied, ranging from about a dozen of very successful projects to a large number of non-effective projects with wide variations in technology, cost and subsidy and implementation processes (Shah, 1998a). All these have resulted into large area of land covered through contour bunds, check dams and tree plantation. What is more important is formation of beneficiary groups or community organisations in large number of villages, especially where NGOs are operating. And, more important than all these is the awareness that has been generated about the need as well as the potential benefits that may result from such programmes.

However, in spite of some positive outcomes, WDPs, in most cases, have yielded only limited or selective impact especially on people's livelihood (Kerr, *et al.,* 1998). As a result, there are situations where some of the successful WDPs have not made even minimum provision for drinking water or fodder. Similarly, development of pasture land and diffusion of various soil-moisture conservation practices have often remained neglected in actual implementation. To a large extent, this might be due to the fact that in spite of the flexibilities, participatory processes and formation of local institutions, the actual implementation of WDPs have still not gone beyond the 'project mode'. This means that in most cases, the composition of project activities, resource allocation, procedural directives, time frame, and above all, impact parameters were more or less pre-determined. Since most of these projects are centrally designed, implementing agencies and even recipient communities treat the project guidelines or the design as largely given thus, leaving a lot of potential linkages as well as benefits untapped[2]. The next phase of WDPs, therefore, may have to increasingly focus on these aspects which are essential for ensuring continuity of watershed-based developmental processes beyond the 'project mode'. *Prima facie,* this would call for (a) creating appropriate incentive structures; (b) benefit sharing mechanism; and (c) location specific adaptation in technologies which can enhance productivity, hence, livelihood support and at the same time ensure sustainable resource use (Jhunjunwala, 1998; Datye, *et al.*, 1998 and Kerr, *et al.*, 1998).

Given this backdrop, the following analysis reviews the experiences of WDPs in Gujarat which is facing not only severe degradation of natural resources but also instability in agricultural growth. WDPs, therefore, become a key strategy for a sustainable economic development in large parts of the state experiencing frequent droughts, dwindling ground water resources, increasing salinity and loss of vegetation. The state also has a distinction of having significant involvement of NGOs in WDPs. The experiences from Gujarat, therefore, may offer significant learning for implementing watershed programmes in other parts of the country, especially those having dryland/semi-arid conditions.

Objectives

The analysis will focus on the following questions:

(i) What are the major challenges for WDPs across different agro-climatic conditions in Gujarat? And, what kind of WDPs are being implemented in different parts of the state?

(ii) What are the initial achievements?

(iii) What kind of improvements are needed to tap the full potential of WDPs on a continued basis?

The analysis is divided into five sections including this introduction. The next section provides a brief overview of the status of natural resources and agricultural growth in different regions in the state. This is followed by a profile of the existing WDPs in the state. Section 4 provides an overall assessment of the achievements and the missing links. The last section discusses the policy implications for the next phase of WDPs in Gujarat.

NATURAL RESOURCES AND TRENDS IN GUJARAT'S AGRICULTURE : AN OVERVIEW

Gujarat is predominantly characterised by dry/semi-arid conditions with large proportion of area facing frequent drought conditions. Of the total land mass, only 50 per cent is put under agricultural uses of which about 30 per cent is irrigated. Since the major source of irrigation (i.e. covering 80 per cent of the irrigated area) is ground water resources, it poses serious problems of rainfall induced uncertainties and depletion of water table reaching dangerous levels in some parts of north Gujarat and coastal Saurashtra regions (Hirway and Shah, 1998). This, in a way, is reflected in more than two-fold increase in culturable wasteland during 1960-1970 and in land kept as current fallow during 1970-1990. By 1993-94 as large as 16 per cent of land was covered under these two categories. Potentially, this land could be brought back to cultivation. For, it is argued that the land, which is neither under managed forests nor under proper cultivation, i.e. the 'uncultivated half', may well be the next frontier of development (Romm, 1981).

Moreover, land capitability is generally low in large number of talukas in the state. For instance, Gujarat does not have even a single taluka covered under land capability category I (i.e. having the highest land productivity), and only 10 per cent of the 184 talukas belong to category II. Nearly one-third of the talukas in Gujarat fall in the lowest capability category of land that can be used for agriculture. The 40 per cent talukas covered under the categories V and VI are actually not considered suitable for cultivation. The task, therefore, is to enhance the land capability status of nearly 75 per cent of talukas covered under the categories III and above (Table 10.2).

Table 10.2 : Distribution of Talukas According to Land Capability* Classification (1979)

Category of Land Capability**	Distribution of Talukas	
	No.	%
I	—	0.00
II	19	10.32
III	28	15.22
IV	63	34.23
V	60	32.60
VI	14	7.61
All	184	100.00

* Land capability is determined by taking into consideration a large number of factors such as soil type, rainfall profile, topography, soil fertility, etc.

** In descending order of land productivity. Categories V and VI generally consist of non-cultivable land.

Source : Government of Gujarat (1979), Report of the Gujarat State Land Commission, Gandhinagar.

Gujarat has about 10 per cent of land under forests, half of which is degraded forests. A similar situation obtains with respect to common property land resources (CPLRs) which are not only reducing in size but also declining in quality (Iyengar, S., p.121). To a large extent, degrading CPLRs is a reflection of the declining productivity of the cultivable land rather than an outcome of increasing livestock population which, in fact, does not show any secular trend of increase since early seventies.

Low land-productivity coupled with (or due to) frequent drought situation leads to further degradation of land because of the poor vegetative cover resulting into increased soil erosion, especially in the hilly terrain of eastern tribal belt.

Non-Sustainability of Agricultural Growth

The declining status of land, water and forest resources in Gujarat have been reflected in terms of low and fluctuating growth rate in the state's agricultural sector. For instance, the annual compound rate of growth in yield was as high as 4.67 per cent in the early phase of Green Revolution. This has declined to 0.90 per cent in late 1980s which was marked by severe droughts, but has recovered to only 2.19 per cent during the early nineties (Desai and Namboodiri, 1997). However, more than declining growth rate (which might be partly due to higher base year yield in the later periods), what is more concerning is the year-to-year fluctuations in yield, as shown in Table 10.3. As a result, SDP from agriculture has fluctuated sharply even during the period of post nineties, which at national level has been marked by normal rainfall situation.

Saurashtra-Kutch Region: A Case of Instability in Growth

The uncertainty in agricultural growth is particularly more prevalent in districts of Saurashtra-Kutch region except Junagadh. The region, which constitutes 27 per cent of the state's population and 43 per cent of the cultivable land, is characterised by semi-arid/arid conditions with average rainfall being less than 700 millimetre (Table 10.4). It is observed that during the 10 years period between 1985-86 and 1996-97, rainfall had dropped below 400 mm. in 4 to 7 years in five out of the seven districts in Saurashtra-Kutch region. The incidence of low rainfall was not so frequent among other districts of the state. Consequently, yields have fluctuated more sharply in some of the major crops grown in the region as compared to the aggregate state level (Table 10.5).

Table 10.3 : Fluctuations in Yield among Major Crops in Gujarat - 1949 to 1967 and 1967 to 1991

Crops	Time Period					
	1949 - 1967			1967 - 1991		
	Growth Rate	CV	Av. Yield* (Kg./Ha.)	Growth Rate	CV	Average Yield** (Kg./Ha.)
Food Grains	3.9	15.3	NA	1.9	22.9	—
Rice	3.2	28.9	616	2.0	23.8	1362** (121.1)
Wheat	3.0	15.2	1165	2.3	11.2	2151 (84.6)
Jowar	2.5	17.8	264	1.8	27.3	967 (266.2)
Maize	4.0	32.6	784	0.1	40.5	1324 (68.9)
Pulses	1.6	14.2	NA	2.5	31.4	—
Groundnut	2.3	25.9	546	0.4	43.6	692 (26.7)
Cotton	2.7	18.5	158	0.7	22.3	238 (50.6)

* Refer to 1966-69; ** Refer to 1990-93.

** Figures in parentheses indicate percentage change over previous period.

Source : Based on Various Tables in Patel, A.S.; Patel, H.F. and Shishodia, Anil (1998), 'Agricultural Productivity Performance in Gujarat', *Artha Vikas*, Vol. XXXIV, No. 1.

The kind of rainfall induced fluctuations in crop productivity has posed a serious problem with respect to economic viability and sustainability of agriculture in this region. Consequently, a large proportion of talukas (ranging from 53 to 100 per cent) in the districts of Saurashtra region have been categorised as drought/desert prone areas. This is so because availability of irrigation is not only low but also uncertain since most of it depends on wells that go dry during unfavourable monsoons. The region, therefore, is poor in vegetative cover.

Evidences, especially since mid-eighties, suggest that the region has undergone significant changes in terms of demographic variables showing lower rates of population growth, increasing sex ratio (thereby indicating male-migration) and faster growth in non-agricultural employment (Hirway and Shah, 1998).

Table 10.4 : Variation in Rainfall across Districts in Gujarat (1985-1996)*

Districts/Category **	Average Rainfall	Range of Rainfall (Millimetre)			
		Upto 400	401-700	701-900	>900
I. Rainfed Commercial				**No. of Years**	
1. Amreli	545.5	5	3	2	–
2. Bhavnagar	595.5	2	6	2	–
3. Jamnagar	497.2	7	2	–	1
4. Junagadh	881.1	2	2	4	2
5. Rajkot	621.1	4	4	1	1
6. Surendranagar	507.0	5	5	–	–
7. Kutch	350.6	6	2	2	–
II. Rainfed Non-Commercial					
8. Ahmedabad	789.0	2	3	3	2
9. Banaskantha	758.4	2	3	3	2
10. Panchmahals	989.1	–	4	2	4
11. Bharuch	883.9	–	4	3	3
III. Irrigated					
12. Mehsana	613.1	3	5	1	1
13. Sabarkantha	796.8	1	5	2	2
14. Kheda	832.2	1	6	1	2
15. Vadodara	1006.1	–	4	4	2
16. Surat	1100.5	–	2	2	6
17. Valsad	1891.6	–	–	–	10

* Except 1985 and 1988.

** Categorisation of districts is based on the data pertaining to early nineties (Shah, Amita and Sah, D.C. 1993), 'Dryland Agriculture Under Changing Resource Environment in Gujarat', *Artha Vijnana,* Vol. 35, No. 3.

Source : Directorate of Economics and Statistics, *Socio-Economic Review*, Gujarat State 1996-97, Gandhinagar.

Table 10.5 : Mean and Variation in Yield of Major Crops in Saurashtra-Kutch (1991-1995)

Districts	Crops					
	Food grains	Pulses	Oil seeds	Bajri	Cotton	Ground-nut
Amreli						
Mean (Kg./Ha)	1534+	483	576	1635+	445	593
CV (%)	36	41	51	40	31	52
Bhavnagar						
Mean (Kg./Ha)	921	442	667+	1245+	2288+	747–
CV (%)	36	29	80	38	31	81
Jamnagar						
Mean (Kg./Ha)	839	584	454	597	2064	441
CV (%)	56	33	88	64	13	113
Junagadh						
Mean (Kg./Ha)	1893+	552	934+	1425+	095	936–
CV (%)	26	40	39	24	11	40
Kutch						
Mean (Kg./Ha)	559	245	1203+	608	250	1522+
CV (%)	43	73	13	63	.25	19
Rajkot						
Mean (Kg./Ha)	1276+	520	507	708	378	461
CV (%)	60	62	93	64	29	103
Surendranagar						
Mean (Kg./Ha)	732	296	607	688	200	823+
CV (%)	39	48	30	50	28	29
Gujarat						
Mean (Kg./Ha)	1015	605	838	716	1517	672
CV (%)	15	12	35	38	19	66
No. of Districts with Higher than the Average Yielded	3	NIL	3	3	7	4

Notes : (i) + indicates higher than the average yield at the state level.
(ii) Yield of cotton is in bales of 170 kgs. each.

Table 10.6 : Change in Livestock Between 1981 and 1992

District/Category		% Change in 1992 Over 1981		Relative Share in 1992	
		A	B	A	B
I.	Amreli	–6.3	–2.5	3.6	1.7
	Bhavnagar	–4.7	–4.2	4.9	6.1
	Jamnagar	–13.6	–9.5	3.9	4.6
	Junagadh	–1.9	–0.3	6.5	5.6
	Rajkot	–0.4	–8.0	5.4	6.2
	Surendranagar	–3.7	–2.3	3.3	3.7
	Kutch	–11.6	–15.0	3.9	7.4
II.	Ahmedabad	7.3	37.1	4.6	4.3
	Banaskantha	–2.1	1.9	7.4	8.6
	Panchmahals	15.8	25.0	11.7	10.8
	Bharuch	17.1	26.9	3.7	3.6
III.	Mehsana	1.3	1.4	7.7	6.5
	Sabarkantha	13.5	17.8	7.4	6.7
	Kheda	11.1	13.1	7.9	6.2
	Vadodara	18.0	30.8	6.3	5.8
	Surat	16.0	15.4	5.1	4.2
	Valsad	28.0	34.9	5.1	4.6

A = Milch animals; B = Total livestock.

Source: As in Table 10.2.

The impact of declining agricultural base has also been reflected in terms of shrinking livestock economy in the region. Table 10.6 indicates that between 1981 and 1992, livestock population has declined in all the districts in the region contrary to the increasing number in most other districts in the state.

The task of putting the agricultural sector on the right track, therefore, would need a strategy that can primarily address the issue of reducing instability in yield. For, evidences do suggest that in spite of low growth in yield, the maximum yield levels in Saurashtra and in most other districts are still higher than that at the end of the second phase of Green Revolution, i.e. in the late seventies (Table 10.7). Thus, stabilising the yield-levels is the crucial task.

Table 10.7 : Changes in Yield of Major Crops and Fertilizer Use

Districts Fertilizer User	Kg/ha	Crops Yield (kg./ ha.)					
		Total Food Grains		Total Oil Seeds		Cotton (bales of 170 lint/ha)	
	88-91(Rank)	81-83	93-95 (Rank)	81-83	93-95 (Rank)	81-83	93-95 (Rank)
Category I							
Amreli	58	1321	1563	881	576@	132	452
	(9)		(3)		(13)		(1)
Bhavnagar	65	1205	1095@	1224	504@	149	432
	(8)		(10)		(16)		(2)
Jamnagar	46	848	987	657	336@	130	391
	(12)		(11)		(17)		(5)
Junagadh	81	1822	2066	894	995	149	363
	(6)		(1)		(11)		(7)
Rajkot	89	1478	1383@	508	509	137	413
	(5)		(7)		(15)		(4)
Surendranagar	25	489	765	827	561@	91	199
	(16)		(14)		(14)		(17)
Kutch	18	636	532@	717	1157	64	267
	(17)		(17)		(6)		(11)
Category II							
Ahmedabad	56	881	1108	1024	1029	75	193
	(10)		(9)		(10)		(15)
Banaskantha*	37	892	658@	1327	1308@	116	193
	(15)		(16)		(3)		(15)

(Contd.)

Table 10.7 *(Contd.)*

Districts Fertilizer User	Kg/ha	Crops Yield (kg./ha.)					
		Total Food Grains		Total Oil Seeds		Cotton (bales of 170 lint/ha)	
	88-91(Rank)	81-83	93-95 (Rank)	81-83	93-95 (Rank)	81-83	93-95 (Rank)
Panchmahals*	42	1038	849@	756	1226	109	310
	(13)		(13)		(5)		(9)
Bharuch*	39	733	701@	689	832	120	203
	(14)		(15)		(12)		(14)
Category III							
Mehsana	54	1235	1423	1502	1374@	141	264
	(11)		(6)		(1)		(12)
Sabarkantha	92	1083	1158	847	1335	155	423
	(4)		(8)		(2)		(3)
Kheda	134	1388	1514	1353	1265@	95	383
	(3)		(4)		(4)		(6)
Vadodara*	70	945	851@	837	1064	151	246
	(7)		(12)		(9)		(13)
Surat	164	1218	1448	845	1147	157	246
	(1)		(5)		(7)		(13)
Valsad	154	1522	1726	528	1091	119	—
	(2)		(2)		(8)		—
Gujarat	**66**	**1056**	**1099**	**878**	**830**	**115**	**277**

* Tribal districts with low irrigation.
@ Indicate decline in average yield.

Tribal-Hilly Region: Problems of Subsistence Agriculture

Gujarat has a moderately hilly terrain in the eastern belt starting from Banaskantha in the extreme north to Dangs in the southern parts of the state. In between, it includes a continuous stretch consisting of parts of Sabarkantha, Vadodara, Panchmahals, Bharuch, Surat and Valsad. To a large extent, this region is inhabitated by tribal population characterised by close links with forest resources and subsistence agriculture. Since the data pertaining to tribal talukas are not readily available, it is somewhat difficult to depict the quantitative measures of agricultural scenario in this region. Nevertheless, to an extent, these realities are being reflected in the district level data.

Table 10.7 provides comparative picture of the yields of major crop-groups across districts in Gujarat. It is observed that most of the districts in the eastern tribal belt are performing fairly good in terms of yields, especially of oilseeds. However, given the relatively better rainfall profile (as compared to Saurashtra-Kutch region), the yield performance, particularly in food grains, is not significantly better (except for Surat-Valsad which are covered under canal irrigation and Sabarkantha which has a fairly developed ground water resources). The relatively low yield-performance is explained partly by predominance of subsistence food crops in the tribal areas where crop cultivation, till recently, was subsidiary to the forest-based economy. Now, when forests have started degrading and population pressure being increasingly building, agricultural sector will gradually start assuming a central place even in the tribal region. At present the two major constraints facing the agricultural sector in the region are: (a) sloppy terrain which is relatively more susceptible to soil-water erosion, and (b) poor infrastructure resulting into low adoption of technology, e.g. fertiliser.

The WDPs need to address these specific needs of the tribal region. To what extent the existing programmes can meet the specific needs across regions? The following section examines this question in the light of the various WDPs in the state.

WATERSHED DEVELOPMENT PROGRAMMES IN GUJARAT: A PROFILE

Soil water conservation, like medium and large irrigation schemes, is considered as basic investment for which the primary responsibility is borne by the state. This was so even during the colonial period when the government had undertaken special programmes for soil-water conservation in the ravenous area and for development of dryland farming[3]. Since these activities cover both private as well as non-private land under different kinds of uses, the basic investment is largely subsidised, though it is presumed that it will induce private investment, particularly on cultivable land. In that sense, soil-water conservation or watershed development programmes can largely be viewed as an important infrastructure for simultaneously promoting agricultural development and environmental sustainability. Accordingly, the governments, both at the centre as well as the state have taken up major initiatives by way of resource allocation, and also in terms of design and implementation of the projects. The NGOs' efforts often become part of these projects and/or they supplement the governments resources by way of mobilising additional funds, especially through charity or donations.

Government's Initiatives

The initial efforts by the government of Gujarat were to establish the Gujarat Land Development Bank with the mandate of providing loans to the individual farmer/co-operatives to take up various measures like land levelling, land shaping, field bunding, etc. Hence, the idea was to help improving the physical structure of cultivable land under private ownership. Conversely, subsidy was not considered necessary. Subsequently, the government started various programmes for soil-water conservation especially in the catchment of the major river basins and also in the drought prone regions as drought prevention and/or relief measures. Both these initiatives were undertaken mainly on non-private land and thereby involved heavy subsidies.

These were some of the precursors to the watershed-based programmes which eventually got initiated in the mid-eighties[4]. By then, soil water conservation programmes had assumed an image of the state-subsidised relief works which do not go beyond creating certain engineering structures having little linkages with measures for promoting farm productivity on a sustained basis. One of the major exceptions was the scheme of land levelling which was directly resulting into productivity gains in undulating land, a large part of which is in the eastern tribal belt of Gujarat. Over time, these activities became more expensive because of the increased capital as well as operational costs. The pervasive nature of the subsidy structure did not permit the government to continue such activities on a large scale because of the resource constraints.

One of the possible solutions, therefore, was to set-up a separate corporation having the required autonomy for mobilising resources, including partial cost-recovery from the owners of private land being covered under the programme. Thus, Gujarat State Land Development Corporation (GLDC) was established in 1978 with the mandate of carrying out all the activities related to soil-water conservation and WDPs. At present, GLDC is vested with the responsibility of implementing most of the WDPs receiving the government's funding. The major exception is the Watershed Development Project (WPR) sponsored by the MoRAE and administered through the District Rural Development Agencies in each of the major states in India.

GLDC's Project Portfolio

Beginning with the special scheme for Rehabilitation of Ravenous Land, the GLDC has substantially expanded its project activities. By mid-1998, it has covered about 11.18 lakh hectares of land under various projects. This works out to be six per cent of the total reporting area in the state. Table 10.8 provides information about the major projects/schemes being implemented by the GLDC. Following observations are important in the context of the GLDC's project portfolio :

(i) The projects are diversed in nature and are designed to cater to some of the region-specific needs like the low lying paddy cultivation areas in the tribal regions, dryland farming especially in the drought prone regions and rainfed agriculture in the plain regions, besides the schemes for problematic areas having saline and alkaline soils.

(ii) There is significant difference in the cost structure across the projects, depending mainly on the nature of activities.

(iii) Most of the schemes have some proportion of loan component which ranges from 15 to 50 per cent. The proportion of subsidy, however, is neither related to the cost structure nor related to the magnitude of benefits as well as type of beneficiaries. For instance, the schemes like soil-water conservation, 'kyaris' on paddy fields and farm ponds mainly benefiting private cultivated land have subsidy components varying from 50 to 85 per cent. Similarly, various components within NWDPRA have more or less same level of subsidies, i.e. of the tune of 90 per cent. Nevertheless, the subsidy structure, though large and adhoc, reflect two broad

Table 10.8 : GLDC's Project Portfolio (As on June 1998)

Scheme (Area and Beneficiaries)	Sponsor	% of subsidy	Type of Treatment	Cost Rs/ha	Basis	Future Management
Soil Water Conservation	GOG	50 (75% in tribal)	CB, NP, TE, LL	7,500	W	Individual Responsibility
Special Component Scheme (All Districts/SC)	GOG	50	"	"	W	Ind
Kyari for Paddy Land (Tribal and Non-Tribal)	GOG	75	"	15,000	S	"
IWDP (Sabarkantha, Baroda, Bharuch, Rajkot)	WB + GOG	85	Veg. Measures + Small WHS + Farming systems	3,500	W	SHG
ACRP (Mehsana)	GOG	50	CB, PA, AL	2,500	W	Ind.
Farm Ponds (All Districts)	GOG	85	Farm Pond on Pvt. Land	17,000	S	"
Reclamation of Alkaline Land	GOI + GOG	50	CB, NP, LL, AL	10,000	W	"
Water Harvesting Structures	GOG	75	WHS	2 lakhs	S	N.A.
Desilting of Village Ponds (All Districts)	GOG	100	Village Ponds on Community Land	2 lakhs	W	N.A.
NWDPRA	GOI	90	Ve. Measures Farming System	3,500	W	SHG

(Contd.)

Table 10.8 *(Contd.)*

Scheme (Area and Beneficiaries)	Sponsor	% of subsidy	Type of Treatment	Cost Rs/ha	Basis	Future Management
Catchment of Mahi River Valley	GOI	100	Veg. Measures Farming System	3,200	W	N.A.
Reclamation of Alkali Land	GOI + GOG	50	CB, NL, TE, LL	1,000	W	Ind.

GOG : Government of Gujarat
GOI : Government of India
WB : World Bank
SC : Scheduled Caste
CB : Contour Bunding
NP : Nala Plugging
TE : Terracing
LL : Land Levelling
SHG : Self Help Group
NA : Not Available
PA : Pasture Development
S : Scattered
W : Watershed Based
Ind : Individual

principles, i.e. higher subsidies for (a) treating non-private land like ravines, village pond, water harvesting structures; and (b) beneficiaries of weaker sections like tribals.

(iv) A large number of projects are being simultaneously implemented on watershed basis having a possibility of overlap in terms of the eligible areas/beneficiaries.

(v) Apparently, there is no mechanism to link-up the various schêmes across the two categories, i.e. those implemented on watershed and on scattered basis.

(vi) Most of the projects have a definite time frame for intervention in a particular locale. The physical activities have to be completed within this time frame. Once this is accomplished and, at the most, some kind of self help groups are formed, the project moves away to the other areas without ensuring continuity of the project's activities in future.

(vii) Being an autonomous organisation, GLDC implements these projects in an independent manner without having any direct linkages particularly for planning and resource pooling from the line departments. At the most, the GLDC gets expert personnel from the departments like forestry, animal husbandry, agronomy, extension education, etc. Beyond this, there is hardly any administrative linkages outside the corporation.

The above observations suggest that in spite of the increasing emphasis on integrated approach, the government's efforts, by and large, remain scheme specific and adhoc. A comprehensive view of the region specific resources and needs are yet to be developed in the form of a hierarchy of watersheds keeping a long term perspective of activities rather than making a one-shot intervention within the project's time frame.

NGOs as PIAs in the Government's Watershed Development Projects (WPR - MoRAE)

As mentioned earlier, the GLDC shoulders the major responsibility of implementing almost all the watershed projects funded by the government except for the one which is sponsored by the Ministry of Rural Areas and Employment (MoRAE). This is a relatively new project which has come into existence by merging several schemes already being implemented by the MoRAE[5]. This project, unlike most other WDPs of the government sector, appears fairly revolutionary because of the three important features viz.; unprecedented devolution of decision making power backed up financial allocation directly to district level and thence to the village organisation level; creation of partnership between government (GO), non-government organisation (NGO) and people; and flexibility in terms of technical as well as financial norms for watershed treatments. Accordingly, the expected outcomes are also more broad-based rather than focusing merely on technical aspects. What is, in fact, envisaged is that social empowerment and resource development have to go hand-in-hand for the later does not sustain without ensuring the former.

A recent study examining the initial experiences of the PIAs in terms of implementing the programme guidelines had observed that while the response from the PIAs is positive and in many cases the project has been adapted to enhance sustainable livelihood among the rural communities, there were, however, shortcomings originating because of the "dichotomy between implementation capacity and the high volume of financial resources made available" (Turton, Cathryn *et al.*, 1998). In terms of actual treatments, this would imply that either a part of the watershed resources remain underdeveloped (e.g. community wasteland or various moisture conservation practices for enhancing the crop yield); or funds are being utilised mainly for constructing high cost structures. Both these may have serious socio-economic as well as environmental implications. The actual constraints would, therefore, depend on the PIAs' capacities in terms of social as well as technical aspects of watershed development. A broad impression is that the NGOs are relatively strong in the former aspect whereas the GOs are relatively strong in the case of the later. Besides this, both the agencies might miss out on some crucial aspects that are generally more difficult to achieve both technically as well as socially. As a result, we may end up with situations where watershed treatment has been carefully carried out following the "scientific" principles, but there are no local organisations strong enough to carry them forward and bring tangible impact to the people's livelihood. Or there may be a situation where only a few large water harvesting structures are built bringing tangible benefits to select households, leaving rest of the resources undeveloped. Of course, it is not possible to achieve an ideal situation where all the resources within watershed are developed, benefiting most of the households. Nevertheless, measures need to be taken to avoid the extreme situations.

By now, 1237 micro watershed projects have been implemented in 16 out of the 19 districts (except Surat, Gandhinagar and Kheda) in the state (Table 10.9). These micro watershed projects are being implemented by about 111 project implementing agencies (PIAs) of which 76 are NGOs. Given the average size of about 500 hectares, these projects together might have covered approximately 2.66 lakh hectares of land — a large part of it is in the arid/semi-arid regions of Saurashtra and Kutch. Since the project is yet to complete its initial tenure of five years, not much is known about the actual implementation of the project. However, initial feedback from some of the NGOs involved as PIAs suggest that the project has created lot of scope and space for undertaking watershed-based development on a potentially continuous basis. This is so because (a) most of the projects have focused mainly on water harvesting structures which yield immediate benefits (than measures like field bunding, plantation or pasture development) and also tend to survive for long; (b) the self-help groups are vested with some amount of funds allocated from the project budget; and (c) people have better access to information about the kind of activities that are needed and undertaken by the project. All these forces are likely to work favourably for sustaining people's interest in the project. Whether and to what extent, this could be actually tapped for establishing the various linkages (that are discussed in section I) needs to be ascertained.

NGOs' Own Initiatives

Apart from being PIA's in the government's project several, NGOs have been working in this field in different parts of Gujarat. Of course, there is no systematic documentation available on the NGOs' initiatives in WDPs in Gujarat. Nevertheless, experiences of some of the successful and hence more visible programmes by prominent NGOs (like AKRSP, KRIBP, VRTI, SEWA, VIKAS)[6] do bring out certain important insights. For instance, AKRSP has a long experience of working through the self-help groups or community organisations for various types of programme initiatives. Their cumulative experiences indicate that these groups operate well and sustain for long even after AKRSP has withdrawn. But this kind of response is obtained primarily around water harvesting measure, e.g. percolation tanks or check dams. People's response for development of community wasteland or pasture land is generally weak. Moreover, it also suggests that people can be persuaded to make and maintain bunds, especially when the fields are receiving irrigation or when basic treatments like land-levelling is done on an undulating field (Shah, 1996). What is more important is that the long drawn work-relationship with a particular community in a region yields significant pay off, especially when it relates to irrigation related activities.[7]

A similar experience of linking field bunds with water harvesting structures was also observed in Bhavnagar district (Iyengar, S., undated). In an another initiative by SEWA, linkages of water harvesting structure like village ponds has been fairly well established with some of the improved agronomic practices like adoption of a suitable pulse crop which eventually got linked-up with household's food security by establishing grain banks. VIKAS has used the opportunity under the WPR (MoRAE) to take up measures for checking salinity ingress especially by creating a Green wall and incorporating a company of groups of villagers which can take up income generating programmes like pond fishing in an economically viable manner.

Such initiatives, however, are fairly limited and scattered. Barring a few NGOs (like AKRSP, KRIBP, VRTI), the reach of even fairly successful NGOs in terms of WDPs is still quite limited. Also, most of these projects were started as soil-water conservation programme, hence yet have to graduate to an integrated approach by linking up the various components within that.

Moreover, most of these NGOs have a fairly long standing in terms of trying and evolving various methods of participatory processes. Also, most of them have long term commitments to the developmental activities in the areas where they are presently working. Therefore, it is too premature to judge and generalise on the sustenance and replicability of the participatory process adopted by these NGOs. Especially, experiences in terms of (a) repair and maintenance of the treatments on both public as well as private land; and (b) extended credit facilities to take up various activities on an interactive basis by the local users' groups are yet to be documented and consolidated before unqualified emphasis is laid on the assumption that the users' group will take care of the future management. If repair and maintenance of field bunds, particularly on unirrigated plots, are any guide, the experiences even from the projects having followed fairly good participatory processes are certainly not very encouraging. Also, there is often a danger that the outcome and impact might get adversely affected because somewhere down the line the participatory processes might become an end rather than an instrument for livelihood support (Shah, Tushaar, *et al.*, 1996). While there is little doubt that participatory approaches work, what is, however, not so clear as to what makes the participatory approaches work. Understanding this is a crucial challenge.

What do these diversed experiences from both the GOs and NGOs add-up to? This has been summarised in the light of some of the available evaluation studies on WDPs in Gujarat.

IMPACT OF WDPS : SOME EARLY ASSESSMENTS

The section collates findings of the evaluation studies pertaining to some of the major WDPs in Gujarat. The projects covered in this analysis range from nationally implemented project, i.e. NWDPRA, a donor agency-funded experimental project, i.e. IWDP, NGO's initiative, i.e. KRIBP, and two scattered schemes like land levelling and farm ponds which are important but so far have remained outside the menu of the major WDPs in Gujarat. The major findings emerging from the evaluation studies are summarised as follows:

National Watershed Development Project for Rainfed Areas (NWDPRA)

NWDPRA is an important programme both in terms of its nationwide coverage as well as its integrated approach. It aims at improving the status of soil-water-vegetation in a manner that enhances productivity of dryland agriculture on a sustained basis. It lays special emphasis on vegetative measures, involvement of village community and a relatively flexible subsidy structure so as to provide incentives for the beneficiary households to carry out the various treatments by using the family labour. Some of the important findings from an impact study of NWDPRA (Shah, and Patel, 1996) have been summarised as follows:

(a) The project has led to significant increase in the yield mainly due to increased water table and availability of irrigation. The yield gain, however, varied across crops and regions. For instance, increase in yield is more consistent among irrigated as compared to unirrigated crops. This observation is largely in confirmly with the findings from several other projects in Gujarat and elsewhere in India (Shah, 1998a; Kerr, *et al.*, 1998).

(b) The gains in terms of net returns (per hectare) was found to be substantially different across the two regions under study, i.e. 17 per cent in Danta (Banaskantha) and as high as 37 per cent in Kapadwanj (Kheda). It may be noted that the former belongs to a drought prone region whereas the later is in an agriculturally developed district. Also, Kapadwanj has better soil profile (i.e. as large as 80 per cent of land belong to land classification category III as against that in Danta where more than 50 per cent of the land belong to the category III and above). This corroborates the earlier findings that yield gains in dryland/semi-arid regions are generally limited, i.e. around 17-20 per cent.

(c) Increased cropping intensity has enhanced on-farm employment generation for additional 39 and 11 persondays respectively in Danta and Kapadwanj micro watersheds.

(d) The above results have been obtained despite some of the inherent constraints in project design and implementation. For instance, the dimensions of the field bunds are quite small hence ineffective. Similarly, quality of water harvesting structures are poor and without any provision of funds for repair and maintenance. The cost-norm for each component is low and rigidly fixed, thus need upward revision. The flexibility in subsidy-structure has been used rarely in actual implementation.

(e) Lack of departmental co-ordination and absence of any programme for livestock development.

(f) Non-involvement of farmers in terms of labour at least on their own farms.

(g) Overall, it was noted that the quantum of benefits was notable but substantially below the desired level.

Integrated Water Development Project (IWDP)

Integrated Watershed Development Project for Rainfed Plain Regions (IWDP) is a manifestation of a shift in the policy approach which emphasised long term environmental sustainability rather than enhancing agricultural productivity *per se*. It deviates from the earlier approach of the model watershed projects for dryland areas which were focused mainly on mechanical measures for soil-water conservation along with a comprehensive package of agronomic practices to bring significant increase in farm productivity.

Unlike the earlier strategy, the new approach adopted by IWDP is to achieve sustainable productivity gains over a longer period of time. Therefore, the project lays special emphasis on *in-situ* conservations and vegetative measures, especially contour vegetative barriers on arable land

and pasture development on non-arable land. Such measures are preferred because they are (a) environmentally more sustainable; and (b) financially viable owing to the low cost of vegetative treatments which, by and large, exclude (a) earth/stone bunding; (b) land levelling; (c) high valued tree species requiring higher doses of nutrients and irrigation; and (c) water harvesting structures.

The major findings of the project impact study (AFC, 1998) are:

(a) There has been a positive but limited impact on yield. For instance, higher yield in the project area was observed in 6 out of 15 crop situations of which 3 were irrigated crops.
(b) There is no significant difference in adoption of HYVs, though there was a substantial increase in water table which has resulted into increase in cropped area. This indicates poor linkages in terms of agricultural extension.
(c) Somewhat similar changes were also taking place in control villages, may be due to favourable monsoon. As a result, the incremental income from agriculture was found to be higher in the control as compared to project villages in the case of two out of the three watersheds.
(d) The measures like vegetative hedges had very poor survival rate. Similarly, farm forestry or plantation on highly degraded soil, without initial waterings and nutrients as well as pest control treatment in required doses were found to have resulted in low rate of survival except for a couple of species for which farmers have very low preference.
(e) People's participation was generally poor because of the top-down approach in project design, planning and implementation.

Overall, the results indicate reconsideration of the low-cost technologies that so far have demonstrated limited economic grains in dryland/semi-arid regions of the state (Shah, 1997).

Kribhco Rainfed Indo-British Project (KRIBP, 1998)

KRIBP was launched in 1991-92 with the primary aim of improving the long term livelihoods of poor farmers in a drought prone region in three districts each in Gujarat, Rajasthan and Madhya Pradesh. The immediate objectives of the project are to promote a replicable, participatory and poverty focused approach to farming systems development. Soil-water conservation programme is considered to be an important initiative of the project. By 1997, the project had completed five years of implementation. According to an internal assessment, the project has made following achievements :

(a) Increase in cropped area by 11 per cent.
(b) Soil-erosion on treated land has reduced to acceptable limits.
(c) Water table has increased by about 1 metre thereby making supplementary irrigation available to many farmers.
(d) Impact on increased yield, except on small patched of paddy, is not reported on a large scale. Even if the potential yield impact (expected to be in the range of 20-30 per cent) is realised, it may still not ensure food security to a large number of households.
(e) Overall, the observations suggest that the SWC-programme is only a beginning towards a more comprehensive strategy to enhance crop-productivity and an overall development of farming system including pasture development and animal husbandary which are by and large missing in the programme.

Farm Ponds on Private Land (Shah, 1999)

There has been, in recent past, a revival of interest in the small water harvesting structures like check dams, village tanks, nala-bunds, etc. If properly introduced, these measures can ensure economic viability which, in turn, may induce private investments. What is, however, missing in these programmes is: (a) mechanism of sharing of benefits with those who do not derive any direct economic gains from such structures; and (b) emphasis on water use efficiency so that it improves the ground water table to a sustainable level. One of the possible ways to overcome this distributional problem is to make smaller structures, like farm ponds, on a large number of privately owned farms. This will spread the benefits among a larger segment of the land owning households, especially those who otherwise, cannot afford investing in private wells and/or remain outside the reach of a small irrigation schemes, like check dams or village ponds, developed on community resources. Moreover, these structures having limited storage capacity and being under the private ownership regime, might promote better efficiency in water use. Also, this may work as an incentive for maintaining these structures, and possibly, for better cost recovery.

Despite these obvious advantages, farm ponds, till recently, have been seen as low priority option by both the farmers as well as policy makers. A priorily, this may be due to the factors like (a) low returns *vis- a-vis* that from canal or lift irrigation schemes; (b) uncertainty about the recharging benefits accruing to the same individual on whose field the structure is made; (c) loss of cultivated land for making the structure; (d) labour intensive operations for maintenance; and (e) lack of information about the potential benefits and the possible adaptations to realise these benefits.

Given these constraints for inducing private investment, the Government of Gujarat has initiated a Farm Ponds Scheme mainly as a device for water conservation (rather than for irrigation) in the dry/semi-arid regions in the state. Obviously, therefore, the scheme involves high intensity of subsidy, i.e. of the tune of 85 per cent of the total cost. A likely corollary of such a high degree of subsidisation might be low incentives for water-use efficiency as well as maintenance. Besides these, it may result into low coverage because of the limited budgetary allocation.

A recent survey of about 800 farm ponds spread over different regions in Gujarat brings fairly encouraging result as far as adaptations in water uses are concerned. Not only that farmers have used the harvested rain water for providing additional waterings to high valued crops like spices, cotton and wheat, but also that they have made additional investment in terms of pitching, pipelines and pumps for lifting water from the farm ponds. What is more noteworthy is that farmers have come out with various means and ways to maximise the return from the harvested water. For example, farmers having sandy soil have pumped out the water to recharge their wells; those in Banaskantha having sandy soil have dug shallow wells inside the ponds; in the coastal area of Jamnagar these ponds have been turned into check dams to stop the salinity ingress from sea water. In yet another situation farmers have used the pond for taking rabi crops with the use of residual moisture and nutrient-rich silt. The project is found particularly relevant in the dry regions where water tables have already gone much below the minimum level and parts of the land are gradually getting abandoned because of the lack of water from any source. Also, the harvested rain water has provided an important source of drinking water for animals and created a scope for growing trees/fodder in the residual moisture. In the context of severely degraded soil-moisture conditions, farm ponds are emerging as an important device for ensuring sustainability of dryland agriculture.

Land Levelling on Moderately Sloppy Land

This is one of the older schemes that has now been relegated to low priority because of the increasing cost of the treatment. This is in spite of the fact that farmers under different soil-crops situations do prefer this treatment especially for improving productivity of the marginal lands. Ironically, land levelling is invariably on high priority among the beneficiary farmers, next only to water harvesting structures and irrigation. Unfortunately, neither NWDPRA nor WPR (MoRAE) have made special provision for this treatment, which in the case of many farmers having smaller holdings, become a basic need or a first step towards enhancing the productivity of their marginal land. This may particularly apply to those relatively less previledged farmers who have received degraded land through redistribution. While the GLDC has certain provision for land levelling in its general schemes of soil-water conservation, it is one of the less subsidised schemes with 50 per cent subsidy. Given the high and increasing cost (i.e. about Rs. 7,500 to Rs. 10,000 per hectare), it might be out of reach for many of the poor households owning marginal land.

In this context, AKRSP has made commendable efforts for carrying out this activity in parts of Surendranagar and Junagadh districts in Gujarat. Similar efforts are also being tried out by Development Support Centre (DSC) under the WPR (MoRAE) in Amreli. The experiences, perhaps, indicate that what farmers need is a good credit facility rather than merely subsidy.

Overall, the evidences from the different WDPs/schemes suggest positive impact on land productivity as well as on household income. Nevertheless, these impacts, by and large, have been realised on selective crops as well as households that get benefited through additional irrigation[8]. While most of the WDPs, especially those implemented through participatory processes by NGOs, have laid special emphasis on water harvesting structure as a key component, they have often missed out on using this economic leverage (created through sure and substantial yield-gains) for extending the linkages to other resources like degraded forest and pasture land, animal husbandary and some of the individual household based schemes like farm ponds and land levelling. In this context, it can be argued that recognising the centrality of water harvesting structures and at least limited irrigation[9] to almost all the land (both cultivated and uncultivated) is a necessary but not sufficient condition for enhancing livelihood support to a large number of households within the watershed area. It may, however, be used as a good starting point as done by several PIAs of WPR (MoRAE) in Saurashtra-Kutch region. Thus, the beginning is fairly good. But there is still a long way before the full potential of the WDPs is achieved covering a larger set of natural resources, activities and above all households. The next stage, therefore, can be built on a more realistic assessment of the achievements made till now.

FUTURE DIRECTION

Some of the important clues emerging from the varied experiences in Gujarat can be listed as follows :

(i) Reduce multiplicity of schemes and evolve mechanism for establishing linkages through cost-recovery, cross subsidisation and pooling of resources from various schemes, especially from minor irrigation.

(ii) Treat the project's funding as a seed money; supplement this through additional resources mobilised in terms of labour-pool and cost-recovery by adopting a more rational rather than adhoc subsidy structure.

(iii) Assess the flow of economic returns from different activities on private resources and work out a strategy for tapping a part of the surplus to be ploughed back in the activities that have low tangible benefits, or use them for cross subsidisation in favour of the economically weaker sections of the community, e.g. those having small and degraded land holdings and the landless.

(iv) Identify a proper sequence of activities rather than taking up all of them simultaneously, however, keep this sequencing flexible.

(v) Try to provide limited irrigation to most of the plots and crops. For, the basic constraint in a dryland farming is water rather than land. Introduce irrigation component as an essential feature; but emphasise efficient use, rational allocation across crops, plants, fodder and drinking water for a larger section of the community. Similarly, provision of drinking water should be seen as an essential component.

(vi) Demonstrate some of the crucial agronomic practices that are environmentally conducive as well as economically viable, e.g. farm ponds and land levelling. Make the initial investments on such activities and mobilise labour contribution for continuing it till a point, when farmers themselves can put in their own labour or pay for hired labour on activities such as composting, manuring, mulching, etc. Extension services need to play a significant role in this context.

(vii) Link-up credit support through various institutional channels like National Bank for Rural Development and Land Development Bank; and also through small saving-credit groups. If funds are limited, revive credit facility rather than drop those initiatives for which farmers have higher preference.

Finally, watershed programme has to work as the basic strategy for developing the farming system, especially in the dryland region. This would imply livelihood security to a large proportion of people rather than merely conservation of soil-water and creating selective impact on regions and households. The participatory approach, especially adopted by some of the NGOs in the state, do indicate possibilities of long term continuity, but they still have to demonstrate impact on a sustained basis and on a larger scale. In any case, one should be careful of the fact that approaches and guidelines should not become substitutes for the ultimate goal of ensuring livelihood support to most, if not to all, of the households within a watershed region.

NOTES

1. In the case of NWPDRA (funded by the Ministry of Agriculture, Government of India), the NGO's role is mainly limited to mobilising people's participation through awareness generation, group formation and co-ordination with the implementing agency. The later i.e. WPR offers a greater scope for the NGOs to design, plan and execute the project, though within the bounds of the project guidelines prepared by the Ministry of Rural Areas and Employment (MoRAE), Government of India.
2. A recent review of implementation of the guidelines of WPR has observed that "wide variability in biophysical and socio-economic conditions means that the guidelines have to be locally adapted by implementing agencies. Few currently have the human capacity to do so, and some operational procedures do not facilitate adaptation .... there is little evidence of cross-learning among the wealth of approaches being developed to implement the guidelines" (Turton, Cathryn *et al.* 1998, p.iv).
3. For further details see Shah, 1998a.
4. Evidently, the importance of soil-water conservation programme was recognised in the early sixties when Gujarat was made a separate state. The

document for the Third Five Year Plan clearly stated the need for field bunding on about 4 million hectares of land i.e. 21 per cent of the total area and 40 per cent of net sown area in Gujarat [Iyengar, S. (undated)]. The systematic planning for WDPs was started with a smaller scale in the late seventies when soil conservation programme was initiated on very small watersheds of 40 hectares. Barring these small schemes the real start for WDPs, however, is marked by NWDPRA in the Seventh Five Year Plan.

5. These schemes are Drought Prone Area Programme (DPAP), Desert Area Development Programme (DADP), Employment Assurance Scheme (EAS) and Jawahar Rojgar Yojna (RJY).

6. These NGOs are: Aga Khan Rural Support Programme (AKRSP), Kribhco Indo-British Rainfed Farming Project (KRIBP), Vivekananda Research and Training Institute (VRTI), Self Employed Women's Association (SEWA) and VIKAS.

7. This has been reflected through a recent development in Garida village of Chotila taluka in Surendranagar district were the village community decided to build their own waterworks by setting up an irrigation co-operative society. To a large extent this is a culmination AKRSP's long drawn approach to help people take initiatives and link-up with the existing (but dis-functional) schemes of the government. This initiative resulted into irrigation of 160 hectares of land and an increased production of 600 quintals of cotton (Mistry, Mihir, 1999).

8. In a larger study in Maharashtra and Andhra Pradesh, Kerr, *et al.* (1998) observe that the projects, that focused on rainfed agriculture, did not appear to perform very well in terms of raising yields (p. 70). Further, they observe that in Maharashtra, primary benefit cited is irrigation .... and an overall percentage of respondents in Maharashtra reporting benefits from a watershed project is only 35 .... the perception of project benefits rises steadily with land holding size (p. 73).

9. It has been widely observed that additional water, that becomes available due to soil water conservation measures, is appropriated by a few. Hence, equity in allocation of water emerges as an important issue that needs innovations in technology as well as social institutions (Datye, *et al.* 1998). In that sense creating water harvesting structures is only a beginning of a long march towards watershed based development.

REFERENCES

Agricultural Finance Corporation Ltd. (1998), "Final Impact Evaluation: Integrated Watershed Development (Plains) Project in Gujarat" (Aided by World Bank), Ahmedabad.

Cathryn, Turton; Coulter, John; Farrington, John and Shah, Anil (1998), *Agriculture in the Indian Semi-Arid Tropics*, (draft), ICAR-World Bank Research Project, World Bank, New Delhi.

Datye, K.R., Gore, V.N., Joy, K.J. and Paranjape, Suhas (1998), Note on a Holistic Approach to Soil and Water Conservation, presented at a Workshop on Small Water Harvesting Structures, Institute of Rural Management, Anand, October 7-8.

Desai, Bhupat, M. and Namboodiri, N.V. (1997), "Development of Agriculture in Gujarat: A Strategic Perspective for Ninth Plan", *Economic and Political Weekly*, Vol. 31, No. 13, March 29.

Hirway, Indira and Shah, Amita (1997), *Liberalisation, Gobalisation and Industrialisation: Conflict and Resolution in a Regional Economy* (mimeo), OXFAM (India), Ahmedabad.

Iyengar, Sudarshan (undated), "Efficiency and Cost-Effectiveness in Implementing Water Conservation Projects through User Groups: Some Evidence from Gujarat, India", Gujarat Institute of Development Research, Ahmedabad.

Jhunjunwala, Bharat (1998), Moderator's Report on the theme Subsidies, Savings and Investment in Ministry of Rural Areas and Employment (ed.), *Proceedings of the National Workshop on Watershed Approach for Managing Degraded Lands in India - Challenges for 21st Century*, New Delhi, April 27-29.

Kerr, John; Pangare, Ganesh; Pangare, Vasudha L. and George, P.J. (1998), "The Role of Watershed Projects in Developing Rainfed Agriculture in the Indain Semi-Arid Tropics", (draft), *ICAR-World Bank Research Project*, World Bank, New Delhi.

KRIBP, Various Reports on the Monitoring and Evaluation of Kribhco-Indo-British Rainfed Farming Project, Dahod.

Mistry, Mihir (1999), "A Village Shown the Way to Self-Reliance", *Times of India*, April 2.

Patel A.S.; Patel, H.F. and Shishodia, Anil (1998), "Agricultural Productivity Performance in Gujarat", *Artha Vikas*, Vol. XXXIV, No. 1, January - June.

Romm, Jeff (1981), "The Uncultivated Half of India", *The Indian Forester*, Vol. 17, Nos. 1 and 2.

Shah, V.D. and Patel, V.G. (1996), "Impact of National Watershed Development Project for Rainfed Areas (NWDPRA) in Gujarat", *Agro-Economic Research Centre*, Vallabh Vidyanagar.

Shah, Amita (1998), "Watershed Development: Integration is Far Behind", in Varma, C.V.J. Rao; A.R.G. Murthy, T.S. (eds.), *International Conference on Watershed Management and Conservation*, New Delhi, December 8-10.

Shah, Amita (1996), "Watershed Project in a Rainfed Region: A Case Study of AKRSP's Interventions in Jalandhar", (unpublished report), Gujarat Institute of Development Research, Gota (Ahmedabad).

Shah, Amita (1998a), "Watershed Development Programmes in India: Emerging Issues for Environment Development Perspectives", *Economic and Political Weekly*, Vol. 32, No. 26, July 27.

Shah, Amita (1999), Evaluation of Farm Ponds - Scheme in Gujarat: An Interim Report (unpublished), Gujarat Institute of Development Research, Gota (Ahmedabad).

Shah, Tushaar; Chandra, Saurabh; Ladbury, Sara; Parthasarathy, R. and Shah, Amita (1996), KRIBHCO, Indo-British Rainfed Farming Project: Report of the Mid-Term Evaluation, Dahod.

11

Employment Trends in the Manufacturing Sector of Gujarat

N. LALITHA and ARTI OZA

Introduction

The share of agriculture in total employment, though declining, accounts for a sizeable share compared to secondary and tertiary sector at the all India level. Bhaduri (1996) observes that the decline in the share of employment of the primary sector has been compensated roughly by the increased share of employment in the tertiary sector. As compared to the tertiary sector, growth rate of employment in the manufacturing sector of India has been sluggish in spite of acceleration in its income growth during the 80s. Bhattacharya and Mitra's (1993) analysis points out that except for Gujarat and West Bengal all other states have recorded a sluggish growth in employment in the manufacturing sector, while most of the states have recorded a fairly high growth rate of income and employment in the services during the '80s.

In Gujarat, the share of the primary sector in the State Domestic Product (SDP) has declined from 30.10 per cent in 1980-81 to 24.71 per cent in 1997-98. As against this, the share of secondary sector increased from 28.21 per cent in 1980-81 to 41.29 per cent in 1997-98 and that of the tertiary sector increased only marginally from 32.69 per cent in 1980-81 to 34.01 per cent in 1997-98. Though the secondary sector has accounted for a sizeable share in the SDP of the state, the scope for employment generation in the industrial sector is seemingly dependent on the small-scale industrial sector. This is because of (1). The highly capital intensive nature of the investments that the state has been receiving since the early '90s. (2) The decline in the textile industry of Gujarat and the emergence of the chemical based industry that is bound to have a strong impact on the state economy due to the linkage effects of these two industries. Particularly, the impact on employment would be severe since the employment generation capacity of the chemical industries is much limited, though they account for a sizeable share in the output. (3) Employment in both public and private organised sector in Gujarat during 1980-98 has been increasing at a rate of 1.73 per cent per annum only (Sudarshan, 1998). However, his disaggregated analysis reports, that while employment in the public sector is slowly declining, the converse is true of the private sector. The decline in public sector employment could be due to the facts that (a) the ban on recruitment of new employment in the government sector as part of the restructuring programme and (b) the state government with the assistance of Asian Development Bank is in the process of closing down some of the state government owned enterprises. This has resulted in retrenching the labourforce in such enterprises. It is possible that such retrenched labour would have been absorbed in the private sector and the rest, especially the semi-skilled and unskilled workers, would have joined the band wagon of casual employees or remain unemployed. These facts are evident in the employment status of workforce in Gujarat (Table 11.1) where we observe an absolute decline in the category of self-employed and an increase in casual wage employment during 1983-1993-94. As compared to this only marginal increase in salaried regular employment is observed. (4) Further, in the context of the reform measures it was debated that given the dualistic nature of the labour market in India, most of the new employment in the restructured economy due to retrenchment and barriers to entry in the organised sector may, therefore, occur in the unorganised sectors[1]. Parthasarathy (1996) observes that the foreign demand led employment growth in manufacturing will lead to decline in employment intensity and faster growth of modern industrial sector using new technology. Ghose (1994) attributes the decline in the employment elasticity in the '80s to the massive capital deepening and modernisation efforts in the organised sector. As the organised sector becomes modern and technology oriented, entry into the organised sector becomes increasingly restricted, therefore workers crowd into the informal sector, or join the army of casual labourers or self-employed where low productivity and decrease in real wages is observed (Ghose, 1992).

Table 11.1 : Employment Status of Workforce in Gujarat

(Percentage)

Status/Year	Rural		Urban	
	Male	Female	Male	Female
Self-Employed				
1983 (38th round)	59.0	60.8	40.3	47.7
1987-88 (43rd round)	47.9	47.8	38.6	40.2
1993-94 (50th round)	46.9	55.4	37.3	42.6
Salaried Regular Employment				
1983 (38th round)	8.3	1.8	44.1	22.3
1987-88 (43rd round)	12.3	3.4	44.8	28.6
1993-94 (50th round)	9.9	1.5	44.9	24.1
Casual Wage Employment				
1983 (38th round)	32.7	37.4	15.6	30.0
1987-38 (43rd round)	39.8	48.8	16.6	31.2
1993-94 (50th round)	43.2	43.1	17.8	33.3

Source : Calculated from the 38th, 43rd and 50th rounds of NSS on employment and unemployment.

Since the nature of the unorganised manufacturing sector is such that it grows either due to the linkage effects provided by the organised sector or by producing cheap substitutes to the products of the organised sector, any change that would have an impact on employment in the organised sector may get reflected in the unorganised sector also. Hence, in the context of the issues mentioned in the above paragraphs, this paper attempts to look at the employment scenario in the state in general with focus on the organised and unorganised manufacturing sectors since the '80s. The paper is divided into three sections. Section 2, which follows this introduction, presents the overall employment trends in Gujarat and section 3 discusses the employment trends in the organised and the unorganised manufacturing sector. Section 4 presents the conclusions.

Data and Methodology

Data on employment has been collected from population census of Gujarat for 1980 and 1990, Employment and Unemployment Surveys of the National Sample Survey Organisation (NSSO) for the years 1983, 1987-88 and 1993-94, follow up surveys on the unorganised manufacturing sector conducted by the NSS and CSO for the years 1984-85, 1989-90 and 1994-95, and the Annual Survey of Industries pertaining to the years 1984-85, 1989-90 and 1994-95 have been used in this paper. For reasons of comparability between the organised and unorganised sectors we have chosen these three years.

Exponential growth rates have been used to calculate the growth rates of employment. Implicit deflators of gross domestic product for the unregistered and registered manufacturing sectors at the two digit level of the base year 1980-81 have been used to deflate the gross value added given at the current prices.

Trends in Employment

Table 11.2 presents the growth rate of employment per annum in the different sectors in rural and urban areas[2]. This table highlights that except for the household manufacturing (HH) in both rural and urban areas where employment has declined by 2.64 and 4.08 per cent per annum respectively, all the other sectors have recorded a positive growth in employment in both rural and urban areas. The decline in urban HH employment is much sharper than the decline in rural HH employment, but the decline in rural HH has been more or less compensated by the sharp rise in the growth of employment (5.51 per cent per annum) in the rural non-household

Table 11.2 : Growth of Employment per Annum by Industries in Gujarat

Sector	Rural	Urban
Agriculture	**1.93**	**2.91**
Mining and Quarrying	3.53	6.16
Household Manufacturing	–2.64	–4.08
Non-Household Manufacturing	5.51	2.72
Construction	3.06	6.56
Trade and Commerce	3.07	4.30
Transport	3.41	1.95
Other Services	3.28	3.58
Total Workers	2.20	3.21

Source: Calculated from the population census of Gujarat for 1981 and 1991.

industry (NHH). It means that the rise in employment could have been in the rural unorganised establishments or in the organised factory sector. In the urban areas, mining and quarrying, construction, trade and commerce are some of the sectors, which have registered a substantial growth in the employment.

A comparison with the NSS data on the working persons (principal +subsidiary) from 1983—1993-94 presents a very interesting scenario (Table 11.3). We observe that in the rural areas the percentage of male workers engaged in primary sector has declined from 78.9 in 1983 to 71.1 in 1993-94. The 43rd round (1987-88) also notes a sharp decline by 10.3 percentage points for rural male workers in the primary sector compared to 1983. This decrease has nevertheless been compensated by an increase in the percentage of rural males engaged in the construction industry, which has registered a sharp decline by 6.5 percentage points in 1993-94. These fluctuations are due to the fact that 1987-88 was a drought year due to which employment in the primary sector has reduced. The increase in employment in the construction industry was due to the large-scale government expenditure on rural infrastructure programme or drought relief programmes. The manufacturing sector, however, shows a steady increase from 7.1 per cent in 1983 (38th round) to 12.3 per cent in 1993-94 (50th round). As compared to this, the percentage of rural male workers engaged in the tertiary sector increased only marginally. As a result of the fluctuations we observed in the secondary sector, the total percentage of males engaged in rural non-agricultural activities that increased from 20.6 in 1983 to 31.4 in 1987-88 reduced to 28.9 in 1993-94. But for the period as a whole, the percentage of male workers in rural non-agricultural activity did increase if we consider the year 1987-88 as an extreme year.

A similar picture is observed with reference to the female employment in the primary sector of the rural areas, where we observe a steeper decline in 1987-88 (43rd round) compared to the decline in the rural male employment. For the period as a whole, decline in female employment has been slower than the decline in male employment. Again, the shock of fluctuations in the primary sector in 1987-88 has mostly been absorbed by the construction sector. This perfectly fits in the Sen's model (Unni, 1997) which establishes the impact of the growth of non-agricultural employment and public expenditure on reduction in poverty. Though we cannot ascertain the issue whether the fall in employment in the primary sector and the consequent rise in the construction·sector due to increase in government expenditure had resulted in reduction in poverty, the data on state governments expenditure on roads and bridges

Table 11.3 : Percentage Distribution of Working Persons by Sector of Usual Activity and Sex for Rural and Urban Areas of Gujarat State During 1983—93-94

Sector	Rural Male			Rural Female		
	38th	43rd	50th	38th	43rd	50th
Primary	78.9	68.6	71.1	92.0	75.9	90.6
Mining	0.2	0.5	0.7	0.04	0.2	0.1
Manufacturing	7.1	9.2	12.3	3.2	3.6	4.1
Electricity	0.2	0.1	0.2	—	—	0.1
Construction	2.4	9.5	3.0	0.8	16.9	1.4
Secondary	9.9	19.3	16.2	4.0	20.7	5.7
Trade	3.5	3.6	4.2	1.2	0.8	1.0
Transport	1.5	2.4	2.5	0.1	0.1	—
Others	6.2	6.1	6.0	2.8	2.6	2.6
Tertiary	11.2	12.1	12.7	4.1	3.5	3.6
Total	100.0	100.0	100.0	100.0	100.0	100.0
Non-Agricultural	20.6	31.4	28.9	7.2	24.2	9.3
Total WPR	55.0	55.9	57.4	41.1	38.1	39.6

Table 11.3 *(Contd.)*

Sector	Urban Male			Urban Female		
	38th	43rd	50th	38th	43rd	50th
Primary	13.4	6.3	4.9	37.2	22.6	20.9
Mining	0.1	0.5	0.6	—	—	0.7
Manufacturing	35.6	33.3	33.7	18.8	23.8	20.2
Electricity	0.5	0.8	0.9	0.1	0.3	—
Construction	1.7	4.2	6.9	2.8	6.2	4.8
Secondary	37.9	38.8	42.1	21.7	30.3	25.7
Trade	16.7	22.8	19.9	8.1	12.0	10.0
Transport	8.2	9.7	9.5	4.2	1.2	1.1
Others	24.1	22.4	23.5	28.9	34.0	42.3
Tertiary	48.7	54.9	52.9	41.2	47.2	53.4
Total	100.0	100.0	99.9	100.0	100.0	100.0
Non-Agricultural	86.5	93.7	95.0	62.9	77.5	79.1
Total WPR	51.7	51.0	53.5	13.2	11.2	14.2

Source : Same as Table 11.1.

during 1987-88 confirms the rise in government expenditure on construction works. It conclusively emerges that there was a rise in the rural non-agricultural employment for both the males and females during 1987-88. While the government's investment in such rural development programmes has decreased during 1993-94, this being a normal rainfall year, there has been an overall decrease in the employment in the primary sector of males and females during 1983—1993-94.

In the urban areas, the percentage of the males employed in primary sector reduced from 13.4 in 1983 (the 38th round) to 6.3 in 1987-88 (43rd round) and further to 4.9 in 1993-94 (the 50th round). Compared to 1983, urban males employed in manufacturing also decreased in 1987-88, and this is maintained in 1993-94. Unlike the rural areas, in the urban areas the percentage of males employed in the construction increased by 2.5 percentage points only. But it was the trade and commerce sector of Gujarat or the tertiary sector, which sponged the reduction in the urban male employment in the primary sector.

The percentage of urban female employment engaged in the primary sector suffered a similar decline (15.5 percentage points) in 1987-88 compared to the percentage seen in 1983 (the 38th round). Urban female employment engaged in transport and communication also reduced by 3 percentage points in 1987-88. However, these urban female workers have found alternative employment in manufacturing, construction, trade, financial and other services as evident from Table 11.3. This explains the higher percentage of (77.5) urban female employment in the non-agricultural sector in 1987-88. However, in 1993-94, besides the primary sector, sectors like manufacturing, construction and trade witnessed a moderate decline in the percentage of female employment. Nevertheless, since the decrease in the primary and secondary sector has, to a certain extent, been compensated by an increase in finance and other services, female employment in total non-agricultural employment in the urban area remained at 79.1 per cent in 1993-94.

From the above analysis, it emerges that there has been a substantial decline in the percentage of male workers in the primary sector in rural and urban areas. For females, employment in rural primary sector has decreased marginally in the case of urban the decline has been substantial. While female employment in manufacturing in both rural and urban has increased only marginally, the percentage of males employed in the manufacturing sector in rural and urban areas move conversely.

Employment and Labour Use in the Manufacturing Sector

The discussion in the earlier section on employment pointed out a decline in employment in the household industry in both rural and urban areas and a positive growth in employment in the non-household industry. One explanation for such a trend could be possibly "due to a negative relation between industrial and informal employment. With an expansion of the formal sector, Hemmer and Mannel (1989) argue that the demand for labour within this sector at a given minimum wage may increase (or decrease) depending upon the technological conditions which in turn, at a given volume of labour supply including the migrants, reduces (or raises) the volume of labour in the informal sector" (as quoted in Mitra, 1994). Further, growth of the formal sector may determine the growth or contraction of informal sector, while it is also possible that informal sector can expand even when the formal sector stagnates (Datta Chaudhry, 1989). Hence, in this section a sectoral analysis has been undertaken to identify those sectors that account for a major share in number of units, employment and gross value added in both organised and unorganised sectors. Besides we have also identified those sectors where employment has grown over the years and the employment elasticities to identify the extent of labour use in different periods.

The following panel presents the growth rate of employment, labour productivity and employment elasticity in the organised and the unorganised manufacturing sector as a whole in Gujarat.

Panel 11.1 reports that the growth rate of employment, gross value added and labour productivity of the organised sector has increased during the second period (1989-95) or during the liberalisation period, while the corresponding figures for the unorganised sector have declined. This implies the liberalisation measures were more conducive for the organised sector rather than for the unorganised sector. Particularly, it may be noted that the growth rates of employment during the liberalisation period, at least in the manufacturing sector, is opposite to the trend that has been predicted by researchers. Though we cannot ascertain the fact whether there has been a shift in the workforce from the organised to unorganised or the other way round, as evident from the panel since the labour productivity is generally much lower in the unorganised than in the organised sector, the shift of labour away from the latter to the former would slow down the growth of output in the economy. This situation, according to Bhattacharya and Mitra (1994), will change only if the productivity of labour in organised and unorganised sectors improves.

Panel 11.1

	Organised Manufacturing Sector			Unorganised Manufacturing Sector		
Indicators\ year	1984-1990	1989-1995	1984-1995	1984-1990	1989-1995	1984-1995
Employment*	0.51	1.61	1.06	19.08	1.47	10.28
Gross value added*	7.12	13.54	10.33	18.71	2.53	10.62
Labour productivity*	6.61	11.93	9.27	-0.38	1.06	0.34
Employment Elasticity	0.06	0.09	0.06	1.03	0.57	0.95

Note : * denotes the exponential growth rates.
Source : Annual Survey of Industries and the follow up surveys on the unorganised manufacturing sector for the years 1984-85, 1989-90 and 1994-95.

For the entire organised manufacturing sector, employment elasticity with reference to the gross value added was as low at 0.06 in 1984-90 and improved marginally to 0.09 in 1989-95. However for the entire period the employment elasticity has been at 0.06. This implies that in the organised manufacturing sector of Gujarat, one unit increase in value added leads to only 0.06 unit increase in employment which in other words refers to the capital intensive nature of production. As compared to this, during 1984-90, for the entire industry in the unorganised sector, the employment elasticity is at 1.03 indicating that during this period, one unit of increase in value added resulted in an increase of more than one unit of employment. It also implies the labour intensive process of production in the unorganised sector. However, during 1989-95, employment elasticity has reduced to 0.57 implying that to produce the same amount of output in 1989-95, only 0.57 labourers were required. While this could imply the improvement in labour productivity, mention should also be made of the fact that growth in gross value added also reduced from 18.71 per cent in 1984-90 to 2.53 per cent per annum in 1989-95. But for the entire period and for all the industries in the unorganised manufacturing sector employment elasticity is at 0.95.

Sectoral Trends in Employment, Productivity and Elasticity of Employment in the Organised Manufacturing Sector in Gujarat

Table 11.4 presents the percentage share of various industrial groups in

Table 11.4 : Share of Enterprises, Employment and Gross Value Added by Industrial Groups in Organised Sector

Industry/Category	No. of Units			Total Employment			Gross Value Added		
	1984-85	1989-90	1994-95	1984-85	1989-90	1994-95	1984-85	1989-90	1994-95
Food Products	9.68	9.69	8.78	9.90	10.36	9.62	4.67	9.71	4.07
Beverages	2.60	2.39	1.83	1.89	1.64	0.93	0.73	0.65	0.26
Cotton	11.61	8.62	6.43	29.27	22.24	14.48	16.95	10.96	6.13
Wool & Silk	4.60	6.13	8.39	7.56	9.33	10.60	8.79	7.06	4.38
Jute	0.00	0.00	0.00	0.00	0.00	0.00	0.00	0.00	0.00
Textiles	1.63	1.70	2.16	1.90	2.38	2.37	1.26	1.01	0.79
Wood	2.50	1.77	1.70	0.42	0.46	0.34	0.16	0.16	0.04
Paper	3.85	4.06	4.18	2.87	2.63	3.18	2.73	1.78	1.99
Leather	0.40	0.18	0.18	0.09	0.11	0.14	0.07	0.02	0.05
Chemicals	9.21	10.65	11.93	12.17	14.48	18.84	39.94	35.55	41.33
Rubber	4.92	5.69	5.85	2.18	2.95	3.86	4.09	11.28	20.35
Non-Metal	13.08	12.35	12.07	8.63	8.09	8.47	3.24	3.91	4.51
Metal Products	6.26	7.19	6.93	4.48	4.20	4.17	2.34	1.95	2.77
Basic Metal	6.59	5.76	6.29	2.54	3.33	3.17	1.65	2.04	1.67
Non-Electrical Machinery	11.33	12.02	12.23	7.21	7.84	8.39	7.31	6.95	4.41
Electrical Machinery	4.19	4.32	3.77	3.64	3.92	3.54	3.51	3.81	3.95
Transport	1.93	2.10	2.51	2.00	1.64	3.36	1.03	0.95	1.58

(Contd.)

Table 11.4 *(Contd.)*

Industry/Category	No. of Units			Total Employment			Gross Value Added		
	1984-85	1989-90	1994-95	1984-85	1989-90	1994-95	1984-85	1989-90	1994-95
Other Manufacturing	3.14	2.91	2.20	1.13	1.41	2.04	0.62	0.91	1.01
Repair of Capital Goods	—	0.18	1.54	—	0.81	2.08	—	0.29	0.62
Repair Services	2.48	2.29	1.01	2.13	2.19	0.41	0.90	1.00	1.10
Cases Not Recorded	—	—	—	—	—	—	—	—	—
All Industries	100.0	100.0	100.0	100.0	100.0	100.0	100.0	100.0	100.0

Source: Calculated from the Annual Survey of Industries, 1984-85, 1989-90 and 1994-95.

units, employment and value added during 1984-85, 1989-90 and 1994-95. It reports that manufacture of chemicals, non-metal and non-electrical machinery have a sizeable share in units and employment, manufacture of cotton, and wool and silk, have a sizeable share in employment in all the three periods. As far as value added is concerned, decline in the cotton textile share is obvious where the share has declined from 16.95 per cent in 1984-85 to 6.13 per cent in 1994-95. However, in 1989-90 and 1994-95 chemicals and rubber account for a major share.

Growth rates of employment have been calculated for the two sub-periods, viz. 1984-90, 1989-95 (referred to as first and second sub-period respectively) and for the entire period 1984-95. Similarly, employment elasticities with reference to the gross value added have also been calculated for the similar periods for the organised manufacturing sector in Gujarat. These are presented in Table 11.5.

At the sectoral level we observe that manufacture of beverages and cotton textiles have registered negative growth in employment during both the sub-periods and hence for the entire period employment has decreased at the rate of 6.03 and 5.97 per cent per annum respectively. In the case of manufacture of wood and repair services due to a steep decline in the employment in the second period, the growth rate for the entire period is also negative for these two industries. On the other hand, in manufacture of non-metal, metal products and transport equipments, employment has declined only during 1984-90.

As far as the employment elasticities are concerned at the sectoral level, in the first sub-period, manufacture of beverages, leather, non-metal, metal products and transport equipments have negative elasticities which are, however, positive during the second sub-period. This is mainly due to the decline in the rate of growth of employment in some of these groups. For the entire period, beverages and cotton textiles show very high positive and negative employment elasticities respectively which could be due to the limitation of the data. Interestingly, only in manufacture of Wool and Silk and Repair services, employment elasticity is more than one implying that in these sectors, one unit of increase in value added leads to more than one unit increase in employment. It also suggests the labour intensive process of production in these sectors.

Sectoral Trends in Employment, Productivity and Elasticity of Employment in the Unorganised Manufacturing Sector in Gujarat

Percentage share in enterprises, employment and value added by industrial

Table 11.5 : Growth Rates of Employment and Employment Elasticities in the Organised Sector

Industry/Category	Employment			Employment·Elasticity		
	1984-90	1989-95	1984-95	1984-90	1989-95	1984-95
Food Products	1.42	0.13	0.77	0.04	-0.04	0.06
Beverages	-2.31	-9.75	-6.03	-0.40	1.72	36.66
Cotton	-4.98	-6.96	-5.97	2.86	-2.92	-28.55
Wool & Silk	4.73	4.16	4.45	1.81	1.05	1.40
Jute	—	—	—	—	—	—
Textiles	5.03	1.47	3.25	2.05	0.14	0.51
Wood	2.35	-4.76	-1.21	0.28	0.42	0.42
Paper	-1.22	5.44	2.11	0.88	0.26	0.22
Leather	4.05	6.66	5.35	-0.42	0.14	0.88
Chemicals	3.98	6.89	5.44	0.81	0.32	0.38
Rubber	6.56	7.03	6.79	0.13	0.17	0.07
Non-Metal	-0.78	2.53	0.88	-0.05	0.11	0.03
Metal Products	-0.75	1.47	0.36	-0.20	0.04	0.02
Basic Metal	5.94	0.61	3.27	0.45	0.05	0.21
Non-Electrical Machinery	2.18	2.98	2.58	0.32	0.65	0.42
Electrical Machinery	2.01	-0.40	0.80	0.19	-0.02	0.04
Transport	-3.53	15.99	6.23	-0.51	0.54	0.26
Other Manufacturing	4.91	9.04	6.98	0.25	0.48	0.28
Repair of Capital Goods	—	20.53	—	—	0.57	—
Repair Services	1.10	-31.87	-15.39	0.10	1.00	1.17
Cases Not Recorded	—	—	—	—	—	—
All Industries	0.51	1.61	1.06	0.06	0.09	0.06

Source : Same as in Table 11.4.

Table 11.6 : Share of Enterprises, Employment and Gross Value Added by Industrial Groups in Unorganised Sector

Industry/Category	No. of Units			Total Employment			Gross Value Added		
	1984-85	1989-90	1994-95	1984-85	1989-90	1994-95	1984-85	1989-90	1994-95
Food Products	16.80	15.26	10.61	10.94	9.28	8.07	10.86	7.05	6.70
Beverages	2.34	1.69	1.10	1.85	1.48	0.92	0.99	0.71	0.36
Cotton	2.42	4.87	4.35	3.19	3.53	3.43	1.86	1.92	1.57
Wool & Silk	1.26	6.76	4.02	4.86	10.56	8.55	12.93	39.54	9.81
Jute	0.00	0.00	0.03	0.01	0.01	0.07	0.01	0.01	0.09
Textiles	25.23	5.03	8.10	13.99	3.95	6.24	10.96	2.55	2.16
Wood	11.72	16.63	12.53	7.89	9.86	7.93	6.56	4.82	2.79
Paper	0.81	1.52	0.86	1.96	1.80	1.06	1.92	1.85	0.89
Leather	2.82	2.38	1.51	1.52	1.21	1.02	1.15	0.64	0.33
Chemicals	0.39	0.78	0.26	0.83	1.24	0.41	2.26	2.00	0.81
Rubber	0.29	1.02	1.21	0.73	1.15	2.03	0.78	1.47	2.94
Non-Metal	5.79	5.91	3.91	5.23	7.49	4.98	3.29	3.13	2.00
Metal Products	0.71	0.49	1.92	1.79	1.26	2.85	1.82	1.38	2.75
Basic Metal	2.40	3.06	3.37	3.44	2.37	5.33	3.79	1.71	4.11
Non-Electrical Machinery	1.82	1.81	2.09	3.78	2.87	2.71	5.43	4.37	2.32
Electrical Machinery	0.28	0.49	0.53	0.90	1.26	0.62	3.41	13.73	0.38
Transport	0.49	0.34	0.12	0.87	0.54	0.16	0.87	0.46	0.12
Other Manufacturing	7.93	14.65	30.95	25.65	30.67	36.02	21.70	34.16	54.62
Repair of Capital Goods	16.48	2.68	3.04	10.57	1.98	2.45	9.43	1.36	1.74
Repair Services	—	14.61	9.34	—	7.49	5.10	—	4.61	3.48
Cases Not Recorded	—	0.00	0.16	—	0.00	0.08	—	0.00	0.04
All Industries	100.0	100.0	100.0	100.0	100.0	100.0	100.0	100.0	100.0

Source: Calculated from the Follow-up Surveys on the Unorganised Manufacturing Sector for the years 1984-85, 1989-90 and 1994-95.

groups in the unorganised sector is given in Table 11.6. We observe that for most of the industrial groups, share in number of enterprises, employment and gross value added has declined in 1994-95, in comparison with the year 1984-85, though a uniform trend could not be identified. Exception to this is 'other manufacturing' whose share has increased in terms of the chosen indicators in 1994-95 as compared to 1984-85. Though industrial groups like, manufacture of wool and silk, rubber, basic metals and metal products show an increase in their share in units and employment, the same is not observed in their share in value added. manufacture of wool and silk and other manufacturing are the sectors that account for a major share in gross value added till 1989-90. In 1994-95 we find the share of other manufacturing to have risen to 54.6 per cent while that of wool and silk has reduced to 9.81 per cent.

The declining share in employment gets reflected in the form of declining rate of growth in employment, which is presented in Table 11.7. At the sectoral level, we find that during 1984-90, but for manufacture of textile products and repair of capital goods, for all others the growth rate in employment has been positive and high. Interestingly, unlike the organised sector, employment in the cotton textiles in the unorganised sector is not negative, though the growth rate has declined in 1989-95. However, during the second period, i.e. 1989-95 as many as eleven industrial groups have experienced negative growth in employment. For the period as a whole, manufacture of transport equipments and repair of capital goods have experienced a negative growth rate.

In order to see whether the decline in the employment has affected the employment elasticities with reference to gross value added, employment elasticities for the two sub periods and for the entire period have been calculated.

At the sectoral level, there has been a general decline in the employment elasticities in many of the industrial groups during 1989-95 compared to 1984-90, with a few exceptions like manufacture of jute and metal products. Some industrial groups like manufacture of food products, cotton, textiles and non-electrical machinery show negative employment elasticities compared to the earlier period, implying that one unit of output could be produced with much less of labour. For the entire period, interestingly we find a steep increase in the employment elasticities of manufacture of beverages, wool and silk, wood, chemicals and non-electrical machinery, while textile products, leather and electrical machinery show a negative employment elasticity.

Table 11.7 : Growth Rates of Employment and Employment Elasticities on the Unorganised Sector

Industry\ Category	Employment			Employment Elasticity		
	1984-90	1989-95	1984-95	1984-90	1989-95	1984-95
Food Products	15.78	-1.33	7.23	1.84	-0.81	1.35
Beverages	14.68	-7.97	3.35	1.33	0.77	9.07
Cotton	21.12	0.92	11.02	1.14	-0.62	1.40
Wool & Silk	34.62	-2.76	15.93	0.68	0.18	3.28
Jute	6.73	49.35	28.04	0.24	0.97	0.50
Textiles	-6.23	10.63	2.20	0.66	-17.97	-0.57
Wood	23.54	-2.90	10.32	2.58	0.39	7.89
Paper	17.44	-9.16	4.14	0.95	0.81	1.49
Leather	14.52	-1.98	6.27	2.57	0.23	-5.52
Chemicals	27.03	-20.51	3.26	2.27	1.19	10.03
Rubber	27.98	12.87	20.42	0.80	0.71	0.68
Non-Metal	26.27	-6.68	9.79	1.91	1.03	2.20
Metal Products	12.06	17.74	14.90	0.88	1.14	1.02
Basic Metal	11.59	17.69	14.64	5.32	0.82	1.55
Non-Electrical Machinery	13.59	0.30	6.95	0.93	-0.64	4.28
Electrical Machinery	25.72	-12.78	6.47	-0.23	0.46	-1.34
Transport	9.53	-22.62	-6.54	1.74	0.96	0.80
Other Manufacturing	22.66	4.68	13.67	0.70	0.32	0.47
Repair of Capital Goods	-14.39	5.67	-4.36	0.81	0.72	0.76
Repair Services	—	-6.23	—	—	1.87	—
Cases Not Recorded	—	132.08	—	—	—	—
All Industries	19.08	1.47	10.28	1.03	0.57	0.95

Source: Same as in Table 11.6.

Summary and Conclusions

From the foregoing discussion, it emerges that in Gujarat since the '80s there has been a decline in the per cent of self-employed and in the salaried regular employment. In contrast to this, there has been an increase in casual wage employment implying the demand for hired labour. Employment trends in different sectors report a steep-decline in the per cent of workforce with the primary sector in the '80s. The share of employment in the tertiary sector is higher than the share of secondary sector, particularly in the urban areas.

The growth rates of employment in the organised and the unorganised sector move in opposite directions. Particularly during the liberalisation period, employment in the organised sector grew while in the unorganised sector it contracted. It emerges that productivity of labour in the organised sector is much higher than the unorganised sector. The employment elasticities clearly bring out the capital and labour intensive nature of production in the organised and unorganised sectors.

As mentioned elsewhere in the paper the shift in the workforce towards the unorganised sector from the original sector might in the long run slow down the growth of output in the economy on the whole unless the labour productivity in both the sectors improve. Since in the absense of increasing labour productivity in the unorganised sector, mostly casual jobs would be created in this sector which in any case is on the rising trend in Gujarat. While the rising share of casual workers within the set of hired workers represents a qualitative deterioration of the hired labourforce (Bhalla, 1996), Visaria (1996) argues that casualisation of labour *per se* need not mean deterioration of labour, provided such labourers are paid proper wages to have a decent standard of living. Hence, a further probe bringing out the linkages between the organised and the unorganised sectors would also highlight the shift in the workforce from one to another and the extent of casualisation of workforce in the manufacturing sector.

NOTES

1. The organised and the unorganised sectors constitute the total manufacturing sector. While those industries that are governed by the Factories Act of 1948 are called the organised sector, those that fall outside the purview of Factories Act, 1948 are called the unorganised manufacturing sector.

2. The exponential growth rates are based on the main workers in different sectors.

REFERENCES

Basant, Rakesh, Kumar, B.L. and Parthasarathy R. (1998), *Non-Agricultural Employment in Rural India*, Rawat Publications, Jaipur.

Bhaduri, Amit (1996), "Employment, Labour Market Flexibility and Economic Liberalisation in India", *The Indian Journal of Labour Economics*, 39 (1), pp. 13-22.

Bhalla, Sheila (1996), "Workforce Restructuring, Wages and Want: Recent Events, Interpretations and Analysis", *The Indian Journal of Labour Economics,* 39 (1), PP1-12.

Bhattacharya, B.B. and Arup Mitra (1993), "Employment and Structural Adjustment: A look at Census Data", *Economic and Political Weekly*, 28 (38), pp.1989-1995.

——— (1994), "Employment, Labour Productivity and Wage Rate in Public and Organised Private Sectors in the Context of Structural Reforms", *The Indian Journal of Labour Economics*, Vol. 37, No. 2.

Chaudhuri, Tamal Datta (1989), "A Theoretical Analysis of the Informal Sector", *World Development*, Vol. 17, No. 3.

Ghose, Ajit K. (1992), "Economic Restructuring, Employment and Safety Nets: A note in Social Dimensions of Structural Adjustment in India", *Papers and Proceeding of Tripartite Workshop held in New Delhi*, Dec.10-11, 1991, ILO ARTEP.

———(1994), "Employment in Organised Manufacturing in India", *The Indian Journal of Labour Economics*, Vol. 37, No. 2.

Iyengar, Sudarshan (1998), 'Gujarat', in Rao, V.M., (ed.) *The Poor in a Hostile Society: Glimpses of Changing Poverty Scenario in India*, Indo-Dutch Programme on Alternatives in Development, Vikas Publishing House Private Limited, New Delhi.

Kashyap, S.P., (1995), "Industrial Scene in Gujarat: A Contrast of Two Patterns", *Anvesak*, 25 (1) January-June.

Lalitha, N., 1998, "State Level Reforms to Promote Industrialisation: A Case Study of Gujarat", *Indian Journal of Regional Science*, 30 (1).

Mitra, Arup (1994), "Industry, Informal Sector Employment and Poverty", *The Indian Journal of Labour Economics*, Vol. 37, No. 3.

Parthasarathy, G. (1996), "Unorganised Sector and Structural Adjustment", *Economic and Political Weekly*, Vol. 31, No. 28, July 13.

Unni, Jeemol (1997), "Non-Agricultural Employment, Livelihoods and Poverty in Rural India", prepared as a background paper for the World Bank Poverty Update on India, Gujarat Institute of Development Research, Ahmedabad.

Visaria, Pravin (1996), "Structure of the Indian Workforce 1961-1994", *The Indian Journal of Labour Economics*, 39(4), October-December.

12

Health for All in Gujarat

Is It Achievable ?

DARSHINI MAHADEVIA

Introduction

Health is a fundamental human right, emphasised the Alma Ata Declaration of 1978. Since the Alma Ata conference on health, which focused on equitable and cost-effective primary healthcare, health has become an important national concern in most countries. Especially, in the developing countries, where health status of large sections of population is still low and population growth rates are high, health sector is very important. Since the sixties, the social development movement and from the beginning of the nineties, human development reports of the United Nations Development Programme (UNDP) have emphasised improvement in the health status of the population as one of the important goals of development.

In the developing countries, health sector policies have tended to lay stress on reducing population growth. Though, population stabilisation is indeed an area of urgency in the developing countries, by now it is known that there are links between overall health status of population and population growth rate. At the same time, many new diseases and challenges are coming up in the developing countries that also require as much attention of the national governments as the population control has received. As the case of India suggests, specifically with reference to some of the states, even population stabilisation is a distant goal due to lower achievements regarding overall health status and social development. This paper, therefore, approaches health status in Gujarat from this holistic perspective for long-term improvement in the health status of people of

Gujarat.

Gujarat has made significant progress in improving the key health statistics: death rates, birth rates, infant mortality rates (IMR) and life expectancy at birth (LEB). The state's performance has been better as compared to all India average in these aspects. However, state's achievements even in these key areas are far behind that of Kerala, a state with lower per capita income than Gujarat, but that has made transition to medium human development level, while India remain in the low human development category as per UNDP's Human Development Index (HDI). While there is still a long way to go regarding improving the key health statistics, new dimensions of health status are emerging which need quick attention now. These are environmental health, occupational health, new contagious diseases such as AIDS, and diseases of prosperity. Also, much needs to be done regarding to women's health. Diseases of poverty continue to afflict a section of population. Urbanisation has brought in new set of health burden in the urban areas. The new dimensions of health area along with the neglected aspects need to be paid attention to simultaneously. Otherwise, there are possibilities of reversal in or slowing down of the achievements regarding key health statistics. At the same time, one needs to understand that sustained improvement in overall health status is also a function of many other factors than just government initiatives.

The second section addresses the question of what is health. Third section is theoretical and looks at the factors that affect health status. Overall health status in Gujarat, observed through key health statistics is discussed in section four. Healthcare expenditures over time in the state, health facilities and health utilisation patterns are discussed in sections five and six. The important emerging areas for concern, which give new areas for public policy focus, are discussed in section seven, the concluding section. This section focuses on how the goal of 'health for all' needs to be addressed in a prosperous state as Gujarat. Achievements with respect to the goal of 'Health for All' can be assessed from various standpoints, such as evaluating achievements of primary healthcare system, coverage of government programmes, and so on. In this paper, focus is on factors determining health status of population and aspects that need to be monitored in Gujarat to move towards improving overall health status of the population.

What is Health?

Health is defined by the World Health Organisation (WHO) as "a state of complete physical, mental and social well-being and not merely absence of disease or infirmity." This definition was accepted by all the signatories to the Alma Ata Declaration on health adopted by the Thirty-first World Health Assembly in 1978. This declaration gave the call of 'Health for All by 2000 AD' and accepted that the Primary Healthcare was a key to attaining this goal. The purpose of this definition was to bring the positive concept of general well-being into focus rather than a negative definition of absence of disease. At the Alma Ata conference the Joint Report of the Director-General of WHO and the Executive Director of UNICEF stated that :

> "...health systems are all too often being devised outside the mainstream of social and economic development. These systems frequently restrict themselves to medical care, although industrialisation and deliberate alteration of the environment are creating health problems whose proper control lies far beyond the scope of medical care" (Tejada-de-Rivero, 1981: 35).

Health is thus not only about diseases and medical care system but also about environment around us, which influences the mental and physical state of a person. It is a multi-dimensional phenomenon (Hema and Muraleedharan, 1993).

The 'basic needs approach' considers health as a basic need along with food, clothing, shelter and education. Starting from Pigou, basic needs approach is utilitarian, "*because and only because* fulfilment" of basic needs "contributes to utility" (Sen 1985: 25). Many subsequent researchers also have built on the concept of health as a utility. For example, the World Development Report, 1993 (World Bank, 1993), considers good health as an input for increasing productivity, leading to economic growth. The National Council of Applied Economic Research (NCAER, 1992: 1) considers, health status as "an important indicator of the level of economic development" and it includes mainly mortality and morbidity. Sen, however, disagrees with this utilitarian approach. He argues that, "value of the living standard lies in the living" (1985: 25) and better health is better living and not because it is an *instrument* for better living or has a *utility*.

Health has importance in three distinct ways: (a) intrinsic importance, (b) instrumental importance at personal and social levels and (c) empowerment importance. In intrinsic sense, health is important because it is a direct measure of human well-being. It is fulfilment of life and a valuable achievement in itself. In the instrumental sense, better health is important in many ways. For example, good health has an economic rationale. Better health reduces medical costs, both of the government and of the households. In the case of children, better health leads to better attendance in schools and to higher level of knowledge attainment. Better education and knowledge lead to better paid jobs and larger benefits to the future generation. For women, better health status is achieved through empowerment. But it also empowers them to participate in economic and public life to fullest extent.

Factors Affecting Health Status

In developing countries such as India, there are number of factors that affect health status. Of these, some are demand side factors such as income, assets, social practices as a result of ethnicity and religion, life style, etc. and some are supply side factors such as the healthcare system, health expenditures, etc. There are also environmental factors and gender inequality related factors that influence health status. These factors are listed below, of which few important ones are discussed in brief:

(i) Poverty, food security, food pricing and malnutrition;
(ii) Environmental pollution and degradation;
(iii) Occupational health problems;
(iv) Reproductive health problems;
(v) Household economy and wages;
(vi) Economic development; represented by per capita income, urbanisation and industrialisation;
(vii) Social development; especially literacy rates;
(viii) Prices of private health care system, and
(ix) Public health care delivery system.

There are two broad categories of diseases, that of poverty and that of affluence. Poverty leads to malnutrition and the resultant diseases, which are common in the developing countries. Lack of food security is another major problem that leads to malnutrition. Other factors related to malnutrition are production and availability of the food grains, level of nutritional knowledge, level of illiteracy and ignorance, consumption patterns, distribution of income and food, level of employment, unsafe drinking water and poor sanitation facilities and non-availability of health services[1]. Good nutrition not only gives adequate calories for functioning but also increases the immunity to resist diseases and infections. Poor tend to live in unhygienic environmental conditions and are at high risk of infections and diseases. Poor are trapped in the vicious cycle of malnutrition, low birth weight female infants, malnourished adolescents, malnourished pregnant and lactating mothers and low weight infants. The specific burdens of malnutrition are (a) Protein Energy Malnutrition (PEM), and (b) Disorders resulting from deficiency of iron (anaemia), vitamin A (keratomalacia or nutritional blindness), iodine (goitre) and vitamin B (angular stomatis, gossitis). Gujarat is a part of the endemic goitre belt (Nutrition Foundation of India, 1983, as quoted in Ali, 1992). Groups that are most vulnerable to malnutrition are infants, pre-school children, especially the girls, pregnant and lactating mothers, landless labourers, urban slum dwellers and tribal communities.

Improvement in the health status is considered as a byproduct of economic growth and of increase in per capita income. Historically, the health status has improved with industrialisation and economic growth. Thus, the population in the developed economies enjoys better health status than in the developing economies. But the relationship between per capita income and health status is not always one to one. Some countries have a relatively high health and status at low levels of economic growth while others have not achieved a higher health status in spite of high incomes. It is argued that urbanisation improves health status because urban areas tend to have better health facilities than the rural areas in a developing country. Also, due to access to relevant information in urban areas, child mortality and fertility rates are lower in urban as compared to rural areas (Murthi, Guio and Drèze, 1995: 9). But even in the highly urbanised developing countries with high per capita incomes, urban environmental conditions are quite poor and industrialisation is causing serious pollution. As a result, overall urban health status is low, especially among the poor households.

Literacy, especially of females, is considered essential for improving the rate of child survival, for bringing down IMR and reducing fertility. It is argued that educated women are more likely to voice resentment against burden of repeated pregnancies and have alternative use of their time. They may have other sources of fulfilment than reproductive performance and may not desire to spend their time unproductively, say for time consuming activities such as childbearing and rearing. They have higher aspirations for their children. Large family may be a hindrance in the achievements of the children. Educated women are more aware of the immunisation programmes and family nutrition, health and hygiene. They are also more likely to use healthcare system in the event of sickness of their child. Hence, child survival rates are higher, which in turn reduce the desire for large family. Female education is also important for maternal health. Hence, female education is more likely to affect infant and child health and through it the family health than the male education. The latter is likely to influence the family health through income effect (Murthi, Guio and Drèze, 1995).

Most health problems of the women are related to their reproductive system or are caused by their reproductive function. Other health problems, such as that of malnourishment or environmental pollution, etc. get aggravated due to their reproductive function. Starting from anaemia to complications of the gynaecological system, women are constantly under health stress. Women's health problems are broadly affected by two factors, biological (natural) and socio-economic and cultural (human-made), besides individual attributes and availability of health and nutritional services. Even access of women to health and nutritional services is partly determined by the socio-cultural factors. Each of these factors influences her health in varying proportions over her life cycle. But, more than others, the socio-cultural factors determine major part of a woman's physical and mental health status. Thus, improvement in woman's health requires change in socio-cultural dimensions of a society and overall improvement in health of a society depends on improvement in women's health status. In short, improvement in overall health situation in any society is also related to socio-cultural dimensions of the particular society.

Environmental health is emerging as new area of concern. The problems of environmental pollution have become all pervasive in the developing countries, especially in the urban areas, because of high concentration of people, inadequate infrastructure for public hygiene, and uncontrolled and unregulated industrial activity. With continuous high rate of urbanisation, provision of basic services such as water supply, sanitation and solid waste collection do not keep pace with the rate of urban growth. As a result, water-borne infectious diseases are pervasive. The population not having access to adequate water does not maintain proper personal hygiene. Skin diseases are common as a result. Risk to schistosomiasis, eye infections and guinea worm diseases also increase due to lack of water supply.

Air pollution, caused by vehicular traffic, thermal plants within the cities, industrial units and use of coal, is the other major environmental health problem in the developing countries. Studies show that in the Indian metropolises, the air pollution levels far exceed the WHO standards

(Environment, 1988). Air pollution damages human respiratory and cardiorespiratory systems. The elderly, children, smokers, and those with chronic respiratory and cardiovascular problems are more susceptible to damages because of air pollution. Finally, malaria, a vector disease, is also common in the urban areas due to stagnant pools of water, water storage systems in the houses, dark and damp houses in the slums and high population density which leads to fast spread of the disease. In rural areas also air pollution due to location of thermal power plants causes respiratory problems.

The rural areas are also affected now due to the effect of industrial pollution. Industrial wastewater and sewage are often released untreated in the river systems. This affects the agriculture down stream. If the river water is the source of drinking water then it affects the health of the rural population down stream. When the untreated wastewater from the industrial estates is released in low-lying areas and in nearby ponds, it leaches in the soil and pollutes the ground water streams. When this water is pumped out for rural use, the population residing far away from the urban areas too gets affected. Situation is serious when untreated chemical wastewater is disposed in this manner.

Environmental degradation leading to malnutrition causes one set of health problems while environmental pollution leads to another set of problems such as respiratory problems, skin problems, cancer, gynaecological disorders among women, vector diseases, etc. It may be appropriate to develop indicators of not only health status based on the reporting of certain health conditions but also epidemiology related indicators or factors causing health problems for appropriate health policy formulation.

Environmental factors affecting health are discussed at length because these are the new challenges faced by Gujarat in the area of health. On the one hand, it is the second most urbanised state and Ahmedabad is the seventh largest metropolis in the country. Urban environmental issues affecting health, therefore, are quite important. On the other hand, large proportion of rural areas face water scarcity, which can manifest in health disorders discussed above.

Occupational health problems due to poor working conditions in the many industries, such as chemical units, tanneries, thermal plants, textile units, potteries, asbestos industries, saw mills, etc. and units undertaking extraction and harvesting of natural resources, such as mining activities (open and closed mines) are known. There is a long list of hazardous industries whose working conditions pose health hazards to the workers, besides posing health hazards to neighbourhood. In addition, those engaged in the petty service sector, such as vending and repairing by the roadside, are constantly exposed to the motor vehicle fumes. Many small eateries and restaurants cook with fire wood or dung cakes, exposing the workers to constant fumes during cooking. Health status of population, therefore, is related to large number of factors, which are tied to the socio-cultural practices, economic systems, production technology, overall environmental conditions, income level and so on, besides public health expenditures and care system. Before importance of these factors in context of Gujarat are discussed, achievements of Gujarat with respect to key health statistics is discussed in the following:

Health Status in Gujarat

Vital Statistics

Gujarat, like India, has made considerable improvement in the health status of the population. In India, the CDR has declined from 27.4 in 1951 to 9.8 in 1991 (Gowarikar, 1993) and the IMR has dramatically reduced from estimated 200-225 per 1000 live births at the time of independence to 79 in 1991 (Visaria and Visaria, 1994). The IMR has declined mainly due to the decline in Neo-Natal Mortality (NNM), an achievement of widespread immunisation programmes in the country. Gujarat's performance is better than that of India's (Table 12.1). The CBR and CDR are lower in Gujarat as compared to India. The MMR is also lower in the state than India. The IMR, child mortality (CMR) and NNM are also lower in the state than in India. However, the pre-natal fertility is slightly higher and projected LEB is lower in Gujarat than in India. Compare achievements of Gujarat with that of Kerala (Table 12.1). It can be seen that the state is quite far from reaching the health achievements of Kerala. For example, IMR in Gujarat is about 3.5 times that in Kerala. Similarly, NNM and PNNM are higher by about three times and TFR double in Gujarat than in Kerala.

The CBRs and CDRs in Gujarat have reduced significantly during the last two decades, much more than at all India level (Table 12.2). In 1971, the CBR in rural and urban Gujarat was 42.1 and 36.1 respectively, against the all India rates of 38.9 and 30.1.

Table 12.1: Health Status, Gujarat Compared to India and Kerala

Health Status Indicators	Gujarat	India	Kerala
Crude Birth Rate, 1999 *	25.6	27.2	17.4 (1994)***
Crude Death Rate, 1997 *	7.6	8.9	6.3 (1993)***
Maternal Mortality Rate 1992-93*	3.89	4.58	2.34 (1982-86)****
Infant Mortality Rate, 1997 *	62	72	17 (1990-92)****
Life Expectancy at Birth, 1996-2000 - Male *	61.53	62.36	68.8 (1990-92)****
Life Expectancy at Birth, 1996-2000 - Female *	62.77	63.39	74.4 (1990-92)****
Neo-natal Mortality Rate 1990-92 **	42.3	48.6	15.5
Pre-natal Mortality Rate 1994*	43.0	42.5	—
Post Neo-natal Mortality Rate 1990-92 **	26.4	29.9	8.2
Child Mortality rate 1994*	20.7	23.7	8.4 (1990-92)**
General Fertility Rate 1996*	106.0	118.3	
Total Fertility Rate 1994*	3.2	3.5	1.8 (1991)****
Net Reproduction Rate 1994*	1.3	1.6	

Source : *Data from Commissionerate of Health, Medical Services and Medical Education.
**PRC and IIPS (1994). ***Government of India (1997).
****Drèze and Sen (1995).

Table 12.2: CBR and CDR Over Time, Gujarat and India

Year	Gujarat				India			
	Rural		Urban		Rural		Urban	
	CBR	CDR	CBR	CDR	CBR	CDR	CBR	CDR
1971	42.1	18.1	36.1	13.1	38.9	16.4	30.1	9.7
1981	36.1	12.4	29.8	10.7	35.6	13.7	27.0	7.8
1986	32.9	11.3	30.8	8.6	34.2	12.2	27.1	7.6
1990	30.2	9.6	28.3	7.2	31.7	10.5	24.7	6.8
1991*	28.2	8.8	25.9	7.9	30.9	10.6	24.3	7.1
1992*	29.5	9.5	24.6	8.3	30.9	10.9	23.1	7.0
1993*	29.1	8.9	25.8	6.8	30.4	10.6	23.7	5.8
1994*	28.5	9.6	24.5	6.9	30.5	10.1	23.1	6.7
1995*	27.9	8.3	24.0	6.2	30.0	9.8	22.7	6.5
1996*	26.9	8.3	23.0	6.3	29.3	9.7	21.6	6.5
1997*	27.0	8.3	22.6	6.2	28.9	9.6	21.5	6.5

* India excludes Jammu and Kashmir.

Source : SRS data from Commissionerate of Health, Medical Services and Medical Education.

These have reduced to 27.0 and 22.6 respectively in Gujarat and to 28.9 and 21.5 respectively in India. The rural CBR, which was higher in Gujarat than in India in 1971, is lower than in India in 1997. Urban CBR continues to be higher in Gujarat than in India, a point that needs an investigation. Similarly, CDRs too have reduced significantly in Gujarat as compared to India. Both rural and urban CDRs were higher in Gujarat as compared to India in 1971, but are lower than that of India in 1997. The CDRs and CBRs have been higher in the rural areas as compared to the urban areas in Gujarat as well as in India. This is expected. Point to note is that the gap between the urban and rural rates has narrowed down over time. Another important observation is that, since 1991, the CBR in the urban Gujarat has remained higher than urban India. Same was the case with respect to CDR between 1991 and 1995, after which the figures for urban Gujarat are lower than that for urban India. In the rural areas, performance of Gujarat has been consistently better than India's.

The IMR in Gujarat has declined more rapidly than in India during the last two decades, in both rural and urban areas (Table 12.3). In 1971, the rural and urban IMRs in Gujarat were higher than that of India, while in 1994, the Gujarat IMRs were significantly lower than that of India. This improvement in IMR in Gujarat can be attributed to the significant decline of infant deaths in rural areas. The IMR has continued declining in rural areas of Gujarat, but in urban areas, there was some increase in 1994 as compared to 1993, after which once again there is a decline. Urban health status, therefore, requires deeper probing in Gujarat.

The decline in the IMR is mainly attributed to the decline in neo-natal mortality due to the immunisation programme, and the extension of healthcare system to take care of complications of deliveries. Trained personnel are assisting more and more deliveries. The decline in neo-natal mortality and hence reduction in the IMR in Gujarat can be seen from the results of the National Family Health Survey (NFHS). In rural Gujarat, NNM rates have declined significantly from 59.2 in 1978-82 (10-14 yrs. before) to 43.6 in 1988-92 (0-4 yrs. before) period (Table 12.4). In urban areas, the NNM has remained almost constant over the last decade and a half with a marginal increase during 1988-92. This is because the IMR during the same period in urban Gujarat has increased from 18.5 to 26.1 for 1000 live births. Once again, urban Gujarat poses special problem.

Table 12.3 : Infant Mortality Rates Over Time, Gujarat and India

Year	Gujarat			India		
	Rural	Urban	Total	Rural	Urban	Total
1971	155	110	145	138	82	129
1981	123	89	116	119	62	110
1986	124	66	107	105	62	96
1990	79	54	72	86	50	80
1991*	73	57	69	87	53	80
1992*	71	54	67	85	53	79
1993*	65	42	58	82	45	74
1994*	70	51	64	80	52	74
1995*	68	47	62	80	48	74
1996*	68	46	61	77	46	72
1997*	69	46	62	77	45	71

*India excludes Jammu and Kashmir.

Source : SRS data based on Commissionerate of Health, Medical Services and Medical Education (1994), Table 2.5, p. 21.

Table 12.4 : Infant and Child Mortlity Trends, Gujarat

Years prior to survey	Infant and Child Mortality Rates				
	NNM	PNNM	IMR	CM 4	CM 5
Urban					
0-4 years	39.3	26.1	65.4	30.8	94.2
5-9 years	39.0	18.5	57.5	22.0	78.3
10-14 years	40.7	19.0	59.7	24.3	82.6
Rural					
0-4 years	43.6	26.6	70.2	40.9	108.2
5-9 years	55.1	32.7	87.7	30.7	115.7
10-14 years	59.2	36.9	96.1	33.2	126.1
All Areas					
0-4 years	42.3	26.4	68.7	37.9	104.0
5-9 years	49.9	28.1	78.0	27.8	103.6
10-14 years	52.9	30.8	83.7	30.2	111.3

Source: PRC and IIPS (1993), Table 8.3, p. 133.

Among the major states in India, in 1994, Gujarat came in the middle order with respect to important indicators of health status. It ranked 16th from the top with respect to CBR, and 14th from the top with respect to CDR out of 29 states and union territories. It is, in fact, surprising that the tribal dominated Tripura and non-urbanised state of Sikkim were doing better than Gujarat with respect to these two indicators of health. Even among the 15 large states, Gujarat was in the middle, seventh in CBR, sixth in CDR and IMR and ninth in LEB in 1991 (Sundar, 1995).

Though the infant and child mortality rates in Gujarat are lower than in India, Gujarat came in the middle order in the state ranking. With respect to the NNM, the state ranked 15th out of 25 states surveyed by the NFHS. As per the SRS data, state ranked sixth with respect to IMR (as per the NFHS data Gujarat ranked 14th in IMR and 19th in under five child mortality). Though various surveys give different pictures of child health in Gujarat, there has been improvement with respect to child health in the state, but not as much as expected. In contrast, Maharashtra, another urbanised state and having similar economic characteristics as Gujarat, is performing well with respect to the child health. The economically not so developed north-eastern states of India too are doing much better than Gujarat in child health, not to talk of Kerala which is showing the best results with respect to most health indicators (Based on PRC and IIPS 1994).

Morbidity

Data on morbidity are difficult to interpret. High morbidity rate can be due to better reporting of illness during a morbidity survey by literate and aware population or due to high prevalence of diseases. In Kerala, it is argued that because of high awareness levels, people avail of health facilities even for minor ailments, leading to higher reporting of illness and higher morbidity rates. In context of Kerala, it is argued that high morbidity rates are due to the decline in the mortality rates (Rajan and James, 1993).

It is also argued that with an increase in the level of development, the prevalence of communicable diseases comes down whereas that of chronic illnesses goes up. This does not seem to be true with respect to Gujarat (Table 12.5). In Gujarat, prevalence rates of serious communicable diseases, in both rural and urban areas, are higher than the same in India, whereas the prevalence rates of chronic diseases are lower than the same in the country. In fact, in rural Gujarat the chronic illness prevalence rate is extremely low.

Table 12.5 : Morbidity in Gujarat

Morbidity Indicators	Gujarat	India
Morbidity rate per '000 population (rural)		
—Total	75.8	106.7
—Male	71.6	105.5
—Female	80.8	108.1
Morbidity rate per '000 population (urban)		
—Total	84.3	103.0
—Male	95.0	98.2
—Female	74.5	108.4
Prevalence of illness by type		
Rural — Serious communicable diseases	21.0	15.6
— Acute illness	49.6	77.9
— Chronic illness	5.2	13.2
Urban — Serious communicable diseases	18.8	14.0
— Acute illness	52.8	70.6
— Chronic illness	12.7	18.4

Notes : Reference period is one year. All India figures include State/Union Territories of Goa, Meghalaya, Pondicherry, Chandigarh and Delhi Rural.
Source : Based on Sundar, (1995) an NCAER survey.

Prevalence of blindness due to Vitamin A deficiency and goitre due to iodine deficiency are high in Gujarat. According to the national goitre control programme, Gujarat forms part of the endemic goitre belt (National Foundation of India 1983, as quoted by Ali, 1992). The prevalence of blindness due to vitamin A deficiency is the highest in Gujarat among all the states in India (based on PRC and IIPS 1994). About 33 persons out of 1000 are either partially or completely blind (Table 12.6). Prevalence of blindness is higher in rural areas than in the urban areas, and among females than males. More than 20 per cent of the population of age 60 and above suffers from partial or total blindness. Prevalence of malaria is also high (32 per 1000 population) in the state. It is higher in the rural than in the urban areas and among females than the males. Cases of malaria and falciparum had increased every year till 1990. From 1991 to August 1997, their incidence declined. However, there was an outbreak of malaria in Banaskantha, Mehsana, and Kutch districts. After August 1997, the outbreak was soon controlled (Health and Family Welfare Department 1998).

Table 12.6 : Prevalence Rates of Specific Health Problems, Gujarat

Demographic Characteristic		Persons per 1000 population suffering from					
		Blindness Parrial	Blindness Complete	Tuber-culosis	Lep-rosy	Phy-sical impair-ment of limbs	Malaria during last 3 months
Urban							
Age	0-14	1.7	5.6	0.4	—	3.8	30.4
	15-59	12.8	3.5	2.1	—	4.6	25.5
	60+	201.5	17.3	1.9	—	15.4	15.4
Sex	Male	20.5	5.6	2.1	—	4.8	22.9
	Female	25.4	4.7	0.9	—	5.6	30.1
Total		22.9	5:2	1.5	—	5.2	26.4
Rural							
Age	0-14	3.3	6.3	0.4	—	5.0	32.1
	15-59	19.5	1.0	5.4	0.4	4.8	34.5
	60+	235.5	16.6	8.3	2.8	12.9	56.3
Sex	Male	28.2	4.5	5.3	0.3	6.6	36.7
	Female	33.8	3.7	2.4	0.6	4.3	34.0
Total		31.0	4.1	3.9	0.4	5.5	35.4
All Areas							
Age	0-14	2.8	6.0	0.4	—	4.6	31.5
	15-59	17.1	1.9	4.2	0.2	4.7	31.3
	60+	224.4	16.8	6.2	1.9	13.7	43.0
Sex	Male	25.5	4.9	4.2	0.2	6.0	31.9
	Female	31.0	4.1	1.9	0.4	4.8	32.7
Total		28.2	4.5	3.1	0.3	5.4	32.3

Note: (–) blank denotes less than .05 per 1000 population.
Source: PRC and IIPS (1993), Table 8.1, p. 126.

About one-fifth of the deaths are caused due to respiratory system diseases in Gujarat and in India (Table 12.7). Senility is another major cause of death in Gujarat and in India. This disease afflicts persons of age

60 and above. Its share in the total causes of deaths has gone up over time in Gujarat till 1994, after which there is quite a decline. Fevers, which include malaria and typhoid, continue to contribute about 7 per cent of total deaths, almost the same as in India. Deaths due to disorders of the circulatory systems, such as heart attack, have declined in Gujarat from 1987 to 1992.

Table 12.7 : Distribution of Deaths by Major Cause-Groups, Gujarat and India

Cause	India	Gujarat**						
	1990*	1987	1990	1991	1992	1993	1994	1996
Coughs (Disorders of respiratory system)	18.8	23.8	19.3	20.4	21.6	19.7	19.4	23.0
Disorders of circulatory systems	11.1	11.2	9.8	8.3	9.0	10.7	9.2	10.4
Digestive disorders	6.2	4.4	3.5	3.0	2.0	2.1	3.0	4.5
Fevers	7.3	8.2	8.7	6.7	6.3	5.2	5.8	4.4
Other clear symptoms	8.5	11.1	7.9	10.1	8.0	8.6	9.3	9.6
Causes peculiar to infancy	9.8	9.8	8.9	9.1	7.7	7.3	9.1	9.4
Child birth and pregnancy	1.0	0.8	0.9	0.9	0.4	1.0	0.6	0.6
Senility	24.4	21.5	29.9	29.5	33.5	34.2	36.6	25.0
Disorders of central nervous system	4.3	3.8	3.4	4.4	3.6	3.1	3.2	3.4
Accidents and Injuries	8.5	5.4	7.7	7.6	7.9	8.1	7.8	9.7
Total	100.0	100.0	100.0	100.0	100.0	100.0	100.0	100.0

Source: *Rajan and James (1993), based on Government of India, 1990, p. 1889.
**Based on data from Commissionerate of Health, Medical Services and Medical Education.

Data is not available for all the diseases of malnutrition. However, a state government document shows that in children under the age of 5, more than 60 per cent were either moderately or severely malnourished (Table 12.8). About half of the under-5 children were in the moderate category and 12 per cent were severely malnourished. As compared to India, proportion of malnourished children was higher in Gujarat. Severe malnourishment was higher among the girls than the boys. The ICDS programme has reduced malnourishment among under-5 children to 4 per cent to 6 per cent in severe category and 25 per cent to 30 per cent in moderate category. Malnourishment is high in the tribal regions, mainly due to lack of food security and water scarcity during drought period.

Table 12.8 : Malnourished Children (1-5 Year), Gujarat and India

	Moderate (%)		Severe (%)	
	Gujarat	India	Gujarat	India
Total	50.8	45.1	11.9	11.1
Boys	54.8	45.6	9.6	11.6
Girls	45.7	44.6	14.7	10.2

Source: Government of Gujarat (1994).

Estimated 60 per cent of the pregnant women and 40 per cent of the children below 6 years of age suffer from anaemia (Government of Gujarat, 1994). Anaemia among young women is a major contributing factor to high maternal mortality. Anaemia among women is caused due to general level of malnourishment, low access to vegetables and other iron rich food, loss of blood during menstruation, worms in the digestive system due to water borne infection, frequent child births and physical stress of daily household chores.

Estimate of the vitamin A deficiency at the state level is not available. But one primary survey on blindness among children of 0-6 years, during 1986-89 period (the drought period in Gujarat), found that 7.6 per cent of children in Gujarat, 9.3 per cent in rural areas and 3.7 per cent in urban areas suffered from vitamin A deficiency. The same surv·y found that in India, these figures were only 6.0 per cent, 6.5 per cent and 9.8 per cent respectively (Government of Gujarat, 1994). Higher prevalence of vitamin A deficiency in Gujarat than in India can be due to scarcity conditions in the survey period. But it is certainly a matter of concern.

Eleven districts of the state have endemic prevalence of goitre due to iodine deficiency (Table 12.9). All but the four districts of these, namely Amreli, Mehsana, Kheda and Surendranagar have high proportion of tribal population. Three districts out of the eleven surveyed—Dangs, Valsad and Bharuch—have severe Iodine Deficiency Disorder (IDD). Dangs is a total tribal district and other two districts have high proportion of tribal population. Three other districts—Sabarkantha, Surat and Panchmahals, which also have significant proportion of tribal population—have moderate prevalence of IDD. It, therefore, appears that the tribal population in the state is still subject to undernourishment and special attention with regards to nutrition is required to improve health status of this section of Gujarat's population.

Table 12.9 : Regions of Iodine Deficiency

District	TGR * (%)	IDD Status **
Dangs	44.00	Severe
Valsad	36.59	Severe
Bharuch	31.70	Severe
Sabarkantha	25.80	Moderate
Surat	22.70	Moderate
Panchmahals	22.40	Moderate
Vadodara	16.83	Mild
Amreli	14.00	Mild
Mehsana	7.40	Mild
Kheda	6.49	Mild
Surendranagar	5.88	Mild

* TGR is the Total Goitre Rate, which is the rate of goitre prevalence among school-age children.

** IDD status classification.

Mild IDD - TGR range 5 per cent - 19.9 per cent.

Moderate IDD - TGR range 20 per cent - 29.9 per cent.

Severe IDD - TGR range > 30 per cent.

Source: Government of Gujarat (1994).

Women's health

Status of women's health is observed through female-child mortality rates, fertility rates and maternal health. The infant and child mortality rates in Gujarat, observed over time, show that in the first year of life more males died as compared to females. Then, in the age group of 0-4 years, slightly more females died than males (Table 12.10).

All the fertility rates are lower in Gujarat as compared to India. Also, there has been a decline in the fertility rates over time, as shown by the two time point data in Table 12.11. Interesting to note is that the gap between Gujarat and India has remained the same in 1986 as well as in 1993. Only in the case of GMFR, this gap has increased in 1993 as compared to 1986.

Table 12.10 : Infant and Child Mortality by Sex, Gujarat

Year	I M R[a]		Death Rate Age 0-4[b]	
	Male	Female	Male	Female
1981	114	118	—	—
1986	—	—	36.1	38.8
1991	—	—	23.1	23.5
1993	70	67	20.3	21.1

Sources : (a) Pathak and Singh (1993).
(b) Commissionerate of Health, Medical Services and Medical Education (Health), Government of Gujarat (1996).

Table 12.11: Fertility Indicators, Gujarat and India, 1986, 1993

Indicator	Gujarat		India	
	1986	1993	1986	1993
1. General Fertility Rate (GFR)	130.5	110.4	136.5	116.6
2. General Marital Fertility Rate (GMFR)	170.9	145.6	175.6	153.7
3. Total Fertility Rate (TFR)	3.8	3.2	4.2	3.5
4. Total Marital Fertility Rate (TMFR)	4.9	4.3	5.5	4.9
5. Gross Reproductive Rate	1.8	1.5	2.0	1.7
6. Mean Age of Fertility	27.4	27.0	27.7	27.4

Source : Government of India (1993), SRS Bulletin.

As per the statistics available from the State Bureau of Health Intelligence, Commissionerate of Health Medical Services and Medical Education, MMR of Gujarat was 450 per 100,000 live births in 1984 which declined to 310 in 1993 (Commissionerate of Health Medical Services and Medical Education 1996: 110). Another state government document gives the MMR as 310 per 100,000 live births in 1985 (Government of Gujarat 1994). Statewise data on the MMR from two other sources give different figures. In Drèze and Sen (1995: Table A.3) the estimated MMR (1982-86 period) was 355 in Gujarat with the state standing third among the fifteen large states. Another source (Pathak and Singh, 1993: 15) gives MMR of Gujarat as 537 per 100,000 live births between 1986-90, with Gujarat coming ninth in MMR. The last data is quite off the trend. In spite of differing estimates of MMR of different sources, it appears that maternal health has improved over time, but not as much as desired. Also, on the whole, discrimination against female child and women continue due to socio-economic conditions, which is reflected in higher death rates of female child as compared to male child.

Public Health Expenditures

The results of government's involvement in health sector are there to see in terms of gains in life expectancy and reduction in overall child and infant mortality rates in the world. Pitt (1993) quotes a World Bank (1980) study which estimates that the life expectancy in the developing countries would have been eight years less in the 1970s without the contribution of the new and inexpensive public health technologies such as vaccinations. This change has come without improvement in nutrition, hygiene, housing and income in the developing countries (Pitt, 1993: 137). In fact, in urban India, the physical conditions of living have deteriorated by all standards over time. In rural India, in spite of the problems of poverty and malnutrition the longevity has increased.

In developed countries, quite high proportion of the GDP is spent by the public sector on health. In all established market economies, 5.6 per cent of the GDP was spent by the public sector on health in 1990. In these countries, another 3.5 per cent GDP was spent by the private sector, including the household sector, taking the total expenditure on health to 9.2 per cent of the GDP. Collectively as well as individually (except the USA), the government's burden in the health sector was higher than the private burden. This was true for most Sub-Saharan African countries, Latin American, Caribbean and Middle Eastern countries and that of the former socialist block, whereas in Asian countries, except China, private sector's involvement was higher than the public sector in the healthcare system (World Bank, 1993: 210-1).

In Gujarat in the mid-eighties, about 8 per cent of the total budget were allocated to the health sector in the state (Table 12.12). By mid-nineties, the proportion came down to about 6 per cent. In the last few years, once again, there is an increase in this share, but not reaching the level that was in the mid-eighties. In terms of the proportion of NSDP, the expenditure on health sector was already very low in the eighties (2.16 per cent in 1986-87) and it has come down gradually since then. A disturbing aspect is that, as a per cent of development expenditure on the revenue as well as capital account, the allocation to health sector had declined for a decade (1987-96). In 1997-98, one can observe slight increase in the proportion of the total budget as well as NSDP spent on health.

Table 12.12 : Trends in Health Sector Expenditure in Last Decade, Gujarat

Year	Expenditure on health as % of							
	On revenue account			On capital account			Total Budget	NSDP
	Social services	Development expenditure	Revenue budget	Social services	Development expenditure	Capital Budget		
1986-87	30.7	15.9	12.1	3.9	0.8	0.3	8.0	2.16
1987-88	32.0	16.1	12.4	1.4	0.3	0.2	8.6	2.78
1988-89	28.2	14.6	10.7	1.6	0.2	0.1	7.1	1.86
1989-90	25.4	13.8	9.9	1.6	0.1	0.1	7.4	1.72
1990-91	25.5	14.2	10.0	2.8	0.2	0.2	7.2	1.70
1991-92	25.3	12.7	9.2	2.1	0.2	0.1	6.2	1.86
1992-93	22.0	10.0	7.1	2.6	0.3	0.1	5.1	1.27
1993-94	22.7	10.7	7.6	1.7	0.3	0.1	5.7	1.36
1994-95	22.7	11.4	7.9	0.8	0.2	0.1	6.2	1.15
1995-96	21.8	11.1	7.8	2.6	0.2	0.2	6.3	1.19
1996-97	22.1	10.9	7.4	3.4	0.4	0.3	5.9	1.14
1997-98	27.3	13.7	9.5	6.6	0.7	0.5	7.8	1.56
1998-99 (RE)	24.7	13.4	9.2	6.2	1.2	0.8	7.5	—
1999-2000 (BE)	25.3	14.1	9.3	7.3	1.5	1.1	7.5	—

Note : Expenditure on heads (i) health and family welfare and (ii) social welfare and nutrition considered here.

Source : Based on state annual budgets.

Concern and expenditure for health are spread across number of ministries and departments. Ideally, health sector expenditures should include five important heads: (a) medical and public health, (b) family welfare (including family planning), (c) water supply and sanitation, (d) nutrition and (e) child and handicapped welfare. Reddy and Selvaraju (1994) have done this categorisation which has been adopted for analysing healthcare expenditures.

In 1990-91, Gujarat incurred much lower per capita expenditure on health than all-India average (Table 12.13). However, if the expenditure of the union territories is excluded, the all India average came to Rs. 63.51

which is slightly higher than the Gujarat average of Rs. 52.18. Gujarat ranked third among the fifteen large states with respect to per capita expenditure on nutrition. It ranked eighth in medical and public health and water supply and sanitation aspects, and ninth in family welfare. On the whole, Gujarat ranked sixth among the fifteen large states. Tamil Nadu was at the top with per capita expenditure of Rs. 77.18 followed by Kerala, with per capita expenditure of Rs. 73.66. Gujarat incurred only 75 per cent of the per capita expenditure incurred by Tamil Nadu. The state paid highest attention to medical and public health aspects followed by water supply and sanitation. In India, family welfare received higher per capita allocation than nutrition, while in Gujarat nutrition aspect received higher per capita allocation than family welfare, which is quite a rational and balanced situation.

Table 12.13 : Healthcare Expenditure in Gujarat and India, 1990-91

Item	Gujarat (Rs.)	India (Rs.)
Per capita Health Expenditure* (total)	57.56	63.51
— medical and public health*	25.92	29.79
— family welfare*	5.16	6.40
— water supply and sanitation*	17.12	19.58
— nutrition*	7.56	4.15
— child & handicapped welfare *	1.32	3.48
Distribution of PC Health Expenditure (total) (%)	100.00	100.00
— medical and public health (%)	46.59	48.62
— family welfare (%)	8.81	9.92
— water supply and sanitation (%)	29.22	30.36
— nutrition (%)	13.55	6.75
— child & handicapped welfare (%)	1.82	4.35
Share of health care expenditure in total government expenditure (%) to total	10.38	6.47
to plan (%)	2.52	2.78
to non-plan (%)	7.86	3.69
% of domestic product to total	1.63	2.18
plan	0.40	0.94
non-plan	1.23	1.24

* at 1980-81 prices

According to Reddy and Selvaraju (1994), the expenditure on health in Gujarat was 10 per cent of the total government's expenditure on all activities in 1990-91 which was lower than that of all the state governments

(12.6 per cent of the total). Tamil Nadu, Kerala and Rajasthan had spent around 15 per cent of their annual budget on health care in this year. The low importance of health sector in Gujarat is also evident from the low share of health sector expenditure in NSDP. Only 1.63 per cent of the NSDP was spent on health in 1990-91 in the state, whereas in India, 2.18 per cent of the GDP was spent on health care[2]. This figure was 3.17 per cent in Kerala and 2.16 per cent for all the states together (Reddy and Selvaraju, 1994). When ranked for the proportion of NSDP spent on health, Gujarat ranked fourth from the bottom out of 25 states and union territories in 1990-91. The high NSDP of Gujarat has not resulted in high government spending on health in the state, perhaps because of the lack of required political commitment. May be, position of Gujarat would have improved in the recent years due to significant increase in expenditure on health sector as discussed above.

In real terms, per capita expenditure on health by Government of Gujarat (GoG) has increased by 60 per cent from 1974-75 to 1990-91[3]. But this increase is much lower than the increase at all India level (98 per cent). Highest increase is in the nutrition sector (1624 per cent), allocation to which increased drastically from 1982-83 onwards. In 1974-75 the per capita expenditure on nutrition was only Rs. 0.44 (1980-81 prices). Allocations for medical and public health increased by 26 per cent, for family welfare by 86 per cent, for water supply and sanitation by 52 per cent and for child and handicapped welfare by 101 per cent. At all India level, allocation to nutrition increased by 501 per cent, towards medical and public health by 42 per cent, for family welfare by 150 per cent, for water supply and sanitation by 166 per cent and for child and handicapped welfare by 596 per cent. It can be seen that emphasis at different state levels and at all India level with respect to components of healthcare is quite different. On the whole, the real total per capita expenditure on health has increased in the state, from 1974-75 onwards. Sharp increase came in the early eighties when expenditure on water supply and sanitation and nutrition increased sharply. This analysis has its limitation as it stops at 1990-91.

Health Facilities and Their Utilisation

As compared to India, Gujarat has much higher level of health facilities (Table 12.14). That is because of urban Gujarat where the level of facilities is quite high. Number of hospitals and dispensaries per lakh population in Gujarat is more than three times that in India. But the difference between

Gujarat and India is not high when sub-centres, beds per lakh population and doctors and nurses per lakh population are considered. With respect to Primary Health Centres (PHCs), Gujarat's performance is lower than that of India. This shows that with respect to high order health facilities, Gujarat's performance is better. High order health facilities are, however, generally located in the urban areas and the low order health facilities, such as the PHCs, sub-centres, etc. are in the rural areas, where the state's relative performance is poor.

Urban-rural difference in high order health facilities is very high in Gujarat as compared to India. For example, in terms of hospitals, urban areas had 16 times higher facilities than rural areas in Gujarat. In India this difference was only 6 times. However, with respect to beds per lakh population, urban-rural difference was 11 in Gujarat as well as in India.

Table 12.14 : Health Facilities in Gujarat and India, 1991

Facilities per lakh population		Gujarat	India
Hospitals	– Total	4.34	1.32
	– Rural	0.70	0.57
	– Urban	11.26	3.51
Dispensaries	– Total	15.22	3.25
	– Rural	9.33	1.86
	– Urban	17.78	5.38
Primary Health Centre's		3.24	3.55
Sub-Centre's		26.41	20.90
Beds	– Total	145.76	78.70
	– Rural	31.34	22.26
	– Urban	363.95	241.96
Doctors		52.98	47.19
Nurses		59.00	36.88

Source : Based on Duggal *et al.* (1995).

Public health facilities in the urban areas are at the initiative of the local bodies, mainly the municipal corporations and municipalities, which incur expenditure on healthcare system from their own funds. For example, Ahmedabad Municipal Corporation runs three general hospitals, 13 maternity hospitals, 25 dispensaries, 5 referral hospitals, one eye hospital, 2 TB clinics, 4 dental clinics and one contagious disease hospital[4]. Employees State Insurance Scheme (ESIS) for the industrial workers also runs three general hospitals and 49 dispensaries. But given that the state is expected to rapidly urbanise and the municipal corporations may not be able to raise funds to meet healthcare demands of the increasing population, state government will have to make budgetary allocation for the urban sector, which is not much at the moment.

With respect to PHCs, Gujarat was tenth among fifteen large states. Nevertheless, with respect to SCs (Sub-centres) Gujarat was first. In terms of doctors and nurses per lakh population, Gujarat was seventh and fifth respectively in 1991 (Based on Duggal, *et al.* 1995). Thus with respect to healthcare infrastructure, Gujarat's performance is fluctuating. Table 12.15 shows that since the seventh plan there is significant increase in number of rural health facilities in the state.

Table 12.15: Development of Health Facilities in Gujarat

Plan	Period	Number of		
		Sub-Centres	PHCs	CHCs
I Plan	1951-56	67	6	—
II Plan	1956-61	288	96	—
III Plan	1961-66	686	142	—
Annual Plan	1966-67	1232	244	—
"	1967-68	1432	244	—
"	1968-69	1780	251	—
IV Plan	1969-74	1920	251	—
V Plan	1974-79	1920	251	12
Annual Plan	1978-79	1920	251	12
"	1979-80	2020	251	17
VI Plan	1980-85	4951	310	47
VII Plan	1985-90	6834	993	161
Annual Plan	1990-91	7132	993	176
"	1991-92	7274	993	180
VIII Plan	1992-97	7274	993	193
IX Plan – 1st yr.	1997-98	7274	993	207

Source: Health and Family Welfare Department (1998).

While the healthcare facilities are at medium level, their utilisation is low. A survey by the National Council for Applied Economic Research (NCAER) conducted in 1994 showed that the dependence of people on private facilities was higher than that on public facilities in rural as well as urban areas, and for both the males and females (Table 12.16). Dependence on private sector for hospitalisation cases is a point to be noted, which is contrary to all India trend and general understanding about the utilisation of healthcare facilities. Hospitalisation involves higher expenditure than out-door treatment. It is expected that people would depend on public facilities for prolonged treatment of chronic illnesses and hospitalisation, which are expensive in private hospitals. Whereas for out-door treatment, time is an important factor. Long waiting, non-availability of medical staff on time and non-availability of quick treatment in government hospitals and dispensaries discourage the outpatients, who turn to private sector. In Gujarat, probably, there are large number of charitable trust hospitals providing hospitalisation at reasonable prices, which makes them popular than government hospitals for in-patient treatment.

Table 12.16 : Utilisation of Health Facilities, Gujarat and India (NCAER data)

		Gujarat		India	
		Public	Private	Public	Private
Out Patient Treatment					
Rural	Male	36.8	62.2	40.2	54.5
	Female	36.7	59.8	43.3	50.8
Urban	Male	38.7	57.7	34.7	58.9
	Female	31.6	63.2	33.2	60.9
Hospitalisation					
	Rural	32.2	67.8	62.0	38.0
	Urban	27.2	72.8	60.1	39.9

Source: Based on Sundar (1995).

An earlier survey by the National Sample Survey (NSS) in 1986-87 gives contrary picture. It shows better utilisation of public facilities for hospitalisation cases in rural as well as urban areas (Table 12.17). Of the hospitalisation cases, about 56 per cent in the rural areas and 62 per cent in the urban areas were in the public hospitals. With the increase in income, the extent of dependence on the public facilities for hospitalisation has declined. The pattern emerging from the NSS data is in consonance with all-India trend and general understanding.

The share of private sector in treating patients outside the hospital was 65 per cent in rural and 80 per cent in the urban areas (Visaria and Gumber, 1994: 135), which is closer to the NCAER trend for the rural areas.

Table 12.17 : Utilization of Public Facilities, Gujarat (NSS Data)

Expenditure	Out patient treatment of						Hospitalised Classes	
Classes	TB		Malaria		Dysentery			
	Rural	Urban	Rural	Urban	Rural	Urban	Rural	Urban
All	55.3	39.8	39.1	20.3	41.3	19.0	56.0	61.8
I	74.9	100.0	48.1	28.5	48.0	2.1	71.5	74.5
II	67.2	3.7	47.0	24.0	43.4	0.0	63.9	67.1
III	51.2	37.0	38.7	15.1	33.7	50.0	63.9	67.1
IV	44.9	100.0	25.7	21.6	49.3	64.4	45.2	55.0
V	30.7	72.6	39.0	10.8	23.6	100.0	39.9	51.7

Source: World Bank (1994), based on NSS data.

In the rural areas, even for non-hospitalised cases, poor households depended greatly on the public facilities than the non-poor households. This was observed for cases of TB, malaria and dysentery. However, in the urban areas, the dependence of the highest quintile of the expenditure classes, on public outpatient treatment was the highest. This may be because of the acceptable level of public health facilities for the treatment of non-hospitalised illnesses. For the inpatient care, the use of public hospitals is high. About 60 per cent of hospital treatment of illnesses in urban areas and about 55 per cent of the same in rural areas depended on public facilities. The public sector hospitals are also well targeted towards the poor, more so in rural than in urban areas. Utilisation of non-governmental care for hospitalised cases increases with the income, in rural as well as the urban areas (Visaria and Gumber, 1994). Still, significant proportion of population has been using private healthcare facilities in the state.

Towards Health for All?

Having analysed the overall trends in health status and public health care intervention in Gujarat, is it possible to conclude whether health for all is achievable soon? Is our understanding of how to achieve that goal adequate and have we done enough to move towards that goal? To be able to answer these questions, we can start addressing the questions in reverse order.

First question is regarding what have been the achievements. Clearly, one can observe that the key health statistics have significantly improved in Gujarat over time, the state improving its performance *vis-à-vis* India. Public expenditure on healthcare has also improved over time, and more so since the mid-nineties with increase in overall awareness about health as an important development issue. However, Gujarat is, strikingly, quite behind Kerala, which has lower per capita income and higher incidence of poverty than Gujarat. Also, though the state has better performance in key health statistics, it comes in the middle order among the states in India. The overall improvement in the health statistics is because of significant improvement in rural areas, while urban areas remain a matter of concern and future policy interventions. Key health statistics have improved because of reduction in CBR and IMR (also reflecting in CDR), indicating reduced fertility and improvement in maternal and child health. Especially progress in reducing PNNM and NNM are noteworthy. This says a lot about the success of immunisation as well as nutrition programmes for mothers and infants in the state. In short, public health intervention towards improving maternal and child health and reducing fertility rates have been successful, especially where required, that is in rural areas.

There are some paradoxes with regards to health situation in the state. On the whole, the state did not fare that well among the states in India with respect to lower order health facilities such as PHCs and sub-centres, which are meant for the rural areas. In spite of that, the rural health statistics have improved. On the other hand, in the urban areas, where the state tops the rank with regards to high order health facilities, the improvement in key health statistics has slowed down. The PRC and IIPS survey shows a reversal of trends in infant and child health in the urban areas in the mid-nineties. Nonetheless, urban areas have better performance in key health indicators than the rural areas. Much detailed investigation is required to understand whether slowing down of improvement in CBR, CDR and IMR in the urban areas is because of increasing exposure of urban residents to environmental pollution or lack of public healthcare system in the cities. As mentioned earlier, public health facilities are run in the urban areas with the funds of the urban local bodies. Health department budget is largely tied to providing rural facilities. The provision of urban public health facilities will, therefore, fluctuate greatly with the fortune of the urban local bodies, many of them, especially in the small and medium towns, are in dire financial conditions. The state government should think of a special cell in the health department to take care of urban health facilities and make funds directly available to the urban local bodies to set up new facilities and run the existing ones.

Another peculiarity of the state is that dependence on private healthcare is quite high, even among the lower expenditure classes and rural areas, especially for outdoor treatment. This suggests that public facilities are being utilised for maternal and child healthcare programmes, especially immunisation programmes, whereas private facilities are being utilised for treatement. Also, in spite of rapid economic growth observed in the state since its formation in 1960, the diseases of poverty continue to have high prevalence. This paradox is observed because of the paradox in the development process of the state itself. There is high inequality in terms of economic and social development aspects between the industrialised and non-industrialised regions and tribal and non-tribal regions of the state (Mahadevia, 1998a). As observed earlier, diseases of poverty, such as goitre, has high prevalence rate in the tribal regions. These paradoxes observed in the area of health need to be investigated seriously and attention paid to for improving the overall performance of the state atleast with regards to key health statistics.

The health area that requires changing the mind set is regarding women's health. Women's health has to be improved not only to ensure better health and survival of children and reduction of population growth rates but also for women themselves and improve overall health status of the society. Till now, women's health has been only viewed from the perspective of maternal health through immunisation and family planning programmes. Women constitute half the population. In Gujarat, as observed, health of female child is neglected, which is reflected in high mortality rate among the female child as compared to male. In other words, socio-cultural change is required to approach women's health as their basic rights and improve their overall health. First step towards that is increasing female literacy. In 1991, only one-third of rural women and two-fifths of all the women were literate in Gujarat. Improvement in female literacy will also significantly reduce fertility and infant mortality rates. Thus, there is a long way to go in ensuring health for all women.

As compared to India, the state has higher level of health facilities, in spite of the fact that the budgetary allocation to health sector continuously declined for over a decade from mid-eighties onwards. For ensuring health for all, it is necessary that utilisation of public healthcare facilities improves. For this, the quality of public health facilities needs to be improved. For this, a new experiment of participation of non-governmental organisations (NGOs) in running public facilities has been initiated. However, these are, at best at the pilot level. These experiments have to be either scaled up or the government on its own initiative has to improve the quality of public facilities.

Health is a broad concept and the health status is a function of large number of factors, besides expenditure by government on public facilities. Industrialisation, urbanisation and economic growth are expected to improve health status. That does not happen automatically can be observed from the case of Gujarat. While Kerala is far behind Gujarat in terms of these three dimensions of development, it is far ahead of Gujarat with respect to the health status.

An emerging area of concern for health professionals is environmental health. First of all, Gujarat faces the problem of ground water in quantitative as well as qualitative terms. Excessive salinity, excessive fluoride and excessive nitrite (Hirway and Patel, 1994 and Mahadevia, 1998b) are responsible for several diseases like fluorosis, leprosy, trachoma and conjunctivitis. Leprosy and scabies are very common in Gujarat. Conjunctivitis erupts during certain seasons. Untreated drinking water in the rural areas also cause water-borne diseases such as amoebic and bacillary dysentery, cholera, diarrhoea, hepatitis, typhoid and guinea worm. These are diseases of poverty, long ago controlled in the developed countries. Industrialisation in Gujarat is based on only single industry group, chemicals and petrochemical units. As per one survey of medium and large industries in Gujarat by the Central Pollution Control Board (CPCB, 1994), 40 per cent to 50 per cent of the medium and large industries in the state came under the list of water polluting units. Around 50 per cent of the units and 84 per cent of the investment in the census sector industries in Gujarat in 1992-93 was in the industries that came under the category of polluting industries (Mahadevia, 1998b). Many of the chemicals used or produced in the state are hazardous. The inputs and by-products of petrochemical industries are non-degradable organic compounds, which are carcinogenic (Greenpeace, 1996). Health impacts of chemical pollution have not yet been investigated, which need to be taken seriously.

The issues discussed above, which emanate from the biased or lopsided development process of the state, are outside the purview of the health department. While these issues are understood and addressed, it is high time that health is viewed in relation to the overall growth process of Gujarat to make health for all a reality in near future. It would require changes in the socio-cultural, economic and political structure and a system that considers prevention as important as cure. A development path is required that is equitous and respects basic rights of all including that of the minorities and other weaker sections, is participative, and does not equate development with consumption (over consumption, alcoholism, etc.). For that to happen the state economy should be free of debt and should not be pressurised to pursue unsustainable development path. And above all, there has to be a political will to pursue a development path that is human-centred and not economic growth centred alone.

NOTES

1. Unsafe drinking water and non-availability of sanitation facilities create disorders of the digestive system, which can lead to chronic indigestion and thus malnutrition. This is called 'nutrition leakage'. If healthcare facilities to treat these disorders do not exist then there can be chronic nutrition problem.
2. These figures do not tally with the figures in Table 12.12 because the latter includes expenditure on only two aspects of health system.
3. Data on increase in allocations are from Reddy and Selvaraju (1994).
4. Based on the data from the municipal corporation.

REFERENCES

Ali, Almas (1992), *Nutrition*, in Voluntary Health Association of India (ed.) State of India's Health, VHAI, New Delhi, pp. 1-50.

Commissionerate of Health, Medical Services and Medical Education (1996), *Health Information of Gujarat, 1996*, State Bureau of Health Intelligence, Government of Gujarat, Gandhinagar.

Central Pollution Control Board (1994), *Inventory of Large & Medium Water Polluting Industries, Volume II (Gujarat)*, CPCB, Delhi.

Department of Health and Family Welfare (1998), *Year Book 1995-96*, Ministry of Health and Family Welfare, Government of India, New Delhi.

Duggal, Ravi, Sunil Nandraj and Asha Vadair (1995), "Health Expenditures Across States - Part I and II", *Economic and Political Weekly*, 30(15 & 16), pp. 834-44 and 901-8.

Drèze, J. and Sen, A.K. (1995, *India: Economic Development and Social Opportunity,* Oxford University Press, New Delhi.

Environment (1988), "Monitoring the Global Environment: An Assessment of Urban Air Quality", *Environment*, 31(8), pp. 6-13 and 26-37.

Government of Gujarat (1994), "State Programme of Action for the Child in Gujart", GoG, Gandhinagar.

Government of India (1997), "Women in India: A Statistical Profile", Department of Education, Ministry of Human Resource Development, New Delhi.

Gowarikar, Vasant (1994), "Demographic Transition in India", *Economic and Political Weekly*, 29(49), pp. 3106-8.

Greenpeace (1996), *The Stranger*, Greenpeace, New Delhi.

Hema, R. and Muraleedharan, V.R. (1993), "Health and Human Resources Development", *Economic and Political Weekly*, 28(43), pp.2328-30.

Hirway, I. and Patel, P. P. (1994), *Dynamics of Drinking Water Problem in Rural Gujarat*, Centre for Water Resources, Utthan, Ahmedabad

Mahadevia, Darshini (1998a), *Development Dichotomy in Gujarat*, Research Foundation for Science Technology and Ecology, New Delhi.

Mahadevia, Darshini (1998b), *Economic Growth and Environmental Degradation: Case of Gujarat*, Research Foundation for Science Technology and Ecology, New Delhi.

Murthi, Mamta, Anne-Catherine Guio and Jean Drèze (1995), *Mortality, Fertility and Gender Bias in India: A District Level Analysis*, The Development Economics Research Programme, No. 61, London School of Economics.

National Council of Applied Economic Research (1992), *Household Survey of Medical Care*, NCAER, New Delhi.

Nutritional Foundation of India (1983), Scientific Report 1, The National Goitre Control Programme - Blueprint for its Intensification, NFI, New Delhi.

Pathak, K.B. and Singh, B.S. (1993), "Adolescent Motherhood and Maternal Mortality in India", in K.B. Pathak and U.P. Sinha (eds.), *Dynamics of Population and Family Welfare*, Himalaya Publishing House, Bombay.

Pitt, Mark (1993), "Analyzing Human Resource Effects: Health", in Lionel Demery, Marco Ferroni, Christiaan Grootaert with Jorge Wong-Valle (eds.), *Understanding the Social Effects of Policy Reform,* The World Bank, Washington DC, pp. 137-54.

Population Research Centre and International Institute of Population Sciences (1993), *National Family Health Survey - Gujarat,* PRC and IIPS, Bombay.

Population Research Centre and International Institute of Population Sciences (1994), *National Family Health Survey,* PRC and IIPS, Bombay.

Rajan, Irudaya, S. and James, K.S. (1993), "Kerala's Health Status: Some Issues", *Economic and Political Weekly*, 28(36), pp. 1889-92.

Reddy, K.N. and Selvaraju, V. (1994), *Health Care Expenditure by Government in India, 1974-75 to 1990-91*, Seven Hills Publication, New Delhi.

Sen, Amartya (1985), "The Standard of Living: Lecture II, Lives and Capabilities", in Geoffrey Hawthorn (ed.) *The Standard of Living*, Cambridge University

Press, Cambridge, New York, New Rochelle, Melbourne, Sydney, pp. 20-38.

Sundar, Ramamani (1995), "Household Survey of Health Care Utilisation and Expenditure", Working Paper No. 53, National Council of Applied Economic Research, New Delhi.

Tejada-de-Rivero, David (1981), "Primary Health Care - World Strategy", Keynote address at the third international congress on Primary Health Care: World Strategy, (Feb. 23-26), organised by the World Federation of Public Health Association and Indian Public Health Association, Calcutta.

Visaria, Pravin and Gumber, Anil (1994), "Utilization of and Expenditures on Health Care in India, 1986-87", Gujarat Institute of Development Research, Ahmedabad.

Visaria, Pravin and Visaria, Leela (1994), "Demographic Transition - Accelerating Fertility Decline in 1980s", *Economic and Political Weekly*, 29(51/52), pp. 3281-92.

The World Bank (1980), *Poverty and Human Development*, Oxford University Press, New York.

The World Bank (1993), *World Development Report, 1993*, for the World Bank, Oxford University Press, New York.

The World Bank (1994), *India, Policy and Finance Strategies for Strenghtening Primary Health Care Services*, South Asia Country Department II, Population and Human Resources Operations Division, The World Bank, Washington DC.

13

The Cultural Context of Development in Gujarat

VIDYUT JOSHI

Introduction

The paper seeks to point out 'non-economic' dimension of development in Gujarat. The idea is to shift the concentration of development argument away from the narrow confines of economic inputs and outputs. As Dreze and Sen (1998:2) put it : "....there must be an attempt to link the strategies of development to something more fundamental, in particular, the ends of economic and social development.... It is only with an explicit recognition of the basic ends that debates on means and strategies can be adequately founded."

The meaning of 'development' has shifted from economic development to human development. Now we prepare human development indicators, which go much beyond market indicators or input-output indicators. Recent trend is to define human development as the process of "enlarging people's choices" (UNDP: HDR. P.III). It is now believed that need is not so much for more consumption or less, but for a different pattern of consumption. This argument has emerged because of growing concern for environment and sustainable development. Now, this 'different pattern' or 'people 's choices' are not reflected in the objective indicators of human development.

This new orientation in the development debate creates confusion. On the one hand, we say that the "more conventional criteria of economic success (such as high growth rate, a sound balance of payment and so forth) are to be valued only as means to deeper ends" (Dreze & Sen, 1998:6). This means that end of any development is people themselves. Now all development indicators (including human development indicators) are collected and maintained according to administrative and economic units. Most of our discussions on development is also centred around such units. Thus, our concept has been shifted from "growth" to "people", but our methods have not changed.

When we talk of ends, we generally mean deeper cultural roots of people that influence their development or lack of it. Development is a process of unfolding people's capabilities, which would result into "increase in creativity and decline in entropy or extent of criminality, which is possible, only when a holistic and symbiotic process of social transformation could be ensured" (Kashyap, 1998:30).

Let me elaborate this unfolding or creativity part of development. 'Work', in fact, has two aspects or values, viz. the instrumental or the economic value and aesthetic or expressive value. If we put emphasis only on instrumental value, the real 'development', as against 'envelopment', or the unfolding of human potential part cannot be explained. All our development indicators, including human development indicators, describe the instrumental part or the external input part. Also, these indicators do not explain differences in development within same policy framework.

The Cultural Area Context

The objective indicators, now known as human development indicators, are not absolute. They are to be seen in relation to a culture area. Within a broad system of culture, there are "regional cultural formations including languages, literatures and lifestyles... the systems have acquired an autonomy of their own" (Singh, : 1987, p.22). A geographical unit may become a culture area in "which characteristic culture patterns are recognizable through repeated associations of specific traits and, usually, through one or more modes of subsistence that are related to the particular environment. As one formulation within the general school of historical particularism, that has developed in anthropology in the United States, the concept of culture area reflects the theoretical position that each culture, on whatever level it may be analyzed, must be examined with regard to its own history and also with regard to the general principles of independent invention, culture borrowing and cultural integration.

Although many factors at the base of any recognizable culture area are ecological in nature, the culture-area concept is one that conforms to the doctrine of limited possibilities rather than to a simple geographic determinism. Viewed in this light and assessed according to the size and character of the geographic units and the degree of complexity of cultural similarities within, and differences between, the units, the culture-area concept takes shape as a classificatory device of marked utility in describing the cultural regions" (*Ency. of Soci. Sci.* 563-4).

Gujarat, within a broad framework of national-Indian-culture is a regional culture area having its own language, lifestyle and literature. Gujarat is generally known as a prosperous, progressive and peaceful state. Gujaratis are known as peaceful people (Shantibhai). In any new investment issue, forty per cent investment is by Gujaratis. Gujarat stands first in new industrial investment plans with a total reaching to Rs. 1.20 lac crores. It is also highly urbanised state. Gujaratis are also known as best entrepreneurs in India, and next only to Jews in the world. One will find Gujaratis in any corner of the world doing some business. Gujarat and Gujaratis are also known as more westernised and modernised than the rest of India and Indians.

Three Sub-Culture Areas

This sort of stereotype of Gujarat and Gujaratis is not true for whole of Gujarat and Gujaratis. For the purpose of better understanding of Gujarat, the region can be divided into three sub-culture areas (Tables 13.1 & 13.2): (1) Plain belt of Central Gujarat, (2) Western Peninsular zone of Saurashtra and Kutch and (3) Eastern belt of hills and forests. Our contention is that all the three areas are different land systems in the past. These differences have shaped different sub-cultures within a broader framework of regional culture of Gujarat, and the sub-cultural traits have facilitated or restricted development potential of people. This context must be kept in mind when we view statistical indicators.

The Central Belt

The central or the plain belt of Gujarat stretches from Palanpur in the north to Vapi in the south on rail and road corridor. It comprises of Banaskantha, Mehsana, Sabarkantha (west), Gandhinagar, Ahmedabad (except Viramgam and Dhandhuka talukas), Kheda, Vadodara (west), Bharuch (west), Surat

Table 13.1 : Regionwise Area

(Sq. Kilometre)

Western Penisula	Area	% TO ZONE	% TO STATE
Jamnagar	10101.69	12.47	5.94
Rajkot	11165.24	13.78	6.57
Surendranagar	10440.27	12.89	6.14
Bhavnagar	9149.78	11.29	5.38
Amreli	6738.53	8.32	3.97
Junagadh	9549.85	11.79	5.62
Kutch	19479.02	24.04	11.46
Ahmedabad (Viramgam & Dhandhuka)	4397.09	5.43	2.59
Cental Belt	**81021.47**	**100.00**	**47.68**
Banaskantha	21309.50	35.83	12.54
Sabarkantha-part	4614.63	7.76	2.72
Mehsana	8993.88	15.12	5.29
Ahmedabad	4105.99	6.90	2.42
Kheda	6916.35	11.63	4.07
Vadodara-part	4406.43	7.41	2.59
Bharuch-part	3554.00	5.98	2.09
Surat-part	1315.00	2.21	0.77
Valsad-part	756.30	1.27	0.45
Gandhinagar	649.00	1.09	0.38
Panchmahal-part	2851.47	4.79	1.68
Eastern-Tribal Belt	**59472.57**	**100.00**	**35.00**
(32 tribal talukas)			
Sabarkantha-part	2645.00	8.99	1.56
Vadodara-part	3387.00	11.51	1.99
Bharuch-part	4209.00	14.30	2.48
Surat-part	6136.00	20.85	3.61
Valsad-part	4379.00	14.88	2.58
Panchmahals-part	5838.00	19.84	3.44
Dangs	1764.00	5.99	1.04
Banaskantha-part	1071.00	3.64	0.63
	29429.00	**100.00**	**17.32**
Total	**169923.00**		**100.00**

Source: Govt. of Gujarat, Tribal Development in Gujarat, 1995, Census 1991.

Table 13.2 : A Comparative View of Three Regions

		Saurashtra & Kutch	Central Belt	Eastern Belt
1.	Area	Jamnagar, Rajkot Bhavnagar, Porbandar, Junagarh, Amreli Surendra Nagar & Kutch distts. & Viramgam & Dhandhuka talukas of Ahmedabad districts.	Banaskantha, Mehsana, Gandhinagar, Sabarkantha (west), Ahmedabad Kheda, Vadodara (west), Bharuch (west), Surat (west), Valsad (west), district.	32 tribal talukas in Sabarkantha, Panchmahals, Vadodara, Bharuch, Narmada, Surat, Navsari, Valsad and Dangs distts. and some pockets.
2.	Terrain	Mostly plain	Plain	Undulating
3.	Landholding system (prior to indepen-dence)	Zamindari (Girasdari, Barkhalidari & Inamdari)	Ryotwari	Community-ownership
4.	Political system (Prior to indepen-dence)	202 feudal states	Some kingdoms and British Rule	Some kingdoms and tribal chiefs under British Tutelage
5.	Dominant Value	Conflict	Co-operation	Subjugation
6.	Political culture	Semi-feudal	Democratic	Semi-tribal
7.	View on human nature	Godly, saintly humanitarian	Interests & goals—means relationship	Reform
8.	Social Organisation	Charity oriented	Development oriented	Liberation Oriented

(west) and Valsad (west) districts. This part of the state had some princely states and British rule. The landholding system in this belt is *Ryotwari* since Mughal period, where the cultivator was the owner and he was paying revenue directly to the state. There was no intermediate authority between him and the state. There was no authority above him in the village and he was an independent decision-maker as far as his agriculture was concerned. This autonomy provided him chance to take decisions for his own development interest. This autonomy, aided by facilitating external factors, led to their agricultural development. Not only it led to an individual's development, it provided ground for people of similar interests to come together to form interest groups. AMUL (Anand Milk Union Ltd.) is a glaring example of farmers coming togather, in form of milk cooperatives, to further their interests (Hardiman, 1981:262). This sort of forming of milk cooperatives has taken place in entire belt (Hirway and Mahadevia, 1998, 24). It was the spirit of cooperation among farmers of this belt which has unfolded in form of successful cooperative venture and they could exercise their might in right type of political climate. Since most of the farmers had actively taken part in nationalist movement in form of Kheda satyagrah, Borsad satyagrah (Hardiman, 1981) and Bardoli satyagrah (Mehta, 1984), they not only developed democratic ethos, but also became dominant pressure group to turn development plans to their benefits. The locations of Ukai, Kadana and other dams gave benefits of green revolution and resultant shift of farmers to business and industry in this belt. In fact, all major industries of Gujarat are located in 402450 sq.kms. strip between Mehsana in the north and Umbergon in the south. This belt has come to be known as golden corridor of industrial development. The overconcentration of industries in this area has reached to a point of saturation and it is becoming economically unviable for a big new enterprise to be located here. This belt of central and south Gujarat attracted more than 92 per cent of the industrial investments in large medium industries in eighties (Hirway and Mahadevia, 1998: 32). Even after saturation in post reform (1991) period, it has received 70 per cent of the total industrial investment.

Three biggest cities of Gujarat (Ahmedabad, Surat and Vadodara) are located in this belt. This belt has also witnessed highest level of urbanisation. This corridor is also known as rail and road corridor as national highway no. 8 and Bombay-Ahmedabad and Bombay-Delhi lines are located in this corridor. Only Banaskantha in the north is not a developed part in this belt. This is not because of lack of conducive culture. Once upon a time, prior to green revolution, all merchants dealing in precious items like diamond, jewellery and precious stones were settled in and around Palanpur, the district headquarter of B.K. district. But because of paucity of irrigation, the fruits of green revolution did not reach this district. All enterprising traders migrated to Mumbai and Surat.

The stereotypes of Gujarat and Gujarati ethos are found in this belt. A progressive farmer, who is independent to take his own development decisions in a village community, invests agricultural surplus in business and industry. Sense of cooperation for furthering their economic interests is more powerful among these farmers. Many a times, this cooperation is on caste line. Caste associations and other such social organisations are development oriented. They developed many institutions also. Out of ten universities in Gujarat, seven are located in this belt, three are located in Saurashtra and none in tribal belt. There are around thirty research institutes in Gujarat. Except one, (CSMCRI of Bhavnagar), all research institutes are located in this belt. There are more NGOs in this belt and Gujarat is known for its NGOs. Almost all of them are development oriented NGOs. The specific term used for them is 'rachnatmak' (constructive) institutions.

Saurashtra and Kutch

Most parts of Saurashtra and Kutch had zamindari system. There were three different forms: Girasdari, Barkhalidari and Inamdari. Girasdari means land or villages given to relatives, generally younger borthers of kings. These garasiyas became feudal lords in Girasdari villages. Inamdari means land or villages given for showing valour in battles or for maintaining religious organisations. Barkhalidari means land given to Brahmins or administrators as a reward to the service rendered to the kingdom. In 1956 land reforms on the line of land to the tillers were brought in Saurashtra and Kutch (Misra, 1964) and all these three systems were legally abolished.

Prior to these land reforms Girasdars, Inamdars and some Barkhslidars—the feudal lords—were owners of these lands. This feudal system, which had divided Saurashtra in 202 independent states and many feudatories, was legally abolished. However, the cultural change takes some time. So, for quite á long time the semi feudal culture and relations persisted in Saurashtra and Kutch. The eulogisation of this cultural traditions by folklorists and pseudo folklorists fecilitated this hangover. Even eminent writers like Meghani could not avoid this. In many populist ways, these feudal values still survive in Saurashtra and Kutch.

The dominant caste in central belt is Patidar, popularly known as Patel. The Kshatriyas are lower to Patel in caste hierarchy in central belt, whereas in Saurashtra and Kutch, the reverse is true. The tiller was a tenant, who was generally a Patel, under a feudal lord in a village where the lord was dictating terms to all tenants in a village. The tenants had to give to the feudal lord half of whatever portion of the produce as decided by the lord. This did not allow autonomy on part of tenants to take their development decisions. Moreover, the tenants had to perform 'veth' (unpaid - forced labour) for the lord as and when required by him (Joshi, Vidyut, 1986). This created subjugation of majority producers to one single non-producer, giving primacy to non-protestant or catholic ethos in Weberian term. As there was ruler-subject relationship between lord and tenant, there was a relationship of conflict between two feudal lords. In a non-productive ethos, if a feudal lord wanted to rise or achieve, the only way for him was to enter into feud and confiscate feudatory of a weaker feudal lord. It is because of this that entire history of Saurashtra and Kutch is full of such feuds and battles valour and conflict have become cherished values. The folklore and folktales are full of eulogisation of such values. If a man dies in a battle, he is remembered by many and prayers are offered to his memories. Not only that son of such a man vows to take revenge. Familial revenge is also considered to be a cherished value.

In such a semi-feudal society, there are only two types of relationships. Either one is a friend or he is a foe. If one is friend, he is supposed to help a friend, irrespective of the nature of help. It could be even illegal act. If one does not grant request for help, the relationship immediately turns into a conflict relationship.

It is not that development efforts were not made in Saurashtra. Prior to independence the Maharaja of Bhavnagar provided land for establishing a university. But it could come up only in 1978. A fine railway network was established prior to independence and it was duly linked with ports, but this infrastructure did not help development of industries in this region. Efforts were also made to establish milk cooperatives in all districts. But they failed for want of co-operative spirit and the government bureaucracy in form of Gujarat Dairy Development Corporation ran all the milk dairies in Saurashtra. Dr. Kurien has a name in cooperative movement. At one point of time the government thought of establishing oil cooperatives. It should be remembered that oil lobby is a very powerful lobby of Saurashtra oil merchants. The task of establishing oil cooperatives was given to the National Dairy Development Board under the tutelage of Dr. Kurien. GROFEDs (Groundnut Growers' Federations) were established in each district. They worked for cooperativising groundnut oil business. Somehow, the structures could not work and there were representations by GROFED staff that they had not got their salaries for more than 8 months. There are many studies about the success of AMUL and operation flood, but there is no study on failure of milk and oil cooperative structures in Saurashtra. The Cooperative Act is the same, the cooperative department's rules and bylaws are also the same, the political will at state level is same, the same works wonder in the central belt, whereas they could not gain ground in Saurashtra.

The author has some experience in forming onion growers' federation in Saurashtra. With sufficient groundwork, first meeting of onion grower farmers was organised at Talaja, the taluka headquarter in Bhavnagar district. Only two farmers came. Their leaders, who were contacted personally, did not come. When further probe was made, it was revealed that they were threatened by ex-feudal elements to face dire consequences if they attend Talaja meeting. Having heard, these two actions were taken. Another meeting was arranged in Sartanpar, a coastal village with only Koli population, and we employed a Paleval Brahmin boy for our work. Palevals are well known in this area for countering the influence of ex-feudal elements. After a long struggle we could form 22 onion growers' cooperatives. Now there is an Onion Gorwers' Federation. But this could be done with great efforts in 1988. Prior to 1980, even a counter cultural strategy would not have worked.

It is the case of NGOs of Saurashtra and Kutch. All the well-known NGOs of Saurashtra and Kutch are charity organisations. Most of them have religoius base. The very concept is this that poor, downtrodden and marginalised people need charity in form of food (sadavrat), work (lowly paid works to sustain life), health and the like. The local words used for such NGOs are 'Dharmada Sanstha'. The value here is sustenance of life at low level and to make them dependent on 'dharmada'. The value of development of human beings as independent citizens do not exist here. In fact, the very concept of citizen is an obedient subject. During my tenure at Bhavnagar University I have seen that teachers treat obedient students as good students and those who raise questions or challenge them are considered as spoiled ones. Educationists and 'Kathakar Bapus' are worried about this sort of students' unrest.

This reminds me of another cultural aspect of Saurashtra. Almost all epic-story tellers (Kathakar Bapus) are from Saurashtra. They are revivalists and they preach to bring the 'satyug' back and want to preserve old values. Morari Bapu, Chote Morari Bapu, Sitaram Bapu and dozens of such Bapus are very good communicators. Then there are folksingers and folklorists. All these people want to preserve semi-feudal Saurashtra culture. All these people are known as good (catholic) men and they have moral authority and influence on Saurashtra and Kutch.

Recently, there are symptoms of change in this sort of semi-feudal culture. Swadhyaya Movement, led by Shri Pandurang Athavale, has made an impact mainly on the lower middle and lower class people on coastal belt of Saurashtra (Sheth and Shah: 1998: 57-73). The Swadhaya movement is asking people to become independent, self-reliant and dignified persons. They are not preaching vegetarianism and totalitarianism. On the contrary, their 'Matshyagandha' project helps fishermen in better fish catching practices.

This is surely the protestant ethics as against the catholic ethics prevalent so far (Max Weber, 1976). This sort of change has taken place also because of the fact that the new generation has been socialised in democratic set up.

This change has come at a time when new frontiers for the development of Saurashtra are opening up. The golden corridor of development between Mehsana and Vapi is being exhausted. No more land for big industry is available at cheap rate. Transportation and affluent discharge have become a problem. The alternative site is the coastal belt of Saurashtra. "The central and south Gujarat (the plain belt) which attracted more than 92 per cent of the industrial investment in large and medium industries in the eighties, received 70 per cent of the investments in the post reform period. The percentage share of Saurashtra increased from a less than 3 to 21 per cent and that of Kutch from less than 1 to 4.7 per cent. The share of Jamnagar (district) has increased from a mere 0.5 per cent in 1983-91 to 13.7 per cent in 1991-96. The committed investments in the other districts of Saurashtra have also jumped up by 6 to 10 times" (Hirway and Mahadevia, 32). This shift of industrial concentration on the coastal belt of Saurashtra and the unparallel reform movement and identity assertion of new generation are related.

The Eastern Belt

The eastern belt running right from north to south and cutting across the boundary of three Indian states, viz. Rajasthan, Madhya Pradesh and Maharashtra is mountainous and covered with forests of varying dimensions. The entire belt is inhabited by various tribal communities. There are 32 talukas in this belt (Table 13.3) where all major tribal communities reside since generations. Their geographical distribution is as under:

Table 13.3 : Talukawise Tribal Population

District	Taluka	Percentage of tribal Population (approx.)	Main tribes
Sabarkantha	Khedbrahma	62.73	Dungri Garasia, Bhil Garasia, Bhil
	Vijaynagar	73.40	Sokla, Garasia, Dungri Garasia
	Bhiloda	53.51	—do—
	Meghraj	37.94	—do—
Panchmahals	Santrampur	79.15	Bhil, Patelia, Naikda
	Jhalod	87.80	Bhil
	Dahod	77.18	Bhil, Patedia
	Limkheda	62.19	Bhil, Patedia, Naikda
Vadodara	Chhotaudepur	88.62	Rathwa, Dhanka
	Nasvadi	84.54	Tavdi, Bhil, Rathwa
	Tilakwada	50.67	
Bharuch	Valia	76.53	Vasava Bhil, Gamit, Dhanka
	Sagbara	91.14	Vasava Bhil, Gamit, Dhanka
	Nanded	66.71	Vasava Bhil
	Dediapada	95.14	Vasava Bhil
	Jhagadia	65.77	Vasava Bhil
Surat	Vyara	86.86	Chaudhary, Dhodia, Gamit, Kokna, Kotwalia
	Valod	74.23	Choudhary, Dhodia, Dubla, Gamit
	Bardoli	51.16	Dubla, Choudhary
	Mahuva	79.69	Choudhary, Dhodia, Dubla, Gamit
	Nijhar	78.83	Vasava Bhil, Dhanka, Gamit,
	Uchhal	97.73	Vasava Bhil, Gamit
	Mandavi	77.33	Choudhary, Dubla, Gamit, Kotwalia
	Songadh	82.50	Gamit, Vasava, Bhil, Choudhary
Valsad	Umbergaon	53.92	Warli, Dubla, Khodia
	Pardi	51.12	Dhodia, Dubla, Naika
	Dharampur	94.91	Konkna, Warli, Dhondia, Naika, Kolgha
	Bansda	90.15	Konkna, Warli, Dhodia, Naika, Kolgha
	Chikhli	70.18	Dubla, Konkna, Naka, Kolgha

(Contd.)

Table 13.3 *(Contd.)*

District	Taluka	Percentage of tribal Population (approx.)	Main tribes
Dangs	Dangs	93.96	Konkna, Kunbis, Bhil Warli, Gamit, Kathodi, Kotwalia
Banaskantha	Amirgadh (Palanpur)	45.07	Bhil, Garasia, Rajput, Garasia
	Danta	79.39	Bhil, Garasia, Rajput, Garasia

Source: R. B. Lal (1998:61.2).

The historical records prove that the Bhils (not 'tribe' in modern parlance) were either subjugated or driven away in interior forests by invading Rajputs. The subjugation or life in forests brought changes in their lifestyle and culture. But it is necessary to remember that this sort of culture is the result of historical experience through which they have passed (Joshi, 1998: 22).

When 'tribals' settled in forests, the modern state did not exist there. It was only "by the end of the nineteenth century, steps were taken for survey and settlement of land revenue in the tribal areas directly governed by the British" (Trivedi, 1998: 151). Prior to that the land where a tribal community had settled was held communally. A tribal farmer, with the permission of the ethnic chief, used to cultivate as much land as was sufficient for his family's maintenance. This sort of practice gave rise to two norms. One, respect for the office of the chief and two, cooperation within the tribal group. The tribals have been traditionally a part of Indian civilisation. But this relationship itself was problematic in the sense that the development model itself created problems for the tribals in the eastern belt. "Many problems concerning tribal development like displacement, poverty alleviation, health and disease, land alienation, indebtedness, criminalisation, etc., in fact, are the resultant effects of such a development model" (Kashyap, 1998: 30). The biggest failure of this sort of consumerist model of development is that it has disintegrated the symbiotic relationship between man and nature in general and between tribals and forests in particular. Moreover, it has also broken the self-generative and self-reliant system, hampered the community's creativity and made them dependent on market forces. The subjugated tribals could not enforce their development ideas against the larger forces. We do not mean to say that development has not taken place in tribal belt. Though there is a strong cooperative movement in the central belt, this has not touched even the fringe of the economic life of the people of this region. Forest labour cooperative societies, groomed mainly by non-tribal Gandhian workers, soon after independence, have benefited some upper stratum tribals. Tribals' enrollments in these cooperatives were more out of respect for Gandhian workers than out of spirit of cooperation. Such a cooperative movement has not taken place from within. It is a part of larger Gandhian reform movement in tribal areas.

Though many big dams have taken place in tribal areas, the irrigation benefits have gone to non-tribals in the plains. Many tribals have lost land and their problem of rehabilitation is alarming. A vast majority of tribals depend on dry agriculture at subsistence level. As agriculture has not developed, the institutional set up and infrastructure for secondary and tertiary sectors are found absent here. "Exceptions may be made in case of few tribal groups such as Dhodias and Chowdhrys of south Gujarat and Patelias of Panchmahals district. But vast majority of them still remain underdeveloped and live a precarious economic existence" (Lal, 1998: 72).

All 32 talukas of tribal area are industrially backward. There are concessions for establishing industrial units in backward areas even then there are very few industrial units in this belt and these, also, have been established by non-tribal industrialists from out side.

There are many NGOs in tribal belt and much has been written about them. Most of them have been established by Gandhian workers. Only recently young educated tribals have started forming their own organisations. Neither a university nor a research institute is located in this belt. Only in the last decade a dozen undergraduate colleges of arts and commerce faculties have been opened in this area.

The school educational scene is not a happy one. Prior to a century there were no schools in tribal area. First Dhanka Vastigrah (residential school) was established in 1885. After the incidence of 'Chaurichaura', Mahatma Gandhi asked his workers to established 'Ashrams'. One of the activities in Ashram was schooling, so it became known as 'Ashramschool' (Joshi, 1980: 7). This contact of Gandhian workers brought a reform movement among the tribals. But this reform movement was led by those outsiders who looked upon tribal culture as inferior and wanted to change it for 'better'. Now the situation was something like this. On the one hand, there was traditional tribal culture. On the other hand, there was westernization or modernisation model which was being followed by larger society. This was third or Gandhian model which was introduced by

Gandhian workers who were outsiders. The tribals were in dilemma. Traditionally, the tribals are habituated to consume liquor (Mahua) and meat. They were taught that teatotalism and vegetarianism are superior norms and if they reform themselves on this line, they will develop. This has created hegemony among outsider-non-tribals and subjugation plus guilt among tribals. They felt that if they have to develop, they would have to adopt a new culture. This was also considered as part of their integration with the main stream. Integration has taken place. The tribals are part of the society, at the same time, they are different. This cultural difference should be understood and respected.

Though special tribal development programmes have been launched and there is a special administrative set up called tribal sub-plan, real transformation is a far cry. On the other hand, the tribal man, "who, once had veritable free spirit, has lost it and has acquired the mental cast of a Hindu of a depressed caste. He has now begun to nurse grievances, on the other hand, to depend more and more on alien agencies. He has fallen prey to the inferiority complex, something which he has never done before. (If) This inferiority ... continues to develop in the tribal areas, it will destroy his art, culture and religion, for he will not hold to his culture for which he was now become ashamed" (Lal, 1998: 79-80).

Conclusion

Thus, there are three sub-cultures in Gujarat, each having different set of ethos within the broader framework of Gujarat culture. The protestant ethic or the 'Mahajan' culture of central belt provides facilitation to individuals to develop on their own lines. The Gujarati entrepreneurship has developed to its full potential in this belt. The semi-feudal culture, which has put more restriction on unfolding of capabilities of human beings uptil now, is changing at a time when development on coastal belt of Saurashtra is becoming a reality. The third or the tribal belt is far behind. Whatever ceremonial development inputs found in this belt are provided by non-tribal developers, resulting in creating a dominant-submissive or patron-client relationship between non-tribals and tribals. They are far from asserting their cultural identity.

REFERENCES

Dreze, Jean & Sen, Amartya (ed.) (1998), "Indian Development", OUP, Delhi.

Hardiman, David, (1981), "Peasant Nationalists of Gujarat", OUP, Delhi.

Hirway, Indira and Mahadevia, Darshini, 1998, *The Gujarat Human Development Report*, (Draft), GLI.

Joshi, Vidyut, (1980), *Ashramshalao - Ek Adhyayan (Guj.),* Ahmedabad, Gujarat Samajik Seva Mandal.

Joshi, Vidyut, (1986), *Bonded Labour in Gujarat*, Ahmedabad, Gandhi Labour Institute.

Joshi, Vidyut, (1998), Genesis of Tribal Problem, in Vidyut Joshi (ed.): *Tribal Situation in India*, Jaipur, Rawat.

Kashyap, Anand, (1998), Parameters of Tribal Development, in Joshi, Vidyut (ed.): *Tribal Situation in India*, Jaipur, Rawat.

Lal, R.B., 1998, Tribal Situation in Gujarati in Vidyut Joshi (ed.) : *Tribal Situation in India*, Jaipur, Rawat.

Mehta, Shirin, (1984), *The Peasantry and Nationalism*, New Delhi, Manohar.

Misra R.R., (1964), *Effects of Land Reforms in Saurashtra*, New Delhi. RPC - Planning Commission.

Shah, V.P. and Sheth, N.R., (1998), "Swadhyaya: Social Change through Spirituality in Dantwada *et al.* (ed.)", *Social change through Voluntary Action*, New Delhi, Sage.

Singh, K.S., (1987), "Anthropology, Culture and Development" in Kalla A.K. & Singh K.S. (ed.) *Anthropology, Development and Nation Building*, New Delhi, Concept.

Trivedi, Harshad, (1998), "Tribal Land in Gujarat", in Joshi, Vidyut (ed.): *Tribal Situation in India*, Jaipur, Rawat.

United Nation's Development Programme, (1998), "Human Development Report", New York, OUP.

Welier, Max, (1976), *The Protestant Ethic and the Spirit of Capitalism*, London, George Allen And Unwin.

14

The Role of Non-Governmental Organisations in the Development of Gujarat

A Review on the Eve of New Millennium

SUDARSHAN IYENGAR

At the turn of the century it is natural for the thinkers in the society to take a hard look at the achievements and failures in its pursuits for the development of mankind. This time, the society is also entering into a new millennium and hence the significance of an overview neightens. The state of Gujarat in India has been in existence for more than twelve centuries, although its geographical boundaries changed a great deal before its formation into the present shape in 1960. Saurashtra and Kutch, which have enjoyed the status of separate states, have their own economic and socio-cultural characteristics, but there are common regional features in practices, traditions, culture and language that cut across all the sub-regions of present day Gujarat. One such characteristic is the humanitarian concern for the poor and weak and also the concern for all living beings, which is expressed as *Jeev Daya*. The father of the nation and the chief architect of the freedom struggle of the country, Mahatma Gandhi, added a very significant dimension to these already existing *Jeev Daya* and philanthropic traditions. This was his idea of creative and constructive voluntarism for human development. Gandhi's influence began from the 1920s and in the last eighty years the voluntary movement in the state continues to be under his influence. However, there have also been significant changes in the ethos and role of NGOs in Gujarat. They have had their share of resounding successes and regrettable failures. The very transition from "voluntary" to "non-governmental" - the word that is now in currency has in it a story of metamorphosis.

One who is not very familiar with Gujarat and its traditions might well wonder as to why a review of development in Gujarat has to contain an analysis of the non-governmental organisations' work. Gujarat has had a tradition and hence a glorious past in voluntary work. Gandhian influence in social reconstruction and the continuing philanthropic proclivity has helped Gujarat in covering a relatively large field for development-related activities.

It is, therefore, appropriate to attempt a review of the role of non-governmental organisations (NGOs) in Gujarat. The main objective of the review is to try to faithfully describe the role NGOs have played during the last eighty years or so in Gujarat. There are not many documents that provide detailed descriptions of the NGOs' development-related activities in Gujarat, especially before independence and up until the 1970s. Hence, more space is devoted here to the period after the 1960s. An attempt will also be made to examine the changes in the role that has taken place and look for reasons. Finally, an attempt will be made to outline the development-related problems that Gujarati civic society is likely to confront in the twenty-first century and to examine whether the role of present day NGOs will have to change. The rest of the paper is accordingly divided into three sections. In section one, role of NGOs or voluntary organisations (VOs) is described during 1920s to 1970. In section two, NGOs' role and work after 1970 is described. In section three, the possible role of NGOs in the 21st Century is projected.

NGOS IN GUJARAT : SOME HISTORICAL ANTECEDENTS

People of Gujarat and Rajasthan are known for their entrepreneurship. Interestingly, both the states are drought-prone. Niggardly nature turns even the human species into hardy varieties and cultivates in them a ruggedness to survive in the most arduous circumstances. People from this region have also been migrating in search of greener pastures. From the second half of the nineteenth century Gujaratis from north Gujarat, Saurashtra and Kutch started migrating to Ahmedabad, Vadodara, Surat, Mumbai and other parts of Maharashtra in the west, Chennai and Bangalore in the south and Calcutta in the east. It was mainly a rural-urban migration. They earned and saved and improved their economic conditions. Their socio-cultural linkages with their native villages continued. Most of those who prospered became philanthropists. Their first welfare acts resulted in the construction of water huts, parks, gardens, and benches for resting in public places. These philanthropic acts elevated the social status of the donors, satisfied their spiritual urges and were consistent with the religious dogmas of promoting well-being in the society. The Bombay Public Trust Act and the Society Registration Act of 1860 were indicators that a need for legalising social organisations was felt much before the economic development activities were taken up by the voluntary organisations in the country. With improved social awareness and the legal framework, the voluntary activities covered health and education—hospitals, dispensaries, school buildings and health education trusts. These activities had taken root by the first two decades of the twentieth century. Other voluntary associations of the educated elite were also formed. The Indian National Congress, registered in 1885, was one such organisation that eventually turned into a political party that has dominated mainstream politics since independence. Similarly, the Servants of India Society and other organisations were also registered. However, political organisations will have to be kept out of the scope of the present discussion.

Towards the end of the First World War, Gandhi entered the political scene in India in a decisive way and began having a major impact. Along with the major political agenda of freeing the country from the British, he also had clear views about the socio-economic development of Indian society. In 1909, he had already penned *Hind Swaraj,* depicting in it the India of his imagination and understanding. More important was his strategy to fight the British. The political movement that he led mobilised a large number of youth full of idealism and commitment for overthrowing foreign rule. This youth force, after spells of intense political activity, had time and energy. They had to be usefully channeled. Gandhi gave a call to the youth to take up rural reconstruction. Hardly any other political leader elsewhere has been able to combine political protest and social reconstruction, as Gandhi was able to do. He effortlessly combined the drafting of ultimatums to the Viceroy, cleaning toilets and tending goats to maintain sound health. Gandhi's call for constructive work for development changed the tenor of voluntary activity in the country completely. Pandey (1991, p. 45), recognising this vital contribution, says, " voluntary social action in India has been grounded partly in a Gandhian response to development and partly in a struggle against the hegemony of macro-organisations (political parties, trade unions) which often discourage people's participation."

Gujarat benefited the most from the Gandhian approach to development. Between 1925 and 1947, a large number of young persons came under his spell, spread themselves in different interior parts of Gujarat and initiated social reconstruction. As a result, even now there are a substantial number of active NGOs that had begun their activities under the influence of Gandhian thought. Their relevance and effectiveness will be examined later. During the pre-independence days, the business class and urban-based entrepreneurs provided the necessary financial support to most of these organisations. Until independence most of these organisations floated on a tide of high idealism. The period could be described as the golden period of voluntary work in rural reconstruction. The British government had hardly any programmes for rural development. Activities that were taken up by the volunteers of the freedom struggle became very visible and important. Urban youth led by idealism entered and settled in remote rural areas. They took up activities relating to khadi and village industries, basic education, women's education and amelioration of the backward castes by working against untouchability. khadi and village industries and basic education took root in Gujarat and a large number of organisations came up in different parts of the state. With independence, however, there was a drastic change in the characteristics of the NGOs in the country as well as in Gujarat.

Independence and NGOs in Gujarat up to 1970

With India winning independence, the perspective underwent a fundamental change. Struggle for freedom from the foreign rule was no longer on the agenda. Economic development and social reconstruction were the tasks ahead for the government. The development paradigm that was accepted by the state and the mainstream politics did not coincide with Gandhian economic thought. India was faced with high and rising population, low food production and high unemployment. Modernisation implied industrialisation. Development and the expansion of capitalism were shunned and the country got wedded to a socialistic pattern of development. Promotion of a mixed economy and development through centralised planning became the main strategy. In this way, Gandhian economic tenets were relegated to the background. However, rural development programmes were planned in the Gandhian mode. The community development programme and national extension services included many aspects of Gandhian rural reconstruction. The Khadi and Village Industries Commission was set up. The chief functionaries of the Commission were Gandhian workers. Similarly, the intensive area development schemes came to be recognised as Gandhian community development programmes (Shah and Chaturvedi, 1983). Thus, although the mainstream efforts for economic development were based on entirely different principles, there was some tolerance of and sympathy towards Gandhian economic philosophy and programmes.

Another fundamental difference that occurred in the 1947-70 phase of NGO participation in development relates to sponsorship. The benefactors who belonged to the business and entrepreneurial class shifted their attention to mainstream economics and the flow of financial support to Gandhian activities slowed considerably. Further, the proposed government programmes required relatively large funds that could not come from the private sector. The Gandhian NGOs in the post-independence era thus came to be patronised largely by governments. Public contributions were made, but they formed only a small part of the total requirement of the organisations. One result of this was that the stranglehold of the bureaucracy tightened. The Khadi and Village Industries Commission (KVIC) became a government organisation. Government patronage also led to expansion and proliferation of NGOs both in the country and in Gujarat. In Gujarat, however, financial support to educational and health institutions continued outside the Gandhian mode also. Support for schools and higher education, hospitals and dispensaries and other individual, community welfare and religion-based activities came forward significantly.

One is not very sure whether the patrons and managers of the Gandhian organisations gave any serious thought to the implications of accepting state patronage. It is quite likely that most of them thought it wise to accept money and survive rather than to close down. However, even those who resisted the temptation of working with government finances, perhaps did not think through the implications of state patronage to the voluntary/NGO activities. There is anecdotal evidence which indicates that Vinoba Bhave expressed total dissatisfaction with the draft First Five Year Plan document. Pandit Nehru, the then Prime Minister of India, had suggested that the other members of the Planning Commission should consult Vinoba Bhave and obtain his comments on the draft Plan. Vinoba's main objection was that the draft Plan was in no way consistent with the Gandhian framework for developing India's economy and society. His suggestion was to discard the entire draft. He was not willing to tolerate small changes. He then went on to take up the *Bhoodan* and *Gramdan* programmes, which he thought were solutions to the ills of the unequal land distribution patterns in the society. But for this evidence, there is no other information that would tell us about the role of

Gandhian organisations in influencing the government's plan policies.

The willingness of most Gandhian organisations to accept state patronage led to a different and perhaps unanticipated consequence. Most organisations lapsed into routine activity whereby they hardly questioned the designs and suitability of government plans and programmes for the proposed clients, i.e., the rural poor. Interestingly, rituals related to Gandhi's and Vinoba's ideology continued. One could see the daily prayers, cleaning of campuses by all inmates (cleaning of toilets—one does not know!) and spinning of khadi, etc. being undertaken as rituals. There is evidences that the new inmates who showed unwillingness to participate in the rituals were asked to pack up and leave. In fact, this attitude of seniors in Gandhian organisations put off many youth, who under the spell of idealism, wanted to join the Gandhian organisations and work. The lack of freedom to question, the lack of an environment in which to think and act and the insistence on participating religiously in all rituals, resulted in promoting mediocrity and sycophancy. The state was comfortable with the overall situation because the mainstream thinking of industrialisation by controlling the commanding heights of the economy could prevail while simultaneously some type of rural development programme could also be pushed. Some staunch Gandhian organisations could see the problem, but they were very small in number and hence could not do much to change the course. They remained like islands. In this phase, i.e. between 1947 and 1970, the NGOs did not succeed in influencing the government's development policy significantly. In fact, because of the culture of routine and rituals that emerged in most organisations, a second line of leadership never came up.

Rajni Kothari (in Bhatt, 1989) states in his analysis that two major steps were taken in India to usher in democratic socialism. The first one was adopting universal adult franchise to facilitate (a) promotion of political plurality in power sharing and (b) making special provisions for the poor and the weaker sections. The second was to initiate a development process that would ensure economic growth in the long run. This second step was aimed at removing poverty, raising living standards and achieving just distribution. According to Kothari, by the mid-1960s, it was realised that the country had failed on both the fronts. Both the left parties and the voluntary agencies that subscribed to radical and revolutionary changes in the society got entangled in the polarisation between the haves and have-nots. He considers the late 1960s as the period when the politics of the country became significantly transformed. It may be remembered that the Congress party broke up for the first time after independence in 1969. Thus, between 1947 and 1970, neither the mainstream politics nor the politics of the NGOs seemed to have succeeded in promoting development policies that would help the large masses of the poor in the country. I shall revert to this point again later.

THE POST - 1970 SCENARIO

1970 may be considered a watershed in the history of NGOs in India as well as in Gujarat. There were important changes in the types and characteristics of the NGOs. Significant changes also took place in politics. An era of populist politics had begun. According to Kothari (in Bhatt, 1989), the populist politics manifested in two ways. Some young ruling party leaders agitated over party policies and management, tried to break away from the party hierarchy and establish rapport with people directly. They also pitched their leadership claims at higher levels. They took recourse to populist politics and gave the slogan of *garibi hatao*. It is well known that in 1971, Indira Gandhi's ruling Congress won the Lok Sabha elections with a thumping majority. Discontinuing the privy purses of the erstwhile maharajahs and nationalisation of the banks were two actions that were taken to announce the pro-people politics. The second manifestation came in the form of grassroots movements. These movements were initiated to obtain local autonomy in issues relating to caste, gender, regional development opportunities and environment. A large majority of them remained non-political and non-governmental. Let us first understand the political processes in some detail. The politics of the time had its impact on the NGOs, both in India and Gujarat.

The ruling Congress led by Indira Gandhi could not deliver what it promised. By the mid-1970s the society witnessed substantial unrest. In 1974, Gujarat witnessed political turmoil. It started with a students' agitation over rising prices. The government had to resign. The unrest spread to other parts of the country, especially Bihar. Indira Gandhi's government came under tremendous pressure and she proclaimed an internal emergency. This move was regarded as highly autocratic and fascist. The Gandhian NGOs in Gujarat, which had always felt some affinity with Congress, reacted very sharply by taking a clear stand in public against the declaration of emergency. Some of the well-known old leaders of NGOs were arrested and jailed. In 1977, the ruling Congress lost elections and a combined opposition front formed the government. In Gujarat, the Janata Party, which consisted of old Congress members and some right wing supporters, had already won the assembly elections and was ruling. The NGOs could establish good rapport with the Janata Government and the state's support to them increased significantly. Thus in Gujarat, the NGOs consolidated their position with respect to state support. However, within two years, the Janata government was brought down at the national level and in the fresh election in 1980, Indira Gandhi and her Congress resumed power. She appointed the Kudal Commission to investigate alleged irregularities in the NGOs. Her target was the Sarvodaya or Gandhian NGOs all over the country which had supported the dissent movement during emergency and subsequently lent support to the Janata government at the centre as well as in Gujarat. Fortunately, in Gujarat, not many NGOs suffered. The state could not remain averse to the NGOs for long. In 1980, Integrated Rural Development Programme (IRDP) was introduced. It involved identification of individual beneficiaries and linking of the economic programmes with bank credit. Government officials could not have identified and implemented the scheme on their own. Similarly, in implementing other rural development programmes including delivery of health and education services, the government could not do without the support of the NGOs. At the national level an autonomous institution, the Centre for Advancement of People's Action and Rural Technology (CAPART) was set up to channel rural development funds to NGOs all over the country. Gujarat took good advantage of the opportunity.

Despite the political turmoil in the mid-1970s, many different types of NGOs came into existence in Gujarat. The number and type increased. Shah and Chaturvedi (1983) divide the secular NGOs into three main categories, techno-managerial, reformist and radical. Hirway (1995) has classified the NGOs in Gujarat into welfare-oriented including health and education, development organisations and empowering NGOs. I have elsewhere classified the NGOs in Gujarat into four categories (Iyengar, 1998). The categories are Gandhian, delivery organisations, professional organisations and mobilisational organisations. The first three mainly belong to the delivery category since they do not question the designs of government programmes. In the context of Gujarat it is interesting that the Gandhian organisations, which initially were created with the main objective of mobilising the masses for political action for gaining freedom from the British, ceased to be critical about the government's programmes and became, in most cases, delivery organisations. It took about twenty-five years after independence to fully realise that the government was not able to improve the conditions of the weaker sections through its programmes. The Gandhian organisations reacted only when emergency was declared. However, even after restoration of democracy in 1977, most Gandhian organisations were content with playing the delivery role and did not find it necessary to question the objectives. During late 1980s and 1990s when the controversy raged over the Sardar Sarovar Project (SSP) on river Narmada, Gandhian organisations divided into two camps. For the first time, some Gandhian organisations came out loudly challenging the development paradigm and dubbed this government project as anti-people. Some of them had been implementing a number of government programmes without ever seriously questioning the framework within which the government had designed its interventions.

As Kothari has suggested, a number of small groups covering one to five villages came into being which took up local development work and issues related to it. These small groups started questioning the designs of the programmes that came from above. Bhatt (1989) has called them 'micro actions by weaker sections'. Although in totality, there were significant limitations of the small group actions, there were some contributions too. The actions have achieved two important purposes. One, they categorically conveyed that the poverty alleviation programmes had not reached the poor and two, the programmes had not been designed with their consultation. Thus, from 1970 onwards, the top-down approach to look for solutions to the socio-economic problems of the weaker sections started being questioned by some. In 1990s the intensity of questioning became high and some NGOs also tried alternative approaches. It should be mentioned that most of the alternatives were tried by NGOs, which had committed professionals. These NGOs also tried out certain innovations in looking for solutions.

The dependence on the state for financial support also increased in the 1970s. As a consequence of the populist or pro-people politics, the state further consolidated its power by intervening in most of the economic development activities. Most of the rural development and urban support programmes were funded only by the state. Finance for NGOs from the non-government sector was limited largely to charity. It became difficult for NGOs to undertake any constructive work without state finances. The characteristics of the NGOs changed. First, most of the NGOs became typical delivery organisations implementing government schemes and programmes. Second, some of them built large empires with state funding. The post-1970 period also witnessed an increase in foreign aid for development. Governmental non-government organisations (GONGOs) from developed countries brought with them huge amounts of monetary assistance. The communication medium also changed from Gujarati and other regional languages to English. Commitment was no longer the value. Professionalism entered and market rate of remuneration to the workers of the NGOs began. Workers of some NGOs got exposure to foreign countries, especially Europe and America. Their value system underwent some change. Korten (1989) points out a political consequence of the working of GONGOs. He notes that the GONGOs pursued the government policies and thus introduced donor government's biases in the programmes. The professional approach was a good garb to conceal the donor country's agenda. The issue is controversial even now. Gujarat has had a fair share of foreign-funded NGOs. Hirway (1995) notes some serious disadvantages of foreign funding. Besides influencing the workstyle and lifestyle among the workers of foreign funded NGOs, a small success transforms these NGOs into internationally acclaimed organisations and soon the key workers lose touch with grass roots reality. However, state support and international NGO funding the NGOs in Gujarat has come to stay.

Networking Among NGOs in Gujarat

The need for networking among NGOs was not felt for quite sometime after independence because initially it was assumed that the desired social change was to be brought about by the government itself and the NGOs had to give a helping hand. The government was committed to ameliorating the condition of the poor to a decent level of living. However, in the first twenty-five years of independence it was realised that government was not able to deliver. By the time internal emergency was declared in 1975, most NGOs had realised that networking around issues and common programmes was necessary. In fact, there were some federations and associations in certain specific activities such as khadi and village industry, basic education and health, etc. but networking to lobby and create pressure over development related issues and conflicts did not appear until the mid-1970s.

Two almost parallel efforts started in Gujarat in the late 1970s and early 1980s. The first federation of the NGOs working for rural development was formed in 1978 under the umbrella of a national level organisation called the Association of Voluntary Agencies for Rural Development (AVARD). The federation was named Gujarat Rajya Gram Vikas Sangh (GRGVS). Mr. Raj Krishna, the then Member of the Planning Commission, had suggested and encouraged the formation of GRGVS. The Gujarat

Institute of Area Planning, Ahmedabad, a social science research institute took the initiative. GRGVS had 225 members including 100 life members.

The second effort was an offshoot of a national dialogue meeting that was held in May 1980 in Delhi. Interestingly, Mr. Raj Krishna, who had inspired the formation of the GRGVS in Gujarat, had also attended this meeting. The move was initiated by Professors Rajni Kothari and D.L. Sheth of the Centre for the Study of Developing Societies, Delhi. It was generally agreed that issues of development cannot be separated from those of social transformation, and hence, there was a need to initiate different sets of actions and research around the socio-economic issues. A project called 'Lokayan' — towards people, was launched as a result of this national level consultation. Professor Ghanashyam Shah of the Centre for Social Studies, Surat and Mr. Achyut Yagnik, a journalist and an activist accepted the responsibility of the Gujarat chapter of Lokayan. A small group of activists and concerned academics was formed to play advisory role for the Gujarat Lokayan activities. A need to combine struggle (sangharsha), reconstruction (rachna) and development (*vikas*) was felt. The Gujarat Lokayan activities eventually, in 1982, converted itself into SETU, meaning a bridge. Thus, by 1982, there were two types of networking that came up in Gujarat: one, which attracted development organisations and two, which attracted the NGOs engaged in mobilisation and social transformation.

Gujarat Rajya Gram Vikas Sangh

The efforts to form a federation for networking were initiated among others by Vimal Shah, the then Director of the Gujarat Institute of Area Planning. It was visualised that a research institute engaged in development research could continuously provide research help and training to the workers of the NGOs. The GRGVS was mainly involved in the following :

- Provide information to members about new projects and programmes and funding sources.
- Conduct training programmes for the workers of the NGOs.
- Obtain recognition for NGOs in the government departments.
- Help member NGOs to prepare project proposals for funding organisations.
- Hold annual conventions to discuss matters of mutual interest

and problems.

- Lobby with the government for better policies for rural development.

With a modest beginning in 1979, the GRGVS functioned effectively for its first ten years. One of its regular features was an annual convention that was co-hosted with one of the member NGOs. As a matter of policy, the GRGVS did not take up project implementation by itself. However, this policy was changed in the 1990s. Presently, the GRGVS undertakes projects and also charges a professional fee for preparing project proposals and getting them sanctioned. Some of the senior and founding members have disassociated from the Sangh over this issue. The GRGVS is active today for those who have common project interests.

SETU

"SETU, which means 'bridge' in several Indian languages, aims to act as a link betweeen social knowledge and social action by facilitating dialogue and interaction between members of marginalised and backward communities, activists, academicians and policy makers. The focus of all its activities is the promotion of social equity and justice, as well as values, which it holds as central to its vision of social transformation" (SETU, 1999, p. 1). SETU's activities in five inter-related areas are, direct action, support action, training, networking and public advocacy, and documentation and research.

Since its inception, SETU has worked towards the çreation of networks of organisations working with backward and marginalised communities. It is to facilitate interaction and cooperation between them as well as create more space in public discourse for their concerns and their expressions. In the past, SETU has facilitated networking on issues such as government's reservation policy (affirmative action), minimum wages for rural labour, natural disasters, problems of women, alterntaive to proposed Forest Bill and National Rehabilitation and Resettlement Policy of the Government of India. Network members could bring neglected areas, sections of population and the issues related to their development into sharp focus. Presently, SETU has turned its attention to the state's enthusiastic plans for industrialising the backward, but ecologically fragile and environmentally vulnerable areas. These areas include the coastal areas of Saurashtra and Kutch. SETU is involved in research and action and networking around these issues.

Janpath

In the 1990s, when the GRGVS was passing though a transition from a networking federation to support agency and project-implementing NGO, small groups and radical social action NGOs felt a need to build solidarity among those sharing a common philosophy and understanding over issues. The need for solidarity was also felt in carrying out protest against the government on policies and programmes that were anti-people or regressive. One of the views was that there ought to be a forum, which should facilitate debates on developmental issues. A need for documentation was also felt in the context. Thus, Janpath was born. It has been functioning now for eight years. It has more than 100 institutional and life members. It performs the following functions:

- Visit the member NGOs and understand their problems.
- Represent their problems at appropriate fora.
- Identify protest issues and help in organising protest movements.
- Collect and collate information and newspaper reports on various sensitive issues, publish a newsletter and circulate among the members.
- Bring out occasional papers on specific development problems and issues.
- Hold an annual convention co-hosted by a member NGO and discuss a relevant theme.
- Award Bhanubhai Adhavaryu Prize every year to one or two individuals for their life time contribution to upliftment of the weaker sections.

Janpath has been able to bring out about fifteen occasional papers on various issues such as Salt pan workers, carriers of human excreta, the drinking water problem, human rights violations in protected areas and forests, etc. It has been able to provide moral support to small groups working in remote rural areas. However, Janpath is yet to make any substantial contribution in lobbying for a major policy change in favour of its cliëntele.

Gujarat Voluntary Health Association

One of the oldest networks is the Gujarat Voluntary Health Association (GVHA). Gujarat has a relatively large number of voluntary initiatives for providing health services in urban as well as rural areas. Christian missionaries form a substantial part of the NGOs in the health sector. The GVHA came into existence in the late 1970s to form a network of those NGOs that were small, catered to very poor sections, functioned in relatively inaccessible interiors of the rural districts and, most importantly, believed in promoting rational practice and a scientific approach to community health. During the last fifteen years, the GVHA has been able to influence policies of the government and to win recognition for its members. It has also been instrumental in promoting production and distribution of low cost standard drugs to be used by the NGOs. The GVHA has also been promoting a workable concept of primary healthcare in which the members of the community are trained to deal with primary illness.

Saksham

In 1996, two new issue-specific networks came into existence. The first was Saksham. It was born out of a need for people-oriented forest policy. Secondly, the concept of Joint Forest Management (JFM) prompted NGOs working in the forestry area to come together to identify problem area and to work out solutions. Saksham was formed with two objectives. One was to lobby the government for solving problems that could not be solved at local levels. The second objective was to help in scaling-up similar activities in a large number of neighbouring villages. VIKSAT of the Nehru Foundation for Development was the originator of the idea and it continues to play a prominent role in Saksham's structure and functioning. According to VIKSAT's own assessment, the attempt is successful but it still has far to go, especially in lobbying the government.

Pravah

A network of NGOs named Pravah (meaning flow) was formed in 1996 with the main objective to enable communities to become self-reliant in accessing adequate and safe drinking water on a sustainable basis. This is to be achieved by promoting and strengthening decentralised, people-friendly technologies in gaining access to and control over water resources, especially by women. It has more than 60 institutional and individual members. Some of its members are recognised by the state water supply board. Pravah tries to lobby the government for (i) changes in the policy in favour of community based alternatives such as ponds, tankas (roof water collection) and other devices for water collection; (ii) improve the water quality; and (iii) allocate financial resources for the suggested alternatives. Pravah is recognised by the Gujarat Water Supply and Sewage Board. The Board seeks Pravah's help in training the NGOs and officials in participatory water supply schemes and in getting exposure to people managed shemes in Gujarat and elsewhere. Pravah has been trying to generate movement around issues in drinking water in the districts of Saurashtra, north and central Gujarat.

Working Group for Women's Initiatives (WGWI), Gujarat

The WGWI, Gujarat, which has been renamed very recently as Mahila Swaraj Abhiyan (MSA), is active since 1997. Although some thinking and discussions among some NGOs, academics and citizens took place in 1994, before the pre-Beijing International Womens Conference in 1995, the activities began only after the Beijing Conference. The WGWI aims at strengthening women's movement in Gujarat and undertake networking of the NGOs, which work on women issues. The WGWI held a Mahila Sammelan (Women's Conference).

Janvikas

During the last seven to eight years Janvikas has emerged as a small but effective network that is engaged in capacity-building of small groups involved in development work. It inculcates a participatory approach to work for development. The attempt is to orient and train small group workers to understand people's problems with the latter's active participation and work out solutions that ensure equity, efficiency and sustainability. Janvikas has also been guiding new organisations in obtaining financial support.

NGOs' Networks in Urban Areas of Gujarat

Some of the most important voluntary initiatives in urban areas of Gujarat have concentrated on women, children, housing and slum improvement. The Self-Employed Women's Association (SEWA) is the best known nationally and internationally. It is essentially a union, which had made highly successful efforts to organise self-employed poor women in a variety of trades in the informal sector of the economy. Unions of women engaged in various trades have been formed to fight for rights to a proper working environment, fair and human treatment by law-enforcing authorities, formation of self-help groups for small savings, a banking facility for poor women and better access to health facilities for working women. SEWA is thus an amalgamation of various types of organisations working to improve the status of women in society. SEWA has also initiated research efforts to undertake studies that would help in analysing the status, scope and contribution of women in development.

Ahmedabad Women's Action Group (AWAG) is another organisation which has successfully worked for raising awareness among socio-economically backward women about their rights, first as women and then as workers in various sectors. It has also organised production centres for the poorest among the slum dwellers including minority communities. Ahmedabad Study Action Group (ASAG), which is engaged in planning development activities in rural and urban areas, has contributed significantly to planning and designing low cost but quality housing complexes for urban slum dwellers and rural poor at alternative sites. It also has a successful programme for developing and strengthening creativity among poor children in cities. VIKAS is another organisation, which has its presence in Ahmedabad and Vadodara in the slum areas. VIKAS has an objective of total slum development in urban areas. It has conducted studies to understand housing, sanitation, civic amenities, economic activities, health and education in the slums and based on the results of the studies has tried to design development interventions. It has also made an attempt to network with other NGOs working for urban communities. The network called 'Samvad' (dialogue), attempts to bring to the fore all the socio-legal complexities of unorganised and urban settlements. VIKAS and the network are closely working with civic authorities such as the Ahmedabad Municipal Corporation.

Campaign Against Child Labour (CACL)

Campaign Against Child Labour (CACL) is part of a national campaign. In Gujarat, NGOs working on the issue of child labour and welfare have come together to form a network. The CACL has been organising statewide programmes to create awareness against the child labour. A public hearing was organised towards the end of 1998 to highlight the plight of child labour in the state. The CACL is lobbying the state government to improve the accessibility of children to primary schools also. About 80 NGOs are part of the CACL, although not all of them are actively and directly engaged in working against child labour.

ROLE OF NGOS

Many scholars have debated the role and relevance of NGOs in a developing country like India. It is fairly well recognised that the state cannot succeed completely in alleviating the status of disadvantaged groups. In fact, even when the state assumed almost total control over the commanding heights of the economy during the planning era, it could not effectively deal a blow to poverty and unemployment problems. Social problems and tensions also could not be resolved to anyone's complete satisfaction. Even when the interventions are conceived on a pro-people paradigm, they very soon get caught in the web of vested interests. Since 1991, the country has made a major decision to shift to market-derived growth and development. The shift may or may not help the poorest of the poor in the society. There are problems such as lack of purchasing power, lack of opportunities to get purchasing power, lack of requisite skills to utilise opportunities that may become available as a result of the operation of market forces, and lack of proper educational facilities in remote rural areas, where most of the poor live, to acquire changing skills required in the market.

In an article written ten years ago, Rajni Kothari (Bhatt, 1989) focused on the "wretched of the earth". According to him, the state, the politicians, the government, the NGOs, investigative journalism, public interest litigants, Naxalites and other aggressive activists have failed to improve the status of the downtrodden. He pins hope on the poor and the unorganised themselves and thought that if at all leadership arose from among them, their lot would improve. However, he was not totally certain and hopeful about the long-term future of the poor organising themselves because there were a lot of questions on the type and nature of group formations that might take place. Kothari (1998) is well aware of developments since 1989 when he wrote about the scope of local groups working for their amelioration. Since 1989, when he wrote about the small local groups, there have been significant changes in the form of NGOs, mentioned in the preceding section. He is not at all comfortable with the present NGO-related scenario. He says, "this new constellation of 'voluntary' effort, encompassing funding agencies and international NGOs, units within government bureaucracies and the Planning Commission meant to assist national and local NGOs, provides a completely new model of both joining-in and containing, co-opting and corrupting the large mass of genuine, grassroots-based, activist efforts. Whether this NGO model of voluntarism will further accentuate the great divides between the haves and the have-nots, or ameliorate the condition of the latter, is still an open question" (p. 186).

Anil Bhatt (1989), in his study of small groups, rated highly the impact of small group organisations on solving critical problems. However, he concluded that their total coverage is extremely limited and the ones that are strong quickly start adopting the tactics of mainstream politicians. Hence, the promise and the prospects, which are visible in the beginning, tend to wither. In his 1995 brief review (Bhatt, 1995) on roles, trends and challenges, Bhatt has expressed concern over some of the trends. One is about how NGOs conduct themselves. According to him, from 1980 onwards, there has been proliferation, competition, conflict and rivalry among voluntary groups. Secondly, there are a few adverse effects of professionalisation also. The spirit of voluntarism is going down yielding to commercialisation. All these trends, according to Bhatt, do not augur well for NGOs and their credibility is at stake. Hirway (1995), too, is worried about the present trend among the NGOs. In section two, Hirway's concerns were described which related to the emerging lifestyle and workstyle of NGOs consequent upon receipt of international funding.

In the context of Gujarat, there has been some thinking going on the role of NGOs. In a statewide convention of NGOs held in November 1994, at Gram Bharti, Amrapur, in Mehsana district, Sanat Mehta, a veteran in politics and social work held that the "last man" has to be identified and reached. He candidly admitted that the government machinery cannot reach the last man and only NGOs have the commitment for the cause. Dr. Anil Patel, a physician and community health expert, who is associated with an NGO, Action Research in Community Health and Development (ARCH), stated that volunteers in the voluntary agencies (and not paid workers in NGOs) were a class by themselves because they were sensitive to the cause of the poor and downtrodden and were above mundane self-interest. They have at times to take up a confrontational approach towards the government when the latter is engaged blatantly in anti-people activities. Responding to a dominant theme for some activists, of capturing power to make governments more accountable and responsive to the people at large, Dr. Patel held that in a democratic framework, the voluntary agencies' function should be to check the power of the state. In the game of power political organisations quickly lose their capacity to make a correct assessment of the situation at the ground level. Voluntary agencies by their continuous and effective presence ensure a realistic assessment.

Formal organisations, especially in developing societies, are likely to fall into a routine and eventually become rigid and reactionary. Mainstream politicians develop heavy stakes and hence vested interests in the *status quo.* Effective voluntary initiatives with their concern and sensitivity are likely to be progressive, flexible and innovative. Being progressive helps them to strive for objectivity and critical rationality in assessing ground realities. It may be difficult for voluntary social activists to retain critical rationality continuously. They tend to become subjective and look for unrealistic or impractical solutions. The question, then, is who keeps the vigil? The responsibility lies with the voluntary agencies themselves. The higher the levels of democratic functioning of the voluntary agencies, the higher will be the chances of retaining the critical rationality.

The relationship between the state and the NGOs is variable. The Amrapur convention brought out this point well. It was argued that while NGOs are, by and large, engaged in constructive work for development of the afflicted sections, there will be situations when the NGOs will have to confront the government on critical policy issues and resort to struggle. In reality, however, there seems to be a polarisation among the NGOs. The delivery organisations (category four) do not join hands with others on the issues of struggle. And the social activists, who take up cudgels against the government, do not like to sit for negotiations and help the government in implementing socially acceptable programmes. The formation of networks and federations are strongly influenced by the types of agenda the NGOs have.

Agenda for NGOs in the 21st Century

Liberalisation and the opening up of the economy have brought a major change in the policy thrust of the country. There has been a conscious decision to reduce the role of the state, to remove unnecessary controls and regulations and to professionalise the public sector. When the power of the state ebbs, market forces become the alternative power centre. Under ideal conditions, the market can operate efficiently and ensure rational allocation of resources and distribute incomes equitably. However, market imperfections can lead to distortions and manipulations. Secondly, and more importantly, the market recognises only those who enter it. The poorest of the poor in India and in Gujarat who survive on subsistence activities have a very low level of interaction with the market as consumers and with negligible transactions for productions they are practically out of the market. They are likely to be neglected. Thirdly, there are certain non-economic factors, which have significant and substantial influence on the performance of services in education and health services. The market is not likely to allocate resources for those who are extremely backward in terms of HRD levels. The state will have to continue to provide support to the social infrastructure. However, the allocation of financial resources will not be enough. Past experience in this regard suggests that the quality of primary education and healthcare is poor and the delivery agents are almost callous and highly negligent. We have already stated that different types of efforts, ranging from efficient delivery of services to efforts to change development strategies in favour of the disadvantaged groups, are undertaken by the NGOs in Gujarat. These activities will have to continue, perhaps, with a higher level of consciousness.

Pandey (1991) has argued that there is a fundamental difference between a development group, which often tries to bring about reforms within a given system, and an action group, which acts to transform social and political conditions in favour of the poor. Similarly, Shah and Chaturvedi (1983) regard development organisations as reformist and argue that such organisations have inherent limitations and hence will not effect a socio-political transformation. Argued differently in the framework of local level planning, it may be said that the delivery organisations are working essentially with a top-down perspective and the action groups work with a bottom-up perspective. The philosophy of the market economy basically gives rise to the top-down approach. It also tends to influence planners and thinkers who do not have access to grassroots assessment. For instance, some people argue that the major problem with the people in resource-poor regions is that they have no skills or access to new production technologies. Their recommendation is for improving the skills. The grassroots assessment may reveal that the critical issue is the control over natural resources. It is here that NGOs have a crucial role. The NGO initiatives in the area of awareness, mass mobilisation and organisation around critical issues are likely to lead towards better problem identification and solutions that involve the active participation of the local population. Such initiatives are likely to make a desirable impact on policy formulations and problem designs. This must be followed by a professional approach to implementation, which would ensure quality delivery.

It has already been argued that the state and the bureaucracy by their very nature are not able to design and deliver for the disadvantaged sections of the population. Hence, the state should give recognition and encouragement to NGO initiatives. Fortunately, Gujarat has a relatively better environment for their purpose.

REFERENCES

ARCH-Vahini, (1992), *Morse-Berger Review: A Search for Truth?,* ARCH, Mangrol, Rajpipla.

ARCH-Vahini, (1993), *Sardar Sarovar Project: An Intellectual Fashion,* ARCH, Mangrol, Rajpipla.

Bhatt, Anil (1989), *Development and Social Justice: Microaction by Weaker Sections,* Sage Publications, New Delhi.

————, (1995), "Voluntary Action in India", in *Economic and Political Weekly*, Vol XXX No. 16 April 22, 1995.

Hirway, Indira (1995), "Selective Development and Widening Disparities in Gujarat", in *Economic and Political Weekly,* Vol. XXX 41 and 42 October 14-21, 1995.

Iyengar, S. (1998), "Voluntary Initiatives for Tribal Development in Gujarat", in *The Journal of Entrepreneurship,* 7, 2 (1998).

Korten, David C. (1989), *Getting to the 21st Century: Voluntary Action and the Global Agenda*, Oxford & IBH Publishing Co. Pvt. Ltd., New Delhi

Pandey, S.R. (1991), *Community Action for Social Justice: Grass Roots Organisation in India*, Sage Publications, New Delhi.

Kothari, Rajni (1998), "The Future of Voluntarism", in Dantwala *et al.* (eds.) *Social Change Through Voluntary Action*, Sage Publications, New Delhi.

SETU, (1999), *SETU: Centre for Social Knowledge and Action - An Introduction*, SETU, Ahmedabad.

Shah, Ghanshyam and Chaturvedi, H.C. (1983), *Gandhian Approach to Rural Development: The Valod Experiment,* Ajanta Prakashan, New Delhi.

15

Panchayati Raj in Gujarat

S. S. MEHTA and PRATUL AHUJA

Introduction

Where there are hierarchies of settlements with varied economic base, inhabited by people with different socio-economic status and backgrounds, having different and conflicting needs, centralised economic systems have not been able to meet the demands and aspirations of different regions and the people. In centralised economic structures, people also have not been able to contribute and participate in the development process. Therefore to make development people-oriented —by the people, of the people and for the people—empowering people is necessary. People need to be given power, resources and financial as well as functional autonomy. These objectives have been sought to be achieved by creating Panchayati Raj Institutions (PRI) under State Panchayat Acts in India.

Panchyati Raj in India

Most of the states in India had enacted Panchayat Act to create three-tier Panchayati Raj Institutions much before the 73rd Amendment in the Constitution of India in 1992. Till 1989, about 14 states and union territories had a three-tier PR system, 4 had a two-tier PR system, 9 had only a single tier PR system and 4 states and union territories had traditional councils of village elders (Hirway, 1989). These enactments provided a legal, administrative, political and financial framework for PRIs. This framework, however, did not fully match with the objective of self-governance, of empowering people and of giving autonomy to people. The framework was largely supply-oriented and not demand-oriented and not as per the needs of the people, regions and sub-regions. Panchayati Raj Institutions were controlled and regulated by the government departments. It was governance from above which had very little to do with self-governance—the objective of Panchayati Raj. PRIs were run through administrative orders and fiats, rather than by the people. Therefore, PRIs made little impact on rural economy and rural life.

Decentralised District Planning

Decentralised District Planning was introduced in most states in the 1980s to give demand/need oriented thrust to Panchayati Raj Institutions, to address the micro level problems of nuts and bolts at the village level. Under this scheme, about five per cent of the Plan outlays were earmarked to address these micro level problems. However, the decision-making body under this scheme was the District Planning Board and not PRIs. While the Decentralised District Planning Scheme did increase the participation and say of the people in the decision-making process, the funds under this scheme were very small and there also a part was transferred to the MLA Development Fund. Therefore, even this innovative scheme had a non-people orientation.

The 73rd Constitutional Amendment Act

In 1989, deliberations started about effective devolution of powers to local bodies for self-governance and these resulted in the 73rd Constitutional Amendment in 1991. In the Statement of objects and reasons published with this Bill, it was stated that "In many states, local bodies have become weak and ineffective on account of various reasons:

(i) the failure to hold regular elections,
(ii) prolonged supersessions, and
(iii) inadequate devolution of powers and functions.

As a result, rural and urban local bodies are not able to perform effectively as vibrant democratic institutions of self-government" [Venkatswamy, G. in the Lok Sabha Debate on Constitution (Seventy-Third Amendment) Bill, December 1, 1992].

The 73rd Amendment in the Constitution of India in 1992 conferred Panchayati Raj Institutions, a Constitutional status of a third-level government to local bodies below the Central and State Governments (Article 243B). So, now along with the Union, State and Concurrent lists under the Seventh Schedule, there is a Panchayats and Municipalities list under Eleventh and Twelfth Schedule under Articles 243G and 243W respectively for rural and urban areas. The Constitution (73rd Amendment) Act, 1992 provides for the institution of Gram Sabha, establishment of Village Panchayat, intermediate tier and Zilla Panchayat at the village, intermediate and district levels. Besides authorising the Panchayats to levy, collect and appropriate suitable local taxes, the Act also provides for making grants-in-aid to the Panchayats from the consolidated funds of the state. As per the provisions of the Schedule IX to the Constitution, preparation of plans/schemes in respect of 29 subjects has been devolved to the Panchayats for their economic development and social justice. The Panchayats are also empowered to implement these schemes and programmes. The implementation of rural development programmes such as JRY, NSAP, EAS, IAY, MWS, etc. will also get a boost as a result of strengthening of the Panchayats (Jain, 1997). There is a provision for a State Finance Commission under Articles 243-I and 243Y to provide finances to the local bodies. The Constitutional Amendment also provides for a limited period of supersession (Article, 243E), reservation for Scheduled Castes, Scheduled Tribes, Other Backward Classes and women (Article 243D). A State Election Commission has also been created for conducting elections (Article 243K). A District Planning Committee has to be constituted in every state at the district-level to consolidate the Plans prepared by the Panchayats and Municipalities in the district and to prepare a Draft Development Plan for the district as a whole (Article 243ZD). This Constitutional Amendment, therefore, led to replacement of the Old State Panchayat Acts by the new one in 1993.

Extension to Scheduled Areas

The provisions of Constitutional 73rd Amendment Act (Part IX) do not apply to the Scheduled Areas unless it is extended to these areas by an Act of Parliament. New Panchayat Acts were not applicable to Scheduled Areas and Tribal Areas under Article 243M. Therefore, the Government of India constituted a committee under the chairmanship of a tribal leader of Madhya Pradesh and former Member of Parliament Mr. Dilip Singh Bhuriya to recommend the ways and means to extend the 73rd Amendment to the Scheduled Areas. Based on the recommendations of the Bhuriya Committee, GoI introduced the Panchayats (Extension to the Scheduled Areas) Bill in the Parliament on December 19, 1996. Subsequently, the President's assent was accorded to the Bill on December 24, 1996, thus making it a part of the Constitution. All the states were supposed to bring their Panchayat Acts in conformity with the provisions of the Extension Act, 1996 within a one-year period that is by December 24, 1997.

The Extension Act, 1996 provides for the establishment of Gram Sabha for every village, comprising persons whose names appear in the electoral rolls of the Village Panchayat. It also lays down that any legislation on the Panchayats for the tribal areas shall be in consonance with customary laws, social and religious practices and traditional management practices of community resources (Singh, 1997). Moreover, grant of prospecting licence of mining lease and concessions for exploitation of minor minerals by auction have to be given on the recommendations of the Gram Sabha or the Panchayats at the appropriate level. The duty of management of minor water bodies in Scheduled Areas lies with the Panchayats at the appropriate level. In order to avoid overlapping of responsibilities between Panchayats at different levels in the three-tier PR structure, the Act highlights the need to ensure that Panchayats at the higher level do not assume the powers and functions of any lower level Panchayat or Gram Sabha.

One of the most striking features of the Extension Act, 1996 is that the Gram Sabha has been made the nucleus of all activities at the village level in order to safeguard tribal identity, traditional customs and practices, community assets and resolve local disputes. Another significant provision made in the Extension Act, 1996, which is not present in the Act of Part IX, is that Gram Sabhas have been mandated to 'approve all plans, programmes and projects for social and economic development, and selection of beneficiaries for all types of programmes to be implemented in the Village Panchayat area' (Singh, 1997, pp. 605). This provision may serve to restrict the influence of the political leadership and bureaucracy over implementation and management of development programmes. It will also ensure a closer monitoring of programmes by people and contribute towards a more transparent and accountable system of implementation. However, making it obligatory for village Panchayats to obtain a certificate of utilisation of funds from the Gram Sabha could further reduce the risk of manipulation by vested interests.

In recognition of the special character of tribal areas the Extension Act, 1996 provides for the Gram Sabha or the appropriate tier of Panchayat to have certain specific powers with regard to enforcement of prohibition, ownership of minor forest produce, prevention of alienation of land, management of village markets, control over money-lending and control over local plans and resources, including tribal sub-plans. Further, land cannot be acquired in these areas without consultation with either the Gram Sabha or the Panchayats at the appropriate level. Similarly, these bodies also need to be consulted at the time of rehabilitating people displaced by a project.

In order to give fair representation to all communities in the Scheduled Areas, the Extension Act, 1996 lays down that at least half of the seats in all tiers of Panchayats should be reserved for tribals as they have a predominant population in Scheduled Areas. Other communities will have a representation in proportion to their population in that Panchayat. In instances where some Scheduled Tribes fail to secure membership at the intermediate or district-level Panchayats, the state government may nominate such tribes to these bodies with the stipulation that these nominated members do not exceed one-tenth of the total elected members. It has been further laid down that all Chairpersons of Panchayats at all levels be reserved for tribals in order to facilitate governance by tribals so as to maintain the tribal character of the Scheduled areas. Although the Extension Act, 1996 mandates that the post of Chairperson at all levels of Panchayats be permanently reserved for the Scheduled Tribes, there are certain districts which are not tribal-majority districts and where tribals do not constitute more than 50 per cent of the total population of the district. In such a case, the other population in the area may resent reserving the above post on a permanent basis.

PANCHAYATI RAJ IN GUJARAT

Gujarat Panchayats Act, 1961

Gujarat took the first step towards decentralisation of power and democratisation of decision-making process with the adoption of Gujarat Panchayat Act, 1961, based on Balwant Rai Mehta Committee's report. The three-tier Panchayati Raj system of Gujarat is recognised as one of the best-decentralised democratic system in India linking the Village, Taluka and Zilla Panchayats. GoG 1961 highlights some of the outstanding features of the Panchayats in Gujarat as follows:

(a) Provision of Social Justice Committee at Gram, Nagar, Taluka and Zilla level for securing social justice to the weaker sections of the society.

(b) Statutory provision for a State Council for Panchayat to advise Government on all policy matters concerning Panchayats.

(c) Transfer of powers, functions and duties in the development sphere within the district to the Panchayats.

(d) Statutory assignment of 100 per cent revenue collection to PRI's.

(e) Creation of non-lapsable funds for assisting weaker sections, encouraging taxation efforts and financing development activities.

(f) Anti-defection provision similar to those for members of Parliament has been provided.

(g) Representation of Scheduled Castes and Scheduled Tribes in proportion to their population in Panchayats.

(h) Representation of women at all levels is ensured through reservation of seats of elected members.

(i) Provision of Nyaya Panchayat and Conciliation Panch.

(j) Provision of Gram Sabha.

(k) Provision of financial stipulation under the Act to provide for own taxes, assigned taxes and shared taxes. Own taxes are assigned to Panchayats and are levied by them. The taxes, which are assigned by statute to Panchayats but collected by the state government and the revenue is then passed to Panchayats are called assigned taxes. Shared taxes are those that are assigned to state government and collected by them but a share of their proceeds go to local bodies.

This Act was amended forty times in thirty years, although it had some very good features as mentioned above (GoG, 1993).

Decentralised District Planning in Gujarat

Despite the fact that Gujarat had a long history with Panchayati Raj Institutions, people in rural areas had not been sufficiently empowered. The large administrative and legal outfits mainly performed a regulatory function and development function was secondary, which defeated the very purpose of the PRIs. Lack of funds with the PRIs, due to limited devolution of resources by the state, constrained their ability to carry out developmental tasks as well as implement poverty programmes of the

Centre. Also, while PRIs are empowered to tax, they are unable to do so in an efficient manner due to inadequate expertise, manpower and infrastructure at their disposal. Therefore, in an effort to give a people-oriented thrust to PRIs, Gujarat introduced a Decentralised District Planning scheme in 1980 to address problems at the village level. This scheme was to earmark about five per cent of the total Plan outlays to address these micro-level problems based on peoples' demands. Financial resources were to be placed at the disposal of the District Planning Boards (DPBs) for the initiation, approval and implementation of schemes. It was envisaged that the DPBs would take up implementation of the Minimum Needs Programme in the initial phase, particularly in villages that were lagging behind. In the second stage, the DPBs would create and improve the production base of villages so that employment, production and incomes could be increased. The scheme was a huge success in its early stages and was able to generate immense enthusiasm amongst people all over the state (Cowlagi and Mehta, 1993).

However, the scheme suffered on account of two important reasons: One, that the decision-making body under this scheme was the District Planning Board and not PRIs. Two, the effective implementation of this scheme was constrained owing to a decline in the share of the Plan outlay allocated to DPBs as can be seen in Table 15.1. While the Sixth Five-Year Plan allocated 5.56 per cent of the total outlay to DPBs, this has come down to a mere 2.3 per cent in the Ninth Plan. Moreover, a portion of these funds was transferred to MLA's Development Fund[1] (Table 15.1), leaving a lesser amount in the hands of the people. Also, most of these funds were in the form of grants-in-aid from the state government for programmes previously decided by the state, hence there was little autonomy regarding the discretionary usage of these tied funds. Therefore, even this innovative people-oriented scheme could not achieve the desired results (*Ibid.*).

It is important to note here that the Five-Year Plan documents of the Government of Gujarat have separate chapters on Decentralised District Planning and Panchayati Raj, without integrating them, whereas the two are complimentary to each other because the objective of both is decentralisation and participation of the people in development.

Despite the initiative taken by Gujarat in adopting the Panchayats Act, certain political economy factors came in the way of successful democratic decentralisation in the state. An intensive study of the working of four village panchayats in four different types of villages in Gujarat by Hirway in 1986 shows that Panchayati Raj Institutions in the state are not as successful as they are made out to be. A number of factors contribute to their limited success (Hirway, 1989):

Table 15.1 : Fund Allocation for DPBs under Various Five-Year Plans

Five Year Plans	Total Plan Outlay (Rs. Crores)	Allocation for DPBs (Rs.Crores)	Share of MLAs Rs.Crores)
6th Five Yr. Plan	3600	200 (5.6)	—
7th Five Yr. Plan	6000	244 (4.1)	—
8th Five Yr. Plan	11500	301 (2.6)	18.5
9th Five Yr. Plan	28000	650 (2.3)	37.0

Note : Figures in brackets indicate percentage share of Plan outlay allocated to DPBs.

Source: Five-Year Plans of Govt. of Gujarat.

(a) *Centralised Decision-making:* There is no rationale behind allocation of functions and responsibilities between PRIs and the development administration. While management of local resources like land, water, forests, grazing land, etc. should be in the hands of local institutions, in reality, the state or central authorities control them. Central and state government schemes, which have increased tremendously in scope and number over the past 25-30 years, have left limited autonomy for the functioning of PRIs. These institutions hardly have expert staff for planning, implementation or monitoring of various development programmes. Such centralisation has also resulted in the finances of PRIs becoming very weak.

(b) *Socio-Economic Political Structure of the Rural Society:* The office-bearers and elected members in PR institutions mostly comprise big farmers and rich traders, usually belonging to higher castes. It is these people who hold the decision- making power in the panchayats and use it to serve and further their own interests. Since this 'elite' group has its own stake in preserving the exploitative structure, their actions do not serve the interests of the poor, so much so that even the SC/ST members of the panchayat are 'selected' by them (Hirway, 1989).

(c) *Unclear Role Demarcation:* There seems to be a lack of clear demarcation of the roles between the bureaucracy and the elected

PR bodies. Implementation of various development schemes suffers on account of the fact that these programmes are prepared either by central or state-level authorities or by bureaucrats at the district and lower levels, with little intervention from PRIs. Officials in the bureaucracy tend to be more loyal to their respective state departments than to elected members in the PR bodies. There is lack of mutual faith as officials feel that they are harassed by PR members wanting to further their own vested interests, while on the other hand, PR members dislike the 'superiority' of officials (*Ibid.*).

Gujarat Panchayat Act, 1993

The PRIs in Gujarat failed to become vibrant institutions of self-governance, because of lack of political and bureaucratic support, irregular elections, inadequate representation of weaker sections of the society, prolonged supersessions, centralised decision-making, unclear role demarcation between the bureaucracy and the elected bodies (Hirway, 1989), absence of functional and financial autonomy, insufficient devolution of powers and inadequate resources. PRIs in Gujarat were largely controlled and run by state bureaucracy with very little autonomy. It provided for representation of women, but only a token one. Elections were held at the will of the state. Supersessions were the order of the day. How PRIs will spend their resources, on what, at what time, all were decided by the state bureaucracy. Neither the state legislature nor the state bureaucracy showed a genuine inclination to share powers with PRIs.

The Gujarat Panchayat Act, 1961 was replaced by the Gujarat Panchayat Act, (GPA) 1993 after the 73rd Constitutional Amendment Act. GPA 1993 adopted all the provisions of the 73rd Constitutional Amendment Act. Gujarat has had for many years a three-tier Panchayati Raj structure similar to the one incorporated in 73rd Constitutional Amendment Act. Thus, GPA 1993 incorporates all the additional provisions required to bring GPA 1993 in conformity with the 73rd Constitutional Amendment Act like constitution of State Finance Commission, State Election Commission, a Panchayat list under Eleventh Schedule, limited period of supersession and additional reservations for Other Backward Classes and women (GPA 1993). The provision of Nyaya Panchayat and Conciliation Panch as in GPA 1961 has, however, been dropped in GPA 1993.

Extension to Scheduled Areas of Gujarat

The provisions of the GPA 1993 were not applicable to Scheduled Areas of Gujarat. It became applicable in 1996 after Parliament enacted Panchayats (Extension to the Scheduled Areas) Act, 1996. Gujarat was supposed to bring the GPA 1993 in conformity with the provisions of the Extension Act, 1996 within a one-year period, i.e. by December 24th 1997. Gujarat State Assembly should have enacted the said law by December 1997. However, instead GOG promulgated an ordinance to that effect on December 20th 1997, which was later on replaced by the Gujarat Panchayats (Amendment) Bill, 1998. This Amendment to Gujarat Panchayats Act, 1993 is applicable to a total of 5055 villages in 33 talukas in 7 districts with tribal population of about 62 lakhs which is 15 per cent of total population living in 28 per cent of the villages in the state.

Major Provisions of the Gujarat Panchayats (Amendment) Bill, 1998

The Gujarat Panchayat (Amendment) Bill, 1998 to amend the Gujarat Panchayats Act, 1993 provides for powerful Gram Sabhas. The Bill lays down that minor forest produce found in the forest area under the jurisdiction of the village shall vest in the Village Panchayat and the sale proceeds from such produce shall be paid into and form part of the village fund. The Bill also provides for reservation of one-half of the total number of seats in all tiers of Panchayats for the Scheduled Tribs. An important provision of the Bill is that the Taluka Panchayats need to be consulted before acquiring any land for any development project under Land Acquisition Act, 1894 and before resettling or rehabilitating persons affected by such project. The duties of the Village Panchayat have been expanded to include planning and management of water bodies. The duties of the Taluka Panchayats have been also expanded to include control over local plan and resources for such plans, including Tribal sub-plan. The Bombay Moneylender Act, 1946, has been amended to protect Scheduled Tribes. Further, the Bombay Land Revenue Code, 1879 has been amended to give primacy to District Panchayats against the existing one to the Collectors (Gujarat Bill No. 5 of 1998).

While the Gujarat Panchayats (Amendment) Bill, 1998 incorporated almost all the recommendations of the Bhuriya Committee Report without many changes, there were certain recommendations which the Bill included, albeit in a diluted form. The Bhuriya Committee had made involvement of the Gram Sabha obligatory in matters of land acquisition, fixing of compensation to affected persons and in provision of a rehabilitation package to the affected. In contrast, the Gujarat Bill of 1998 has completely played down the role of the Gram Sabha by suggesting that all decisions in regard to land acquisition be made 'in consultation' with the Taluka Panchayat. It has thus sought to restrict to the local people, the very autonomy, which it was meant to provide. Moreover, certain provisions, as given hereunder, of the Bhuriya Committee Report have been completely overlooked by the Gujarat Panchayat (Amendment) Bill, 1998. According to the provisions of the Bhuriya Committee:

(a) It is mandatory to take the recommendations of the Gram Sabha or the Panchayats at the appropriate level prior to the grant of prospecting license or mining lease for minor minerals in the Scheduled Areas, or for grant of concessions for the exploitation of minor minerals by auction (GOI, 1996 & Singh, 1997).

(b) Administrative boundaries in Scheduled and Tribal areas need reorganisation based on geographic, ethnic and demographic considerations since these boundaries were determined during colonial times and need to be changed.

(c) Actions of the functionaries of police, excise, forest and revenue departments have often been found regressive and exploitative of tribal people. The Bhuriya Committee suggested that there should be no police interference in cases not involving non-heinous offences. In case of development functions, the Autonomous District Councils (ADCs) should discharge such functions. Administration of justice should be largely dealt with by the traditional legal bodies and jury-based systems evolved by the tribal communities.

(d) In certain districts, Scheduled Tribe population may be less than 50 per cent of the district's total population, but it may be concentrated in a part or parts of the district. The Committee has recommended that sub-district councils may be constituted for such areas and designated as Autonomous Sub-District Councils (ASDCs), which will be at par with ADCs.

Thus, a number of significant recommendations having far-reaching implications on the lives of the tribal population in Scheduled Areas were either watered down and/or omitted in the Bill 1998.

SOME ISSUES CONCERNING PRIS IN GUJARAT

Evolution of PRI's in Gujarat and India raises several issues with regard to its implementation and efficacy. The first issue concerns functional and financial autonomy of PRI's in Gujarat — in particular the role of Gujarat Finance Commission set-up under Article 243 I of Constitution of India. The second issue concerns the extension of 73rd Constitutional Amendment to the Scheduled areas.

Functional and Financial Autonomy of PRIs in Gujarat

The most important issue concerning PRIs in Gujarat and even in other states of the country is with respect to functional and financial autonomy. All efforts so far in the Panchayat Act have been made towards this area. The necessary condition for autonomy is to match the functions and the funds. Unfortunately, this very condition for autonomy is the most disregarded. As Rani (1999) observes: "A one-to-one correspondence between functional responsibilities and financial resources at various levels of government is impossible in any federation. The problem is compounded when the Constitution provides for a deliberate mismatch as in India. A further worry is added as the 73rd and 74th Constitutional Amendments have left the tasks of devolving more powers, authority, functions, finance etc. to the State Legislatures......"

Responsibilities Allotted to the Panchayats

(i) The State Government has transferred to the District Panchayats, powers, functions and duties as are exercised by the 10 departments of the state, along with funds and personnel under Section 175.

(ii) The State Government can also entrust to District Panchayats, 29 schemes of the state government (same as Eleventh Schedule to the Constitution of India) for economic development and social justice, with funds and personnel under Section 180.

(iii). Under the Gujarat Panchayat Act, 1993, Schedule I (Section 99) with a total of 109 duties, Schedule II (Section 130) with a total of 87 duties and Schedule III (Section 154) with a total of 86 duties, elaborate the duties of Village Panchayats, Taluka Panchayats and District Panchayats respectively. However, adequate provision of funds and personnel has not been made for carrying out these duties, especially in case of the Village Panchayats.

In the above framework, PRIs largely function as extended wings of the state government departments. PRIs receive large funds for fulfilling the responsibilities mentioned above in (i) and (ii). However, this is for departmentally determined specific projects and purposes and not as per the needs of the region and people. It is largely supply-oriented and not demand-oriented. The control of the funds is with the departments. These funds are not available for fulfilling the duties assigned to Panchayats in Schedules I, II and III. PRIs have to generate and mobilise additional resources for fulfilling the duties mentioned in the above Schedules. At present, 98 per cent of the total expenditure incurred by Panchayats come as grant-in-aid from the government for transferred departmental functions. The own income of Panchayats accounts for only 2 per cent of the total budget of the Panchayats, which is available for fulfilling the duties under Schedules I, II and III (GOG, 1999). There is thus a need for rationalisation and a clear-cut demarcation of responsibilities between the Central, State Governments and District, Taluka and Village Panchayats. At present, it is all concurrent.

ROLE OF STATE FINANCE COMMISSION

Undue Delay in submission and implementation of the recommendations of the State Finance Commission

The responsibility for providing financial autonomy to PRIs has been entrusted to the State Finance Commission under Article 243-I of the Constitution of India, which has to be set up every five years. The Government of Gujarat set up Gujarat Finance Commission under Article 243-I of the Constitution of India on September 15th, 1994. It submitted an interim report with respect to the recommendations of Tenth Finance Commission, Government of India, in September 1997. The final report should have been placed before the Assembly in 1998/1999, which has not been done (Shah, 1999 and GOG, 1999). This means that the State Finance Commission has already taken about four-and-a-half years in completing and submitting its report to the Government, which is against the spirit of the 73rd Constitutional Amendment Act. This delay reflects the indifference of the state. This also denies the benefit to the tune of Rs. 1778.16 crores to PRIs, arising due to the recommendations of the State Finance Commission (GOG, 1999), which would have given some financial autonomy to PRIs. In this context, it is important to note that nearly a dozen SFCs have already submitted their reports to the Government (Rani, 1999).

Variations in the terms of reference

The Terms of Reference as stipulated in Article 243-I of the Constitution of India, and as mentioned in the Notification issued by the Government of Gujarat on 30th September, 1994, differ from the Terms of Reference laid down by the Gujarat Finance Commission for its functioning. There are certain areas of commonality between the Terms of Reference issued by the above:

(i) The first is with regard to the distribution between the State Government, Panchayats and Nagarpalikas of the net proceeds of the taxes, duties, tolls and fees leviable by the State Government.
(ii) The second area deals with determination of the taxes, duties, tolls and fees, which may be assigned to, or appropriated by the Panchayat.
(iii) The third is with regard to the grant-in-aid to Panchayats from the Consolidated Fund of the state and the measures needed to improve the financial position of the Panchayats.

Despite these commonalities, there are other areas where the Terms of Reference suggested by the three sources differ distinctly:

The Constitution of India stipulates that "the Legislature of a state may, by law, provide for the composition of the Commission, the qualifications which shall be requisite for appointment as members thereof and the manner in which they will be selected" (Constitution of India). Besides determining the procedure, the Commission will also have powers in regard to the performance of their functions.

The Notification issued by the Government of Gujarat mentions that the Commission should check for the level of financial self-dependency of local self-government institutions and give recommendations regarding the following matters:

- Ways to increase assets from the fiscal levy, taxes, fees, etc. obtained from institutions of local self-government.
- To improve the method of collection of taxes with regard to public amenities like water.

- Rules determining ceiling on borrowings made by these local institutions from state government.
- To look at ways to compensate the possible decline in allocation of funds by the government.

The Terms of Reference laid down by the Gujarat Finance Commission for its functioning, however, emphasised the need for a more efficient usage of the existing taxes, instead of levying new taxes, so as not to put excess load of taxation on the general population. Also, the Commission suggested reducing delays on the part of the state government in releasing grants to the local bodies. While the Constitution, in its Terms of Reference, highlighted the importance of creation of a divisible pool, there is no provision for such a pool by the Commission, which may be disadvantageous to the PRIs. This is also against the Constitutional spirit and mandate (GOG, 1994, GOG, 1997 and Bakshi, 1998). The question arises as to 'can a State Finance Commission alter the Terms of Reference as laid down in the Constitution and Government Notification?'

Delay in the implementation of the recommendations of the Tenth Finance Commission with respect to PRIs

The Tenth Finance Commission, Government of India, gave an untied grant of Rs.192 crores to PRIs in Gujarat for the period 1996-2000 at the rate of Rs. 48 crores per year. However, Gujarat Panchayats will get this money from the year 1999-2000 to 2003 because of the delay in the recommendations of the Gujarat Finance Commission. This delay means that the real value of Rs. 48 crores will go down to Rs. 30 crores only, which is a loss to PRIs (GOI, 1994 and GOG, 1997).

Gujarat Finance Commission was expected to provide the necessary financial autonomy, but it seems that it was not a matter of concern and urgency for the Finance Commission, which caused unnecessary delay. This delay is against the spirit of the 73rd Constitutional Amendment. A proper and timely recommendation by the State Finance Commission would have gone a long way in giving Panchayats some financial autonomy. Even the major recommendations of the Gujarat Finance Commission are largely with respect to existing provisions only. It hardly makes an attempt to project the needs and incomes of the Panchayats over time and how that gap could be filled.

Grant-in-aid for Transferred and Delegated works to District and Taluka Panchayats

One of the major and most important sources of funds for the Panchayats is the grant-in-aid from the state government for transferred departmental schemes to be implemented by the Panchayats. Table 15.2 and Table 15.3 show the grant-in-aid to Panchayats in Gujarat. Government of Gujarat transfers about 20 per cent of its revenue to Panchayats, amounting to over Rs. 2000 crores. Even in 1976-77, in Gujarat, the share of assigned taxes worked out to 29.60 per cent of the state's own resources and grants to Panchayats accounted for 22.90 per cent of the total (GOI, 1994). This is more than a minimum of 15 per cent of the total resources of the state recommended by the Ministry of Rural Development, Government of India, in its memorandum to the Tenth Finance Commission in the State Panchayat's context. However, this massive transfer of funds (mentioned under Section 175 and not under Schedules I, II and III to the Constitution of India) is for the transferred and delegated works of the state departments. The transfer of these funds is for non-Plan purposes to the extent of 83 per cent. Moreover, this transfer is supply-oriented and not demand-oriented. The transfer of funds is also very complicated and the process is very slow. District Panchayats receive them at the end of the financial year, and sometimes, even later than that. In this three-tier framework of PRI, District Panchayats have become a new centre of power after the state government and Government of India. It, therefore, does not provide any autonomy to Panchayats. In spite of so much of funds, PRIs have made little impact on rural economy and rural life since they are not need-based.

The total resources transferred to PRIs are quite large, which they have been receiving since 1963. However, 98 per cent of the funds are tied. If 40 to 50 per cent of these funds are made available in un-tied manner, with a provision of contribution by the people in equal proportion, then it would lead to financial autonomy. The functional autonomy also can be achieved by rationalising the list of responsibilities of the PRIs, state and central government.

Table 15.2 : Total and Per Capita Grant-in Aid to District and Taluka Panchayats in Gujarat, 1989-90 to 1998-99

Year	Grant-in-aid (Rs. crores)	Per capita grant	% of grant-in-aid to total budget
1989-90	460.41	169.89	—
1990-91	612.27	225.93	—
1991-92	970.52	358.13	—
1992-93	956.63	353.29	—
1993-94	1117.17	412.57	14
1994-95	1329.20	490.87	16.2
1995-96	1322.57	488.03	16.1
1996-97	2026.76	747.88	20.7
1997-98(R.E.)	2040.67	753.01	18.5
1998-99(B.E.)	2299.39	848.48	17.6

Source : Budget Publication No:- 4, 11, 18 (part II), 19, 21, 23 (part 1, 2 & 3), 9, 24, 3 and 22 (part 2).

Recommendations of the Gujarat State Finance Commission

GOG (1999) highlights some of the recommendations given by the State Finance Commission of Gujarat in order to augment the resources of the Panchayats. While the report of the SFC of Gujarat has not been made public, its major recommendations have been reproduced in the Memorandum to the Eleventh Finance Commission (GOG, Jan. 1999). Our comments are largely based on this:

1. Panchayats should be given a share from such state taxes, which have hitherto been denied to Panchayats, e.g. Professional Tax.
2. Instead of sharing all tax proceeds with the Panchayats, the state should levy a surcharge on the tax and then pass on the proceeds to the Panchayats.
3. The share of the Panchayats in case of taxes like Land Revenue and Local Cess may be increased.
4. The state may impose new taxes on items like agricultural produce and surcharge on stamp duty.
5. Taxes regarding land revenue, entertainment tax and pilgrim tax, which were withdrawn in the past, are to be re-imposed.

Table 15.3 : Schemes-Wise provision for grant-in-aid and loan to District and Taluka Panchayats by Departments 1996-97 (Actual), 1997-98 and 1998-99

(All figures are in crores)

No.	Department	1996-97 (Actual)			1997-98 (Revised Estimated)			1998-99 (Budget Estimate)		
		Plan	Non-Plan	Total	Plan	Non-Plan	Total	Plan	Non-Plan	TOTAL
	1	2	3	4	5	6	7	8	9	10
1.	Finance	—	0.2	0.2	—	0.2	0.2	—	0.2	0.2
2.	Narmada Water Resources & Water Supply	33.4	16.1	49.5	52.3	16.6	68.9	55.2	17.7	72.9
3.	Food, Civil Supplies and Consumer Affairs	—	—	—	—	—	—	—	—	—
4.	Home	—	—	—	—	—	—	—	—	—
5.	Sports, Youth and Cultural Activities	—	—	—	—	—	—	—	—	—
6.	Gujarat Legislation Secretariat	—	—	—	—	—	—	—	—	—
7.	Panchayat, Rural Housing and Rural Development	82.0	145.5	227.5	1.5	131.5	133.0	4.2	129.7	133.9
8.	Road and Building	51.1	120.2	171.4	58.1	120.3	178.4	108.9	139.7	248.6
9.	Industries and Mines	—	—	—	—	—	—	—	—	—

(Contd.)

Table 15.3 *(Contd.)*

1	2	3	4	5	6	7	8	9	10
10. Social Welfare and Tribal Development	88.9	77.6	166.5	89.4	97.0	186.4	103.9	98.3	202.2
11. General Administrative	0.03	1.3	1.3	0.03	1.4	1.5	0.1	2.3	2.4
12. Education	27.6	1075.2	1102.7	48.1	1028.5	1076.6	70.8	1180.1	1250.9
13. Legal	—	—	—	—	—	—	—	—	—
14. Labour and Employment	—	—	—	—	—	—	—	—	—
15. Urban Development & Urban Housing	—	—	—	—	—	—	—	—	—
16. Ports and Fisheries	—	—	—	—	—	—	—	—	—
17. Legislative and Parliamentary Affairs	—	—	—	—	—	—	—	—	—
18. Revenue	—	32.6	32.6	—	32.3	32.3	—	26.3	26.3
19. Forests and Environment	—	—	—	—	—	—	—	—	—
20. Energy and Petro-chemicals	—	—	—	—	—	—	—	—	—
21. Receipt under Consolidated Fund & Transactions Under Contingency Fund & Public Accounts etc.	—	—	—	—	—	—	—	—	—

(Contd.)

Table 15.3 *(Contd.)*

	1	2	3	4	5	6	7	8	9	10
22	Information, Broadcasting and Tourism	—	—	—	—	—	—	—	—	—
23	Health and Family Welfare	40.6	165.5	206.1	88.8	176.6	265.4	63.5	188.8	252.3
24	Agricultural and Corporation	9.4	59.4	68.8	16.0	81.9	97.9	16.0	93.5	109.5
(a)	Welfare of SC, ST and OBC	0.02	0.1	0.1	0.04	0.1	0.1	0.04	0.1	0.1
(b)	Crop Husbandry	3.6	26.6	30.2	9.5	45.3	54.9	8.4	46.4	54.7
(c)	Animal Husbandry	4.7	20.9	25.7	5.8	24.1	29.9	6.5	30.4	36.9
(d)	Dairy Development	0.7	—	0.7	0.3	—	0.3	0.3	—	0.3
(e)	Co-operation	0.4	11.1	11.5	0.4	11.9	12.3	0.7	15.9	16.6
(f)	Others	—	0.7	0.7	—	0.6	0.6	—	0.9	0.9
	TOTAL	**333.2**	**1675.1**	**2008.3**	**354.3**	**1665.9**	**2020.2**	**422.7**	**1883.3**	**2305.9**
			9791.1 (20.7)				**10920.9(18.5)**		**131081.8 (17.6)**	

Source : Budget Publication No: 4, 11, 18 (part II), 19, 21, 23 (part 1, 2 & 3), 9, 24, 3 and 22 (part 2).

6. Increase in taxation by Village Panchayats themselves in matters of local and irrigation cess are proposed.
7. Distribution of land revenue should be based on the relevant year's land revenue and not on the last three years' average. Also, deduction of 35 per cent towards the salaries of Talati-*cum*-Mantri needs to be dispensed with.
8. For the maintenance of roads handed over to the Panchayats and for construction of new ones, a part of the total cost needs to be kept aside as an annual maintenance fund. Similarly, for the maintenance of buildings, 5 per cent of their present cost of construction should be provided as grant-in-aid by the state.
9. The SFC has recommended making levying of property tax, water tax and conservancy tax mandatory for the Gram Panchayats.
10. Since tax recovery is poor, monetary incentives can be given for their better and improved recovery.
11. The Panchayat Finance Board should be reconstituted. Giving it an independent status will ensure that there is minimum interference in its day-to-day functioning by the government.
12. The grant of Rs. 20 lakh per MLA from the Decentralised District Planning Scheme should be abolished.

The above recommendations consist of :

(a) Recommendations that impinge on the state government's budget, and

(b) Recommendations which do not affect the state government budget, but pertain to redistribution of grants, tax recovery of local bodies, income generation through direct taxes by local bodies and motivation of public donations to local bodies.

The major recommendations of the State Finance Commission of Gujarat concern land revenue and local cess on it. It may be noted that Section 203 of GPA, 1993 states that a village panchayat is entitled to levy and collect upto 25 paise as 'cess' on every rupee payable to the state government as land revenue (GOG, 1993). However, the Government of Gujarat has abolished land revenue (w.e.f. 1997) and its benefit to Panchayats is dependent on reimposition of land revenue by the Government of Gujarat.

Table 15.4 : Minimum Budgetary Implications of the Recommendations of the State Finance Commission

Point No.	Recommendation	Financial Impact on State Budget (Rs. lakhs)
5.2	35% pay and allowance expenses of Talati-cum-Mantri	2432
5.3A	5% more on Jungle Upaj to District Panchayat	80
5.3B	Special Grant instead of Land Revenue	45
5.4	Profession Tax	275
5.5	Maintenance of roads and buildings	7600
6.1	20 paise District Planning share	685
7.2	Travelling allowance to primary teachers	220
7.2	Datum Grant from Rs. 4/- to 5/- per student	35
7.4	1% Contingency charges	1330
7.7	Salary of DDO and his staff 100%	66
13.1.21	(a) Village roads	4400
	(b) Primary school rooms	46800
	(c) Drinking water	80700
	(d) Building of PHCs	28201
13.1.2	Maintenance of primary school rooms	4947
Total		177816

Source: Memorandum to Eleventh Finance Commission, GOG, pp. 75, January 1999.

It has been found that the three-tier Panchayats have been receiving less than their total entitlements, for example, District and Taluka Panchayats have been receiving only 50 per cent of their share from land revenue and Village Panchayats only 25 per cent. However, the Gujarat Finance Commission (GFC) is largely silent on this issue. It is imperative, therefore, that the three-tier Panchayats demand their due share after reimposition of land revenue.

In the present scheme of things, Village Panchayats have the largest responsibilities (as much as 106) (Section 99, Schedule I, GPA 1993) as well as the largest number of taxes and fees that they are entitled to levy (as many as 21 taxes and fees) (Section 200, GPA 1993). However, their administrative infrastructure to fulfil these two obligations is negligible. As against this, District and Taluka Panchayats are given both funds and personnel to fulfil their obligations. If Village Panchayats are supposed to mobilise additional resources by better imposition and collection of taxes, then their administrative structure needs to be urgently upgraded. GPA 1993 has incorporated the Eleventh Schedule introduced under the 73rd Constitutional Amendment Act as Section 180 in GPA 1993 and the responsibility for this has been entrusted to District Panchayats along with funds and personnel. These could be transferred to Taluka Panchayats with the approval of the state government. In this context, it is suggested that the schemes under the Eleventh Schedule incorporated in Section 180 of GPA 1993 should be entrusted to the Village Panchayats along with the funds and personnel for carrying out these functions. In fact, there is a commonality between Schedule I elaborating duties of Village Panchayats and the Eleventh Schedule of the Constitution of India and, therefore, it is advisable that the Village Panchayat itself performs these functions. This change will strengthen the Village Panchayat significantly, which at present is the weakest unit of PRIs, albeit with the largest and the widest responsibilities and the minimum resources.

That Village Panchayats have been entrusted with an equal, if not greater, magnitude of responsibilities than District and Taluka Panchayats — without provision of such supporting administrative infrastructure as will enable them to carry out these tasks — is a reflection of the strong tendency of centralisation of power, which still pervades all levels of government functioning in the country. Despite the best intentions of the 73rd Constitutional Amendment, the state still remains the nodal decision-making agency, with the District Panchayats becoming the new centres of power in the hierarchical structure of PRIs. It is unfortunate that the Act, which sought grassroots empowerment, has failed to provide any endowment to the most fundamental unit of self-governance—the Village Panchayat.

Interesting features of other State Finance Commissions

Although Gujarat prides itself as being the pioneer of democratic decentralisation in the country, owing to its strong three-tier Panchayati Raj system, certain other states like Rajasthan, Kerala, Karnataka, Punjab and West Bengal have shown some remarkable efforts towards providing functional and financial autonomy to the PRIs (Rani, 1999). The State Finance Commissions of these states, in their reports, have suggested some very innovative measures regarding tax assignment to Panchayats and their functional and financial responsibilities.

The Karnataka State Finance Commission (KSFC) in its recommendations on fiscal devolution with reference to PRIs has suggested abolition of regional development boards and the scheme for allotting funds to MLAs for spending on development works in their constituencies. It has also proposed setting up of an upgradation grant, based on certain norms to improve the quality of public services. The provision of transfer of 36 per cent of gross state revenue to local bodies, with a scheme of *inter se* distribution of resources to PRIs giving weightage to backwardness etc. needs special mention.

The report of the State Finance Commission of Punjab (PSFC) has clearly demarcated the financial powers of each tier of PRIs, with the maximum of Rs. 5 lakhs to Gram Panchayats, Rs. 10 lakhs to Panchayat Samitis and above Rs. 10 lakhs to the Zilla Panchayats. The power for framing of by-laws has been given to PRIs. The PSFC has also tried to spell out in detail, the specific functions each tier has to undertake. While the functions of Gram Panchayats have been classified into six categories, those assigned to Panchayat Samitis and Zilla Panchayats are in the nature of supervision and control. Further, the PSFC recommends the creation of public accounts committees at the district level for ensuring public accountability in the same manner as the public accounts committee of the state does at its level.

In an effort to rationalise the local tax structure, the PSFC has analysed the resources of local bodies during the pre- and post-73rd and 74th Amendment periods. Gram Panchayats are assigned house tax and 40 per cent of state land revenue, while the Panchayat Samitis and Zilla Panchayats are not given any tax assignments. The PSFC recommends that PRIs should be given freedom to levy taxes and fees and also to fix the rates thereof. The West Bengal State Finance Commission (WBSFC) suggests an entitlement approach or a revenue sharing formula for the PRIs. It has recommended a new regime of tax collection in which the tax administration works in co-operation with the Panchayats, giving a portion of the tax collected as entitlement to these bodies (Rani, 1999).

Extension to Scheduled Areas in Gujarat

Undue delay in extending the benefits of the 73rd Constitutional Amendment

The second issue is with regard to the extension of the 73rd Constitutional Amendment to Scheduled Areas of Gujarat. In Gujarat, the provisions of the Constitutional 73rd Amendment Act were extended to the Scheduled Areas through an ordinance in December, 1997, one year after the Amendment in the Central Act. The Gujarat Panchayats Amendment Bill 1998 replaced this ordinance. The very fact that the Scheduled Areas were denied the benefits of the 73rd Constitutional Amendment Act for more than three years reflects the sheer indifference of the state towards empowering people's institutions in these backward areas.

Features of Gujarat Panchayats (Amendment) Bill, 1998

Need for Amending Land Acquisition Act, 1894

The Gujarat Panchayats (Amendment) Bill, 1998 provides that the "Gram Sabha or Panchayat at the appropriate level shall be consulted before making the acquisition of land in the Scheduled Areas for development projects and before resettling or rehabilitating persons affected by such projects in the Scheduled Areas; the actual planning and implementation of the projects in the Scheduled Areas shall be coordinated by the State Government". The implication of this provision is that it is only a consultative process and not a mandatory one. It is, therefore, unlikely to make any impact on acquisition of land under the Land Acquisition Act, 1894 and the people affected by land acquisition.

There is also a need to reexamine the Land Acquisition Act, 1894. At present the compensation for land acquired by the Government is fixed within the framework of Land Acquisition Act, 1894. The main focus of the Act is to compensate the land acquisition in terms of the market prices. Since the rural agricultural land is not widely traded, ready market prices are not available. Effort is made to find a suitable proxy for the market price of the land, superstructure and other movable and immovable properties, affected due to acquisition of land. There is a general tendency on the part of the Land Acquisition Officers to consider the conservative values observed among the transactions in arriving at the base value and therefore the compensation based on it is a very poor proxy for the actual land value. It has been also found that the Land Acquisition Officers do not update the amount of sales transactions in different years for computing the base values. Given this method of determining the base values, the compensation so paid would not enable the cultivator to actually buy the land of the order of the quantity forgone. The present compensation formula also does not differentiate between those who lose all their land and those left with less than two hectares of land. This method of fixation of market price and compensation does not take into account, either the agricultural or the development potential of the land. Also, as land is not regarded as a productive asset, the income loss is not estimated and compensated. Therefore, the present method of determining compensation for acquiring land is totally inappropriate in comparison to the assets and incomes actually forgone by the cultivator. This compensation is invariably much lower than the true market value of those assets. As a result of this, it leads to impoverishment of the affected persons.

When a farmer's land is acquired, he is losing

(1) his basic productive asset,
(2) his future income, and
(3) his family employment.

However, the present Land Acquisition Act, 1894 provides the compensation package merely as an asset, but not as productive asset, nor does it take into consideration the loss of future income as also of family employment. An amended Land Acquisition Act needs to provide for all these three types of losses, which will ensure the standard of living enjoyed by affected persons before acquisition (Srivastava *et al.*, 1991).

Another lacuna in the Land Acquisition Act, 1894 is that it is based on the principle of individual land ownership and does not take cognizance of the customary regulation of common property resources in tribal areas. Among many tribal areas, land and such other natural resources are owned jointly by the community and the community itself sanctions its use by individuals. In not recognising this basic principle in tribal areas, the Land Acquisition Act is premised on unrealistic ground (Sharma, 1995).

Managing Water Bodies

Water bodies are an integral resource to village Panchayats with the rural populace depending on them, both for their daily needs as well as for augmenting their income by rearing fish. While the Gujarat Panchayats (Amendment) Bill, 1998 provides for planning and management of water bodies in the Scheduled Areas through Panchayats at the appropriate level, it is important that the state provides the necessary wherewithal to Panchayats in matters of :

(1) Identification of water bodies in un-exploited areas and maintenance of existing ones, and
(2) Provision of funds and technology for the optimum utilisation of these resources.

Common Property Resources

Among many tribal areas, land and such other natural resources are owned jointly by the community and the community itself sanctions its use by individuals. One of the most powerful means of giving autonomy to Panchayats is to let them have control over the Common Property Resources (CPRs) of land, water and forests in their jurisdiction. It is important to note here, the various provisions in the Constitution of India, regarding ownership of community resources, and the protection and improvement of the natural environment. Article 39B of the Constitution of India states that "Ownership and control of the material resources of the community are so distributed as best to subserve the common good". Article 48A of the Constitution of India lays down that "The State shall endeavour to protect and improve the environment and to safeguard the forests and wildlife of the country". Also, the Fundamental Duties mentioned under Part IVA [Article 51A (g)] of the Constitution of India state that "It shall be the duty of every citizen of India to protect and improve the natural environment including forests, lakes, rivers and wild-life, and to have compassion for living creatures."

These resources, which vest with the respective departments at present can be developed in an efficient manner only when the right to do so passes on to the tribal people, who have been taking care of these natural resources since a long time. Income accrued from the development of these CPRs can be further utilised by the Panchayats to fund development programmes in the village, thereby improving the overall economy of the area. As a safeguard, the ownership of the CPRs can remain with the state, so that Panchayats are not able to transfer this land.

Conclusion

Gujarat, despite its long tradition of Panchayati Raj Institutions, has not been very successful in providing to its village-level institutions, the functional and financial autonomy, which is integral to self-governance. The Gujarat Panchayat Acts of 1961 and 1993 and the Panchayats

(Amendment) Bill, 1998 have fallen far short of providing meaningful empowerment to Panchayati Raj Institutions. The dilution of the Decentralised District Planning Scheme introduced in 1980, the disproportionate provision of duties and resources to the Village Panchayats, watering down of the recommendations of the Bhuriya Committee Report, delay in submission and implementation of the Gujarat State Finance Commission's recommendations and the half-hearted measures suggested by the Commission for devolution of powers and functions to the Panchayats — all point towards the reservations of the state in reducing its hold over the local institutions.

The existing legal, administrative and financial framework of Panchayats overlooks the glaring mismatch between their means and responsibilities. Sadly, this mismatch is more glaring at the Gram Panchayat level, which is the crucial component in the empowerment of rural areas. The 73rd Amendment through the Eleventh Schedule (Article 243G) sought to create an opportunity for strengthening the Village Panchayats. However, Gujarat did not utilise this opportunity and instead, entrusted schemes under this Schedule to the District and Taluka Panchayats with funds and personnel by inserting Section 180 in Gujarat Panchayat Act, 1993. This provision needs to be amended by substituting in Section 180, 'Village Panchayats' in place of the District and Taluka Panchayats, both in non-Scheduled as well as Scheduled Areas. Also, in order to ensure financial autonomy to the Panchayati Raj Institutions, about 40 to 50 per cent of funds received from the state should be in the form of untied funds, with a provision of contribution by the people in equal proportion.

The Panchayats (Amendment) Bill, 1998 should transfer the powers with regard to ownership of local forest produce, management of water bodies and minor minerals and the issue of adequate rehabilitation of people displaced under the Land Acquisition Act, 1894 to the Gram Sabha instead of the Taluka Panchayat. Further, there is an urgent need to amend the Land Acquisition Act, 1894 in order to arrive at a more rational formula for determining compensation for acquisition of land. Finally, the weak and inadequate administrative structure at the Village Panchayat level needs to be strengthened to enable it to carry out the above functions.

NOTES

1. The recommendations of the Gujarat SFC (reproduced in the Memorandum to the Eleventh Finance Commission, GOG, 1999) seek to abolish transfer of funds to the MLA Dvelopment Fund.

REFERENCES

Bakshi, P.M. (1998), *The Constitution of India,* Government of India, Universal Law Publishing Company, Delhi.

Cowlagi, V.R.S. and Mehta, S.S. (1993), "Lessons from Panchayati Raj in Gujarat", *The Administrator - Special Issue on Panchayati Raj*, Vol. XXXVIII, No. 4, Oct.-Dec., 1993, Wiley Eastern Limited, New Delhi.

Datta, Abhijit (1995), "Municipal Reform in India - Comparative Models and Processes", *Economic and Political Weekly,* Sept. 23, 1995, Mumbai.

Girglani, J.M. (1993), "Financial Resources of Panchayati Raj Institutions", *The Administrator - Special Issue on Panchayati Raj,* Vol. XXXVIII, No. 4, Oct.-Dec., 1993, Wiley Eastern Limited, New Delhi.

Gopalakrishnan, R. and Sharma, Amita (1998), "Education Guarantee Scheme in Madhya Pradesh - Innovative Step to Universalise Education", *Economic and Political Weekly,* Sept. 26, 1998, Mumbai.

Government of Gujarat (Legal Department) (1961), *Gujarat Panchayats Act, 1961,* Gandhinagar.

Government of Gujarat (Panchayat and Rural Housing Department) (1991), "Annual Report of the Office of the Development Commissioner 1991", Gandhinagar.

Government of Gujarat (Panchayat and Rural Housing Department) (1992), *Panchayati Raj in Gujarat,* Gandhinagar.

Government of Gujarat (Legal Department) (1993), *Gujarat Panchayats Act, 1993,* Gandhinagar.

Government of Gujarat (Panchayat and Rural Housing Department) (1993), *Panchayati Raj - Gujarat blazes the trail,* Gandhinagar.

Government of Gujarat (Panchayat and Rural Housing Department) (1994), *Notification with regard to the Terms of Reference of the State Finance Commission,* Gandhinagar.

Government of Gujarat (Panchayats and Rural Housing Department) (1997), *Gujarat Panchayats Amendment Ordinance 1997.*

Government of Gujarat (1997), *Interim Report of the Gujarat Finance Commission,* Gandhinagar.

Government of Gujarat (Legal Department) (1998), *Gujarat Panchayats Amendment Bill 1998,* Gandhinagar.

Government of Gujarat (Finance Department) (1999), *Supplementing the Resources of the Panchayats*, Memorandum to the Eleventh Finance Commission, Gandhinagar.

Government of India (Ministry of Finance) (1994), *Report of the Tenth Finance Commission for 1995-2000,* New Delhi.

Government of India (Ministry of Law) (1996), *The Provisions of the Panchayats (Extension to the Scheduled Areas) Bill 1996,* New Delhi.

Hirway, Indira (1989), "Panchayati Raj at Crossroads", *Economic and Political Weekly,* July 22, 1989, Vol. XXIV, No. 29.

Institute of Social Sciences (1998), *Facts about PRIs in India,* Panchayati Raj Update, New Delhi.

Jain, S.P. (1997), Editorial, *Journal of Rural Development* – Special Issue on Panchayati Raj, Oct.-Dec. 1997, Vol. 16, No. 4, NIRD, Hyderabad.

Lok Sabha Debate on Constitution (Seventy-Third Amendment) Bill, (December 1, 1992): Mr. G. Venkatswamy, the then Minister of Rural Development, while moving the Bill to further amend the Constitution of India - pp.713 - 718.

Mehta, S.S. (1997), *Augmentation of the Panchayat Resources,* Gandhi Labour Institute (GLI), Ahmedabad, mimeo.

Mukherjee, Amitava(1993), The Seventy-Third Amendment: Next Steps and Conflict Resolution, *The Administrator - Special Issue on Panchayati Raj,* Vol. XXXVIII, No. 4, Oct.-Dec., 1993, Wiley Eastern Limited, New Delhi.

Narayan Rao, K.V. (1982), "Finances of Panchayati Raj Institutions", *Journal of Rural Development,* Vol. 1, May 1982, NIRD, Hyderabad.

Oommen, M.A. (1998), "Eleventh Finance Commission and Local Bodies - Tasks and Options", *Economic and Political Weekly,* Dec. 19, 1998.

Rajaraman, Indira, Bohra, O.P. and Renganathan, V.S. (1996), "Augmentation of Panchayat Resources", *Economic and Political Weekly,* May 4, 1996, Mumbai.

Rani, P. Geeta (1999), "State Finance Commissions and Rural Local Bodies - Devolution of Resources", *Economic and Political Weekly,* June 19, 1999, Vol. XXXIV, No. 25.

Shah, Ramesh, M. (1997), "73rd Constitutional Amendment - A Victim of Reluctance and Reticence", *Vishleshan,* Vol. No. 22, July-Sept. 1997, Ahmedabad.

Shah, Ramesh, M. (1999), "Summary of the Recommendations of State Finance Commission", *Sarpanch,* Oct.-Dec. 1998 / Jan.-March 1999.

Sharma, B.D. (1995), *Whither Tribal Areas? – Constitutional Amendments and After,* Sahyog Pustak Kutir, New Delhi.

Singh, S.K. (1997), "Self-Governance for the Scheduled Areas", *Journal of Rural Development* – Special Issue on Panchayati Raj, Oct.-Dec. 1997, Vol. 16, No. 4, NIRD, Hyderabad.

Society for Participatory Research in Asia (PRIA) and Network of Collaborating Regional Support Organisations (NCRSOs) (1999), *Status of Finances of Panchayati Raj Institutions.*

Srivastava, U.K., Seetharaman, S.P. and Mehta, S.S. (1991), *Compensation to Canal Affected People of Sardar Sarovar Narmada Project,* Indian Institute of Management, Ahmedabad, mimeo.

Thimmaiah, G. (1976), *Raison D'etre of State Finance Commissions*, Federal Fiscal Systems of Australia and India, Associated Publishers, New Delhi.

UNNATI (1999), *Finances of the Panchayats in Rajasthan*, Ahmedabad, mimeo.

16

Poverty
Its Concept and Incidence in Gujarat

N.C. SHAH

This paper consists of two sections. First section discusses some of the issues in measurement of poverty and develops an alternative measure, while in second, trends in poverty and its correlates in Gujarat are analysed.

MEASUREMENT OF POVERTY

There are three different ways of defining poverty. The first is income or consumption poverty which defines poverty as a relationship of a person to a bundle of commodities of the nature of basic needs with a norm or threshold recommended for each basic need and the person then is considered to be poor if his level of consumption falls below the norm or the threshold for the bundle of basic needs. A second way to define poverty is in terms of capability to lead a long life, to enjoy good health, to have access to knowledge and above all freedom of choice. The third way of looking at poverty is by social deprivation approach. This view of poverty leads to formulating special anti-poverty measures at the local level. For a low income country like India at that time, Dandekar and Rath started with income or expenditure poverty concept. They defined 2250 kilo calorie level as minimum requirement as reported by a Nutrition Advisory Committee (1958).

The Planning Commission Methodology

The "Task Force on Projections of Minimum Needs and Effective Consumption Demand" of the Planning Commission (1979) estimated that, on an average, 2400 and 2100 kilo calories per capita per day met the energy requirements of the population residing in rural and urban areas of the country respectively. It was further estimated, on the basis of all-India rural and urban consumption distributions of the National Sample Survey (NSS) 28th round (1973-74) data on household consumer expenditure, that on an average an expenditure of Rs. 49.09 and Rs. 56.64 per capita per month at 1973-74 prices satisfied the said calorie norms for the rural and urban population respectively. These expenditure cut off levels or the poverty lines were applied on the NSS size distribution of population by consumer expenditure classes for 1973-74 to segregate the poor from the non-poor for that year (Planning Commission, 1993).

This method of deriving the poverty line, for a given year, aims at estimating the purchasing power at current prices required to meet the expenditure associated with the consumption basket that satisfies the calorie norm in the base year 1973-74. A few characteristics of the poverty lines, so defined, need substantiation. First, the base year (1973-74) poverty lines are partly normative and partly behavioral as they are based on a certain specified calorie requirement of the population and are estimated using the observed consumption expenditure pattern of the population from the NSS distribution for that year. This, however, is not true about the poverty lines for subsequent years. The estimation of poverty line for the base year and its mere updation thereafter amounts to holding the consumption basket implicit in the poverty line and which meets the normative requirement constant over time. In the process, ignoring changes in the consumption expenditure pattern of the population, thereby freezing the behavioral aspect of estimating the poverty line thus, for any year after 1973-74 so long as an individual has the requisite purchasing power to afford the reference base year consumption basket even though he chooses to actually spend on a different basket which may fetch him lesser calories than the calorie norm, the individual would be classified as non-poor. Secondly, besides accounting for the calorie intake, the poverty line makes a certain allowance for non-food consumption, including clothing, footwear, fuel and light and other miscellaneous goods and services though not necessarily the respective normative minimum.

The Expert Group Methodology

Both the Expert Group and Planning Commission have adopted the monthly per capita total expenditure of Rs.49.00 and Rs.56.6 as the base lines for rural and urban areas respectively, at the all-India level for the year 1973-74. To facilitate comparability of the poverty estimates across states and over time, the all India basket corresponding to the base year implicit in these lines, has been used as a standard and applied to all the states. There are, however, two major departures. First, the Expert Group has recommended the valuation of this standardised consumption basket , i.e. the adopted base lines at the prevailing state-specific prices to estimate state specific poverty lines. These state specific poverty lines along with the statewise NSS consumption distribution give the state level proportions of poor. Second, at the all-India level for both rural and urban areas, the poverty proportion has been derived as a ratio of the aggregate state-wise number of poor to the total all-India population for rural and urban areas respectively.

Issues in the Estimation of Poor

The average caloric intake for all sections of the population has been observed to be declining over the years as per the NSS consumption data. This has necessitated revision of calorie norms and taking a fresh look at the consumption basket implicit in the base poverty lines. Table 16.1 gives the per capita calorie intake in different states for three decades which clearly exhibits the declining trend in most of the states.

More importantly, it has been pointed out that the use of a single set of calorie norms across the states does not allow for either the inter-state variation in climate and topography which has a bearing on the energy requirement of the individual or the intra and inter-personal adaptations over time by the same person to varying calorie availabilities and needs. In this regard the observation made by Sukhatme on influence of external temperature on maintenance of body weight may be considered extremely important. His arguments run as follows:

The energy released from food is transformed and expanded within body to perform different activities. The efficiency with which the food intake is converted depends on several factors such as age, sex, etc., as well as on environment. Thus, there exists a functional relationship relating calorie intake to energy expenditure through above factors and hence one needs to know the parametric values of these factors in order to separate the effect of environment. With available evidence he say that at least fifty per cent of the energy released from food is being dissipated as heat the rate depends among other factors on external temperature. To elaborate, he adds , "in the tropical coastal region external temperature is close to body temperature; heat dissipation is negligible and body weight can be maintained at relatively low level of calorie intake". Further, he argues that "even in circumpolar regions too, person dissipates heat through breathing and body weight has to be maintained at relatively higher level." This suggests that given other things calorie requirement increases with increase in absolute difference between body temperature and external temperature.

Table 16.1 : Per Capita Caloric Intake

	RURAL			URBAN		
STATE	1973	1983	1994	1973	1983	1994
A.P.	2103	2204	2052	2143	2009	1992
Assam	2074	2056	1983	2135	2043	2108
Bihar	2225	2189	2115	2167	2131	2188
Gujarat	2142	2113	1994	2172	2000	2027
Haryana	3215	2554	2491	2404	2242	2140
H.P	2954	2636	2324	2961	2429	2416
J.K	3151	2569	2507	2467	2234	2392
Karnataka	2202	2260	2073	1925	2124	2026
Kerala	1559	1884	1965	1923	2049	1966
M.P.	2423	2323	2164	2229	2137	2082
Maharashtra	1895	2144	1939	1971	2028	1989
Orissa	1995	2103	2199	2276	2219	2261
Punjab	3493	2677	2418	2783	2100	2089
Rajasthan	2730	2433	2470	2357	2255	2184
Tamil Nadu	1955	1861	1884	1841	2140	1922
U.P.	2575	2399	2307	2161	2043	2114
West Bengal	1921	2027	2211	2080	2048	2131
India	2266	2221	2153	2107	2089	2071

In a big country like India there exists substantial interstate variations in geographical conditions, particularly in latitude and distance from sea; the two major factors determining the climatic conditions in general and temperature in particular. We have tropical coastal regions like Kerala, where the average external temperature is not away from body temperature and the variation therein is also relatively low. On the other hand, U.P., Rajasthan, Bihar, etc. are characterized by extreme climatic conditions and other near to Himalayas like Jammu and Kashmir and Himachal Pradesh by extremely low temperature zones.

In order to capture the effect of climate we fitted the following function to the data related to the 27th round of NSS :

$$C = a + bx + c\,TA + d\,TE$$

Where C = per adult calorie intake in a region.

X = per capita expenditure in the region.

TA = Average external temperature as deviated from body temperature (absolute).

TR = Range of external temperature.

The estimated equation is as under :

$$\text{Log C} = 4.7512 + .4934\,\text{LogX} + 0.1576\,\text{LogTA} + 0.2101\,\text{LogTR}$$
$$(6.53) \qquad (3.99) \qquad (3.54)$$

$R2 = 0.7989$

Note: All the coefficients are statistically significant at 1 per cent as per the t-value given in the brackets.

It can be observed that about eighty per cent of the inter-regional variation in calorie intake is explained jointly by expenditure and temperature variable. Coefficient of per capita expenditure is, of course, positive as expected and significant, but more crucial are the results of temperature variables. Both of these variables are positive and significant which confirms the hypothesis set earlier.

Further and most important, the analysis of variance of the above equation showed that about seventy per cent of the explained variation in calorie intake is due to the two temperature variables, which implies that the calorie intake does not vary so much with purchasing power as with climatic condition in the region. Using the above equation, we estimated the calorie requirement and in turn incidence of poverty in each state. The calorie requirements derived varied between 75 per cent of average norm for Kerala to 115 per cent for U.P. and J&K. An interesting result was obtained regarding the association of new poverty estimates with PQLI. A significant rank correlation of the order of –.5449 between revised poverty estimate and PQL was obtained as against 0.0824 between the latter and poverty estimates based on fix calorie requirement.

The Issue of Calorie Norms

The decline in the average caloric intake across nearly all sections of the population is largely a result of significant changes in the consumption pattern since mid-seventies. This decline is particularly sharp for rural population in lower consumption strata. In both rural and urban areas, there is a shift of expenditure from coarse to finer cereals, from cereals in general to non-cereal quality food like meat, eggs, fruits, etc. and from food as a whole to non-food items in almost all expenditure groups. Further, even for people who fall in the lower expenditure strata, i.e. people who form the hard-core of poor, the proportion of expenditure on cereals, as also on total foodgrains is falling and at the same time proportion of expenditure on quality food is rising. As a result, where these shifts in consumption pattern are predominant the cost of requisite calories is going up on account of individuals paying a higher price per unit of calorie. This suggests that people not only at the poverty line but also those below it appear to prefer more expensive calories to cheaper ones even if they, in the process, get inadequate calories. Despite the possibility of inevitability of the changing composition of the consumption basket due to changes in availability of commodities (per capita) the behaviour may not be quite in keeping with common sense (Rath, N. 1996)). In view of the rational behaviour it is unlikely to expect the people much below the poverty line to obtain an adequate level of calories (or a stomach full of meal) at much higher the cost than could be obtained at relatively lower cost by rearranging his basket to allow more of cereals (cheaper source of calories) in place of non-cereals like milk, oil, etc. In any case this leads to doubt regarding either the validity and reliability of consumer expenditure data or the validity of recommended calorie intake level to be used as cut off point for arriving at poverty line in different years. With regard to the former, Visaria (1996) has recently drawn attention to such possibility saying that period of survey has too long a reference period and hardly any other country in the world has such a long reference period.

The other, and more important, is the calorie norm itself used to estimate poverty lines. The average calorie norm for the population is calculated on the basis of age, sex and activity type. It is possible that over the years due to advancement in technology the activity status of the rural population is becoming such that it does not require as large an input of calories as was the case earlier. It is evident that conditions of living and working in almost all parts of India have undergone a change that requires less physical efforts than decades ago. For example, progress in availability and access to various sources of water has reduced the work of long distance travel by rural women for fetching water. So is the case for the task of collection of fire wood from forest and so on. It may be interesting to observe that if the poverty estimates be determined on the basis of calorie information of 1993-94 consumer expenditure survey it would exceed 80 per cent for number of states which, in view of other progressing indicators of living standard, will not be accepted .

It is evident from the above discussion that the debate regarding any externally fixed calorie norm is subject to serious conceptual difficulties. In order to overcome the problem Minhas (1993) has attempted a behavioral approach to the estimation of the calorie level for calculation of rural and urban poverty. He uses the 1983 Consumer Expenditure Survey data of the NSS for the purpose.

Minhas considers the calorie level at which the meals received and meals given out by households on an average just balance to be significant. The households above this level are net givers of food and therefore are considered by him to be food abundant households, and those below this level are considered as food deficient households. The poverty line may, according to him, be defined at this 'net zero displacement' level. The just adequate calorie norm obtained by Minhas from the behaviour of the surveyed households does not depend upon any nutritional standards, but is determined by the observed level of calorie intake at which the given received meals just balance. The calorie level so determined comes to about 70 per cent of the recommended norm for Gujarat.

I have attempted yet another behavioral approach. I define the level of per capita calorie intake as cut off point art which the behavior of consumers in regard to food expenditure and calorie intake as income (Total expenditure) rises change sharply. In other words, a threshold or a point of inflexion is obtained at a particular calorie level which may then be used to derive poverty line and, in turn, poverty. The logic is as follows. It is known that at very low level of income (expenditure), calorie elasticity rules high and higher than food expenditure elasticity due to dominance of cheap sources of calories. As income increase both the elasticities declines but calorie elasticity declining faster than that for food expenditure and hence a point of inflexion is obtained at which the two curves cut each other. The threshold level in terms of calorie intake then may be considered as minimum required level. Analytically, since the food elasticity is sum of calorie elasticity and calorie cost (preference) elasticity, the threshold calorie level may be defined as that beyond which preference elasticity turns positive. On the basis of 1983 (38th round) data the threshold is obtained at about 2000 k. calories per capita for rural and about 1600 k. calories for urban India. Similar analysis at state level data is in progress. The method, like that by Minhas, is also free of imposing any external norm of calories and depends on self-revealed behaviour.

UNDERSTANDING POVERTY IN GUJARAT

In this section we present some of the features of incidence of poverty and its economic, social and demographic correlates over time and space in Gujarat using NSS data from 1960-61 onwards. It was observed from Table 16.2 that till 1966-67 poverty showed increasing trend and thereafter it has declined with some exception. Nevertheless, have succeeded the share of Gujarat in total poor has remained almost constant at 4.5 per cent over four decades which is close to its population share. On the other hand, some of the southern states like A.P., Kerala and Tamil Nadu in

Table 16.2 : Profile of Poverty in Gujarat Over Time

Year	Rural	Urban	Trend Equations		
			Variable	Rural	Urban
			Constant	60.19*	45.87*
1960-61	50.05	46.95	Trend	−1.32*	−.70*
1961-62	47.86	39.25		(5.9)	(3.3)
1963-64	53.98	32.89			
1964-65	60.07	49.45	Dummy	5.38	7.15
1965-66	60.35	48.64		(1.3)	(1.8)
1966-67	63.71	44.74			
1967-68	59.82	52.79	R^2	0.75	0.36
1968-69	52.21	55.01			
1969-70	56.66	49.85			
1970-71	53.03	45.60	Where dummy = 0 for 1960-1966		
1971-72	50.25	41.96			
1972-73	55.99	34.43		= 1 for 1967	
1973-74	46.79	40.01			
1977-78	41.76	40.02		onwards	
1983	39.23	39.14			
1990	36.98	37.26			
1994	35.39	30.66			

reducing their share in total poor to the extent of fifty per cent over the same period.

I fitted a simple linear trend equation to see, if any, significant declining trend in both rural and urban areas. The Equations are as follows.

It is evident that there exists significant declining trend in both the areas irrespective of dummy variable inserted to demarcate the pre-green revolution period. However, significance of intercept term in both the equation indicates the contribution of real factors to changes in poverty.

Further analysis of time series data on poverty in Gujarat, in consistency with all India and other developing countries, has indicated that while the intensity of poverty falls with growth in per capita state income and consumption sectoral composition of growth does matter to the overall rate of reduction. During 1990-97 over all SDP has grown by 7.88 per cent (6.02 per cent per capita) while agricultural income has grown by only 2.59 per cent (1.32 per cent per capita) with non-farm sector contributing (9.55 per cent) for the entire growth.

Following Equations show the impact of overall SDP and agriculture income on poverty.

$$\text{Log(HR)} = 6.35 - \underset{(2.56)}{\overset{**}{.3379}}\,\text{Log(SDP)} \qquad R2 = .3823$$

$$\text{Log(HU)} = 10.58 - \underset{(8.23)}{\overset{*}{.8795}}\,\text{Log(SDP)} \qquad R2 = .8812$$

$$\text{Log(HR)} = 5.08 - \underset{(7.45)}{\overset{*}{.6772}}\,\text{Log(AG)} \qquad R2 = .7145$$

$$\text{Log(HU)} = 6.74 - \underset{(3.92)}{\overset{*}{.5976}}\,\text{Log(AG)} \qquad R2 = .6304$$

Where (1) HR and HU are the Head count poverty measure of Rural and Urban Gujarat respectively. (2) SDP and AG are income at 1980 prices. (3) Figures in brackets are T values. (4) * indicates Significance at 1 % and ** at 10%.

The above results show that growth in SDP led by non-farm sector has reduced poverty in urban areas and has not affected rural areas significantly, while growth in agriculture has reduced poverty in both the sectors. Thus, secondary and service sectors brought no discernible gains to rural sector.

Agriculture, Employment, Prices, Govt. Exp. and Poverty

Ravallion and Dutta(1995), through a two stage least square model showed that higher agricultural output reduces the incidence of poverty both directly and through its positive effect on the wage rates, while inflation affects poverty only indirectly and temporarily through its impact on money wages. This was a more sophisticated version than most other versions including that of Tandulker and Jain (1995) in that it was a two equation model where by the incidence of rural poverty was explained by agriculture real wages and the lagged and current agriculture output per net sown acre. In addition, the model included the lagged dependent and a time trend among explanatory variables. In turn, the real agriculture wages were explained by the inflation rate and earlier output variable in addition to lagged wage term. However, their model was fitted at all India level data and could not explain either increase in poverty in 1992 nor the decrease in it in 1993. Also the agriculture productivity variable turned out to be insignificant when the model was extended to include the post-reform period. In a latter study, Sen (1997) estimated the above model including the relative price of cereals, proportion of non-agriculture workers in rural population and commercialization variable in addition to agriculture output and real wage rate. An interesting result was that the time trend and lagged dependent variable used by Dutt *et al.* turned insignificant and the relative price and commercialization variable turned out to be significant indicating a faster adjustment of poverty to the omitted real factors than merely a trend factor. Also, the model predicted with complete accuracy the massive increase in poverty during 1992. This model, thus, highly emphasized the importance of relative price variable and of non-agriculture factor. Further, in order to provide more strength to the results the model was estimated using time series of cross-section of state data where poverty was regressed on agriculture productivity, per capita SDP, relative food price index, inflation index based on SDP deflator and per capita real state development expenditure. The result showed that the relative price was most significant variable and having highest impact in magnitude on poverty followed by the state development expenditure and agriculture output, in that order. Further, it was very interesting to observe that, when fitted to the time series data (1971-92) for individual state, again the relative price variable was found to be of utmost importance for changes in poverty in states followed by state development expenditure and agriculture output in that order. Thus, the same conclusion may follow for Gujarat too, of course, with some change in magnitude of the coefficients of the model with out altering the relative importance of the variables. Following Table 16.3 gives the estimated model.

Table 16.3 : Rural poverty equation (Head count)

Variable	Coefficient All India	Coefficient Pooled state data
Constant	–0.1	5.80
	(.67)	(6.59)
Ag.prod.	–0.4	–0.20
	(4.21)	(3.67)
Real wages/State devp.exp	–0.4	–0.2
	(3.29)	(7.61)
Relative food price	0.9	0.6
	(7.69)	(5.45)
Non-agriculture	–.4	
Employment	(3.97)	
Commercialization	0.9	
	(4.92)	
R2	0.97	0.88
D.W.	2.37	2.22

Source: Sen Abhijit (1997).

The important point to note was that the expansion of rural non-agriculture employment was based largely on increasing government expenditure and hence the decline in plan outlay since sixth plan for programme sectors and sub-sectors containing anti poverty schemes was of considerable concern (Iyengar, S. 1998). However, the allocation to social services has been substantially raised during ninth plan as well as annual plan (1997-98) to about 35 per cent of total plan outlay which was only about 24 and 20 per cent during seventh and eighth plan respectively. Even in absolute term it has increased nearly three-fold over eighth plan.

Further, it is evident from the significance of the productivity variable in all India as well as state equation that acceleration of growth in agriculturally stagnant states is a development of major importance because of the fact that rapid growth in the agriculture is likely to percolate to the large population dependent on agriculture thereby making significant dent on rural poverty. Analysis of performance of agriculture during 1983-95 reveals that there was a marked acceleration in the growth rate of agriculture output as compared to the earlier period in India. The period marks a turning point in Indian agriculture development. At all India level the growth rate of crop output accelerated from 2.38 per cent during 1973-83 to 3.4 per cent during 1983-95. Most of the states in all parts of India, except Gujarat, registered significant increase in productivity and output following a regionally diversified input pattern as well as changes in cropping pattern from low value crop to high value crops. For example, in the eastern region it was primarily the growth in rice productivity which was the main source of development while in the central region and also to some extent in southern region the main source of growth was change in cropping pattern involving shift from low value coarse cereals to oilseeds. In the southern region the rapid increase in both rice and oilseeds production contributed to high output growth. Table 16.4 gives growth performance of different regions of India versus Gujarat during three decades.

Table 16.4 : Growth and Agriculture Output (Value)
(At 1990-93 Constant Prices)

Region	1962-65 1970-73	1980-83 1970-73	1992-95 1980-83	1992-95 1980-83
North-west	3.60	3.21	3.29	3.35
Eastern	1.57	1.09	3.01	1.98
Gujarat	1.78	3.12	1.96	2.30
Central	0.73	3.13	3.62	2.68
Southern Region	2.40	1.36	3.58	2.52
All India	2.08	2.38	3.40	2.71
CV	85	86	45	34

Source: Bhalla, G.S. and Gurmil Singh (1997).

However, Gujarat is among the few states where growth rate recorded sharp deceleration during this period. On the other hand, West Bengal, Rajasthan, Haryana, M.P., Tamil Nadu, Karnataka and Punjab recorded, in that order, high rate of growth. These states also recorded a high rate of growth in the use of modern inputs in general and fertilizer in particular. In this regard, the achievement of West Bengal has been most remarkable and a case for Gujarat. West Bengal achieved an unprecedented output growth of 5.39 per cent and yield growth rate of 4.39 per cent as against 1.96 and 2.28 per cent respectively for Gujarat. The cropping intensity in West Bengal increased to as high as 1.62 as against 1.14 in Gujarat. Table 16.5 gives the relative picture of two states with respect to output growth and input use in agriculture.

Table 16.5 : Output Growth and Input in Agriculture

Output	Year	West Bengal	Gujarat
Yield Rate (Rs./hect)	1980-83	5943	5693
	1992-95	9958	7460
	1970-73 to 1980-83	1.56	7.78
% contr. to incremental output	1980-83 to 1992-95	8.83	3.27
Inputs Fertilizer (Kg./hect.)	1980-83	48.02	40.38
	1992-95	139.36	76.60
Irrigation (% of GCA)	1980-83	24.57	22.93
	1992-95	54.25	29.33

Source: Bhalla, G.S. and Gurmil Singh (1997).

It can be seen that within a decade more than half of the cultivated area received irrigation which was only a quarter during early eighties. Consequent to irrigation, the fertilizer application too increased very rapidly to 139 kg./hect. which stood at only 77 kg. in Gujarat. The high growth in output in West Bengal was made possible because of rapid increase in area under irrigation brought about through substantial private investment in pumpsets and tubewells. Thus, if the experience of West Bengal and other fast growing states is of any significance, Gujarat needs to strengthen its credit facilities to the farmers to induce more investment in modern inputs by increased public investment in institutional infrastructure, on one hand, and bridging the gap between realized and potential yield level of important crops like oilseeds through better extension services, on the other.

Poverty and Discrimination

As an outcome of history of social discrimination the burden of deprivation has fallen with disproportionately high severity on Scheduled Cast (ST) and Scheduled Tribe (ST) in Gujarat. It is observed (NCAER, 1994) that while the mean income in rural Gujarat is about 20 per cent higher then the rest of rural India, that of ST is not different from their counterpart in India. In case of SC, it is marginally higher (7 per cent). This reveals a high inequality in distribution of high growth in the state. Consequently the incidence of poverty among these groups is very high as per the latest NSS information (1993-94). There is an indication (Jayaraj and Subramaniam, 1999) of the possibility that as the state becomes less poor in an average sense, cast discrimination tends to rise. Taking country as a whole, between group (ratio of poverty among SC/ST to Others) is 141 per cent which is not a negligible reflection of relative disadvantage suffered by SC/ST group. However, it is heartening to note that in Gujarat the ratio is as high as 207 and highest among the states including Orissa and Bihar (150).

Basic Minimum Services

Provision of basic minimum needs in a time bound manner has been one of the major objectives of Ninth Five Year Plan for removal of poverty. Starting from 1996-97 additional allocations have been made to the states for removing the gaps in basic minimum services. The package includes education, health, rural roads, rural housing, rural water supply, nutrition and public distribution of essentials through fair price shops. Gaps between targets and achievement at the end of eighth plan have been worked out for each factor in each state as percentage to all India gap which in turn are used to arrive at state-wise weights. These weights then may be used for resource allocation to the states under this scheme. However, in what follows, I have attempted to show that due to some of the methodological problems weight of Gujarat is drastically reduced affecting adversely the allocations to the state.

There are seven components under the scheme. However, while calculating weight for the states only five components have been considered. The two important components, viz. gaps in fair price shops and uncovered beneficiaries under the supplementary nutrition projects under (ICDS) have been excluded for unknown reasons. In particular, it is known that government has attached high priority to the public distribution system. The scheme is being constantly revised in terms of retargeting poor by excluding non-poor, commodity based targeting and establishing fair price shops in remote and hilly regions [Revamped PDS and Targeted PDS (TPDS]. Hence, it needs to form a integral part of the Basic Minimum Services.

A close scrutiny of the data on gaps in components of services revealed the plausible explanation for excluding these two components because their inclusion would complicate the calculation of final weights for the states. Some of the states (12 out of 25) have exceeded their targets showing negative percentage. Now if allocation is made on the basis of percentage gap the negative figure would imply taking the funds from the concerned state and allocating it to the deficit state which is meaningless. The appropriate policy in such case, therefore, is not to allocate funds under FPS to the state showing negative gap which would amount to replacing negative figure with 0. Similar is the case with nutrition component.

Thus, it seems that in order to avoid the complication arising out of the aforesaid anomaly these two components have been simply dropped despite their importance. For example, if these two components are included then the state of U.P. will have negative overall weights implying flow funds from U.P. to Centre.

We have recalculated the weights for each state by correcting the individual component gaps as discussed above and presented in Table16.6 column 9 gives the weights on the basis of all seven components. Column headed TW shows old weights.

In the above analysis the individual components have been aggregated by using reciprocal of standard deviation of individual component as weight.

It is evident from the table that statewise individual components weights change substantially and meaningfully when negative gaps are replaced with zeros. Also, the inclusion of nutrition and PDS components while deriving aggregate weights, alters state-wise weights. In case of Gujarat, it is observed that the average weight increase from 2.71 per cent to 4.75 per cent on the basis of implicit weights. Although the increase of about 2 per cent point looks small, considering the volume of central budget for BMS, this would imply a substantial and almost double the amount in absolute terms. The additional fund thus obtained would certainly help narrowing the existing gaps in basic services in Gujarat.

Table 16.6 : Inter-State Gaps in Basic Minimum Services

	Education	Health	Water Supply	Road	Housing	FPS	Nutrition	WGT	TW
Andhra Pradesh	9.13	6.89	5.27	3.66	7.91	0.00	7.51	5.48	6.57
Assam	3.59	2.92	5.42	2.17	18.87	0.00	6.66	5.50	6.59
Bihar	12.84	10.78	2.97	14.25	32.35	0.00	12.76	12.20	14.64
Goa	0.03	0.05	0.10	0.01	0.07	0.02	0.27	0.05	0.05
Gujarat	4.25	4.61	2.71	0.52	1.78	13.67	5.72	4.59	2.71
Haryana	1.38	2.00	0.00	0.01	0.11	1.92	0.00	0.90	0.70
Himachal Pradesh	0.46	0.58	0.79	3.03	0.10	3.00	0.18	1.33	0.99
Jammu & Kashmir	1.32	1.00	1.20	0.74	0.00	8.86	0.47	2.19	0.85
Karnataka	5.38	4.85	2.23	4.50	3.02	5.85	0.00	4.30	4.00
Kerala	0.04	1.48	10.15	0.00	2.56	0.70	4.62	2.49	2.84
Madhya Pradesh	8.35	10.10	4.95	16.73	0.00	18.66	7.02	9.80	8.03
Maharashtra	7.17	7.78	0.87	6.20	4.56	0.00	17.38	4.43	5.32
Orissa	4.40	4.65	6.20	9.46	4.97	0.00	3.71	4.95	5.94
Punjab	1.67	1.99	4.44	0.01	0.27	0.00	0.44	1.40	1.68
Rajasthan	7.30	6.28	6.22	6.93	0.00	8.31	5.92	5.84	5.35
Tamil Nadu	4.44	5.05	10.85	2.56	1.19	9.25	0.00	5.56	4.62
Uttar Pradesh	18.20	20.82	24.39	20.34	8.16	0.00	19.55	15.32	18.38
West Bengal	8.64	7.43	9.73	6.50	8.64	25.64	7.26	11.10	8.19

Household Characteristics of Poor

The household level correlates of poverty in Gujarat have been determined by two cross sectional study by Murty and Shah (1985) and Visaria (1996). In a detailed household level analysis of 1983 (38th round) and 1987-88 (43rd round) NSS survey data, Visaria (1996) identified the important characteristics contributing to the classification of household as poor through logistic regression both in rural and urban regions of Gujarat. Three types of characteristics, namely, household characteristics such as social groups, size dependency ratio, number of female workers, highest educational attainment and per capita land, characteristics of household head and physical environment including region and the seasons.

In rural areas size of the household, region, activity status of the head and per capita land possessed were the most important factors followed by dependency ratio, highest educational level of female member, education of head, social/caste status and season. However, in urban areas the four most important factors were size of household, highest educational level of female member, the region and educational level of the head. They were followed by activity status of head, dependency ratio, social/caste status and number of married males. The number of female workers (usual status), sex and marital status of the head turned out to be least significant in both the region. Interestingly, although the relative importance of different factors explaining incidence of poverty differed between rural and urban areas, their ranks did not change between 1983 and 1987-88. Similar pattern may likely be obtained for 1993-94 too. Further, the findings in terms of correlates of poverty as revealed by the earlier study for 1972-73 and 1977-78 by Murthy and Shah (1985) were more or less similar to what obtained by Visaria. The former found that persons engaged in agriculture activity belonging to household possessing land up to 5 acres with the household size ranging from 5 to 9 and working head having below primary level of education constitute a significant part of the rural poor population. Also, high importance of education level of head and highest education level of female member suggest the need for eradication of illiteracy and raising the level of education to amelioration of poverty.

Summary and Conclusion

This paper discusses some of the conceptual issues in defining poverty and its incidence in Gujarat over four decades. While discussing the measurement issues and difficulties in their interpretation an alternative measure based on threshold of calorie and food expenditure behaviour of the people has been developed. Analysis of time series state level data on poverty has indicated that while the growth in income and consumption helps reducing absolute poverty, the sectoral composition of growth is of immense importance. Poverty reduction has been affected more by rural economic growth than the urban oriented one. Although the agricultural terms of trade has turned favourable since nineties in terms of better agriculture prices due to lack of growth in public investment and real wages, our agricultural sector has been lagging behind other states and the poor are affected adversely at least in the short run. The slow growth of per capita agricultural output, which was responsible for lack of progress in reducing poverty in fifties and early sixties, seems to be operative during nineties too. For this, increased investment in irrigation and other improved technical inputs along with soil conservation measures are called for. In view of high impoverishment among socially backward groups in comparison to other parts of India social sector resources need to be more targeted towards these groups in terms of building social infrastructure as also employment generation.

It has been observed that growth of non-farm employment and earning has high potential for poverty reduction. However, in Gujarat most of the growth has taken place in non-farm labour and wage earners as compared to self-employment which has resulted in low growth in non-farm income. Finally, the state has to represent convincingly to the Centre for appropriate and rightful allocation of resources under various anti-poverty programmes.

REFERENCES

Alagh, Y.K. & Shah, N.C. (1998), *Basic Minimum Needs: A Note.*

Bhalla, G.S. & Singh, G. (1997), "Recent Development in Indian Agriculture", *Economic and Political Weekly* No. 1, 32 No. 13.

Dev, Mahendra, S. (1997), "Growth, employment poverty and human development", *Review of Development and Change* Vol.11 No. 2 July-Dec. 1997.

Dandekar, V.M. & Singh (1997), *Poverty in India*, Indian School of Political Economy.

Dutt and Ravallian, M. (1995), *Why have some states done better than others at reducing poverty policy,* Research Department, World Bank (Mimed).

Dubey, A. and Gangopadhyay, S. *Counting the poor*, Sarvekshan analytical report, Government of India.

Iyengar, Sudarshan, 1998, *Gujarat, in the poor in a Hostile society*, (ed.) V.M. Rao, Vikas Publishing House.

Jayaraj, D. and Subramanian, "Poverty and Discrimination: 1999 Measurement and Evidence from Rural India", in Barbara Harris White and Subramanian (eds.), *Illfare in India,* Sage Publication.

Malhotra, Rajiv (1997) "Incidence of poverty in India", *Indian Journal of labor Economics* Vol. 40, No. 1.

Minhas, B.S. 1993, "On Estimating the Inadequacy of energy intakes" *Journal of Development Studies*, Vol. 28 No. 1.

Planning Commission (1979), *Report of the Task force on projection of minimum needs*, PPD.

————, (1993), *Report of the expert group on estimation of proportion and number of poor,* PPD Govt. of India.

Murthy, G.V.S.N., Shah, N.C. (1985), *Levels and patterns of Living in Gujarat*, Sardar Patel Institute of Eco. & Social Research, Ahmedabad.

NCAER (1994), *Human Development Profile of India.*

Rath, N. (1996), "Poverty in India Revisited", *Indian Journal of Agriculture Economics*, Vol. 51 No. 182.

Sen, Abhijit (1997), "Structural Adjustment and Rural Poverty", in Chadha, G.K and Sharma, N. (ed.) *Growth Employment and Poverty,* Vikas Publishing House.

Shah, C.H., Niresh Shah (1988), "In Search of Demand for Nutrition", *Anvesak.*

Shah, N.C. (1988), "Measurement of Poverty an Interstate Profile", *Anvesak* Vol. 118. No. 12

Sukhatme, P.V. (1981), "On Measurement of Poverty", *Economic and Political Weekly*, Vol. XVI, No. 32.

Tandulkar, S.D. & Jain (1995), "Economic Reforms and Poverty", *Economic and Political Weekly* June 10.

Visaria, Pravin (1996), *Levels of Living in India Correlates and Determinants*, Gujarat Institute of Development Research.

INDEX